Black History

Black History

A Guide to Civilian Records in the National Archives

Compiled by Debra L. Newman

NATIONAL ARCHIVES TRUST FUND BOARD
GENERAL SERVICES ADMINISTRATION
Washington, D.C.
1984

Published for the National Archives and Records Service
By the National Archives Trust Fund Board

Front cover photos. Clockwise from uppermost right:

John Tats, West Virginia coal miner. Date unknown. Lewis Hines, photographer. RG 69, Records of the Work Projects Administration. (69–RP–125).

Coal miner's widow, Gilliam, McDowell County, W. Va. This is one of several hundred photographs taken to document the living conditions of coal miners following World War II. This woman was living on an old-age pension. August 13, 1946. Russell Lee, photographer. RG 245, Records of the Solid Fuels Administration for War. (245–MS–1501L).

Leaders of the Civil Rights March on Washington on August 28, 1963. Left to right, front row: Whitney M. Young, executive director, National Urban League; Roy Wilkins, executive secretary, NAACP; A. Philip Randolph, founder of the demonstration; Walter P. Reuther, president, UAW and vice-president, AFL-CIO; and Arnold Aronson, secretary, Leadership Conference on Civil Rights. RG 306, Records of the U.S. Information Agency. (306–SS–77A–46–14).

World War II industrial labor. Anna C. Larchand was one of hundreds of young black women who were able to get jobs in war production plants during World War II. She is shown working in an aircraft factory in a large eastern navy yard. May 1942. Liberman, photographer. RG 208, Records of the Office of War Information. (208–NP–3Y–8).

The original Fisk Jubilee Singers. Date and photographer unknown. The Jubilee Singers were organized in 1867 by the treasurer of Fisk University in Nashville, Tenn. In an effort to raise money for the newly founded university, the singing students toured parts of the United States and introduced black spirituals to royal audiences in Europe. The singers raised nearly $100,000 in less than three years and made it possible to build the school's first permanent building, named Jubilee Hall. Jubilee Hall and the Jubilee Singers are lasting Fisk University traditions. RG 69, Records of the Work Projects Administration. (69–GU–7641).

Frontispiece: Detail from a drawing by Charles Alston. Date unknown. RG 208, Records of the Office of War Information. (208–COM–8).

Library of Congress Cataloging in Publication Data

Newman, Debra L.
Black history.

Includes index.
1. Afro-Americans—History—Sources—Bibliography—Catalogs. 2. United States. National Archives—Catalogs. I. Title.
Z1361.N39N576 1984 [E 185] 016.973′0496 84–16597

Hardcover ISBN 0–911333–21–5
Paperback ISBN 0–911333–31–2

Table of Contents

*There may be restrictions on the use of the records in this Record Group. Consult the NARS staff for specific information.

List of Illustrations

Preface

This book, *Black History: A Guide to Civilian Records in the National Archives,* is one of a large number of publications designed to make the records in the National Archives better known and easier to use. Essentially it is a specialized supplement to the general *Guide to the National Archives of the United States* (1974).

From time to time the National Archives and Records Service has published other subject guides to Federal records that have research value to a broad spectrum of scholars. In this category are *Federal Records of World War II* (2 vols., 1951), *Civil War Maps in the National Archives* (1964), *Guide to the Archives of the Government of the Confederate States of America* (1968), *Guide to Federal Archives Relating to the Civil War* (1962), *Guide to Cartographic Records in the National Archives* (1971), *Guide to Materials on Latin America in the National Archives of the United States* (1974), *Guide to Records in the National Archives of the United States Relating to American Indians* (1981), and *Guide to Genealogical Research in the National Archives* (1982). Two other subject guides, *Documenting Alaskan History: Guide to Federal Archives Relating to Alaska* (Alaska Historical Commission Studies in History No. 23, University of Alaska Press, 1982) and *Guide to Federal Archives Relating to Africa* (African Studies Association, Crossroads Press, 1977) were also compiled by National Archives staff but published privately. For finding aids and other publications, see the most recent *Select List of Publications of the National Archives and Records Service,* General Information Leaflet No. 3.

The records listed in this guide are of special importance because, taken as a whole, they are probably the single greatest resource for the study of black history in the past century. Since the Civil War (1861-65), the Federal Government has figured prominently in the lives of American blacks. The records created by this involvement—whether official bureaucratic reports and instructions or letters and depositions from former slaves—amply document black culture and society. Here, comprehensively for the first time, are listed records that have the potential to fill a gap in American historic knowledge as they illuminate the role and importance of blacks in American society.

It is hoped that the publication of this guide will focus the attention of researchers on the vast research potential of materials relating to black history in the records of the nonmilitary agencies of the Federal Government in the National Archives of the United States and aid prospective researchers in the use of this material. If it serves either or both of those purposes, the effort that went into the preparation of this guide will be considered well spent.

ROBERT M. WARNER
Archivist of the United States

Introduction

The purpose of this guide is to assist the researcher in locating within the National Archives of the United States those records of civilian agencies that have been concerned with the black population. For the most part, coverage in this guide has been limited to records that can be identified with existing finding aids. Some isolated files or documents concerning blacks undoubtedly can be found in the records of many civilian agencies but have not been included in this guide because there is no practical way of identifying them. This guide is not a comprehensive listing of every document among the civilian records that pertain to black history. The term "black" is used most often to describe black Americans, but "Negro" and "colored" are used when these terms will facilitate locating the records.

The National Archives of the United States consists of permanently valuable records of the Federal Government. They are housed in the National Archives Building in Washington, D.C.; in the Washington National Records Center, Suitland, Md.; in eleven regional Federal archives and records centers; and in the Presidential libraries.

The basic organizational unit to which all records in the National Archives and Records Service (NARS) are assigned is called a record group (RG), and each record group is assigned a number. A record group most frequently consists of the records of a single agency, such as the Committee on Fair Employment Practice (RG 228). The records of the head of an executive department and units with departmentwide responsibility may be assigned to a general record group, such as General Records of the Department of Labor (RG 174). Records of a number of agencies are sometimes brought together on the basis of similar function or other relationship. An example of a collective record group is Records of Temporary Committees, Commissions, and Boards (RG 220). This guide is arranged by record group number.

NARS endeavors to keep records in the order in which they were maintained by the creating agency, in the belief that this best preserves their integrity and interrelationships. The agency filing systems were designed for administrative purposes and not for the benefit of future researchers. A major reason for the preparation of guides such as this is to assist subject-oriented researchers in understanding the complexities of recordkeeping systems and in locating material of interest among the vast quantities of records.

Within record groups, the basic archival unit of control for records is the series, which is a body of records arranged in some serial order or logically grouped together for some other reason. For many record groups, NARS has prepared preliminary inventories or inventories, which describe the records series by series. Typical information in an entry includes series title, covering dates, quantity, types of records, and perhaps some indication of content. In this guide many of the same records are described, but there has been an attempt to present a different viewpoint, with more emphasis on subject matter, specific examples, and practical guidance on using the records. There is expanded discussion of basic records and more summary treatment of records having less significance. When information about blacks is dispersed among records relating to other subjects, an effort has been made to identify as specifically as possible the black-related materials.

In this guide, series titles appear in boldface type. This and other important elements of the format are illustrated in the following key.

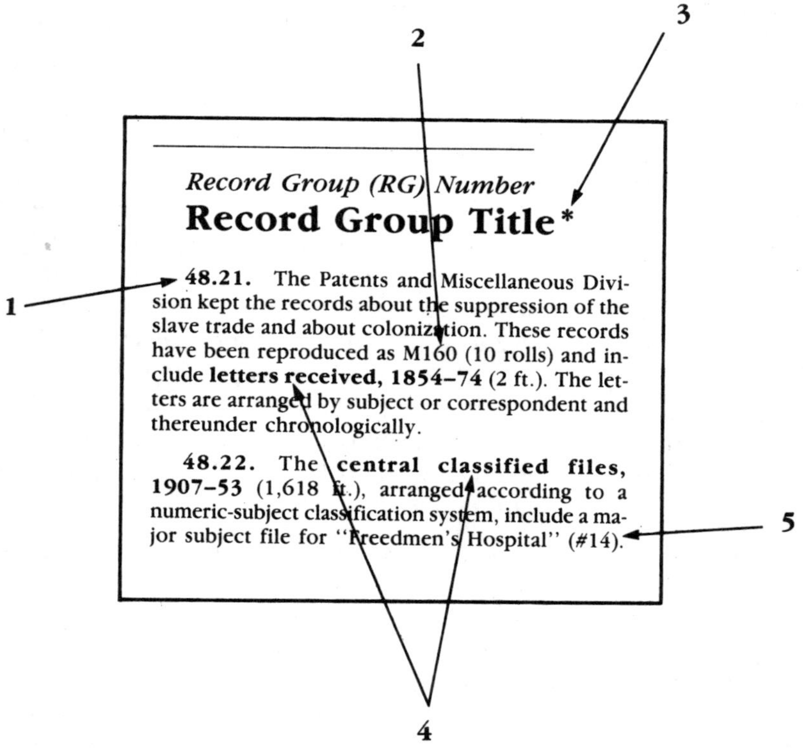

1. 48.21. 48 is the record group number, 21 is the paragraph number. You should cite this composite number when requesting records.

2. M160. M160 is the number of a NARS microfilm publication. Most of the microfilm publication numbers begin with the letter "M," but some begin with "T." Some records, such as the population census schedules, come into NARS on microfilm, and these are not always assigned microfilm publication numbers. Microfilm is 35mm unless there is a notation that microfilm is 16mm.

3. *. This symbol after the record group title (also appearing after the RG title in the Table of Contents) indicates that there may be restrictions on the use of the records described. The researcher should consult the NARS staff for specific information.

4. Bold Type. Boldface type is used for the title of a series of records within a record group and for the date of those records. Information about the volume and the arrangement of the records follows the bold face type. The volume is usually given in linear feet, but in some instances the number of items, volumes, or microfilm rolls is given.

5. #. This symbol precedes a file number (e.g., correspondence file number; case number; docket number; map number; photograph, film, or sound recording number).

Most of the records are readily available and researchers are not required to make arrangements in advance to consult them. Some records, however, may be temporarily unavailable (they may be being reproduced for another researcher, for example) and there are restrictions on access to some of them. It is suggested, therefore, that before traveling any extended distance to visit a repository, researchers write and describe as specifically as possible the subject of their interest and the records that they may wish to consult.

This guide should be used in conjunction with the *Guide to the National Archives of the United States* (GPO, 1974). The National Archives *Guide* gives descriptions of all of the holdings that were in NARS' custody at the time of its publication, as well as a detailed explanation of the record group concept, regulations for the use of NARS records, detailed administrative histories of agencies, and the titles of finding aids available for each record group.

Several other publications were helpful in the compilation of this guide. The *Guide to Federal Archives Relating to Africa,* by Aloha South (Crossroads Press, 1977), provided information about the slave trade,

African colonization, and back-to-Africa movements. *The Guide to Federal Archives Relating to the Civil War,* by Kenneth W. Munden and Henry P. Beers (GPO, 1962), supplied information about records relating to black Americans during the Civil War and the Reconstruction period. Many black history records are on microfilm. These are described in *Black Studies: A Select Catalog of National Archives Microfilm Publications* (NARS, 1984). This catalog lists microfilm of records of both civilian and military agencies, including the extensive records of the Freedmen's Bureau, which was administered by the War Department. Another helpful volume is *Afro-American History, Sources for Research,* edited by Robert L. Clarke (Howard University Press, 1981); of particular interest in this volume is the article "Presidential Libraries as Sources for Research on Afro-Americans," by J.C. James. For information about Africans, see South's guide; for information about Latin American blacks, see *Guide to Materials on Latin America in the National Archives of the United States,* compiled by George S. Ulibarri and John P. Harrison (GPO, 1974).

Many members of the NARS staff have helped with this publication. Finding aids prepared by staff members have provided invaluable aid in the compilation of this guide. A number of staff members read and commented on the entries in this volume. Most of the descriptions of audiovisual records were taken from an unpublished NARS finding aid entitled "Audiovisual Records in the National Archives Relating to Black History," by Leslie Waffen, Nancy Malan, and Charles Thomas (1972). Information about recent motion pictures and sound recordings was supplied by Donald Rowe. All of the photographs in this guide are from record groups described in this volume and were selected, with the aid of exhibit specialist Lillian E. Grandy, from a large collection of NARS black history photographs. Constance Schulz, a photographic research specialist, and the staff of the Still Pictures and Photography Branches were very cooperative in processing the illustrations reproduced in this volume. Mark Allnatt, a student volunteer from Houghton College in New York, aided in the description of the records of the Departments of Justice and Treasury.

The NARS Publications Division, R. Kevin Flood, Director, published this guide. The meticulous attention of Shelby G. Bale, who edited this guide, was invaluable to its completion. The Publications Development staff including Katherine Coram, Gwen Cyrkiel, Richard Smith, Mary Ryan, Constance Potter, Kevin Hardwick, Starr Oaddams, and Camille Cormier, scrupulously guided this project through the publication process. The extreme care of the copy editor and indexer, Susan Carroll, and the creativity of the designer, Christopher Jones, resulted in a publication that is attractive and easy to use.

Dr. Virginia C. Purdy, who supervised this project, provided unfailing encouragement. James W. Moore, who has been an active supporter of the black history guide project for many years, has inspired me by his confidence in my ability to complete it. I extend my thanks to all of the Civil Archives Division staff members who patiently aided me in the preparation of this guide.

Debra L. Newman

Record Group 1
Records of the War Labor Policies Board

1.1. In January 1918 the President appointed the Secretary of Labor as War Labor Administrator, and the Secretary in turn appointed an advisory council to help deal with labor problems involving war production. On the recommendation of the council, the War Labor Administrator established the War Labor Policies Board on May 13, 1918, to standardize labor policies of Government agencies.

1.2. The Board formulated uniform policies for war labor administration, promoted better housing conditions for war workers, and, after the Armistice, considered proposals for canceling Government contracts. It also made studies of domestic and foreign wartime labor conditions and of labor policies relating to immediate postwar conditions in the United States. Because blacks moved from the South to become part of the work force in northern defense industries, a few of the Board's records relate to policies addressed to those black workers. The Board was discontinued in March 1919.

1.3. Among the **correspondence of the Chairman and of the Executive Secretary, May 1918–February 1919** (9 ft.), arranged alphabetically by name or subject, is a folder entitled "Negro Economics" (1/4 in.). The folder contains primarily correspondence with George E. Haynes, Director of the Division of Negro Economics in the Department of Labor (see RG 174), and the correspondence covers subjects such as the actions of the Labor Department that affected black workers, recruitment of black workers, German propaganda among blacks, and union discrimination against them. Among these records of the Board's Chairman and Executive Secretary is also the correspondence of the Committee on Conditions of Living (1 ft.), which includes scattered information about living conditions for blacks.

Record Group 2
Records of the National War Labor Board *(World War I)*

2.1. The National War Labor Board, composed of representatives from labor, management, and the general public, was appointed in March 1918 by the Secretary of Labor (in his capacity as War Labor Administrator) to arbitrate, mediate, and conciliate labor disputes that might interfere with the effective conduct of the war. Some of these cases involved black workers. The Board was formally dissolved in August 1919.

2.2. The **case files, 1918–19** (75 ft.), are arranged numerically by case number. A typical case file contains a copy of the original complaint, notices and transcripts of hearings, briefs, exhibits, the examiner's report, a summary of the case and statement of disposition, a copy of the agreement negotiated by the parties in dispute, and related correspondence. Some cases involved occupations in which blacks were heavily employed, such as shipbuilding, lumbering, coal mining, tobacco growing, longshoring, metal casting, and building trades. For example, one case file (#213, 8 pp.) relates to a dispute involving black railroad workers and is entitled "Colored Bagmen and Mail Porters of Philadelphia Terminal Division vs. Employers." The points at issue were a 20 percent increase in wages and discrimination against black employees. Another case (#233, 3 in.) involved labor conditions in laundries in Little Rock, Ark., where 65 percent of the women employed were black. In eight laundries, women constituted over 66 percent of the work force and 75 percent of the union membership.

Record Group 3
Records of the U.S. Housing Corporation

3.1. The U.S. Housing Corporation (USHC) was incorporated July 8, 1918, to provide housing, local transportation, and other community facilities for industrial workers. Black-related material is found among the records of five components of the Corporation: the Service Division, the Homes Registration and Information Division, the Surveys and Statistics

Division, the Industrial Relations Division, and the Operating Division. After several administrative transfers, the Corporation was dissolved in 1952.

Records of the Service Division

3.2. Among the records of the Service Division—which had charge of supplies, mail, files, and stenographic services—are the **general files, 1917–20** (36 ft.), arranged numerically. The folder entitled "Negro Housing" (#1691, ¼ in.) consists mostly of correspondence from the Division of Negro Economics of the Department of Labor (see RG 174 for additional information about this Division) for the years 1919 and 1920. The principal subject covered by the correspondence is poor housing conditions among black people, particularly those in northern industrial centers such as Newark, Philadelphia, Pittsburgh, Detroit, and Chicago. There is also an album that contains photographs, September–October 1918, depicting slums in Chester, Pa., and portraying black residents in dilapidated housing.

Records of the Homes Registration and Information Division

3.3. This Division was to fully exploit all existing housing and boarding facilities so that the need for Government housing and construction could be reduced to a minimum. Room registries listed available rooms for rent and the names of whites who needed accommodations. The Division of Negro Economics advocated the establishment of room registries for black workers. The **reference file, 1918–19** (7 in.), arranged by subject, is part of the records of the Division's Homes Registration Section. The file includes a folder entitled "Negro Registries." Material in the folder pertains to the establishment of registries, race relations in the area of housing, problems encountered by black workers trying to find accommodations, and Division of Negro Economics' cooperation with the Urban League on matters of housing. The folder also contains registries for black women and a list of the Division of Negro Economics supervisors and agents entitled "Negro Workers Advisory Committees, State and Local." The names in this list identify black field agents who generated correspondence contained in the series **USHC field agencies and committees, 1918–19** (4 ft.). The correspondence is arranged alphabetically by name of field agent or town and relates chiefly to the establishment, operation, and closing of local homes registration service committees; activities of field agents; housing for black workers; and rent profiteering.

Records of the Surveys and Statistics Division

3.4. This Division conducted general surveys of industrial communities. Among the **records relating to industrial housing surveys,**

1918 (23 ft.), arranged alphabetically by name of city, are questionnaires on housing and employment that include information about the race of the respondents. The Division's records also include daily reports of investigators, surveys of the labor force, and information about the extent and adequacy of housing facilities.

Industrial Relations Division

3.5. This Division handled labor problems on housing projects for USHC employees, contractors, and employees of war industries who were living in temporary quarters provided by USHC. Scattered through the **general correspondence of the Division, 1918–19** (2 ft.), arranged alphabetically by name of project location, are complaints of discrimination against nonunion laborers and members of minority groups in the building trades.

Records of the Operating Division

3.6. The Operating Division planned and contracted construction projects to provide housing and other facilities to war workers; it also operated all buildings constructed or otherwise acquired by USHC. Among the **records relating to the operation of projects, 1918–20** (14 ft.), arranged alphabetically by name of project location, is information (10 in.) about Project 150–C in Truxton, Va. Project 150–C was a housing development built by USHC contractors specifically for black workers. The Truxton, Va., material includes correspondence (chiefly with project representatives), reports, maps, and newspaper clippings. The material pertains to inspection, repair, furnishing, equipment, utilities, collection of rents, miscellaneous complaints, and other matters of routine project administration. There is also an album of photographs of the buildings in the project.

Record Group 4

Records of the U.S. Food Administration

4.1. The U.S. Food Administration (USFA) was created by an Executive order of August 10, 1917, to assure the supply, distribution, and conservation of foods; facilitate their movement and prevent monopolies and hoarding; and maintain governmental control over foods, chiefly by means of voluntary agreements and a licensing system. It assumed jurisdiction over commodities when they reached commercial channels. The USFA components that created records most closely related to the study of black

The Charlie McGuire family of Poke County, Ala., and their new wagon. Date and photographer unknown. RG 16, Records of the Office of the Secretary of Agriculture. (16-G-97-S30346).

history were the States Administration Division and the Educational Division.

4.2. After November 11, 1918, rules and regulations of the Food Administration were revoked, and its organization was gradually dismantled. An Executive order of August 21, 1920, terminated all branches of the Food Administration still in existence.

States Administration Division

4.3. This Division directed USFA activities in various States. One of the components of this Division was the Negro Activities Section. **Records of the Section, 1917–18** (1½ ft.), arranged alphabetically by subject, include correspondence with clubs and black organizations and interoffice memorandums. The materials cover various aspects of food conservation in the black community and the establishment and operations of various State and local groups that worked on behalf of the Food Administration.

Educational Division

4.4. One of the chief functions of the Educational Division was to conduct publicity campaigns to promote food conservation. The Division included a Negro Press Section. A. U. Craig headed the Negro Press Section; E. T. Attwell worked with Craig. About the first of October 1918, the Section was abolished and its duties were transferred to the Copy Desk Section. During its period of existence, the Negro Press Section aimed to reach every group of blacks through the black press, schools, moving picture theaters, fraternal institutions, and churches.

4.5. The records of the Negro Press Section include several correspondence files. The **general correspondence file of A. U. Craig, 1917–18** (10 in.), is arranged alphabetically by correspondent; the **general correspondence file of E. T. Attwell, 1918** (3 in.), is arranged alphabetically by subject or person. The combined **general correspondence file of both Craig (to Oct. 1918) and Attwell, Aug. 1917–Dec. 1918** (1 ft., 4 in.), is arranged alphabetically by subject. **Correspondence regarding black theaters and fairs and other publicity, Jan.–Aug. 1918** (5 in.), is a file that was maintained by Craig; it is arranged alphabetically by subject.

4.6. There are also in the records of the Negro Press Section a **miscellaneous data and correspondence file, 1918** (6 in.), arranged alphabetically by subject, and a **miscellaneous mimeographed and printed material file** (n.d., 11 in.) arranged by agency of publication. The Section's records also include lists of black ministers, schools, and fraternal and other organizations; these lists are accompanied by **correspondence, 1917–18** (1 ft.), which is arranged alphabetically by organization and thereunder alphabetically by name of official who submitted a list. There are **lists of ministers** (n.d., 3 in.) of the Colored Methodist Episcopal, the African Methodist Episcopal, and the Colored Baptist Churches; the lists are arranged by churches indicated and thereunder by State.

Record Group 7

Records of the Bureau of Entomology and Plant Quarantine

7.1. The Bureau of Entomology and Plant Quarantine was established in the Department of Agriculture by authority of the Agricultural Appropriation Act of 1934. Consolidated under the Bureau were entomological research and plant quarantine work formerly conducted by various Department of Agriculture agencies. Entomological work had originated in the Office of the Entomologist, established in the Agricultural Section of the Patent Office in 1854. Legislation to prevent importation and interstate transportation of insect-infested plants was first enacted in the Plant Quarantine Act of 1912. The Bureau of Entomology and Plant Quarantine cooperated with the States in studying and controlling insects to prevent plant diseases and damage. It was responsible for the enforcement of the Plant Quarantine, Insect Pest, Honeybees Importation, Mexican Border, and Export Certification Acts. The Bureau was abolished in 1953 and its functions were given to the Agricultural Research Service.

7.2. Scientists at Tuskegee Institute were interested in various areas of experimental entomological work and corresponded with the Bureau. Among the entomological records is a series of **letters received relating to silk culture, 1901–4** (3 ft.). These letters are arranged alphabetically by name of correspondent and pertain to requests for information concerning methods of producing silk for silkworm eggs and requests for seeds and cuttings of silkworm food plants. Included are letters from George Washington Carver of Tuskegee, Ala. (¼ in.).

Record Group 9

Records of the National Recovery Administration

9.1. The National Recovery Administration (NRA) was created by an Executive order of June 16, 1933, under authority of the National Industrial Recovery Act. Its purpose was to rehabilitate industry and trade in the United States, expand employment, and improve labor conditions. Special codes of fair competition were drafted under its supervision to govern industries and trades, and a blanket code (the President's Reemployment Agreement) was offered for voluntary acceptance by employers, pending the approval of specific codes. On May 27, 1935, mandatory codes were declared unconstitutional by the U.S. Supreme Court. The NRA was terminated on January 1, 1936.

9.2. Records about black workers are scattered among the records of NRA. Many black individuals and organizations wrote protests to NRA officials because agricultural and domestic occupations—the occupations that included the vast majority of black workers—were not included in the codes of fair competition. Another major issue addressed by black workers was the problem of unequal pay for equal work, commonly known as wage differentials. Since black workers sometimes were subjected to these differentials and some employers wanted to keep it that way, several NRA code hearings were called to settle the problem. Some employers, when forced to pay black workers the same wage as whites, fired the black workers and hired whites only. In other cases, black workers were displaced because whites were attracted by the minimum wages.

9.3. The **classified general files of NRA, 1933–35** (160 ft.), arranged by numerical classification scheme, contain two file categories that specifically identify race. One category is labeled "Negro," with the subheading "Negro Labor" (#581, 4 in.), and the other is labeled "Wage Differentials–Negro and White" (#542, 1 in.). Most of the records in these categories concern the effect of the National Industrial Recovery Act on the black population, especially the problems associated with minimum wage provisions, the exclusion of agricultural and domestic work from the codes, and the displacement of black workers.

9.4. Similar information about black workers also appears in other parts of the classified general files. Some category headings are "Learners and Apprentices" (#561), "Shipping–Stevedores" (#395), "Bagging Cotton" (#429), and "Labor" (#567).

9.5. A series entitled **"Volumes 'A' and 'B'," 1933–35** (157 ft.), arranged numerically by code number 1–557, is in the records maintained by the Code Record Unit and contains a selection of the more significant papers filed in the process of drafting codes of fair competition. There are two "volumes" for each code: "Volume A," consisting of unbound papers dated between the time of the submission of the code and the time of the public hearing, and "Volume B," consisting of unbound papers dated between the time of the public hearing and the time of the code's formal approval. Some of these papers include information about industries in which blacks were heavily employed. For example, papers about the code of fair competition for the raw peanut milling industry (#203, 3 in.) state that 90 percent of the workers employed in that industry were black and that 80 percent of the workers in peanut mills were women; the papers give a description of the work, the cost of living for blacks in some areas, and some comparative wages for black farm laborers. The planters felt that an increased wage would result in the replacement of blacks with white wage earners.

9.6. Among the **consolidated files on industries governed by approved codes, 1933–36** (2,200 ft.), arranged alphabetically by name of the industry or trade, is scattered information on black workers. Generally included, with statistics, is information about the racial composition of a given industry's work force. The lumber and timber, tobacco, cotton and textile, and shellfish industries, and related occupations such as stevedoring, tended to employ large numbers of black workers. There is information about wages, working conditions, and the effect of the NRA codes. There is similar information in the **consolidated files for industries whose proposed codes were never approved, 1933–36** (268 ft.), which are arranged in the same manner as those for industries with approved codes.

9.7. The **consolidated administrative files, 1933–36** (124 ft.), arranged alphabetically by subject or name of author, contain scattered information on black workers. Several specific folder titles are "Differentials," "Negro Workers," and "Negro Material"; all three total less than 1 inch. The folder "Negro Material" includes a few documents pertaining to the Federal Government's Interdepartmental Group Concerned With the Special Problems of Negroes and a "List of Colored Local Unions Affiliated with the American Federation of Labor."

9.8. The **transcripts of hearings, 1933–35** (109 ft.), which were maintained by the Library Unit, are arranged by code registry number, 101/23–1754/01. There is a card index to the hearings; the index is arranged alphabetically by the name of the industry. The hearings relate to proposed codes and code amendments or modifications. Some of the hearings pertain to requests for exemption from minimum wage provisions. Of special interest are the hearings in which employers argued that black workers should receive less pay because they could not perform as efficiently as white workers. Examples of these hearings are *Application for Exemption from Code of Fair Competition for the Textile Industry in the United States* (Nov. 24, 1933) and *Hearing on Appeal by Central Weaving and Spinning Corporation of Fayetteville, North Carolina* (Oct. 8, 1934).

9.9. The records of the Research and Planning Division include the **office files of John E. Hamm, 1933–35** (4 in.), arranged alphabetically by subject. Hamm was successively understatistician, liaison officer between the NRA and the Reconstruction Finance Corporation, senior economist, and assistant to the Director of the Division. In Hamm's files is a folder captioned "Negro Problems," which includes one document dated March 2, 1934, entitled "Inter-Departmental Group Meeting for Discussion of Problems of Negro Laborers."

9.10. The **records of the Tobacco Unit, 1933** (5 in.), arranged by subject, are a part of the records of the Industries Studies Section. There are materials among the records of the Tobacco Unit pertaining to hours and wages in the tobacco industry. Included are unpublished studies entitled "Negro Laborers in the Tobacco Industry in North Carolina," by C. Tinsley Willis, 1931; "The Tobacco Industry in North Carolina," by Robert C. Weaver, n.d.; and "The Negro and Wage Differentials Under the Codes," by Lawrence A. Oxley, n.d. There is also a 1935 survey of tobacco workers' families, including information about their racial composition. Many were black families.

9.11. The Labor Advisory Board was appointed in 1933 by the Secretary of Labor to ensure that all labor, organized and unorganized, was adequately represented in all matters concerning the NRA. The records of the Labor Advisory Board include a **subject file, 1934–35** (4 ft.), arranged in two parts—each part arranged alphabetically by subject. There are two separate folders entitled "Negro Labor" (¼ in. and 1 in.) and one

Roy Wilkins, executive director of the National Association for the Advancement of Colored People, emphasized the case for strong civil rights legislation at a press conference in Philadelphia, Pa. Date and photographer unknown. RG 306, Records of the U.S. Information Agency. (306-ST-867-64-515).

entitled "Negro Displacement" (½ in.). The materials in these three folders include correspondence from black organizations and individuals concerning wage differentials; a report by Gustave Peck entitled "The NRA and the Negro Worker"; extracts from a study by John P. Davis, Chairman of the Joint Committee on National Recovery, on conditions of black workers in cotton mills in North Carolina, South Carolina, and Georgia; and other letters and reports from Davis. These folders also include complaints of job displacement and lowered salaries, including the complaint that the minimum wage became the maximum wage for black workers. A January 27, 1934, letter from Roy Wilkins of the National Association for the Advancement of Colored People (NAACP) to Matthew F. Boyd of the Labor Advisory Board includes some specific information about the displacement of black workers. There are some copies of newspaper clippings. One headline reads: "Colored Women at $4.50 a Week Replaced by Whites at $12."

9.12. The records of the Labor Advisory Board also include the **of-**

fice files of Henry H. Collins, 1933–35 (2 ft.), arranged alphabetically by subject. The folder captioned "Differentials" (¼ in.) contains several documents relating to black workers. One such document is the "Statement of the Negro Industrial League Concerning the Code of Fair Competition for the Lumber and Timber Products Industry," by John P. Davis and Robert C. Weaver, July 21, 1933.

Record Group 10

Records of the National Commission on Law Observance and Enforcement

10.1. The National Commission on Law Observance and Enforcement, popularly known as the Wickersham Commission, was appointed by President Hoover under provisions of an act of March 1929 to inquire "into the problem of the enforcement of prohibition under the provisions of the eighteenth amendment of the Constitution and laws enacted in pursuance thereof, together with the enforcement of other laws." The Commission was terminated in 1931.

10.2. Information about blacks is scattered among the documents, reports, and correspondence in many of the series of this record group. Among the **general correspondence of the Office of the Chairman, 1929–31** (11 ft.), arranged alphabetically by name or organization, is one folder for the NAACP (¼ in.). Most of the letters from the NAACP to the Commission are from Walter H. White, the executive secretary of the organization, who was urging that the problems of mob violence and racial crimes be investigated and that the findings be included in the Commission's reports.

10.3. Most statistical information about criminals and juvenile delinquents includes racial breakdowns. For example, the **circulars to the commissioners, 1929–31** (2 ft.), arranged numerically by circular number, include various memorandums, reports, pamphlets, and publications. Circular 51, a report entitled "Juvenile Delinquency," includes two sections detailing the race, nationality, age, and sex of juvenile delinquents. The author of the report states that "Negro children are more likely than white children to come to the attention of juvenile courts." Circular 53, "Prisoners in State and Federal Prisons and Reformatories," gives information about the race and nativity of the prisoners.

10.4. Among the records of the Research Staff is the summary of a

study of the Juvenile Court in the District of Columbia, 1931–32 (1 in.). The study includes information about court proceedings involving black youths.

Record Group 11

General Records of the United States Government

11.1. This record group consists of the Constitution of the United States, the Bill of Rights and other amendments, and related records; laws of the United States and related records; international treaties and agreements; Indian treaties; Presidential proclamations, Executive orders, and other Presidential documents; rules and regulations of Federal agencies; electoral records; and the Great Seal of the United States.

11.2. The **Constitution of the United States,** 1787 (5 sheets); the **Bill of Rights,** 1789–90 (1 sheet and 1 vol., 4 in.); **ratified and unratified amendments,** 1795–1961 (3½ ft.), arranged by amendment; and related records include information about the enumeration of slaves in the population and about the slave trade as well as the 13th, 14th, and 15th amendments. These three amendments abolished slavery, defined citizens as all persons born or naturalized in the United States or subject to the jurisdiction thereof, and established the right to vote to all males regardless of race, color, or previous condition of servitude.

11.3. The **enrolled acts and resolutions of Congress, 1789–1962** (134 ft.), arranged by Congress, are original engrossed copies of laws of the United States and of joint resolutions signed by the Speaker of the House, the President of the Senate, and the President of the United States. Many of these laws pertain to matters directly affecting black Americans. Examples are the Act to Prohibit the Importation of Slaves, 1807; the Missouri Compromise, 1819–21, which prohibited slavery in all the Louisiana Territory north of latitude 36°30′; the Compromise of 1850, which provided for the abolition of the slave trade in the District of Columbia and for the passage of a stricter fugitive slave law; the Act to Establish a Bureau for the Relief of Freemen and Refugees in 1865; and the Civil Rights Acts of 1866, 1875, 1957, and 1960.

11.4. Some of the **perfected treaties, 1778–1945** (201 ft.), arranged numerically, such as the Webster–Ashburton Treaty of 1842, had specific provisions relating to slavery.

11.5. Presidential proclamations, 1791–1951 (17 ft.), arranged numerically, include the Emancipation Proclamation, which went into effect January 1, 1863, and freed the slaves in those States that had seceded from the Union. **Executive orders, 1862–1958** (22 ft.), arranged numerically, that pertain to black history are those establishing the Committee on Fair Employment Practices in 1941 (#8802); terminating segregation in the Armed Forces of the United States in 1948 (#9981); ordering an end to segregation in the Little Rock, Ark., Central High School in 1957 (#10730); and authorizing the use of Federal troops in integrating the University of Mississippi in 1962 (#11053).

Record Group 12
Records of the Office of Education

12.1. A Department of Education, headed by a Commissioner, was established by an act of 1867. In 1868 it was abolished as an independent agency and reestablished as the Office of Education (also headed by a Commissioner) in the Department of the Interior. The original statutory functions of both the Department and the Office were to collect and disseminate information on education in the United States and abroad and to promote better education throughout the country. Later legislation and Executive orders have added functions, including responsibility for Federal financial assistance to education and special studies and programs. In 1939 the Office of Education was transferred to the Federal Security Agency, which in 1953 became the Department of Health, Education, and Welfare. The records contain information about education for black youths and adults.

Records of the Office of the Commissioner

12.2. The Commissioner of Education, appointed by the President with the advice and consent of the Senate, had general direction of the programs and operations of the agency under its various designations of department, bureau, and office. Among these records is the **historical file, 1870–1950** (50 ft.), arranged according to a duplex-numeric classification scheme; the file includes records of the Commissioner, administrative officials, and specialists. The records pertain to the history, organization, programs, policies, and activities of the agency and to educational standards, methods, facilities, problems, and trends in the United States and elsewhere. There are several file categories that include data on black education. The records about the adult education program, which was designed to eradicate illiteracy among native American people, include material about education of black adults (#420, 5 in.). The category labeled "Negro Education" (#901, 10 in.) consists of some surveys of black education in the United States, such as "Thirty-Two Years of Educational Pioneering, A Statement of the Philosophy, Organization and Administration of the Bethune-Cookman College Program for the Education of Negro Youth, 1904–36," and a general survey of black education made by the Office of Education in cooperation with the Phelps-Stokes Fund. The Negro education category also includes some correspondence with Booker T. Washington of Tuskegee Institute; folders entitled "Negro Education," 1920–40; records pertaining to a December 1928 race relations conference in Washington, D.C.; and information about black participation in the World War II defense effort at home and abroad.

12.3. The **office files of Ambrose Caliver, 1946–62** (4 ft.), arranged by subject or name of conference or organization, are also among the records of the Office of the Commissioner. Caliver, a black educator and a national leader in the field of black education, was the principal official in the Office of Education concerned with the education of blacks for more than 30 years. Caliver served as senior specialist in the education of blacks, 1930–46; specialist for higher education of blacks, 1946–50; assistant to the Commissioner, 1950–62; and Chief of the Adult Education Section in the Bureau of Adult, Vocational, and Library Programs, 1955–62. Caliver's records concern his liaison work with organizations interested in the education of blacks and of adults. The materials document the Office of Education functions of formulating national education policy and of advising and cooperating with State, local, and private institutions on educational matters. Included are parts of a lengthy report by Caliver prepared at the request of the U.S. Attorney General on the feasibility of implementing a possible Supreme Court decision for the desegregation of schools.

12.4. The Major Surveys Division of the Office of the Commissioner was established in 1929 to do a series of national factfinding surveys on aspects of U.S. education. One of them was the National Survey of the Education of Teachers, and the results of the survey were published in six volumes. Volume IV is *Education of Negro Teachers in the United States,* by Ambrose Caliver, 1933. The **survey materials** for these volumes, **1930–32** (5 ft.), arranged by the name of the author, include background and research materials (1 in.) collected for Caliver's volume. The **manuscripts of survey reports, 1932–33** (1 ft.), which are arranged by volume number, include some material (3 in.) deleted from Caliver's study before publication. Records relating to the **personnel who conducted the studies, 1930–33** (1 ft.), arranged alphabetically by the name of the employee, include information (¼ in.) about Caliver's personnel. The materials include personnel action forms and job classification sheets.

12.5. The Education Media Branch was established in 1962 to collect audiovisual materials useful for education. **Sound recordings relating**

Girls sitting on the steps of the Little Zion Church, Montgomery County, Ala. Date and photographer unknown. RG 145, Records of the Agricultural Stabilization and Conservation Service. (145-AAA-5012W).

to historical events, 1937–50 (10 items), include excerpts from addresses before the Mid-Century White House Conference on Children and Youth (#12.20), including an address by black sociologist Ira DeA. Reid. **Sound recordings of the White House Conference on Education in 1965** (87 items, #12.31–12.55)—consisting of recordings of general sessions, panel discussions, and a press conference—contain discussions on such topics as school desegregation and management of urban schools. Among the participants was Kenneth B. Clark, a professor of psychology at the City College of New York. In addition, Whitney M. Young, Jr., executive director of the Urban League, served as vice-chairman of the Conference. Young participated in many of the panel discussions and delivered a report entitled "Education and the World of Work" during the final general session. The records of the 1965 Conference are among the materials for the Office of Information, as are **photographs of handicapped children, 1938–65** (about 500 items), which are arranged alphabetically by type of handicap. The prints, which sometimes depict black children, show handicapped children in educational and therapeutic situations.

Records of the Office of the Assistant Commissioner

12.6. The Assistant Commissioner acted for the Commissioner in his absence and directed educational research. In 1929 he was placed in charge of the Division of Research and Investigation, which included the following component divisions: American Schools, Higher Education, Special Problems, Foreign Education, and Statistics.

12.7. The Morrill Act of 1862 provided that each State was to receive a certain amount of public land or land script and that the proceeds from the sale of the land were to constitute a permanent fund for the establishment of colleges of agriculture and the mechanical arts. Some of the schools that were established were for the education of blacks.

12.8. Among the materials for the Division of Higher Education are the **office files of the specialists in land-grant college statistics, 1912–22** (2 in.), arranged chronologically. The specialists in land-grant college statistics were responsible for collecting educational and financial data about the colleges and for auditing their expenditures of funds provided by the Federal Government. The records relate to an exhibit about the colleges, some of which were all-black, at the San Francisco Exposition, February 1915; a study of college financial administration and courses in military training and forestry; and other matters. **Annual reports received from land-grant colleges, 1929** (1 ft.), are arranged in several categories and thereunder alphabetically by name of institution. There are folders among the annual reports labeled "Negro Schools" (totaling about 2 in.). Also among the records of this Division are the **files of Walter G. Daniel, Specialist for Higher Education of Negroes, 1951–53** (10 ft.), arranged by subject. The materials include data about the availability of college, university, and vocational training for blacks.

Records of the Vocational Education Division

12.9. Federally aided vocational education in secondary schools originated with the Smith-Hughes Act signed by President Woodrow Wilson on February 23, 1917. The act provided a grant for the promotion of vocational education and created the Federal Board for Vocational Education to administer the program. The Board was transferred to the Office of Education in 1933. At the time it was transferred, the Commissioner established the Vocational Education Division. The **State files, 1917–37** (213 ft.), arranged in chronological segments and thereunder alphabetically by State, constitute the central files of the Washington office of the Division and document its principal function, namely, the development of State programs for vocational education. Included are State plans for vocational education and interpretations of State laws; annual descriptive, statistical, and financial reports from State boards; similar records for State rehabilitation programs; and reports from Federal agents on State vocational activities. There is also correspondence on vocational guidance and occupational information, the annual contests of the American Royal Livestock Show, and the Future Farmers of America and their black counterpart, the New Farmers of America. There are sometimes separate reports on vocational programs for blacks in segregated school systems.

Records of Special Projects and Programs

12.10. The Civilian Conservation Corps (CCC) was established by an act of Congress in 1933 as an emergency measure for the relief of unemployment. The CCC camp education program in the Office of Education was established to strengthen and broaden the educational activities that developed in the CCC camps under the immediate direction of the War Department and under the general supervision of the CCC Director. The Office of Education acted in an advisory capacity to the Secretary of War in all matters relating to education in the camps. It was responsible for selecting and appointing all educational personnel and for recommending teaching procedures and instruction materials. The **central file of the CCC education program, 1934–42** (48 ft.), arranged alphabetically by name and subject in three chronological segments, consists chiefly of correspondence, memorandums, and reports of the director of the CCC education program, Howard Oxley. They relate to virtually all activities of the program. Because there were some all-black CCC companies, some of the records (6 in.) relate to the education of black youths and the employment of black advisors.

12.11. Another special project of the Office of Education was the National Survey of Vocational Education and Guidance of Negroes. The records relating to it are divided into three series: **general correspondence, 1934–38** (3 ft.), arranged alphabetically by surname and subject; **correspondence with the regional directors of the survey, 1935–37** (5 in.), arranged by the name of the regional director of the project and thereunder chronologically; and **inquiry forms, 1935–37** (7 in.), arranged alphabetically by form designation Ac–Z. The Office of Education was authorized to conduct this survey with funds provided by the Emergency Relief Appropriation Act of 1935. Caliver directed the survey. The principal staff consisted of Caliver, an associate director, four regional directors, and a technical advisory committee. Aside from its research function, the survey was designed to provide employment for white-collar blacks on relief. The major part of the interviewing and the collection of data was performed by approximately 500 local investigators with experience in teaching, social work, and office operations.

Record Group 13
Records of the National Mediation Board*

13.1. The National Mediation Board was created by the amended Railway Labor Act of 1934 to mediate railroad labor disputes. This function evolved from an 1888 act that authorized the President to establish temporary commissions to investigate and report on railroad labor controversies and provided for voluntary arbitration of disputes between carriers engaged in interstate commerce and their employees. In 1894 the President appointed the U.S. Strike Commission to investigate the Pullman strike. Under the Erdman Act of 1898, responsibility for mediation was assigned jointly to the Chairman of the Interstate Commerce Commission and the Commissioner of Labor, who were known in their mediatory capacity as the Board of Arbitration, Interstate Commerce Controversies. This Board was not officially abolished until 1926, but most of its jurisdiction was transferred in 1918 to the U.S. Railroad Administration and was assumed by the Railroad Labor Board in 1920. The Railroad Labor Board—representing management, labor, and the public—was created by the Transportation Act of 1920. It was superseded, under the terms of the Railway Labor Act of 1926, by the Board of Mediation, which was superseded by the present National Mediation Board. Information concerning black employees of railroad companies is found among the records of this Board and its predecessors.

13.2. Erdman Act case files, 1899 and 1907–13 (10 ft.), are arranged numerically by case; some unarranged material pertaining to arbitration cases is at the end of the series. Two cases primarily concern racial issues. Case 20 involves the use of black locomotive firemen by the Georgia Railroad Co. and its stations at Atlanta, 1909 (1 in.). Case 42, 1911 (1 in.), also involves black firemen and their use on preferred runs by the Cincinnati, New Orleans, and Texas Pacific Railroad. A typical case file includes the following: correspondence regarding the existence of a dispute, agreements to mediate or arbitrate, mediator's notes or reports, a copy of the terms of the mediation settlement, correspondence relating to the selection of arbitrators, notification of hearings, verbatim transcripts of testimony at hearings and related briefs and exhibits, awards and related dissenting opinions and interpretations, and press clippings.

13.3. Docket case files among the records of the Railroad Labor Board, **1920–26** (396 ft.), are arranged numerically by docket, 1–5300, and indexed. Some of the cases most obviously relating to blacks are those involving the Association of Colored Trainmen. In 1920 the association was involved in a controversy with the Illinois Central Railroad Co. and the Yazoo and Mississippi Valley Railroad over employment and seniority (#138, 2 in.). Local 2 of the association, located in Lufkin, Tex., was involved in a case with the Southern Pacific trains in Texas and Louisiana and the West Texas Railroad of Houston and Shreveport (#353-29-2, ¼ in.). The association raised the seniority issue again with the Illinois Central Railroad Co. and the Yazoo and Mississippi Valley Railroad Co. in 1924 (#4092, 1 in.). Another case pertained to discrimination on account of color brought by the Protective Order of Railway Trainmen against the Missouri Pacific Railroad. The case involved alleged discrimination against black trainmen and yardmen and collective bargaining representation (#2032, 2 in.).

13.4. The records of the Board of Mediation, 1926–34, include **wage and representation case files, 1926–35** (29 ft.), arranged numerically by case. One representation case (#C1207, 1 in.) involved A. Philip Randolph's Brotherhood of Sleeping Car Porters of Chicago, Ill. A typical case file contains the application for mediation, the mediator's reports and the final report, a case digest or summary and recommendations by the Technical Division of the Board of Mediation, statistical memorandums prepared for Board members or mediators, submissions by unions and carriers supporting their claims, ballots in representation cases, transcripts of proceedings and interpretations of mediation agreements, an agreement to arbitrate, an arbitration award, a digest of the settlement of the case, and related correspondence and memorandums.

* *Restrictions may apply to this Record Group. Consult NARS staff.*

Record Group 14

Records of the U.S. Railroad Administration

14.1. Under the authority of the Army Appropriation Act of 1916, President Wilson took full control of railroads and certain allied activities on December 28, 1917. Later proclamations extended Federal control to specified steamship lines, canals, and the American Express Co. Control was exercised through the Director General of Railroads and the U.S. Railroad Administration (USRA), which was organized into eight main divisions (including the Division of Law and the Division of Labor) and seven regional offices. Federal managers were in charge of the most important groups of railroads. Government operation continued, except on short lines that were released, until March 1920, when this control was ended by the

Transportation Act of 1920. Thereafter the Director General's staff was concerned chiefly with liquidation of assets and final settlement of USRA affairs. Most of these activities were completed by 1927, but a skeleton force functioned until 1937. Necessary clerical duties were performed by the Treasury Department, and in 1939 the remaining functions of the Director General were transferred to the Secretary of the Treasury. Some information in the records pertains to black railroad employees and passengers.

Records of the Office of the Director General

14.2. The Director General of Railroads had jurisdiction and control over every system of transportation within the boundaries of the United States except street and interurban railways. The **subject-classified general file of the Director General, 1918–27** (200 ft.), is arranged according to a USRA classification scheme. One file, P19–3 (3 in.), concerns a controversy in the 1920's over the barring of black people from purchasing prepaid rail tickets and the reaction of the NAACP to this ruling, improvement of conditions for black passengers on southern railroads, and discrimination against black passengers. Another file, E38–30 (1/8 in.), includes information relating to the pay of "colored trainmen, firemen and switchmen."

14.3. There is a **card index to the Director General's records, 1918–27** (16 ft.), that is arranged alphabetically by subject, name of correspondent, and Government agency. Some of the index cards refer to only one letter and its reply. Others refer to may pieces of correspondence. Various headings that refer to blacks are: "Colored American Council Re Elimination of Separate Cars for Negroes" (#P19–3); "Colored Association of Railroad Employees" (#38–18/17); "Trainmen–Colored" (#ES38–18/12); "National Association for the Advancement of Colored People" (#P19–3); "Passengers–Colored" (#P19–3); and "Negroes" (#01–15, #ES–18, #E13–11). Some of the subjects under "Negroes" include discrimination; effect of State laws on interstate passengers—the Jim Crow laws; employment and wages of Negroes as firemen and hostlers; facilities; use of Pullman cars in Arkansas by Negroes and whites; and Negro employees of USRA.

Records of the Division of Law

14.4. The Director General created the Division of Law, headed by a General Counsel, in 1918. The Division's functions included general supervision over all legal activities of railroads under Federal control, the preparation of contracts, work relating to claims and property protection, and the dissemination of information and advice on legal matters both to the public and to officials of the Railroad Administration. The **general file of the General Counsel, 1918–37** (53 ft.), is arranged numerically by file number 1–19963. There is a card index to this file; the **index 1918–37** (53 ft.), is arranged alphabetically by subject and name of firm or individual. A few of the index cards refer to such topics as claims of "colored" porters and Jim Crow laws.

Records of the Division of Labor

14.5. The Division of Labor was created in 1918 against a background of labor discontent. The formulation of a labor policy was one of the first tasks to confront the Director General upon the assumption of Federal control. Before Federal control, the railroad labor unions had agreements with the management of individual roads regarding wages, hours, and working conditions. When these agreements came up for renewal or revision, disputes often flared up and sometimes resulted in strikes and lockouts. The Director General felt that if a means could be found for adjusting such disputes methodically and expeditiously, this would increase the efficiency of railroad labor and help promote the successful prosecution of the war. A bipartisan board consisting of an equal number of representatives of labor and management was regarded as the most suitable tool for adjusting any differences between the two factions. Accordingly, three railway boards of adjustment were set up in the Division of Labor to settle all controversies stemming from the interpretation or application of the provisions of wage schedules or agreements that were already in effect between labor organizations and the railroads.

14.6. The subject-classified general file of the Division of Labor, 1918–22 (66 ft.), arranged according to a USRA classification scheme, includes one category entitled "rates of pay—colored employees' complaints and questions concerning general wage increases granted railroad employees by Government and special cases thereunder" (#E–38–11, 3 ft.). The records in this category pertain to black trainmen, boilermaker helpers, individual railroad workers, brakemen, and porters.

14.7. Also among the records of the Division of Labor is the **general subject file of the Women's Service Section, 1918–20** (12 ft.), arranged numerically by file number, 1–295. The Section was established to deal with complaints of female employees on railroads under Federal control. When complaints were received, investigators were sent to inspect women's working conditions and to propose methods of alleviating objectionable conditions of employment. The records include a group of forms that were completed during inspections. The forms contain information about the town or shop, division, railroad, occupation of the women, number of women, number of women under 21 years old, number of black women, date first employed, hours, wages, and union membership. Some narrative reports are also among these files. They describe the type of facilities available to women, and, if segregated, the type of facilities available to black women. The primary focus of the records is wage rates. Inspection forms are scattered from file 55 to file 220. The files also include some correspondence and some complaints.

Record Group 16

Records of the Office of the Secretary of Agriculture

16.1. The Department of Agriculture, established by an act of 1862, continued and expanded the agricultural activities that had been performed by the Patent Office since 1836. The Department was headed by a Commissioner without Cabinet rank until an act of 1889 enlarged the agency's powers and duties and made it an executive department under a Secretary. For several decades the Department was engaged chiefly in the distribution of seeds and plants and in scientific and educational work to increase agricultural production or decrease unit costs, to prevent damage by disease and insects, and to select the best varieties of plants and breeds of animals. The work of the Department has steadily expanded, and numerous changes have been made in its organization to provide for new functions, to bring together related scientific and economic work, and to coordinate various research, extension, and regulatory activities.

16.2. The vast majority of the black population of the United States was engaged in agricultural pursuits before the large-scale migrations to the North during the two World Wars. Many issues about blacks have been raised with the Secretary of Agriculture. Some pertain to agricultural education and improved training for black farmers; others concern the political affairs of blacks in general, not only farmers.

Records of the Office of the Secretary of Agriculture

16.3. The **letters sent by the Secretary's Office, 1893–1941** (1,129 vols. and unbound material, totaling 300 ft.), are arranged alphabetically by the name of the office or bureau that prepared the letter and thereunder chronologically. Many of the volumes include correspondence to George Washington Carver that pertains to agricultural education and experimental techniques for the cultivation of various crops. There is some biographical information about Carver. There are a number of indexes to these records.

16.4. The **general correspondence of the Office of the Secretary, 1906–70** (3,543 ft.), is arranged by year and thereunder by subject. This series is the best primary source of information on the relationship of the Federal Government to agriculture. It relates primarily to

County agent, home demonstration agent, and rural nurse with Tuskegee Institute bus, Alabama, in 1923. Booker T. Washington conceived the idea of a movable agricultural school to carry new ideas, methods, and equipment to farmers in rural areas near Tuskegee Institute. The first demonstration wagon began operation in May 1906. Success with this venture led to acceptance by the Federal Government and the hiring of the first black demonstration agent. The scope of the service rendered by the Booker T. Washington Agricultural School on Wheels expanded to include a home demonstration agent in 1914 and a registered nurse in 1920. Photographer unknown. RG 16, Records of the Office of the Secretary of Agriculture. (16-G-280-S2544C).

policy, organization, and procedure and often summarizes the results of work done in constituent units of the Department. It contains letters sent and received, memorandums, and reports by the Secretary, the Assistant or Under Secretary, and other officials in the Secretary's immediate office.

16.5. There are a number of black history topics interspersed among the correspondence files of the Office of the Secretary. Although the records in general are arranged by year, those under the heading "Negroes" for the years from 1917 to 1955 have been extracted from the files and boxed together (1 ft., 3 in.). For later years black history topics can be found under headings such as "Civil Rights," "Personnel–Discrimination," "Farm Tenancy," "Economic Opportunity," "Equal Employment," and "Contracts." An important aspect of the Secretary's files is that they reflect the activities of various bureaus and offices of the Department in relation to the black population. The correspondence and reports are especially helpful in documenting the growth of Federal Extension Service (FES) activities in black farm communities and the Department's employment of black staff to serve these areas. Many students were recruited for the FES from black colleges such as Tuskegee Institute, Hampton Institute, and the Florida Agricultural and Mechanical College (now Florida A&M University). The 1921 folder includes a departmental publication entitled *Exten-*

sion Work Among Negroes, 1920 (24 pp.), which gives a history of the work as well as the names of the black extension agents. The report states that "altogether 224 agents, 157 men and 67 women, are employed" (p. 6). (See also RG 33.)

16.6. Many of the letters in the correspondence files of the Office of the Secretary refer to the establishment of an office or a position within the Department to deal with specific needs of the black farmer. Giles B. Jackson, a black attorney from Richmond, Va., submitted proposals for a Federal Government office concerned with the needs of black Americans, especially farmers. Other letters pertain to the black press, black land-grant colleges, tenancy, sharecropping, the distribution of the black population, and black employees in the Department. Correspondence during the two World Wars and the period in between is concerned with black farmers and soldiers in the defense effort, migration of blacks to the North, protests against lynching from the NAACP and other black organizations, the Marcus Garvey movement and other colonization efforts, blacks and New Deal agencies, black farmers organizations, and the Fair Employment Practice Committee. Post-World War II records document various aspects of the civil rights movement. Although many records relating to black history are not in these folders, there are usually cross-reference sheets that give the location of other letters.

Records of the Office of Information

16.7. The Office of Information was responsible for the general direction and supervision of publications and other informational policies and activities incident to the preparation and dissemination of the results of the Department's work. This Office produced a series of farm radio programs originally presenting crop and market news and weather reports and then expanding to informational and educational programs that reported departmental activities. In 1930 the "National Farm and Home Hour" was inaugurated; it became a popular radio program, which was broadcast for many years. The Motion Picture and Exhibits Service became part of the Office in 1942, and in 1953 a television service was begun.

16.8. The **index to correspondence and press or radio releases, 1913–44** (190 ft.), is arranged according to a subject-numeric scheme. Under "Negroes" (#3.0 and #3.04) are a number of index cards. Each card gives the date of the communication and a digest of its contents. The color of the card indicates the type of communication; for example, blue: radio; pink: general; white: correspondence; and yellow: press release. A later **index to press and radio releases, 1945–63** (168 ft.), is arranged in two chronological breakdowns, 1945–54 and 1955–63, and thereunder by subject. There are many cards for black history under "Racial Relations."

16.9. The **general correspondence, 1913–44** (87 ft.), is arranged

Men bringing bags of cotton from the fields on the G. B. Walker plantation, Washington County, Miss. October 1941. L. C. Harmon, photographer. RG 16, Records of the Office of the Secretary of Agriculture. (16-G-116-2-4).

according to a subject-numeric filing scheme and thereunder chronologically. There is a folder, "Negroes" (#3.0, ½ in.), that includes information about farming activities among blacks; reports from black staff members such as Sherman Briscoe, Thomas M. Campbell, Claude A. Barnett, and Albon L. Holsey; and information about black farmers' relations with the Farm Security Administration, the Federal Extension Service, and the Agricultural Adjustment Administration. There is also some correspondence about the benefits of the school lunch program for black youths.

16.10. Press releases, 1913–63 (194 ft.), are arranged by year and thereunder by number. (The indexes for these press releases are described in paragraph 16.8. The file number given on an index card might be 20–2111 (282–42). The number 20–2111 indicates that it is a press release; 282 is the number of the release; and 42 is the year.) Many press releases addressed to black Americans cover such topics as black personnel in the Department, black land-grant colleges, wartime food production, agricultural development at Tuskegee Institute, blacks in the Extension Service, the school lunch program, tenant farmers, sharecroppers, blacks and the Agricultural Adjustment Administration, income and living expenses of black farmers, and Department relations with the black press. A few random titles of press releases are "Negro Farmers in Wartime Food Production" (#20–2111 (1006–44)); "Sixteen Years Ago the First Negro Agricultural Demonstration Agent Employed. Now 285 Negro Men and Women—Serving 14,000 Negro Farmers" (#20–2111 (651–23)); and "Booker T's Granddaughter" (#20–2111 (681–43)).

16.11. Radio releases, 1926–54 (33 ft.), are arranged chronologically. These are mimeographed copies of scripts for programs such as "Farm Flashes" and the "National Farm and Home Hour." The indexes (described in paragraph 16.8) include only a few blue cards, which indicate radio releases. Some of the radio releases for the "National Farm and Home Hour" that relate to black history are: Thomas M. Campbell, "Historical Sketch of Negro 4–H Club Work," May 2, 1936; John M. Gandy, "What the Negro Land Grant Colleges Are and What They Are Doing," December 18, 1935; and Thomas B. Patterson, "Extension Work Among Negroes in Virginia," December 18, 1935.

16.12. The Information Office produced a film entitled "Henry Brown, Farmer" (#16.655) for the Agricultural Adjustment Administration. The film is narrated by Canada Lee and depicts the life of a black farmer and his family during wartime. Black aviators are highlighted. There are a few press releases about the film. There is also an Italian-language version of the film.

Office of Civilian Conservation Corps Activities

16.13. This Office was established in July 1938 as a unit of the Office of the Secretary of Agriculture. It was responsible for the administration and coordination of Civilian Conservation Corps programs carried on by various bureaus of the Department. The Office had a chief liaison officer who served as coordinator between the War Department and the other Departments cooperating in CCC work. The **correspondence of the chief, 1933–42** (16 ft.), is arranged by subject. There is a folder entitled "Personnel–Assignment–Negro Camps" (¼ in.), and additional information about black history is interspersed among the records. (See also RG 35.)

Record Group 21

Records of District Courts of the United States

21.1. U.S. district and circuit courts were created by an act of 1789. The district courts had exclusive, original jurisdiction in civil cases involving admiralty and maritime matters; the circuit courts were given appellate and original jurisdiction in certain cases. The United States is currently divided into 11 judicial circuits, and each State is assigned to one of the circuits. For each circuit there is a U.S. Court of Appeals, which is an intermediate court having the right to review all final decisions and some interlocutory decisions of district courts. Each State has at least one district court, which is the trial court having general Federal jurisdiction.

21.2. These court records, 1789–1944 (about 90,000 ft., located in regional archives branches), are arranged geographically by name of district or circuit court and thereunder by type of record. The records include dockets; indexes; minutes; judgments and decrees; final records; and equity, civil, criminal, and admiralty case papers. Court cases involving black Americans are interspersed throughout these records; however, most of them can only be located by name of case, by the nature of the case, or by racial designations within the records. The most easily identifiable records for black history are those pertaining to various aspects of slavery, such as the slave trade, slaving vessels, fugitive slaves, manumissions, emancipation, and the enfranchisement of freed slaves. The records of the Federal courts of the northeastern part of the country are the richest in this kind of record.

Slavery and the Slave Trade

21.3. Admiralty case files concerning the slave trade generally contain court proceedings relating to the seizure, condemnation, and sale of vessels engaged in the trade. Criminal case files concerning the slave trade pertain to the outfitting of slave ships and to the prosecution of the masters and crews of the ships.

21.4. The records of the district and circuit courts for the district of Massachusetts include cases for Massachusetts, Connecticut, and Rhode Island and contain about 200 cases involving violations of the slave trade laws. They are arranged chronologically. The records include case papers, docket books, and final records. Some of the district and circuit court records for the State of Connecticut relate to the capture of the slave vessel *Amistad* in 1839 and subsequent trials to declare the slaves that were on board legally free. A few other examples of cases relating to the slave trade

Daguerrotype of one of Thomas Jefferson's former Monticello slaves, Isaac, taken when he was an elderly man. Date and photographer unknown. RG 306, Records of the U.S. Information Agency. (306-ST-721-62-2962).

concern the seizure of the brig *Malaga* at Kabinda Bay in West Africa by the U.S.S. *Boxer* for engaging in the slave trade, 1846; the *Porpoise,* a slaver seized at Rio de Janiero, 1845; the *William G. Lewis,* taken at Newport, R.I., 1856; the *Laurens,* captured at New London, Conn., 1859; and the *Wanderer,* seized at Boston, Mass., 1859.

21.5. Among the records of the **southern district of New York** are **criminal cases, 1790–1912** (55 ft.) and **1845–68** (4 ft.), arranged numerically by case number, which include some district and circuit court cases about ships and crews engaging in the slave trade. **Admiralty records, 1790–1912** (620 ft.), are arranged chronologically by year to 1828 and thereunder by the name of the vessel involved; after 1828 the cases are arranged by docket number. Most of the admiralty cases concern seizure and forfeiture of vessels and cargo for violations of customs laws, nonpayment of seamen's wages, and physical abuse of seamen; some cases relate to ships engaged in the slave trade, including the seizure of slave trade vessels. Both criminal and admiralty case files include narratives and information explaining the nature of the suits.

21.6. The **minutes, trial notes, and rolls of attorneys of the circuit court for the southern district of New York, 1790–1841,** have been reproduced as M854 (3 rolls). There are some black history materials among the minutes, which are the proceedings of the court. They are arranged chronologically by date of session and relate to the evasion of customs duties; trespass laws; salvage, privateering, and prize laws; mutinies and revolts; and slavery and the slave trade.

21.7. Some of the **criminal files for the eastern district of Pennsylvania, 1791–1883** (6 ft.), arranged alphabetically by defendant's name or chronologically by the session of the court, include cases concerning persons who were engaged in the slave trade. The **law (civil action) records** of this court, **1787–1844** (M1057, 40 rolls), arranged chronologically, pertain to actions for forfeitures arising from violations of customs and internal revenue laws, but there are also some cases concerning the illegal transportation of slaves.

21.8. Among the **minutes of the Maryland district court, 1790–1911** (M931, 7 rolls), arranged chronologically, are references to slavery and the slave trade. The minutes are a record of the activities of the court, showing dates of sessions; names of presiding judges, marshals, and clerks; and, usually, judgments and orders of the court arising from the litigation of cases before it. In almost all cases the minutes simply list the case and give a brief account of the action taken.

Fugitive Slave Records

21.9. There are court records concerning fugitive and emancipated slaves. The writ of habeas corpus was generally used by masters to reclaim fugitive slaves. This writ is generally considered as the most famous writ in law, having been employed for many centuries to remove illegal restraint on personal liberty. Cases arising from the Fugitive Slave Law of 1850 are closely related to the habeas corpus cases involving runaway slaves. Sometimes cases resulting from this law are filed with the habeas corpus cases. A part of the Compromise of 1850, enacted by Congress on September 18, 1850, provided that claimants of fugitive slaves might recover them by applying to Federal judges and commissioners for warrants for the arrest of the fugitives, or by arresting them and taking them before the judges or commissioners to establish ownership. The testimony of the fugitives was not to be admitted in evidence. The act provided for the punishment of anyone who interfered with its enforcement.

21.10. Most of the **habeas corpus cases for the District of Columbia circuit court, 1820–60** (2 ft.; M434, 2 rolls), arranged chronologically, involve persons alleged to have been fugitive slaves.

21.11. The **records of the clerk of the district court for the southern district of New York, 1746–1932, and of the U.S. commissioners of the same court, 1837–60** (M938, 1 roll), are arranged chronologically. These records relate solely to fugitive slaves. They consist of affidavits, petitions, and proofs filed by owners of runaway slaves; the owners were seeking to reclaim the fugitives, who were believed to have fled to areas under the jurisdiction of the court. The names of the slaves are Nat; James Hamlett; John VanOrden; Stephen, Robert, and Jacob Pembrook; Abraham Harris; Edmund Dye; Josiah Hoy; and Allen Goff.

21.12. The **habeas corpus records for the district court for the eastern district of Pennsylvania, 1848–62** (6 in.), arranged chronologically, include petitions for writs of habeas corpus, writs of habeas corpus endorsed with the returns of the marshal, depositions, and warrants. Most of the cases originated in the arrest of fugitive slaves or people opposed to the Union cause in the Civil War. The **criminal case files** of this court, **1791–1840** (5 ft.; M986, 7 rolls), arranged chronologically, include cases referring to the harboring of fugitive slaves.

21.13. The **general records of the district court for the eastern district of Pennsylvania, 1795–1850** (1 in.), arranged by subject, include a letter from the Secretary of the Navy to the judges enclosing a copy of a Presidential order relating to the possibility of military aid to the court in the enforcement of the Fugitive Slave Law of 1850. Also included is a letter to justice Robert C. Grier from Charles Gibbons, accompanied by a draft of Grier's reply, concerning the right of alleged fugitive slaves to present witnesses in their behalf, 1850.

21.14. Fugitive slave case files for the eastern district of Pennsylvania, 1850–60 (1 in.), arranged chronologically, include affidavits of ownership of fugitive slaves, depositions, records of proceedings in the claimant's State to establish ownership of the slaves, warrants for the arrest of the fugitives, and certificates of ownership issued by the court. An interesting case is that of the fugitive Moses Honner in 1860, which includes notes of testimony, an opinion of the judge, an affidavit of the claimant that he feared a rescue of the slave would be attempted, and the marshal's account for extra expenses incurred in preparing to resist such an attempt.

Manumission and Emancipation Records

21.15. Some court records refer to the manumission and emancipation of slaves. Manumission papers for the U.S. Circuit Court of the District of Columbia (covering the period from 1820 to the passage of the act of April 16, 1862, that abolished slavery in the District of Columbia) reflect the voluntary freeing of slaves by their owners. Some slaves were freed by their owners for good service, other slaves paid for their freedom, and some were freed by wills. After the act of 1862, owners were required to file a schedule of their slaves with the court and the court then issued certificates of freedom to all freedmen. A subsequent act of July 12, 1862, provided for the filing of the schedule by minor and absentee owners or by the slave if any owner neglected to file.

21.16. The **minutes for the circuit court of the District of Columbia, 1801–63** (30 vols., 10 ft.), are arranged chronologically. They record information about the manumission of slaves and various other aspects of slavery and the slave trade. In most cases, the minutes give only a brief account of the action taken.

21.17. The records of this court include both bound and loose manumission and emancipation records. All of the emancipation records are dated 1862 or after, while all of the manumission papers are for the period between 1821 and 1862. The **bound manumission and emancipation records, 1821–62** (6 vols., 1 ft.), arranged chronologically, include the name of the person freed and such information as occupation, whether the person paid the master for freedom, whether freed by will, or any other conditions. There is an **index to the manumissions, 1821–28** (1 vol., ½ in.), arranged alphabetically by the initial letter of surname. **Loose manumission papers, 1857–63** (6 in.), are arranged chronologically, and **loose emancipation papers, 1862–63** (10 in.), are arranged alphabetically by the initial letter of surname. Many of the records pertaining to slavery and emancipation for this court have been reproduced as M433 (3 rolls).

Other Black History Records

21.18. The District of Columbia circuit court records also include chancery cases. Chancery jurisdiction was exercised by this court from the time it was founded in 1801 until it was dissolved in 1863. The **index to the chancery cases, 1801–63** (2 vols., 5 in.), arranged alphabetically, occasionally includes racial designations.

21.19. Other black history materials include some **census schedules** among the **records of the clerk of the court for the eastern district of Pennsylvania, 1820–30** (5 vols., 6 in.), arranged by ward. The census of 1820 for the New Market Ward and the Lower Delaware Ward in Philadelphia shows the names of heads of families and the number of people in the families, addresses, occupations, sex, age group, and race, including free black and slave. (Although there are sections on the schedules for information about slaves, they are blank.) The schedules also list the number of black persons who were blind and dumb.

21.20. The **records for the Maryland district court, 1790–1911** (M931, 7 rolls), arranged chronologically, include cases pertaining to efforts to enforce voting rights for blacks during the Reconstruction era. Some records of the U.S. District Court for the Eastern District of Virginia concern the supervision of elections. Among them are **registers of white and black voters** in Clay, Jackson, Jefferson, Madison, Marshall, and Monroe Wards **in the city of Richmond, 1886–92** (41 vols., 1 ft.), arranged by ward and thereunder by surname.

Record Group 25

Records of the National Labor Relations Board*

25.1. The National Labor Relations Board (NLRB) was created by the National Labor Relations Act (the Wagner Act) of 1935. The NLRB was preceded by two earlier boards, the first of which, the National Labor Board (NLB), was established in 1933 by the President to adjust industrial disputes arising from the interpretation and application of the President's Reemployment Agreement or of any approved code of fair competition under the National Industrial Recovery Act. The NLB was replaced by the first National Labor Relations Board, established by authority of a public resolution of 1934. The first National Labor Relations Board continued many cases and enforced decisions of the NLB. Both these Boards utilized a system of regional boards to deal with labor controversies in the field; both regional and national boards engaged in the settlement of labor disputes, enforced collective bargaining requirements, and conducted elections for employee representatives. After the National Industrial Recovery Act was declared unconstitutional in 1935, the first National Labor Relations Board virtually ceased to function.

25.2. The Wagner Act affirmed the right of employees to organize and to designate representatives for collective bargaining purposes. The second NLRB was authorized to determine the unit of employees appropriate for bargaining, conduct secret elections for employee representatives, and require employers to end specified unfair labor practices that frustrated collective bargaining in industries other than the railroads and, after 1936, the airlines. The War Labor Disputes Act of 1943 (the Smith-Connally Act) authorized the Board to hold strike vote elections in labor disputes that seriously threatened to interrupt war production. The Labor Management Relations Act of 1947 (the Taft-Hartley Act), as amended, defined some labor practices forbidden to organized labor and restricted the Board to a primarily judicial and policymaking role. NLRB operations, particularly administrative procedures, were further modified by the Labor-Management Reporting and Disclosure Act of 1959 (the Landrum-Griffin Act).

25.3. Most NLRB records are **case files, 1933–59** (5,900 ft.). There are headquarters case files and regional records (which are available at various regional archives); all case files are arranged by case number. The NLRB published a multivolume series of its decisions, which can be used as an index. It is arranged by the name of the company and union involved.

Though many cases involve industries in which blacks were employed, only a few specifically concern racial issues. For example, among the records of the second National Labor Relations Board is a case involving the Atlanta Oak Flooring Co. and the United Brotherhood of Carpenters and Joiners of America, Local Unions 2281 and 552, June 29, 1945 (#10–R–1464, 1 in.). One of the issues was that the company declined to recognize the petitioning unions because they engaged "in illegal and discriminatory segregation of employees on the sole basis of race and color in contravention of the National Policy as expressed by the President of the United States in violation of the fifth amendment to the Constitution of the United States." In the case of Larus and Brother Co., Inc., and the Tobacco Workers International Union Local 219, American Federation of Labor, June 21, 1945 (#5–R–1413, 4 in.), "there was bargaining along racial lines from 1941–43; the white workers represented by the A. F. of L. and the colored workers by the C.I.O. . . ." The file includes transcripts of the case, copies of agreements with the separate locals, lists of employees, and correspondence. The major question was union representation at the bargaining table.

* *Restrictions may apply to this Record Group. Consult NARS staff.*

Record Group 26

Records of the U.S. Coast Guard

26.1. The U.S. Coast Guard, established in the Department of the Treasury in 1915, was formed by consolidating the Department's Revenue-Cutter Service (established in 1790) and Lifesaving Service (established in 1878). It took over lighthouse administration in 1939. In April 1967, the Coast Guard became a part of the Department of Transportation.

26.2. The Coast Guard, which operates on the high seas and navigable waters of the United States and its territories and possessions, is a military service and operates as part of the Navy in time of war or when the President directs. Its major duties include enforcing customs and navigation laws, supervising vessel anchorages and movements, reporting marine casualties, protecting life and property at sea, installing and maintaining aids to navigation and to transoceanic aviation, and carrying on oceanographic observation as part of an interagency program. Material pertinent to the study of black history is among the records of several Coast Guard components.

Records of the Bureau of Lighthouses and Its Predecessors

26.3. The maintenance of lighthouses was performed by Treasury Department officials from 1789 until the Light-House Board, created in

1852, was transferred to the Department of Commerce and Labor in 1903. The Light-House Board was superseded in 1910 by the Bureau of Lighthouses, which remained in the Department of Commerce when the Department of Labor became a separate agency in 1913. It was consolidated with the Coast Guard in 1939.

26.4. The **correspondence of the Bureau of Lighthouses, 1911–39** (639 ft.), is arranged according to a subject-numeric system and relates to the location, building, and maintenance of lighthouses. A **subject index to the Bureau of Lighthouses correspondence, 1901–39** (159 ft.), includes a card entitled "Negroes" with several entries. These entries refer to correspondence containing information about Civil Service requirements for blacks, discrimination, and black political appointees; the correspondence also contains queries about the number of blacks employed in the lighthouse service. One letter (#1633E) dated July 5, 1928, states that there were 308 "Negro appointees or employees" in the lighthouse service with salaries totaling $228,339.68.

26.5. Also among the records of the Light-House Board are the **muster rolls of the light tender *Pansy*, 1895–1901,** and **of Light Vessel No. 43, 1881–84** (¼ in.). These muster rolls give for each crew member such information as name, monthly pay, date of entry, residence, birthplace, age, height, complexion, color of eyes and hair, marital status, and next of kin. Some of the cabin boys, stewards, cooks, and mess attendants are listed as colored under the column for complexion.

Records of the Revenue-Cutter Service

26.6. A 1790 act of Congress authorized the construction and equipment of cutters to enforce laws governing the collection of customs and tonnage duties. Customs collectors supervised the cutters from 1791 until 1843, when the Revenue Marine Division of the Office of the Secretary of the Treasury took over that function. In 1849, control of cutters was again transferred to the collectors, but in 1871 a new Revenue Marine Division was established. It became the Revenue-Cutter Service in 1894. Its functions included suppressing the slave trade.

26.7. Information about the work of the Revenue-Cutter Service in the prevention of the African slave trade appears in various series. For example, one volume, designated **"Extraordinary Operations and Legislation," 1789–1871** (2 in.), includes copies of correspondence from various components of the Service on the subject. One entry states that on July 8, 1820, the brig *General Ramirez* was captured off St. Augustine by the cutter *Dallas*. The brig was carrying a cargo of about 280 African slaves.

26.8. One man of African descent achieved very prominent status in the Service. Michael Healy, the son of an Irish immigrant and a mulatto slave woman, was accepted into the Revenue-Cutter Service in 1865. He became a first lieutenant in 1870 and second lieutenant in 1886. In 1886 he took command of the polar ship *Bear*. The following series include some Healy correspondence and some information about the ship he commanded. The **letters sent, 1790–1897** (212 vols., 43 ft.), arranged chronologically, consist of copies of letters sent to collectors of customs, captains of cutters, officials in other Government departments, and private persons. **Letters received, 1836–1910** (308 vols., 55 ft.), arranged chronologically, include those from officials in other Government agencies, collectors of customs, captains of cutters, and private persons. There is an index in the beginning of each volume of the letters sent and received.

26.9. Healy commanded the *Bear* until 1895. The **logs of cutters and Coast Guard vessels, 1819–1947** (2,907 ft.), arranged alphabetically by name of vessel, include logs maintained by Healy for the *Bear* (2 ft.). Information about the vessel's expeditions is also in *Alaska File of the Revenue-Cutter Service, 1867–1914* (M641, 20 rolls).

26.10. Other records with information relating to black history are the **letters from officers of cutters, 1833–69** (90 vols., 14 ft.), arranged chronologically. One volume for the years 1834–36 consists of a survey of lighthouses and revenue boats on the Atlantic coast. Each attendant described his staff, and some attendants mentioned that they held slaves or employed free blacks who worked with their lighthouse operation.

26.11. Among the personnel and payroll records are **muster rolls, 1848–1910** (47 ft.), which consist of ships' copies of lists of the officers and crews of cutters. The muster rolls are arranged alphabetically by name of vessel. Information about crew members generally includes name of ship, date, name of crew member, rank or rate, number of days present this month, date of enlistment, where enlisted, where born, personal description (age, occupation, eyes, hair, complexion), and remarks (whether detached, transferred, discharged, deserted, or died—and date and place the event occurred). Various forms were used to record this information, but most often it appears on muster roll form 2016. Many cooks, stewards, and mess attendants are identified as black, mulatto, Negro, or colored under the personal description column.

Records of the Lifesaving Service

26.12. This Service was established in 1871 in the Revenue Marine Division of the Treasury Department to construct and maintain lifesaving stations and assist shipwrecked vessels and crews. It was placed under a general superintendent immediately responsible to the Secretary of the Treasury in 1878.

26.13. The correspondence of this Service includes **letters received, 1847–1914** (113 vols., 242 ft.). They are arranged numerically by assigned number and chronologically thereunder. One letter, from Charles F. Shoemaker, assistant inspector, to Sumner J. Kimball, General Superintendant of the Lifesaving Service, dated January 6, 1880 (#S102, vol. 9, 19 pp.), gives a history of the establishment of an all-black staff at the Pea Island, N.C., lifesaving station under the direction of Richard Etheridge, the first black appointed to "keepership" in the Service. The letter also gives information about other black men in the Service. The **logs of lifesaving stations, 1873–1945** (23,554 vols., 2,169 ft. in the Archives Branch, Philadelphia Federal Archives and Records Center), include volumes for Pea Island (78 vols., 6½ ft.). The Pea Island volumes contain information about weather conditions, vessels sighted, lives saved, and members of crews and patrols.

Records of the U.S. Coast Guard

26.14. The **miscellaneous reference materials, 1910–41** (15 ft.), arranged by subject, include a small alphabetical subject file. Under "N" is a folder entitled "Negroes in the Coast Guard" (¼ in.). The folder contains information about the participation of black coastguardsmen in wars, names some who received decorations, and gives general statistical information.

26.15. Among the audiovisual records for the Coast Guard is the **activities, facilities, and personalities photograph series, 1886–1967** (15,000 items), arranged alphabetically by subject or name. Some photographs show black coastguardsmen training, on duty, in combat, and relaxing; others show black marines and soldiers on transports operated by the Coast Guard in war zones during World War II. Prominent black personnel in the Coast Guard can also be located by using the personalities section of the series, which is arranged alphabetically by last name.

Record Group 28
Records of the U.S. Postal Service

28.1. The Office of the Postmaster General was created by an act of September 22, 1789, which continued regulations that originated with the appointment on July 26, 1775, of Benjamin Franklin as Postmaster General by the Continental Congress. The first act to provide in detail for a Post Office Department was passed February 20, 1792, and subsequent legislation enlarged its duties. Although the Postmaster General has been a member of the Cabinet since 1829, the Post Office Department did not attain the status of an executive department until June 8, 1872. Assistant Postmasters General, authorized by acts of 1792, 1810, 1836, and 1891, were assigned administrative supervision over specific functions of the Department.

28.2. The records of the immediate office of the Postmaster General include **letters sent from 1789 to 1952** (502 vols., 90 ft.), arranged chronologically. These are fair, press, and carbon copies of letters relating mainly to post offices, postmasters, mail transportation, mail contracts, and postal laws and regulations. Included among the earlier correspondence are a few letters pertaining to the establishment of laws forbidding black men to work as mail carriers. Some letters relating to blacks are dated January 13, 1800; February 10, March 23, and April 14, 1802; and December 10, 1828.

28.3. Another early record is the **journal of Hugh Finlay, Surveyor of Post Roads and Post Offices, 1773–74** (1 vol., 1 in.), which includes a May 17, 1774, entry pertaining to the use of black riders as mail carriers. A **scrapbook of circulars, notices, instructions, regulations, and newspaper clippings, 1823–71** (1 vol., 2 in.), includes information on the distribution of antislavery publications.

28.4. The Solicitor was appointed to take charge of contracts and other legal matters. The Post Office accumulated case files relating to the denial of second-class mailing privileges to periodicals and other publications under section 12 of the Espionage Act of June 15, 1917 (40 Stat. 217). The act provided that any publication advocating treason, insurrection, or forcible resistance to any law of the United States was nonmailable. The **records relating to the Espionage Act, World War I, 1917–21** (94 ft.), arranged numerically, include some files about black-owned periodicals and newspapers and about propaganda directed to black Americans: Robert Abbott's paper the *Chicago Defender* (#B–349, 2 in.); *Crisis*, the NAACP magazine edited by W. E. B. DuBois (#B–123, ¼ in.); *The Messenger*, edited by labor unionist A. Philip Randolph (#B–240, 1 in.); Negro propaganda, miscellaneous (#B–398, 2 in.); *Negro World*, an organ of Marcus Garvey's Universal Negro Improvement Association (#B–500, 2 in.); *New York News* (#B–210, ⅛ in.); and *The Veteran* (#B–397, ⅛ in.).

28.5. There are also a few fliers, pamphlets, and books among the records relating to the 1917 Espionage Act: "Justice for the Negro" (#28); "Why the Negro Should Vote the Socialist Ticket" (#51); "Chicago Race Riots" (#207); *The Black Man's Burden*, by E. Morel (#495); "The Black Evil" (#593); "Greetings from the Negro People of America" (#619); "Colored Workers of America, Why You Should Join the IWW" (#598); and "To Colored Working Men and Women" (#B192). Copies of many of these pamphlets are also available in a series called the unnumbered file.

28.6. The **records relating to the Espionage Act of World War II, 1943–45** (25 ft.), are case files, similar to those described in paragraph 28.4, pertaining to the denial of mailing privileges to certain publications.

Files pertaining to periodicals published by blacks include the National Negro Council letter, (#E–178, ¼ in.); *New Negro World* (#E–208, 1¼ in.); *Black Dispatch* (#E–280, ¼ in.); and *Philadelphia Afro-American* (#E–419, 2 in.).

28.7. The **records of appointment of postmasters, 1832–90** (98 vols., 33 ft.), are arranged in chronological periods, thereunder by name of State or Territory in rough alphabetical order, thereunder by name of county, and thereunder by name of post office. These records contain the names of postmasters for each post office and dates of their appointments; the dates of discontinuance and reestablishment and name changes of post offices; and, occasionally, dates of changes in location or site of post offices. These records have no racial designations, but blacks did serve as both postmasters and postmistresses. The researcher would need to know the name and the place of service except in the cases of black towns and settlements such as Mound Bayou, Miss.

Record Group 29

Records of the Bureau of the Census*

29.1. The Census Office was established in 1902 as a permanent bureau in the Department of the Interior. The first nine censuses were taken by U.S. district marshals. The 1790 census returns were submitted directly to the President, those from 1800 to 1840 to the Secretary of State, and those from 1850 to 1870 to the Secretary of the Interior. From 1880 to 1900 the censuses were taken by enumerators under supervisors responsible through the Superintendent of the Census to the Secretary of the Interior. In 1903 the Census Office was transferred from the Department of the Interior to the Department of Commerce and Labor. Since 1913 it has been in the Department of Commerce. The terms "Census Office" and "Census Bureau" were used interchangeable until the term "Bureau of the Census" was formally fixed by law in 1954.

29.2. The Census Bureau is responsible for providing basic statistics about the people and economy of the Nation to assist the Congress, Government, and public in planning, carrying out, and evaluating programs. It collects, tabulates, and publishes a wide variety of statistical data for Government and private users. Because of the nature of the census records, statistical data about the black population in the United States is interspersed throughout the records.

Administrative Records of the Census Office

29.3. Summaries of the 1850 census returns (3 vols., 2 in.) are arranged by the name of the marshal's district and thereunder by subdivision number. For each enumeration subdivision, the summary shows the subdivision number; the "civil division" (county and towns) composing the subdivision; and the number of dwellings, families, inhabitants by sex and color, deaths, farms, and industrial establishments in the subdivision. Among the records of the Office is a **report on population, 1870** (3 vols., 4 in.), arranged alphabetically by State and thereunder alphabetically by name of county or other civil division. The report consists of photostatic copies of (1) tables showing aggregates of white, free colored, slave, Chinese, and Indian inhabitants by county for the censuses of 1790–1870 and (2) tables showing, for the census of 1870, aggregates of native and foreign inhabitants and white and colored persons and, for the censuses of 1850 and 1860, the aggregates of white and colored inhabitants in civil divisions smaller than counties.

Administrative Records of the Bureau of the Census

29.4. There are some records about the black population in the **subject file, 1889–1950** (55 ft.), of the Geography Division. The records are arranged alphabetically by subject. Information about blacks (1 ft.) appears under headings such as "Slaves and Slaveholders"; "District of Columbia, Percent of Negro Population by Police Precincts: 1920"; "Distribution of Aggregate Foreign Born and Negro Population by Mean Annual Temperature: 1880–1890 and 1900"; "Center of Population: White and Negro for the South Atlantic and South Central States, 1900, 1890 and 1880"; and "Drainage Basins: 1910 Aggregate, Foreign-Born White and Negro."

29.5. Also among the records of the Geography Division is the **record set of decennial maps, 1860–1953** (1,600 items, 10 in.). This record set includes maps, atlases, and graphs, arranged chronologically by census, depicting the findings of the decennial censuses as to population, agriculture, irrigation, drainage, manufacturers, vital statistics, mines and quarries, cotton, financial status of cities, religious bodies, the hospitalized insane, and marriage and divorce. Also depicted are the distribution of the slave population in the Southern States (1860) and the distribution and density of population by age, sex, race, nationality of foreign born, physically and mentally handicapped groups, and religious bodies.

29.6. The Chief Statistician of the Census Bureau, Joseph A. Hill, collected a series of **memorandums and notes, 1905–40** (6 ft.), which contains some relevant documents. Among Hill's materials, arranged alphabetically by subject, are folders entitled "Negro Enumeration of 1920"

James and Ernest Solomon of Sumter County, Ga., and their pet pigs on their grandfather's farm. October 1947. Forsythe, photographer. RG 16, Records of the Office of the Secretary of Agriculture. (16-N-9614).

(⅛ in.) and "Negro Migration, Recent Northward" (1 in.). The first folder includes a 10-page article by LeVerne Beales, an expert special agent of the Bureau, entitled "The Negro Enumeration of 1920. A Reply to Dr. Kelly Miller." Miller's article, "Enumeration Errors in Negro Population," had been published in the February 1922 issue of *Scientific Monthly*. The second folder consists of tables, correspondence, and the manuscript and printed article by Hill entitled "The Recent Northward Migration of the Negro," which was published in the *Monthly Labor Review* of March 1924.

29.7. Among the **correspondence of Joseph A. Hill, 1911–40** (3 ft.), which is arranged by name or subject in two chronological groups, 1911–32 and 1924–40, is scattered correspondence pertaining to census reports on black Americans. One folder, "Negro Report–1910" (¼ in.), contains some instructions for the preparation of Census Bulletin 129, "Negroes in the United States," as well as letters commenting on the bulletin. The bulletin is not included in the folder.

29.8. The position of attorney-advisor was established in the Statistical Reports Section of the Office of the Director of Statistical Standards, probably in 1948. When the legal advisory duties were transferred to that Office from the Governments Division, Robert H. Holley, a black man who had been an attorney in the Governments Division, served as attorney-advisor from 1948 until he retired in 1953. Holley produced several series of records. The records of the Governments Division, which was under the Assistant Director for Economic Fields, include the **office files of Robert H. Holley, 1924–44** (3 ft.), arranged alphabetically by name or subject in two chronological segments, 1924–42 and 1943–44. The files consist chiefly of memorandums to Bureau officials relating to the drafting of census legislation, the confidentiality of census schedules, and interpretations of State laws dealing with such matters as taxation, the issuance of bonds, pension funds, voting, elections, and the nature of public records; Governments Division issuances; Holley's monthly activity reports; and correspondence relating to blacks.

29.9. Holley also created records relating to State taxation and revenue laws and several series about election surveys that do not specifically relate to black history but are of interest because they demonstrate Holley's contribution to the Federal Government.

29.10. Holley's **comments on bills, 74th–81st Congresses, 1936–52** (3 ft.), arranged numerically by Congress and thereunder by subject or bill number, include information about proposed Federal legislation that concerned the Census Bureau.

29.11. There are two series that have some information about blacks among the records of the Assistant Director for Demographic Fields. The **first-count tabulations of enumeration districts,** n.d. (8 ft.), arranged alphabetically by State and thereunder by county or other civil division, include population totals by color, sex, and farm residence. The categories of color consist of native white, foreign-born white, Negro, and "other colored." The **special count of data for nonwhite foreign-born persons,** n.d. (6 in.), arranged alphabetically by State and thereunder by county or other civil division, consists of tabulations of citizenship data for States in alphabetical sequence from Maryland to Wyoming, summary sheets of citizenship data, and summary sheets of data about country of birth.

Census Schedules and Supplementary Records

29.12. Information contained in the **decennial population schedules, 1790–1910** (about 25,000 rolls of microfilm), became progressively more detailed with each succeeding census. All of the population schedules are arranged chronologically by census year and thereunder, for the most part, alphabetically by State. The 1790 schedules contain the names of the heads of families and, for each household, the number of white males 16 years of age and above, the number under 16 years, the number of white females, the names of other free persons (most of whom where free blacks), the number in their families, and the number of slaves. A greater breakdown of the black population did not begin until the census of 1820, which numbered male and female slaves and free colored persons under 14 years, 14 to 24, and 25 years and upward. Schedules for censuses before 1850 give only the name of the head of each family, followed by such family information as the number of dependents by age and sex. Beginning with the 1850 census, the schedules contain the name of each individual as well as age, sex, State or country of birth, and occupation. The censuses of 1850 and 1860 include separate schedules of the slave population. The census of 1870 was the first to contain information about all blacks as free persons. More than 99 percent of the 1890 census was destroyed by fire in 1921.

29.13. The **population schedules for the 1900 census** (1,854 rolls), arranged by State, thereunder by county, and thereunder by city, give for each person: name; address; relationship to the head of the household; color or race; sex; month and year of birth; age at last birthday; marital status; if a wife is listed within the household, then the number of years married, number of children born of that marriage, and number of children living; places of birth of each individual and of the parents of each individual; citizenship; if the individual is foreign born, then the year of immigration and the number of years in the United States; the citizenship status of foreign-born individuals over age 21; occupation; whether or not the person can read, write, and speak English; whether the home is owned or rented; whether or not the home is a farm; and whether or not the home is mortgaged.

29.14. A **card index of heads of household for the 1900 census schedules** (7,846 rolls), arranged according to the Soundex coding system, was prepared by the Work Projects Administration during the 1930's. Information was abstracted from the census schedules and placed on filecards. The cards give name, race, month and year of birth, age, citizenship status, place of residence by State and county, civil division, and, where appropriate for urban dwellers, the city name, house number, and street name. The cards also list the volume number, enumeration district number, and page and line numbers of the original schedules from which the information was taken.

29.15. The **population schedules for the 1910 census** (1,784 rolls), arranged by State, thereunder by county, and thereunder by city, are detailed, but not as detailed as those for 1900. The 1910 census is only partially indexed (4,642 rolls for 21 States). The index is arranged according to the Soundex coding system.

29.16. Other census schedules that include information about blacks are the **territorial population schedules for Minnesota, 1857–58** (5 vols., 10 in.), arranged alphabetically by county, and **for Seminole County, Okla., 1907** (5 in.), arranged by enumeration district number. The schedules for the **Special Census of 1885** (about 40 vols., 5 ft.), arranged alphabetically by State and thereunder alphabetically by county, are for the States of Colorado, Florida, and Nebraska and the Territories of Dakota and New Mexico. Schedule 1, inhabitants, and schedule 5, mortality, give information about color. The **schedules of special municipal population enumerations, 1932–38** (167 vols., 2 ft.), arranged chronologically and thereunder alphabetically by State, show the name, address, relationship to the head of the family, sex, color, and age of every inhabitant of 15 municipalities in North Carolina, Indiana, Pennsylvania, Alabama, Illinois, and Missouri.

29.17. Mortality schedules, 1850–80 (40 vols., 5ft.; 30 rolls), arranged alphabetically by State or Territory, contain descriptions of persons who died within the year preceding the enumeration. The **social and population schedules, 1935–36** (11 ft.), of the 1935 Special Census of Puerto Rico, arranged alphabetically by municipality and thereunder by enumeration district, include information about race.

29.18. The **tobacco schedules, 1910** (2 ft.), arranged alphabetically by State, are special schedules that supplement the general farm schedules and relate to the tobacco crops of 1909. These schedules, submitted by the tobacco growers in 15 States, contain information on the production of tobacco by variety and type, the use of fertilizer, land ownership, and crop yield. These records do not have specific racial designations, but tobacco farming was often performed by black sharecroppers. The schedules ask if the informant was an owner, tenant, or manager; if the land was leased from others; and who paid for fertilizer, "the owner, tenant or cropper, or both equally."

29.19. Schedules of the **1929 census of business distribution, 1930** (1,100 ft.), are in two groups—for wholesale and for retail establishments—each arranged alphabetically by State and thereunder alphabetically by name of industry. The schedules give the name of the owner, the location, the date of its establishment, a description of it and its type of business, the number of employees, expenses, stocks on hand, sales of merchandise and products, a list of net sales by commodities, and whether the business was "owned and operated by Negroes."

29.20. The schedules of the **census of religious bodies, 1926–28** (92 ft.), arranged alphabetically by denomination or organization and numerically thereunder, show for each locality the number of churches or local organizations, membership by age and sex, total value of church buildings and parsonages, debts on church properties, church expenditures, and the number of Sunday schools, teachers, and students. The schedules also give information on missions and benevolences and on the education of ministers. In some denominations the membership was consolidated by county. There are records for some black churches, such as the African Methodist Episcopal Church (3 ft.), the African Methodist Episcopal Zion

Church (1½ ft.), the Colored Methodist Episcopal Church (1 ft.), and "Negro Baptists" (10 ft.).

29.21. The supplementary records of the Bureau of the Census are (1) statistical records not taken by the Census Bureau, (2) copies of abstracts and reports of census returns, and (3) indexes to population schedules. Among the supplementary records is a **typed copy of the 1789 tax lists for Lincoln County,** which was in the State of Virginia in 1789 and is now in Kentucky. The lists contain the names of taxable persons, the number of white males in each household over 21 years old, the number over 16 and under 21, the number of slaves, and the number of horses, colts, and mules owned by each person liable for taxes. The lists are arranged by district and thereunder alphabetically by name of taxable person. The supplementary records also include **microfilm copies of 1792–1917 census publications, 1948–49** (42 rolls). Many of the Census Bureau publications relating to the population include information about race.

* *Restrictions may apply to this Record Group. Consult NARS staff.*

Record Group 30

Records of the Bureau of Public Roads

30.1. The Bureau of Public Roads had its origin in the Office of Road Inquiry, created by the Secretary of Agriculture on October 3, 1893, under authority of an act of 1893. Within the Department of Agriculture it was known successively as the Office of Public Roads Inquiries, 1899–1905; Office of Public Roads, 1905–15; Office of Public Roads and Rural Engineering, 1915–18; and Bureau of Public Roads, 1918–39. The Bureau became part of the Federal Works Agency in 1939 and of the General Services Administration in 1949. It was transferred to the Department of Commerce later in 1949 and to the Department of Transportation in 1966. Beginning with a large-scale plan of Federal-State cooperation in roadbuilding in 1916, the administration of federally aided highway construction has been the major function of the Bureau. It also administers the highway beautification program and is responsible for administering a highway safety program.

30.2. The **general correspondence, 1893–1912** (40 ft.), arranged according to a numeric-subject classification scheme, includes a file (#97, 2 in.) on convict labor. There are several references in the letters to the use of black convicts on roadbuilding projects, with comparisons drawn between the treatment of convict labor and the treatment of blacks under slavery. A letter to a Senator from James W. Abbott of the Office of Public Road Inquiries, dated June 24, 1904, states "whenever they use convict labor in the South it is nearly all colored, and they control them with the lash." In another letter to the Senator, dated June 27, 1904, Abbott states that "a Negro convict is a slave. His condition is more deplorable than it ever was in ante-bellum days."

30.3. Later **general correspondence files, 1912–50** (2,272 ft.), arranged according to a modified Dewey classification system, also include some files about convict labor (#712, 2 in.), but specific references to blacks are rarely made. The correspondence files contain some 1932 inquiries from Tuskegee Institute (#481, ⅛ in.) about the construction of a road to the Veterans Hospital at Tuskegee.

30.4. Although most photographs in the still picture collection of the Bureau of Public Roads relate to highway engineering, there are scattered items identifiable as pertinent to black history. These are photographs of black convicts working on public roads in Florida between 1929 and 1946 and several pictures showing homes of poor blacks and former slave quarters.

Record Group 31

Records of the Federal Housing Administration

31.1. The Federal Housing Administration (FHA) was created by the National Housing Act of 1934, and, after several reorganizations, it became part of the Department of Housing and Urban Development in 1965.

31.2. The FHA carries out programs authorized by the National Housing Act to insure private lending institutions against loss on mortgage loans for one-to-four family dwellings, rental housing projects of eight or more units, and property repair or improvement. It also insures advances for housing in nonurban and disaster areas, for the elderly and military personnel, for nursing homes, and for the improvement of housing standards—with particular emphasis on the rehabilitation of slums and blighted areas. During World War II, FHA field offices accepted, processed, and forwarded to the War Production Board applications from private sources for scarce materials to be used in war housing and utility lines and systems, issued allotments and preference ratings for priorities, and inspected projects for conformity with regulations regarding the use of critical materials.

31.3. The Research and Statistics Division gathered current economic and housing market data for cities with a population of 5,000 or more in order to forecast housing demands and market values. The resulting records are called the **city data files, 1938–54** (30 ft.), which are arranged by State and thereunder by city. The study of each city is divided into four large sections: general characteristics, demand factors, supply factors, and demand versus supply. The second and third sections contain detailed information, which is sometimes broken down into race, wealth and income, and wages and employment. The city data file should be used in conjunction with the Home Owners Loan Corporation city survey file (see RG 195).

31.4. Among the **cartographic records for the Division of Research and Statistics, 1934–42** (3,855 items), are manuscript, annotated, and published maps, prepared to show the results of the Real Property Surveys conducted in about 260 cities throughout the United States. Most of the maps are large-scale, cadastral maps showing by blocks certain aspects of housing, such as physical condition of structures, average rental price, occupancy by owner or tenant, occupancy by race, income of occupant, age of structure, duration of occupancy, number of persons per room, extent of mortgages, and sanitary facilities.

Record Group 32

Records of the U.S. Shipping Board

32.1. The U.S. Shipping Board was established by the Shipping Act of 1916 to regulate carriers by water and to develop a naval auxiliary and merchant marine. The Board established the U.S. Shipping Board Emergency Fleet Corporation (known after 1927 as the U.S. Shipping Board Merchant Fleet Corporation) to procure, construct, charter, equip, man, operate, and dispose of merchant vessels for the Board. Under the Merchant Marine Act of 1920 and subsequent legislation, the Board was charged with regulating rates charged in waterborne interstate commerce, trade practices, the transfer of ships from U.S. registry, and insurance matters; investigating the adequacy of port and water transportation facilities; subsidizing private construction of ships; and determining the steamship lines necessary for U.S. commerce and the characteristics of vessels to be operated on those lines. The Board was abolished by Executive Order 6166 of June 10, 1933, and its functions, including those with respect to the Corporation, were thereafter administered through the U.S. Shipping Board Bureau in the Department of Commerce until that Bureau and the Corporation were abolished by the Merchant Marine Act of 1936. Some of the records pertain to blacks who owned shipping lines or who were employed by shipping companies.

Records of the Shipping Board and the Shipping Board Bureau

32.2. The official minutes of the Board contain file number references to the dockets maintained by the Board's secretary. These **dockets, 1917–33** (400 ft.), arranged according to a subject-numeric system, contain supplementary materials (such as reports and memorandums) that relate to subjects under discussion by the Board. In these dockets there are reports about the purchase of some ships by Marcus Garvey, a black activist who organized the Black Star steamship line and the Black Cross Trading Co., Inc. The following dockets relate to Garvey's movement: 728.5 K13, which consists of two documents about the application for transfer of the vessel *Kanawha* to Garvey's line; 796.2 Or4 (1 in.), which contains information about the sale of the *Orion*; and 796.2 M71 (1 in.), which contains information about an offer to purchase *Porto Rico* for operation between New York and Africa. There are indexes to the dockets, arranged, for the most part, by subject.

32.3. The **subject-classified general files, 1916–36** (2,203 ft.), include correspondence, memorandums, reports, and charts relating to all aspects of the operation and activities of the Shipping Board, the Shipping Board Bureau, and the Emergency (later Merchant) Fleet Corporation. These records, maintained by the office of the Secretary of the Board and Bureau, include what were considered the most important records of both the Board and the Fleet Corporation. Until September 1, 1917, the records are arranged according to a numerical system, 1–550. From September 1, 1917, to March 1, 1920, the records are arranged numerically, 100–108019. From March 1, 1920, to October 25, 1936, the records are arranged according to a subject-numeric system. There is a subject index to these records. The black history related records pertain mostly to Marcus Garvey's steamship line. However, there are a few documents pertaining to the Liberia Transportation and Steamship Co., Rev. J. E. Lewis, president. A December 29, 1921, letter describes this company (which was located in San Pedro, Calif.) as "a colored organization (somewhat similar to the Black Star Line in character) . . ." (#605–1–899). There is a subject category for "colored stewards/ship personnel/marine cooks and stewards" (#631–6, 2 in.), and one for "colored labor/labor and labor conditions/longshoremen and stevedors–re Texas ports" (#621–3–10, 3 in.).

32.4. Materials about the Black Star Line and the Black Cross Trading Co., Inc., in the subject-classified general files range from 1919, when the earliest attempts to purchase ships were made, to 1936, when the Shipping Board aided in the settlement of claims of investors, creditors, and employees of the company. Interim records concern ship maintenance, personnel difficulties, and attempts to purchase additional ships. For example, a June 18, 1924, letter from the manager of the Department of Ship

Sales to the president of the Fleet Corporation pertains to the offer of the Black Cross Trading Co., Inc., to purchase the steamship *Susquehanna*. The company was described as "a negro [sic] enterprise, fostered by the Universal Negro Improvement Association, Marcus Garvey being the head of both organizations and apparently the moving spirit." This letter is part of a collective file of Garvey information created by the Shipping Board (#605–1–653, 3 in.), but there are also several other categories that have information about the Garvey companies (#553–1410, 1 in.; #1091–1250, 3 in.; #1091–4805, 4 in.; and #1091–3520, ¼ in.).

Emergency Fleet Corporation

32.5. The records of the Investigations Department include **case files of the home office, 1918–26** (170 ft.), arranged numerically (100–3737) by number assigned when the first report was made for each case. Individual case files contain correspondence, reports of special agents, exhibits, notes, and memorandums pertaining to the case. A file for Marcus Garvey, 1921–25 (#1494–15, ¼ in.), includes correspondence, clippings, and reports about various ships. Another file, "Colored Cooks and Stewards," 1923–25 (#3436, ¼ in.), gives information about the Colored Cooks and Stewards League and other labor organizations formed by black cooks and stewards.

32.6. The **general records of the Industrial Relations Division of the Construction Organization, 1917–19,** arranged according to a numerical filing scheme, consist of correspondence, reports, and memorandums pertaining to labor relations, labor conditions, labor administration, and all phases of the work of the Division. There is a file entitled "Negro Labor" (#53818–1, 1 in.) that includes reports about the percentage of blacks working at various ports, reports from some shipping companies about the numbers of blacks employed, training available for black seamen and dockworkers, and labor problems between white and black workers. The file also includes cross-references to other files that have scattered information about black workers.

Record Group 33

Records of the Federal Extension Service

33.1. The Extension Service of the Department of Agriculture was organized in 1923 to bring together Department extension activities handled by the States Relations Service, the Office of Exhibits of the Assis-

Tying tobacco to be cured on a farm owned by a black resident of Wildwood, Fla. June 1940. Hunton, photographer. RG 33, Records of the Federal Extension Service. (33-S-6712).

tant Secretary's Office, and the Office of Motion Pictures of the Division of Publication. The States Relations Service had been established in 1915 as a consolidation of the Office of Experiment Stations and the farmers cooperative demonstration work of the Bureau of Plant Industry. The Secretary of Agriculture renamed the Extension Service the Federal Extension Service in 1953, but in 1970 its name reverted to Extension Service.

33.2. The Service coordinates extension activities of the Department bureaus with those of State agricultural colleges, helps farmers carry out new farming and home enterprises through the services of county agricultural and home demonstration agents, makes known results of agricultural research, and presents displays and exhibits at fairs and expositions. In periods of crisis, such as drought, depression, or war, local agents of the Service perform emergency activities.

33.3. Beginning in 1905, the Department of Agriculture showed an increasing interest in the development of extension activities among black farmers (see also RG 16). With money furnished by the General Education Board, a private institution, two black agents were employed in 1906, and the number increased rapidly thereafter. The subsidies made by this board to farm demonstration work in the early 1900's did much to extend and popularize the movement.

Records of the Extension Service and Its Predecessors

33.4. The **annual narrative and statistical reports, 1908–44,** constitute one of the chief sources of documentation of the activities of the Extension Service. These reports are on microfilm (T845–T897, 3,577 rolls). They are arranged alphabetically by States, Territories, possessions, and the District of Columbia; thereunder by year; and thereunder usually as follows: those of subject-matter specialists, those of the Director and Assistant Director, those of State leaders, and those of county agents. The reports of subject-matter specialists (such as soil use or sheep production specialists) are in turn arranged alphabetically by field of specialization. The annual reports of State leaders are arranged alphabetically by title of leader; those of county workers are arranged alphabetically by county and thereunder in roughly the following sequence: agricultural agent (white) and, where present, agricultural agent (Negro); home demonstration agent (white) and, where present, home demonstration agent (Negro); and club agent (white) and, where present, club agent (Negro).

33.5. There are some annual narrative and statistical reports that are not on microfilm. **Textual records for 1945** (151 ft.) continue the series of microfilmed reports. They are arranged alphabetically by State and thereunder in the same order as the microfilmed reports. The **annual narrative and statistical reports for North Carolina, 1908–17** (4 ft.), arranged by year and thereunder alphabetically by county, consist largely but not exclusively of county agents' reports that could not be successfully microfilmed for one reason or another.

33.6. The **national indexes to annual narrative reports of field workers, 1924–28** (12 vols., 1 ft.), are arranged by year. They show where to find information in the previously described reports. They were prepared by Washington staff members according to an elaborate classification scheme.

33.7. The **general correspondence of the Extension Service and its predecessors, 1907–43** (402 ft.), is arranged by year and thereunder alphabetically by State, Territory, and the District of Columbia. This series consists of correspondence of the Special Agent in Charge of Cooperative Demonstration Work, Bureau of Plant Industry, 1907–15; correspondence of the States Relations Service, 1915–23; and correspondence of the Extension Service, 1924–43. It includes letters received and copies of letters sent, telegrams, memorandums, annual and other administrative reports, and informational materials. The records concern all phases of extension work, including certain special activities undertaken during World Wars I and II and relief work carried on during the Depression. There is correspondence from black extension workers in the South. Although there are indexes to the correspondence, it is easier to find black history materials by using names taken from the annual reports. The correspondence gives a great deal of information about the administrative aspects of extension work, while the annual reports describe programs and activities. There is much correspondence for Thomas M. Campbell of Tuskegee Institute. He was one of the first black extension workers and later coordinated the activities of many black extension agents in the South. For example, his file for 1942–43 (2 in.) includes information about 4–H Clubs for black youths, publicity, radio programs, payroll problems, war production, black extension workers, black land-grant colleges, and many other subjects.

33.8. The work of the Extension Service in the South is illustrated in the film "Helping Negroes to Become Better Farmers and Homemakers," 1921 (#33–157). The progress of a black family of tenant farmers is traced through their participation in Tuskegee Institute's "movable school" and through aid received from Extension Service agents. The audiovisual records also include photographs, 1906–42 (5,000 items), illustrating rural life and farm activities in all the States of the Union. Some photographs depict extension work among blacks, others include shots of black farm laborers or domestic workers. There are no indexes or other finding aids for these photographs.

Record Group 35

Records of the Civilian Conservation Corps

35.1. The Civilian Conservation Corps (CCC) was created by an act of 1937 to succeed the Emergency Conservation Work that had been established by Executive order in 1933. In 1939 the CCC became part of the Federal Security Agency. An appropriation act of 1942 provided for the termination of the CCC not later than June 30, 1943. The CCC and its predecessor provided employment and vocational training for unemployed youths and, to a limited extent, for veterans and Indians through conservation and national resources development work. Many black youths and some black veterans participated in the CCC programs. Usually, separate camps were established for black enrollees, but in a few cases camps were integrated.

General Records

35.2. The **general correspondence, 1933–42** (427 ft.), is arranged by numerical classes, 100–900, and thereunder alphabetically. There is an index to the **general correspondence, 1933–40** (127 ft.), which is arranged in segments titled "Agency," "Congressional," "Personal," and "Precedent" and thereunder alphabetically by surname and/or subject. In the "Congressional" segment of the index are some cards for Oscar DePriest, a black Congressman from Illinois. The "Personal" segment includes a few cards for black individuals, such as Robert R. Moton, president of Tuskegee Institute, and Claude A. Barnett of the Associated Negro Press. There are a number of index cards with the heading "Negroes" and a few "Colored" in the "Precedent" segment of the index. The subjects most often covered in this correspondence are the enrollment of black youths into the program, the employment of black staff in the camps, and the location of black camps. There was a degree of controversy over each of these subjects. Black activists wanted to ensure that black youths were not discriminated against in the enrollment process. Much of the correspondence about the locations of black camps came from whites who did not want these camps to be located near their communities.

35.3. Annual, special, and final reports, 1933–43 (13 vols., 4 in.), arranged chronologically, include some statistical information about black participation in the CCC program. The final report covers the period April 1933–June 1943 and presents a detailed account of CCC objectives and accomplishments.

Records of Divisions

35.4. The records of the Division of Selection include **monthly reports of enrollment, 1941–42** (1 ft.), arranged chronologically and thereunder alphabetically by State. These are statistical reports that were submitted by the State selecting agencies and that include information on the number, race, age, education, employment status, and urban-rural distribution of enrollees.

35.5. The Division of Planning and Public Relations formulated plans for the operation of the CCC and initiated and directed public relations for the Office of the Director and for the CCC activities of the cooperating Federal agencies. The staff also selected or prepared all speeches, radio broadcasts, and material for newspapers. The Division directed the preparation of motion pictures and the creation and maintenance of photographs. The **general correspondence of the Division, 1933–42** (22 ft.), is arranged alphabetically by subject or name of individual or organization. There is a file entitled "Negroes" (2 in.), which includes the 1940 report "The Civilian Conservation Corps and Colored Youth." The report states that in 1935 there were 2,652 CCC camps, of which 265 were all-black. There is a report by Edgar G. Brown, Adviser on Negro Affairs, entitled "Colored CCC Camps by State." The file also includes CCC correspondence and press releases relating to blacks and copies of some articles in the CCC newspaper *Happy Days* concerning black youths. One article for July 18, 1936, by G. Lake Imes, is entitled "Fourth Corps Negro Contingent,

Black corpsman at a Civilian Conservation Corps camp in Yanceyville, N.C., mapping a contract farm area. Enrollee is drawing a line on the plane table to represent the boundary of the field. May 5, 1940. Photographer unknown. RG 35, Records of the Civilian Conservation Corps. (35-G-255).

12,000 Strong, Went From Plow Handle to Pencil and Grasped Opportunity's Hand.''

35.6. The records of the Division of Planning and Public Relations also include a **general photographic file, 1933–40** (1,300 items, 2 ft.). The file is arranged alphabetically by subject. The photographic prints depict all aspects of the Corps operations, including vocational training, conservation and natural resources development work programs, and recreational activities. One of the subject categories for the photographs is Negro enrollees. There is also a **general photographic file** for the period **1940–42** (2,900 items, 25 ft.). These prints are arranged alphabetically by subject. They show the full range of CCC programs and activities, including operations during the 1937 flooding of the Mississippi and Ohio Rivers. Among the subjects are Negro–Beltsville, Md.; Negro–Yanceyville, N.C.; Negro–Winnetka, Ill.; and Negro–miscellaneous. There is also a series of **photographs of black enrollees, 1936–39** (150 items, 5 in.), arranged by geographic area. Photographic prints showing enrollees in vocational training sessions, recreational activities, and conservation and other work programs are included in this series.

35.7. The Division of Research and Statistics planned, collected, analyzed, and distributed all types of data on the CCC for administrative and general informational purposes. Field personnel of the cooperating agencies supplied the data to the small Washington staff, which performed necessary processing and summarizing work. The **station and strength reports, 1933–42** (46 vols., 4 ft.), are arranged numerically by the Army corps area. Each report includes a numerical list of companies that serves as an index. The reports, which are monthly and contain some gaps, include the camp number; company number; local camp name; number of enrollees; State of origin of enrollees; whether the camp was for white (w), "colored" (c), or mixed (m) enrollees; number of Army and technical personnel; post where the company was organized; date the company occupied the camp; and the nearest post office, telegraph office, and railroad.

35.8. The Division of Investigations sent out investigators to make special inquiries to determine the treatment of enrollees by company commanders and supervisory personnel; they noted companies that had high discharge rates or absenteeism. Another aspect of the routine inspection involved reporting on the efficiency and fiscal responsibility of persons performing the work. The **camp inspection reports, 1933–42** (103 ft.), are arranged alphabetically by State and thereunder by camp number. Forms completed by special investigators contain information concerning the general welfare of the enrollees and general camp conditions. The forms provide information on the company number, race of enrollees, date of camp establishment, camp location, names of military personnel, condition of buildings and sanitation facilities, medical services, religious services, safety, discharges, and brief descriptions of work projects.

Record Group 36

Records of the U.S. Customs Service

36.1. The Customs Service, created by an act of July 31, 1789, became part of the Department of the Treasury when it was established in September 1789. The Office of the Secretary of the Treasury and later the Division of Customs, created in the 1860's, administered the Service until the establishment of the Bureau of Customs in 1927. Other functions of the Bureau relate to import and export of merchandise, collection of tonnage taxes, entrance and clearance of vessels and aircraft, regulation of vessels in the coastal and fishing trades, and protection of passengers. The Bureau assists other agencies in the export control program, the control of persons entering or leaving the United States, and the enforcement of restrictions on the importation of certain plants, foods, and drugs.

36.2. Some early records of the Customs Service relate to the enforcement of the slave trade laws that were passed from 1794 to 1820. The law of 1794 prohibited ships from being built in the United States for use in the slave trade; it required sureties of owners or masters of vessels suspected of trading in slaves; and it imposed on sellers of imported slaves a fine of $200 for each slave sold. An act of 1800 prohibited any American from having an interest in any ship used in the slave trade, subject to a penalty of double the amount of his financial interest, and forbade U.S. citizens to serve as seamen on ships engaged in such trade. An act of 1807 provided that U.S. naval vessels would be used to stop the slave trade after January 1, 1808; that all ships seized would be treated as enemy ships and sold as prizes; and that half the money thus obtained would go to the crew of the capturing ship. An act of 1818 levied a fine of $5,000 on anyone building ships for the slave trade or assisting in the loading of slaves on such ships; it also imposed on importers a fine of $10,000 and an additional fine of $1,000 for each slave sold to a U.S. citizen. A law of 1819 reaffirmed the use of U.S. naval vessels to halt the slave trade. Another law, passed in 1820, declared slaving to be an act of piracy and authorized the execution of anyone convicted of participation in the slave trade.

36.3. Section 8 of the law of 1807 prohibited the transportation of slaves in any vessel under 40 tons except on the rivers of the United States. Section 9 of the same act required that all vessels of 40 tons or more carrying slaves in the coastwise trade file duplicate manifests (at the port of origin and at the port of destination) showing name and age of each slave, the names and residences of exporter and consignee, age and description of the slave, and pledge that the slaves had not been imported after 1807.

36.4. The records of customhouses include **slave manifests** for four ports: **Philadelphia, 1790–1840** (¼ in.); **New Orleans, 1819–52** and **1860–61** (15 ft.); **Mobile, 1822–60** (4 ft.); and **Savannah, 1801–60** (6 ft.). These manifests are arranged chronologically by date of arrival and thereunder by name of vessel. They show name, tonnage, and nationality of vessel; date of arrival; name of master; name (usually Christian name only), age, and sex of slave; name and address of consignee; and name of owner.

36.5. Customs collection districts were established at more than 100 ports in accordance with the act of July 31, 1789. These districts were changed from time to time until 1913, when districts were established in each State and Territory. In each district there was a headquarters port with a customhouse. There were also various ports of entry and delivery with a collector, naval officer, surveyor, and other minor officials as needed. The collector was responsible for collecting duties and keeping records of and reporting his financial transactions. He was also responsible for the protection of U.S. seamen and marine passengers.

36.6. The records of the collectors vary in type and completeness. However, for many of the ports there are crew lists and shipping articles that document the participation of many black men as sailors. For example, **crew lists for New York, 1803–1919** (585 ft.), arranged by port, show the name of each crew member and his age, place of birth, personal description, and most recent address. Some members of the crew are described as "black" with "wooly" hair, "mulatto," or "colored." The **shipping articles for New York, 1840–72** (46 ft.), arranged chronologically, are agreements between masters or owners of vessels and seamen, showing for a particular voyage its length, origin, and destination. They usually include, after the general agreement printed on the form, the signature of each seaman and his age, nationality, personal description, name of State or country of birth, address, rating and salary, and name and address of next of kin. Race is indicated in the personal description column. Similar records are the **seamen's protection certificates for Philadelphia, 1797–1861** (35 ft.), arranged chronologically. These records were essentially proof of citizenship for U.S. seamen for the purpose of protecting them from impressment into the British Navy. The certificates indicate race. Some of these records have been quantified and published as M972, *Computer-Processed Tabulations of Data From Seamen's Protective Certificate Applications to the Collector of Customs for the Port of Philadelphia, 1812–1815.* The tabulations include information about "race and status if nonwhite."

36.7. The volume and completeness of correspondence with collectors of customs varies for each port. Some black men served as collectors (see RG 56), and correspondence for some ports includes information about them. For example, Robert Smalls served as collector for Beaufort, S.C., from 1889 to 1894 and from 1898 until his death in 1913. **Letters received at Beaufort, 1910–21** (2 ft.), and **letters sent, 1867–1926** (10 in.), both arranged chronologically, include some of his correspondence.

36.8. The **letters sent by the collector at Mobile, Ala., 1835–1912** (16 ft.), and the **letters received, 1815–1934** (35 ft.), both arranged chronologically, include some letters concerning the enforcement of laws against the slave trade.

36.9. The **outward foreign manifests, 1789–1918,** are arranged geographically by name of port and thereunder chronologically. The volume of records varies with each customhouse. These manifests list the cargo of vessels engaged in foreign trade, including trade with African countries, and give the following information: name of vessel and master, port of embarkation, description of merchandise exported, name of consignee, and date of clearance. Among the **outward foreign manifests for**

Charleston, S.C., 1844–1930 (30 ft. of inward and outward manifests), arranged chronologically, is an outward manifest for the barque *Azor* and its black U.S. passengers on their way to settle in Monrovia, Liberia, in April 1878. Other records (½ in.) concerning this voyage of the *Azor* include the **passenger list, 1878;** which gives the name, sex, and age of each passenger, and the **baggage list, 1878;** which gives the amount or type of possessions taken on board by each family (e.g., "two barrels," or "one bedstead").

36.10. The **registers of foreign arrivals and clearances of vessels, 1789–1899** (various footage for each port), are arranged geographically by name of port and thereunder chronologically. Information given in the registers includes name of vessel and master, port of origin or destination, country of registry, type of vessel, tonnage, and number of crew. The type of cargo is also given in the earlier volumes. Emigration of black Americans to Liberia and supplies sent to settlers in Liberia are reflected in some entries showing clearances for Monrovia. The volume of **clearances to foreign ports from Baltimore, 1856–57,** gives information on various vessels that were departing for Liberia, including the barque *Shirley,* the schooner *Fawn,* the ship *Mary Caroline Stevens,* the barque *Juniatta,* the ketch *Mary Atwell,* the barque *Dorchester,* and the ketch *President Benson.*

Record Group 40

General Records of the Department of Commerce

40.1. The Department of Commerce and Labor was established by an act of 1903, which transferred to it a number of previously existing offices. Separate Labor and Commerce Departments were established in 1913. The functions of the Commerce Department are to promote foreign and domestic commerce, the manufacturing and shipping industries, and the transportation facilities of the United States. Most of these functions are performed by bureaus of the Department, whose records constitute separate record groups. This record group includes general records of the immediate Office of the Secretary of Commerce and of officials and offices performing staff and administrative functions for the Department as a whole. It also includes reports of various related commissions, boards, and other special bodies. Some of the records pertain to black businesses.

40.2. There is an **alphabetical subject index, 1903–50** (84 ft.), divided into 5-year segments, to the **general correspondence of the**

Office of the Secretary, 1903–50 (1,167 ft.), arranged by a subject-numeric filing scheme. The index lists individual documents and gives the numerical arrangement within the general correspondence. The index sometimes provides more information than the records themselves. The 1903–7 segment of the index includes a card for "Colored Employees"; the 1908–12 segment under "Negro" lists correspondence relating to the appointment of blacks as enumerators for the 13th census, black population, the black census of Oklahoma, the exclusion of U.S. blacks from Canada, deportation of blacks to Africa, blacks residing in alleys in Washington, D.C., and immigration of blacks from Africa to America; the segment 1913–17 under "Negroes" includes information about race discrimination in the Bureau of Foreign and Domestic Commerce, segregation in Government departments, and protests against the use of lowercase "n" for the word "Negro" in census publications. Many of the documents listed in the 1913–17 segment of the index are in correspondence file 67001.42 (¼ in.), a few are in 71315, and others are scattered in various other files. File 71315 includes a clipping from the *Washington Times,* November 12, 1914, entitled "Colored Delegate Rebuked by Wilson," which relates to a meeting between black activist William Monroe Trotter of Boston, Mass., and President Woodrow Wilson.

40.3. For the 1918–22 segment of the index, under the heading "Negroes," are entries relating to lynchings, World War I, discrimination, black employment, publications about blacks, and the employment of blacks by the Department of Commerce. The 1923–27 segment notes only a few letters under the heading "Negro," including one from Robert R. Moton of Tuskegee Institute pertaining to the 14th census and another from R. J. Bryant about the rights of blacks. For the segments from 1928 to 1950 there are entries about the Department's Negro Advisory Council; the Negro Affairs Section, headed by Charles E. Hall; problems unique to blacks; black chambers of commerce; the appointment of Eugene Kinckle Jones, former executive secretary of the Urban League, as an advisor to the Department; blacks and the Texas Centennial celebration; the purchasing power of blacks; publications about black newspapers and periodicals; black participation in Civil Aeronautics Administration aviation programs; and black businesses, particularly banks. Most of the records for this period appear in correspondence file 88449 (5 in.).

40.4. In the Office of the Secretary, Emmer Martin Lancaster was appointed advisor for the Division of Negro Affairs on May 23, 1940, by Secretary Harry L. Hopkins. The Division had been established in 1933. Lancaster filled a vacancy created by the resignation of Eugene Kinckle Jones. The National Negro Business Advisory Council was formed to serve the Division of Negro Affairs. Lancaster's records include **correspondence with insurance companies owned and operated by blacks, 1942–53**

(2 ft.), arranged in two parts: one, alphabetically by the name of the insurance company, and two, alphabetically by geographiclly be geographic location. **Correspondence with banks owned and operated by blacks, 1942–53** (1 ft.), is arranged in the same way. The **correspondence with black lending institutions, 1942–53** (8 in.), is arranged alphabetically by the name of the institution. There is **correspondence with State lending departments, 1942–53** (4 in.), which is arranged alphabetically by the name of city. **Correspondence pertaining to "Conferences on the Negro in Business," 1940–53** (2 ft.), is arranged alphabetically by name of correspondent.

40.5. The Division of Negro Affairs correspondence on small business and inquiry reference service, 1940–53 (1 ft., 2 in.), is arranged alphabetically by subject, such as awards, agenda, colleges, universities and business schools, programs, official proceedings, committee on entertainment, and conference publicity. **Reports on conferences on the Negro in business, 1940–53** (8 in.), are arranged by subject. **General correspondence, 1945–53** (2 ft.), is arranged by the name of the correspondent and consists of requests for information, publications, or business advice and of complaints of discrimination. Lancaster's **special reading-subject file, 1941–53** (2 ft.), consists of correspondence and reports and is arranged by subject, such as Committee on Negro Defense Contracts, national defense correspondence and contractors, Negro chambers of commerce and trade associations, Negro periodicals and publications, postwar planning, housing, the emergency program, and real estate brokers.

40.6. Annual reports of the Division of Negro Affairs, 1943-51 (3 in.), consist of the first to the sixth *Annual Report of Banking Institutions,* 1943–51. There are other periodic reports on black business associations, insurance companies, and postwar planning for blacks in business, as well as a directory of black businesses in the United States.

Record Group 41

Records of the Bureau of Marine Inspection and Navigation

41.1. Navigation laws were passed by the First Congress in 1789 and were enforced by customs officers under the supervision of the Treasury Department. Federal circuit courts directly handled matters relating to shipment, care, and discharge of seamen until this work was taken over in 1872 by shipping commissioners appointed and supervised by the courts.

In 1884 responsibility for the administration of navigation laws, including those administered by the shipping commissioners, was given to the Commissioner of Navigation, who, with the Bureau of Navigation established under his control, was placed under the general supervision of the Secretary of the Treasury. By the Steamboat Act of 1852, the Steamboat Inspection Service was formally established to formulate rules and regulations for uniform administration of steamboat inspection laws. The two units were combined in 1932 to form the Bureau of Navigation and Steamboat Inspection, to which was transferred in 1934 the Sea Service Section of the U.S. Shipping Board Bureau of the Department of Commerce. In 1936 the Bureau of Navigation and Steamboat Inspection was renamed the Bureau of Marine Inspection and Navigation. Some of the records pertain to blacks who owned shipping lines or who were employed by shipping companies.

41.2. The **general correspondence file of the Bureau of Navigation, 1906–35** (1,572 ft.), arranged numerically, includes some files about vessels owned and operated by Marcus Garvey's Black Star Line and Black Cross Trading Co., Inc. There are several files on the steamship *Kanawha,* mostly for the period 1920–27 (#116430–N, #122539–N, #123858–N, #139262–N, and #161123–N, totaling about 3 in.). There are also several folders pertaining to the steamship *General G. W. Goethals,* 1925–56 (#143611–N, #144621–N, #145301–N, #145456–N, #154580–N, and #215106–N, totaling about 1 in.). The records refer to purchase, maintenance, upkeep, personnel problems, and various claims made either by the Black Star Line or against it. There is correspondence from State Department officials in Cuba and Jamaica, from stockholders of the Black Star Line, from owners of other vessels, and from the Black Star Line. There are two *New York Daily News* clippings (Jan. and Feb. 1925) entitled "Garvey's Second Steamer Rides the Waves" and "Harlem Weeps Over Garvey—Jailbound; Black Star Proves Ill Star for Colored Hopes."

41.3. The records relating to merchant vessel personnel include **applications for seamen's protection certificates, 1916–40** (375 ft.), arranged by name of port. These applications, with affidavits and occasionally other material offered as proof of citizenship, were submitted by seamen in the U.S. merchant marine to collectors of customs acting as field agents for the Commissioner of Navigation (later for the Director of the Bureau of Marine Inspection and Navigation) in the issuance of seamen's protection certificates required by law for sailing in foreign waters. The applications usually contain name and address of the seaman, date and place of his birth, place and date of naturalization if applicable, name of ship on which last employed, and name of ship of prospective employment. In addition, they contain the applicant's signature, left thumb print, photograph, and description of physical characteristics. Photographs of black seamen are scattered throughout. Similar records for the 19th century are among the records of the Bureau of Customs (see RG 36).

41.4. Records of U.S. shipping commissioners, 1872–1938 (5,000 ft.), are arranged by port and thereunder chronologically. Since July 1872, shipping commissioners in various ports have administered laws on protection and welfare of seamen, including those relating to their shipping and discharge. The records consist of most of the shipping articles collected by the shipping commissioners and of official merchant marine logbooks filed with the commissioners at the conclusion of voyages. In many instances these are the only extant proof of a seaman's service. Coverage for individual ports varies greatly, and these records do not include articles and logs for all U.S. ports. Most of the records before 1915 are for Baltimore; Boston; New York; Portland, Oreg.; and San Francisco. The shipping articles for each voyage usually give name and type of vessel, date and port of departure, destination, and the signature, rank or rating, birthplace, height and complexion, wage, date of signing on, and name and address of next of kin of each crew member. Copies of the articles were filed at the port where crewmembers signed on and at the port where they were paid. Official logbooks contain crew lists; crew slop and cash accounts; loadline information; entries relating to events on the voyage, such as conduct, health, and discipline of the crew; and information about deaths, marriages, and births. Blacks are usually described as "colored" in the column on complexion. References to blacks are scattered.

Record Group 42

Records of the Office of Public Buildings and Public Parks of the National Capital

42.1. The Office of Public Buildings and Public Parks of the National Capital had its origin in 1791 when the Board of Commissioners for the District of Columbia was appointed to plan and construct a capital city. In 1800 the capital was moved from Philadelphia to Washington, D.C., and in 1802 the Board was abolished. Part of its functions and its records were inherited successively by the Superintendent of the City of Washington, 1802–17; the Commissioner of Public Buildings, 1816–67 (who was placed after 1849 under the Department of the Interior); and the Office of Public Buildings and Grounds under the Chief of Engineers in the Department of War, 1867–1925. The functions of the Office of Public Buildings and Grounds and of the Office of the Superintendent of the State, War, and Navy Building (created in 1883 as an independent agen-

Demonstrator during the August 28, 1963, March on Washington. Photographer unknown. RG 106, Records of the U.S. Information Agency. (306-ST-821-63-4521).

cy to maintain the building) were transferred in 1925 to the newly established Office of Public Buildings and Public Parks of the National Capital. The Office or its predecessors acquired the records of temporary agencies established to erect buildings or monuments in the District. The Office was abolished in 1933. Some of these records concern black employees and segregated facilities such as Howard University.

42.2. The general records include **letters received, 1791–1867** (39 vols., 10 ft.), arranged chronologically. Among the letters of the Commissioners of Public Buildings and Grounds is a letter of January 5, 1793, from Thomas Johnson, et al., to Samuel Blodget, which mentions that "we have a good many Negro laborers . . ." (Vol. 1, p. 142).

42.3. The **letters received** by the Office of Public Buildings and Grounds, **1899–1906** (11 ft.), are arranged for the most part chronologically and numbered 1–1975. File 790 relates to the buildings and grounds of Howard University in Washington, D.C. (2 in.), and pertains to maintenance needs and the use of university facilities by other members of the community.

42.4. The **general correspondence of the Office of Public Buildings and Grounds, 1907–21** (126 ft.), is arranged by subject and numbered 1–313. This is chiefly the correspondence of the officer in charge and relates to the duties and responsibilities of the Office. Some of the records pertain to personnel matters. File 95/288 includes a report of November 5, 1915, accompanied by a "Table Showing Ratio of White and Colored Employees under the Office of Public Buildings and Grounds during the First Two Weeks in October 1915." The table shows 137 white and 133 black employees (including one who worked in the Executive Mansion).

42.5. See also RG 66, Records of the Commission of Fine Arts.

Record Group 43

Records of International Conferences, Commissions, and Expositions

43.1. Since 1826 the United States has participated in numerous international congresses, conferences, committees, commissions, and international exhibitions and expositions. This participation has been, for the most part, under the auspices of the Department of State as authorized by the Congress, and the resulting records have usually been preserved by the Department.

43.2. Scattered records relate to the participation of black Americans in fairs and expositions. For example, the *Official Catalogue of United States Exhibitors* at the International Exposition in Paris in 1900 includes a list of the materials in the "Negro Exhibit." The list indicates that bound volumes of the *Colored American* newspaper, a collective exhibit on the results of W. E. B. DuBois' study of blacks in Georgia, writings from black pupils at Fisk University, a photograph of a cotton mill owned and operated by blacks, and an exhibit of black medal of honor winners were included in the Negro Exhibit. The list indicates that there were exhibits pertaining to black professionals, blacks in education, housing for blacks, civic and religious organizations led by blacks, books written by blacks, and musical compositions by black composers.

43.3. The motion pictures for this record group include a black and white documentary entitled "Voyage to America," 1964 (#43.2). The film, through the use of drawings and still pictures, describes immigrant groups that have been assimilated into U.S. society. It points out that early settlers came to America seeking political and religious freedom and that some obtained passage in exchange for indentured servitude. It also describes the importation of black slaves.

Record Group 44
Records of the Office of Government Reports

44.1. The Office of Government Reports was created in 1939 as an administrative unit in the Executive Office of the President to succeed the Executive Council, 1933–34, and the National Emergency Council, 1934–39. The general functions of these agencies were to coordinate Federal relief and recovery programs and, later, the homefront aspects of the defense and war effort; to provide a clearinghouse for Government information; and to serve as a liaison between Federal and State Governments, including assistance in the preparation of State legislation. In 1942 the Office of Government Reports was consolidated with other agencies to form the Office of War Information. The Office of Government Reports was reestablished in 1946, but reduced appropriations in 1947 restricted its activities to advertising, motion picture liaison, and operation of a library. Liquidation of the Office was completed June 30, 1948. Many of the reports prepared by this Office pertain to activities of black Americans, particularly during World War II.

44.2. The records of the Executive Division include the **correspondence of Director Lowell Mellett, 1936–43** (2 ft.), arranged in part by agency and in part by subject. There is one file folder for the Urban League, which contains only a few letters and two Urban League pamphlets: *The ABC of Labor Problems, A Primer for Negro Workers* (1934) and *Handbook for the Emergency Advisory Council for Negroes* (1933).

44.3. The records of the Division of Field Operations include **correspondence with State directors, 1939–41** (18 ft.), arranged chronologically by year and thereunder alphabetically by State. The correspondence relates to defense activities and the distribution of Government publications. Some of the reports and correspondence, especially from Southern States, give information about homefront programs addressed to the black population.

44.4. The United States Information Service (USIS) was established in March 1934 to make available to the public factual information regarding Government departments and agencies. The USIS Research Division produced **weekly media reports, 1942–43** (1 ft.), arranged by report number. These reports on editorial opinion dealing with the war effort were based on news and editorial comment of daily and weekly U.S. newspapers; special analyses of various Government departments; analyses of the labor press, black press, and foreign language press; and analyses of magazine contents, radio commentaries, and newsreels.

44.5. The USIS Surveys Division made public opinion surveys at the request of Office of War Information media bureaus and policy-determining officials to aid in the solution of operational and policy problems. The **reports of the Surveys Division, 1942–44** (7 ft.), arranged by report number, include the following reports on blacks: "Negroes and the War: A Study in Baltimore and Cincinnati" (54 pp.), "Anti-British Attitude of Negroes" (7 pp.), "Special Report on Negro Housing in Detroit" (19 pp.), "March on Washington Movement Among Negroes" (9 pp.), and "Current Problems on Negro Morale" (11 pp.).

44.6. Special memorandums of the Surveys Division, 1942–44 (4 ft.), arranged by memorandum number, include reports entitled "Harlem Riot" (11 pp.), "Opinion in Detroit—Thirty-Six Hours after the Race Riot" (31 pp.), "A Preliminary Test of an Office of War Information Pamphlet: The Negro and the War" (23 pp.), "Negro Attitudes toward Certain War Connected Problems" (38 pp.), "The Negro Looks at the War" (65 pp.), "Memphis Negroes and the War" (74 pp.), "White Attitudes toward Negroes" (20 pp.), and "The Negro Problem" (16 pp.).

44.7. Project case folders for public opinion surveys, 1942–44 (4 ft.), are arranged by project number. The case folders contain copies of questionnaires, tabulations of results of surveys, copies of completed reports of surveys, and memorandums regarding interview schedules and conduct of surveys. Some of the black history topics covered by these surveys are draft evasion by blacks; the social dynamics in Detroit, including the situation of blacks in the city; blacks in Medford and Boise; and a preliminary study on blacks during the war period, much of which is in longhand.

44.8. Intelligence reports of the Surveys Division, 1941–43 (10 in.), arranged by report number, contain summaries and analyses of editorial comments and information regarding U.S. attitudes toward war news, of military developments, of homefront war efforts, and of conditions brought about by the war. The report "White Attitudes Toward Negroes" (16 pp.) includes the following subheadings: "Basic Attitudes Toward Negroes"; "Opportunities Open to Negroes"; "Views on Negroes' Ability"; "Segregation"; "Negroes in the War Effort, in War Production, and in the Armed Forces"; and "Negroes' Willingness To Make Concessions." Also among the intelligence reports are the following titles: "Civilians and the War, Pacific Coast Attitudes Toward Aliens, Taxes, Race Problems" (17 pp.), "Negroes and the War, Price Control and Rationing" (15 pp.), and "Negroes in a Democracy at War" (30 pp.) with its supplement "Memphis Negroes and the War" (12 pp.).

44.9. Background material for reports of the Surveys Division, 1942–43 (8 ft.), is arranged alphabetically by subject and includes one folder entitled "Detroit Housing Riot—Negro" (⅛ in.). The folder contains a report on events leading up to the riot and on some of the aftermath of the disturbance.

44.10. The **field reports of the Surveys Division, 1942–43** (1 ft.), are arranged alphabetically by name of field officer and thereunder chronologically. Some reports relate to the reactions of persons in various sections of the United States to the draft, rationing, bond drives, and other aspects of the U.S. war effort on the homefront. Other reports are about problems such as racial tensions, race riots, the public school situation, and labor unrest and housing. For example, among the field reports of Walling Keith is the memo "Alabama Racial Relations" (4 pp.), dated January 25, 1943. The reports of Margo McConnell from Indiana discuss some aspects of racial tension. A weekly report dated March 3, 1943, mentions "Negro groups forming Randolph Movements" for a march on Washington. McConnell also sent a copy of the *Indianapolis Weekly Recorder* for January 30, 1943, which includes an account of William H. Hastie's resignation as special assistant to the Secretary of War.

44.11. The records of the Bureau of Intelligence of the Office of War Information (OWI) include the **records of the Chief of the Bureau, 1942–43** (6 ft.), arranged by division of the Bureau and thereunder alphabetically by subject. There are the following reports about black Americans among the Chief's records: "The Islam Cult and Negro Psychosis—Two Types of Adaptive Reacting Among the Lower Class Negroes of Chicago" (32 pp.); "Negro Civilian Attitudes and the Morale of Negro Troops" (42 pp.); "Statement of Negro War Aims," submitted by the Negro Newspaper Publishers Association (2 pp.); "Recommendations Made by the OWI Advisory Committee on the Negro Press" (3 pp.); "Washington Committee on Jobs for Negroes in Public Utilities" (4 pp.); "Race and Rumors of Race" (14 pp.); and a copy of the *NAACP Bulletin* for February 1944.

44.12. Reports and special memorandums of the OWI Bureau of Intelligence, **1942–43** (2 ft.), are arranged by division of the Bureau and thereunder in part by city or State and in part by number of report or memorandum. Some of the numerous black history topics among these reports and memorandums are the arrest of black cult leaders in Chicago, black-white conflicts, criticism by blacks who found it difficult to reconcile their treatment with the announced war aims of the United Nations, a rally of blacks in New York City one year after Pearl Harbor led by Adam Clayton Powell, Jr., black attitudes toward the war, the Sojourner Truth Housing project conflict in Detroit, a conference of blacks held at Lincoln

University, morale of blacks in Boston, the March on Washington movement, black organizations in the North and South, minority groups in Baltimore and Cincinnati, the question "Is the Negro Press Pro-Axis?," southern reactionaries and war policies, editorial emphasis of the black press, Axis propaganda on the race question, and Government spokesmen on blacks. There are studies entitled "Northern Negro's Most Aggressive Politician, Adam Clayton Powell, Jr.," "Race Tensions in Texas," and "Community Tensions in Three Army Camp Campaign Areas—Indiana, North Carolina and Mississippi." There is also information about radio programs directed to blacks in the series of reports entitled "Daily Radio Digest."

44.13. See also RG 208, Records of the Office of War Information.

Record Group 46

Records of the U.S. Senate*

46.1. The U.S. Senate and the House of Representatives were established by article 1, section 1 of the Constitution as the legislative branch of government. The Senate is empowered to try all impeachments and to judge the elections, returns, and qualifications of its Members. The Constitution also provides that the President share executive responsibility with the Senate by requiring its advice and consent in the negotiation of treaties and the appointment of certain Federal officials.

46.2. Many congressional records have been published by the U.S. Government. In some cases, no unpublished records pertaining to particular actions have survived. Included among the printed records are the *Journals* of the Senate, which are the official record of business transacted on the floor. They give summaries of discussions on the floor, indicate the committees to which matters were referred, and give summaries of committee actions and legislative proposals and actions. The *Journals,* which are indexed, are helpful in locating information about blacks. The following description of black history materials among the records of the Senate is based primarily on information from the *Journals* and covers primarily unpublished Senate records.

Journals of Legislative Proceedings

46.3. The ***Journals* of legislative proceedings and minute books, 1789–1970** (250 ft.), are arranged by number of the Congress. Under article 1, section 5, of the Constitution, the Senate is required to keep and publish a journal of its proceedings and of Senate executive business.

Religious service. Date and photographer unknown. RG 208, Records of the Office of War Information. (208-PR-26B-6).

46.4 Black history topics in *Journal* indexes from the 1st Congress (1789–91) through the 35th Congress (1857–59) pertain to aspects of slavery such as the suppression of the African slave trade; the abolition of slavery in the Nation, in Washington, D.C., and in the territories; claims for slaves taken by the British during the Revolutionary War and the War of 1812 as well as claims for slaves taken or lost in wars with Native Americans, particularly with the Seminoles; the repeal of the Fugitive Slave Law; and propositions to levy a slave tax.

46.5. The earliest agitation against slavery listed in the *Journals* was generated by Quaker groups. Most Congresses during the antebellum period include memorials and petitions from Quakers. During the 16th Congress (1819–21) the question of the admission of slave and free States into the Union was temporarily settled by the Missouri Compromise. Under the terms of this compromise, Missouri was admitted as a slave State. However, slavery was prohibited from that time onward in all of the Louisiana Territory north of latitude 36°30′. In spite of the compromise, the number of petitions for the abolition of slavery continued to increase. During the 24th and 25th Congresses (1835–39) there were many petitions from citizens, including many signed by women only, protesting against slavery in general, the slave trade, slavery in the District of Columbia and in the territories, and the kidnapping of free blacks. In addition to these concerns, petitions from the 27th through the 29th Congresses (1841–47) protested against the admission of Texas as a slave State. Resolutions and memorials relating to slavery were also sent by various State legislatures. For example, during the 18th Congress (1823–25) the General Assembly of Ohio recommended that Congress consider the gradual emancipation of all slaves.

46.6. The colonization of free blacks in Africa was also a subject that appeared often in the *Journals* during the pre–Civil War years. During the 13th Congress (1813–15) Paul Cuffee of Westport, Mass., presented a memorial "praying the aid of the government in execution of a plan which he hopes may ultimately prove beneficial to his brethren of the African race within their native climate." The American Colonization Society was formed for the purpose of colonizing free people of color on the West African coast. During the 17th Congress (1821–23) the Colonization Society sent a memorial to the Senate asking the aid and support of the Government in their efforts to send free blacks to their colony in Liberia. The members of the society were able to attract the support of a number of State legislatures, which, during many succeeding Congresses, sent resolutions favoring colonization. A few States sent resolutions urging that no Federal monies be used for colonizing blacks. One example, during the 20th Congress (1827–29), was a resolution sent by the legislature of South Carolina "to oppose all appropriations in favor of the Colonization Society."

46.7. There are several other aspects of the colonization movement documented by the Senate records. When slave ships were caught, the Africans (called "recaptives") who were on board were freed and subsequently sent, in most cases, by the U.S. Government to the Colonization Society's Liberian Colony. The records of various Congresses include deliberations about annual appropriations for the transport (and a short period of maintenance) of the recaptives, for U.S. naval vessels that patrolled the Liberian coast from time to time, and for the support of ships that were used in the suppression of the African slave trade. In the exceptional case of the slaver *Amistad*, which had been captured by the Africans on board, the Senate received petitions about the disposition of these Africans during the 33d (1853–55) and 35th (1857–59) Congresses.

46.8. Colonization has been a recurring theme for the history of blacks in America. While Liberia continued to be the primary location for emigrants, during the 21st Congress (1829–31) there was a proposal to colonize blacks in Canada; during the 35th (1857–59) and 37th (1861–63) Congresses, emigration of blacks to South or Central America was advocated. Blacks petitioned for suffrage and colonization during the 39th Congress (1865–67) and for emigration to Liberia during the 51st Congress (1889–91). Some petitions during the Reconstruction era also called for acquiring or setting apart territory in Northern or Western States for blacks or for the emigration of blacks. During the 58th Congress (1903–5) there were memorials favoring the establishment of a colonization bureau. Petitions of blacks urging colonization in Africa were also received during the 74th (1935–36) and 79th (1945–46) Congresses.

46.9. The *Journals* include many entries about black people during the prelude and aftermath of the Civil War as well as during the war itself. Violence erupted in the year before the war when John Brown, a militant abolitionist, led a group of 13 whites and 5 blacks in an attack on the U.S. arsenal at Harpers Ferry, Va., in October 1859. During the 36th Congress (1859–61) the Senate established a select committee to inquire into the facts attending the invasion and seizure of the arsenal. The committee's hearings, reports, and correspondence have been reproduced as M1196. Other activities during the 36th Congress were the formation of a special committee of 13 to investigate grievances between slaveholding and nonslaveholding States and the establishment of a select committee of 5 to "discuss the differences which now disturb the peace of the union." There were petitions from black individuals and citizen groups requesting various rights and filing claims for war losses during the 36th and many subsequent Congresses during the 19th century.

46.10. During the Civil War many Senate discussions involved slavery, freedmen, the use and treatment of black troops, and colonization of freed blacks. Some of the slavery issues during the 37th and 38th Congresses (1861–65) were the right of slaves or former slaves to file claims for property used or destroyed by Union troops, the abolition of slavery, and the suppression of the slave trade. The Senate established a select committee on a bill to confiscate the property and free the slaves of the rebels. Some of the many issues involving freedmen were the plight of black refugees in Kentucky, Tennessee, and Alabama; the franchise; civil rights; employment of freedmen; establishment of the Bureau of Refugees, Freedmen, and Abandoned Lands (Freedmen's Bureau), the Freedman's Savings and Trust Co., freedmen's hospitals, and Freedmen's Village; the activities of various Freedmen's Aid Societies; and the removal of the "disqualification of color" in the carrying of U.S. mail. During the 37th Congress, the Select Committee on Slavery and the Treatment of Freedmen was established.

46.11. Affairs of blacks in the District of Columbia addressed by the Senate during the Civil War were the activities of the Colored Benevolent Association of D.C. and of the National Association for the Relief of Colored Women and Children, the education of black children, and equal treatment of blacks on the railroad between the District of Columbia and Baltimore. Matters relating to black troops detailed in the *Journals* were equality of treatment and pay of black and white troops and the "massacre of colored soldiers" at Fort Pillow, Tenn., 1864. During the Civil War Congresses and many subsequent Congresses there were numerous claims of black soldiers and sailors for pay, pensions, bounties, and prize money.

46.12. During the Reconstruction period, from the 39th through the 44th Congresses (1865–77), a variety of black history issues are included in the *Journals.* The Freedmen's Bureau was continued until 1872. The Freedmen's Savings and Trust Co. failed in 1874. Many duties, problems, and investigations of the Freedmen's Bureau were reviewed by the Senate. As a result of the failure of the Freedman's Savings and Trust Co., petitions and claims were filed and appear among the records until after the turn of the century. Institutions such as Freedmen's Hospital and Howard University, both in Washington, D.C., were established during this period, and various matters pertaining to them appear in the Senate records into the 20th century. There are petitions and claims from freedmen who lived among the Five Civilized Tribes. Many records concern the welfare of freedmen in matters such as homes for the aged, education, employment, care of orphans, purchase of land, and protection of life.

46.13. Much of the legislation during the Reconstruction period involved the rights of black Americans. The *Journals* give information about the ratification of the 13th, 14th, and 15th amendments to the Constitution. Civil rights bills, political rights, and equal protection under the law were all important considerations of the Senate. Many petitions were received from blacks asking for equal rights with white Americans. There was much violence against blacks during this period. During the 41st and 42d Congresses (1869–73) the Select Committee on Alleged Outrages in Southern States was active. During the 42d Congress black citizens of Frankfort, Ky., petitioned for "enactment of laws for the better protection of life in that State."

46.14. Between the end of the Reconstruction period and the turn of the 20th century, the *Journals* reflect the continuation of many black history concerns, such as colonization, migration to the North and West, treatment of black soldiers and sailors and claims made by them, agitation for civil and political rights and for equal protection under the laws, claims against the Freedman's Savings and Trust Co., relief of black aged and poor, and land and employment for blacks. There were petitions from black citizens on each of these matters. During the 52d Congress (1891–93) Frederick Douglass and others petitioned "for a hearing in respect to lawless outrages upon colored people in certain southern states." There were also petitions for a "Colored People's World Exposition in Chicago" during the 48th Congress (1883–85) and for a "commission to inquire into the mental progress of the colored race" during the 50th Congress (1887–89).

46.15. During the 57th Congress (1901–3) black history concerns included in the *Journals* consist of petitions to the Committee on Education and Labor asking for an investigation of conditions in the South, memorials of blacks asking for legislation to see that their rights were enforced, petitions for a home for aged and infirm blacks, and petitions and memorials in support of numerous actions such as an exposition for blacks, the creation of a commission to inquire into their condition, the establishment of a memorial home in honor of black soldiers, and the creation of pensions for black people who had been enslaved. From the 59th through the 61st Congresses (1905–11) there are unpublished records, printed hearings, and petitions about the "Affray at Brownsville, Texas," August 1906, an incident that led to members of the all-black 25th U.S. infantry being dismissed because of violence against whites in Brownsville. Petitions from blacks protested the Government's treatment of the soldiers, and many called for the reenlistment of the soldiers.

46.16. Some of the major areas for black history during and after the World Wars that are listed in the *Journals* are matters relating to blacks in the District of Columbia, discrimination against blacks, denial of their civil rights, emigration to the North, and colonization in Africa. The records also concern protests against lynching and mob violence, equal protection under the laws, miscegenation, higher education, blacks in the Armed Forces, the establishment of black National Guard units, blacks in industry, blacks in the war effort, the establishment of the Committee on Fair Employment Practice (see RG 228), equal employment, voting rights, and race riots. The Senate records also include information about expositions, monuments, and memorials for blacks. Matters relating to these subjects were considered by many Congresses.

46.17. For example, records relating to blacks in the District of Columbia include proposals for a home for the aged, laws against intermarriage with whites, inadequate housing of blacks in alley dwellings, blacks in the civil service, the operations of Freedmen's Hospital and Howard University, dissolution of the Colored Benevolent Association, and appropriations for the Industrial Home School for Colored Girls. These issues and other subjects pertaining to blacks were usually addressed by the Committee on the District of Columbia and can be found for almost every Congress.

46.18. *Journals* of Senate executive business include the names of Presidential appointees presented to the Senate for confirmation. Most nominations were handled as routine cases. Sometimes, however, if a nomination was contested, a file was generated. Some of these files about contested nominations relate to blacks. For example, there are records for Frederick Douglass, a nominee for U.S. marshal for the District of Columbia, during the 45th Congress (1877–79); for William D. Crum, a nominee for collector of customs for the district of Charleston, S.C., during the 58th Congress (1903–5); and for Robert H. Terrell, a nominee for judge of the municipal court of the District of Columbia, during the 63d, 64th, and 67th Congresses (1913–15, 1915–17, 1921–23).

Committee Records

46.19. There is a rough similarity between the committees and the standing committees of the House and the Senate. (See the description of RG 233 for information about House committee actions in the area of black history.)

46.20. Senate committee records and reports, 1789–1968 (6,889 ft., 1,436 items), comprise records created and received by standing and select Senate committees and consist of minutes, dockets, correspondence, memorandums, transcripts or prints of hearings, and prints of committee reports, bills, and resolutions. They are arranged by the number of the Congress and thereunder alphabetically by the name of the committee. During its early history, the Senate established various select committees, which, after carrying our specific tasks, were abolished. Although the Senate continued to establish select committees, by the 1820's a group of standing committees had been created. The names and jurisdictions of these committees varied somewhat during the history of the Senate.

46.21. The *Journals* can be used to locate information about committee action concerning black Americans among the Senate records. Among the standing committees whose records are important for the study of black history are the Committee on the Judiciary, which dealt with the legal status of blacks both in slavery and freedom; the Committee on the District of Columbia, which debated the many racial questions that have arisen during the history of the United States and in many ways was therefore a microcosm of the Federal Government's racial policies; and the Committee on the Military, which addressed itself to the suppression of the African slave trade and to colonization of blacks in Africa.

Petitions and Memorials

46.22. Petitions and memorials, 1789–1970 (2,637 ft.), are arranged by the number of the Congress and thereunder alphabetically by name of the committee to which they were submitted. These records, which include supporting documents, are from individuals and organizations and deal with private and public matters. Most petitions were referred to committees for action. However, there is also a group of petitions that was not referred to any committee. There are hundreds of petitions about slavery and colonization. After the Civil War, many black groups petitioned for protection from racial violence and for equal rights with white citizens.

Printed Records of the U.S. Congress

46.23. From its origin, Congress has published a large quantity of the records it has created. Consequently, many of its records are available as

Federal Government publications. Debates of Congress, for instance, are recorded in the following publications: the *Journals*, 1789 to the present; *Annals of Congress*, 1789–1824; *Register of Debates*, 1824–36; *Congressional Globe*, 1833–73; and *Congressional Record*, 1873 to the present. Information about the activities of black representatives in Congress can be located in the post-Civil War volumes. All of these publications have indexes in which various black history topics can be found.

46.24. The *Serial Set*, 1817 to the present, represents the congressional attempt to publish important documents. This set is very extensive (currently over 13,000 volumes) and includes Senate and House committee reports, most executive branch reports and communications, and other congressional documents. The *American State Papers* consist of legislative and executive documents of Congress dating from 1789 to 1838; congressional bills and resolutions, 1789 to the present; and congressional hearings, 1824 to the present. These two published series contain information about black history. (See also RG 287.)

46.25. Information in congressional records can be supplemented by examining the private papers of congressmen. To learn of the existence and location of legislators' papers, researchers should consult the *National Union Catalogue of Manuscript Collections*, compiled by the Library of Congress in Washington, D.C.

* *Restrictions may apply to this Record Group. Consult NARS staff.*

Record Group 47

Records of the Social Security Administration

47.1. The Social Security Act of 1935 established a three-member Social Security Board as an independent agency. The Board administered provisions of the act relating to Federal old-age and survivors insurance and authorizing grants-in-aid to States for administration of unemployment compensation, old-age assistance, and assistance to the blind and to dependent children. The Board also made studies and recommendations for providing economic security through social insurance. In 1946 the Social Security Board was abolished and its functions transferred to the Federal Security Administrator. In the same year the Social Security Administration was established under the direction of the Commissioner of Social Security. The Social Security Administration became part of the Department of Health, Education, and Welfare in 1953. Some of these records relate to the participation of blacks in social security programs.

47.2. The Committee on Economic Security (CES) was created by Executive Order 6757 on June 29, 1934, to study economic and social security and to develop a legislative program. The CES was a predecessor of the Social Security Board. Among the **general records of the CES Executive Director and his staff, 1934–35** (5 ft.), arranged by subject, are published transcripts of congressional hearings pertaining to social security bills. Included are statements of Charles H. Houston of the NAACP; T. Arnold Hill and Reginald Johnson of the Urban League; Rosa Rayside of the New York Domestic Workers Union; Manning Johnson of the League of Struggle for Negro Rights, New York City; and George E. Haynes of the Federal Council of Churches. These persons testified against the lack of provisions for agricultural and domestic workers in the various social security bills. Three-fifths of the black working population were employed in these two occupational areas.

47.3. The **master files of the Social Security Board, 1935–40** (48 ft.), which are arranged according to a decimal classification scheme, include several files concerning blacks: "Social Security Board Publicity to Negroes" (#060.5), "Hiring of Negroes" (#214), "Public Assistance Problems for Negroes" (#600.113), and "Personnel–Race and Nationality Qualifications" (#222.2). Although the filing scheme is helpful, the materials for black history are interspersed throughout the files. There are a large number of cross-reference sheets in the folders. Information about blacks can also be found by using these file numbers in most of the other series of Social Security Board records because the same filing scheme is used throughout.

47.4. There are separate **alphabetical files** (#095) **for the Board, 1935–40** (6 ft.), **for the Executive Director, 1935–40** (2 ft.), and **for** a segment of **the central file, 1935–47** (32 ft.). The alphabetical files include headings such as the "NAACP," "National Urban League," and "Negro Land Grant Colleges." Subjects include unemployment centers, civil service status, merit system, race discrimination, public relations, and questions about the indication of race on applications for old-age benefits.

Record Group 48

Records of the Office of the Secretary of the Interior

48.1. The Department of the Interior was established by an act of March 3, 1849, which provided that the Secretary of the Interior should assume powers previously exercised by the Secretary of War over the Commissioner of Indian Affairs, by the Secretary of the Treasury over the General Land Office, by the Secretaries of War and the Navy over the Commissioner of Pensions, by the Secretary of State over the Commissioner of Patents, and by the President over the Commissioner of Public Buildings. Jurisdiction over census taking, marshals and court officers, Federal buildings and grounds throughout the United States, and charitable and penal institutions in the District of Columbia was also placed in the Department.

48.2. Agencies that have since been transferred from the Department include the Patent Office, Pension Office (Veterans Administration), Census Bureau, Office of Education, Office of the Commissioner of Railroads, Capitol Buildings and Grounds, Freedmen's Hospital, St. Elizabeths Hospital, the Columbia Institution for the Deaf (Gallaudet College), and Howard University. Separate record groups have been established for the records of many operating units of the Department. The records relate to various aspects of black history, including slavery, the slave trade, slaves held by Indians, colonization of blacks, the Civil War and Reconstruction, the health and education of the black population, segregation, and the civil rights movement.

Pre-1907 Records

48.3. There are no general records of the Office of the Secretary of the Interior for the period from the establishment of the Department in 1849 until a central filing system was started in 1907. The records series described below comprise records for the pre-1907 period, although some of the series include some records dated after 1907.

Records of the Appointments Division

48.4. The Appointments or Appointment Division (the exact title varied) was formally established in 1861, but there are records of the Division from the organization of the Department of the Interior in 1849. The Division handled business concerning appointments, promotions, reductions, transfers, removals, resignations, and other changes in the status of employees appointed by the President and the Secretary of the Interior. It handled matters relating to charges against employees, claims of debt against employees, oaths of office, official bonds, leaves of absence, time reports, the establishment and location of field offices, and the preparation of orders and circulars and of registers of departmental employees. In 1907 most of the recordkeeping activities of the Division were transferred to the Mails and Files Division.

48.5. There are no systematic racial designations among the various application and appointment files. Generally, blacks can only be identified by name or by indication of race in their correspondence. The **central office appointment papers, 1849–1907** (40 ft.), are arranged by office or bureau, thereunder by position, and thereunder for the most part alphabetically by name of applicant or incumbent. Files consisting of applications for unspecified positions are arranged alphabetically by name of applicant. Two examples of blacks who applied for unspecified positions are Henry F. Downing and Edwin Belcher. Downing, who identified himself as a black man, in a September 18, 1893, letter to President Grover Cleveland asked for a position in Oklahoma. He was a resident of Chicago, Ill., at the time and stated in his letter that in spite of the fact that he had not supported Cleveland in the last election, he would like a patronage position. Edwin Belcher of Augusta, Ga., applied in 1877 for "some position under the government." He stated that he had served in the Union Army, 1861–65, and was the only black man to command a company of white soldiers. There are various indexes and registers to the central office appointment papers that can be used to find the names of other black applicants.

48.6. The **field office appointment papers, 1849–1907** (346 ft.), are arranged alphabetically by State or Territory, thereunder by position, and thereunder alphabetically by name of applicant or incumbent. This series includes appointment papers for certain officials of the District of Columbia, such as the Recorder of Deeds, and of institutions located in the District, such as Freedmen's Hospital. The hospital records contain information about many black health professionals, including Surgeon-in-Chief Daniel Hale Williams, who was a pioneer in open heart surgery. (Other records pertaining to the hospital are described in paragraphs 48.12 through 48.15 and 48.34.) Blacks were often appointed to the position of District of Columbia Recorder of Deeds. An 1893 newspaper clipping in the file of Recorder Charles H. J. Taylor states, "It has been the fashion for some time to appoint a colored man to this post." Some blacks other than Taylor who served as Recorder of Deeds for the District of Columbia were Frederick Douglass, James M. Trotter, Blanche K. Bruce, James C. Matthews, and Henry P. Cheatham. Many other blacks applied for the position. The file for each applicant generally contains only a few documents, such as letters of application, oaths, endorsements, and related records.

48.7. Names of blacks who served as Recorder of Deeds and of other black officials appointed in the District and other parts of the country can be found in the **indexes to nominations, commissions, designations, and suspensions or removals, 1849–1922** (10 ft.). The index is arranged in three alphabetical sequences: one by name of person concerned, one by position, and one by location of position. The latter two parts are incomplete. Each card gives name of person, position, location of position, and volume and page reference to the appropriate records. Some black nominees and appointees included in the name index are P. B. S. Pinchback, who was nominated and confirmed as the register of the Land Office in New Orleans; Mifflin W. Gibbs, nominated for register of the Land Office in Little Rock; and John R. Lynch, nominated for census supervisor in the Third Census District. These indexes are useful for finding names in several series, including **executive nominations, 1849–94** (13 vols., 2 ft.) and **confirmed executive commissions, 1849–94** (10 vols., 2 ft.), both arranged chronologically.

48.8. The **departmental appointment papers, 1879–1906** (180 ft.), are arranged by year and thereunder by file number assigned for the most part in order of receipt of the earliest document in the file. There is an alphabetical **card index to the names of applicants and appointees, 1879–1907** (65 ft.). Many of the letters among the appointment papers are from heads of bureaus recommending personnel actions. Most of the positions were in Washington, D.C.; they included jobs as clerks, copyists, examiners, messengers, watchmen, and laborers.

48.9. Lists and registers of appointees and employees, 1849–ca. 1909 (49 vols. and unbound papers, totaling 8 ft.), include a volume entitled "Appointments by the Secretary, March 4, 1885 to March 4, 1889, Volume 1." It is arranged by State and congressional district. There is a note on the top of many pages in the volume that the symbol "+" indicates that an appointee was "colored." Some of the other volumes also use this symbol. By using these registers, some names of blacks can be located among the departmental appointment papers.

Records of the Patents and Miscellaneous Division

48.10. There are records of the Patents and Miscellaneous Division dating from 1849, although the Division was not formally established until considerably later. The Division handled all of the work that was not specifically assigned to another division. There are records concerning Patent Office business, including agricultural work until 1862, and Pension Office business from 1849 to 1907. This Division also handled most of the work of the Office of the Secretary concerning public buildings and grounds, welfare institutions, penal institutions, and matters relating to the District of Columbia. Some of the records of the Division grouped separately by subject or function relate to hospitals, schools and charitable institutions, suppression of the African slave trade, and the U.S. Penitentiary for the District of Columbia.

48.11. Records concerning funds for agricultural colleges, 1890–1907 (2 ft.), are arranged for the most part alphabetically by name of State or Territory. By an act of Congress of August 30, 1890, funds from the proceeds of sales of public lands were made available to qualifying land-grant colleges of agriculture and the mechanical arts. The principal requirement was that each State or Territory provide equal facilities for "white and colored" students. Evidence of compliance with this requirement had to be submitted to the Secretary of the Interior, and each State or Territorial legislature had to assent to the provisions of the congressional act. The records include letters received, reports, memorandums, circulars, lists, copies of State laws, college catalogs, congressional documents, certificates, affidavits, and clippings. The file jackets state whether there were "separate colleges for white and colored students, funds equitably divided" or "white and colored students admitted to college on same footing, no division of funds." There is some information given about separate black schools.

48.12. There are several series of records for Freedmen's Hospital among the records of the Patents and Miscellaneous Division. Letters received and other **records relating to Freedmen's Hospital, 1872–1910** (2 ft.), are arranged for the most part chronologically. Starting in 1879, many items also have assigned file numbers. The records relate to the transfer of the hospital from the War Department to the Department of the Interior in 1874, appropriations and other financial matters, rental of buildings from Howard University, conflicting authority of the Department and the government of the District of Columbia over the hospital, investigations, admission policy, personnel, supplies, and other subjects.

48.13. There are **records relating to an 1877 investigation of the treatment of black patients at Freedmen's Hospital** (1 ft.). The testimony is arranged chronologically, and the exhibits are arranged numerically by assigned number. Charges were brought against Surgeon-in-Chief G. L. Palmer alleging that he was guilty of "maladministration of the hospital's pecuniary affairs;" that "superannuated, slovenly and unskillful persons . . . employed as cooks at four dollars a month" served "revolting food . . . in quantities insufficient to satisfy the hunger" of the patients; and that there were "beds . . . infested with multitudinous and repulsive vermin." The records are primarily transcripts of testimony accompanied by a report of the Board of Inquiry regarding their findings. The exhibits consist of letters received, printed documents, affidavits, and copies of contracts.

48.14. Records relating to the new Freedmen's Hospital building, 1903–9 (2 ft.), are arranged roughly by assigned number. There are letters received, specifications, estimates, bids, contracts, vouchers, plats, plans, and related records concerning the selection of a site for the new hospital building, the competition of architects to furnish plans for the new building, the solicitation by potential contractors, the construction of the new building, the science hall for Howard University, and other subjects.

48.15. Some correspondence relating to Freedmen's Hospital is interspersed among the **miscellaneous letters received, 1881–1907** (50 ft.), which is arranged by year and thereunder by file number. There is an **index to the letters received, 1881–1907** (11 vols., 2 ft.), arranged by chronological periods of varying length and thereunder alphabetically by the first two letters of surname or official position of writer or by subject. There is a manuscript topographic map of the proposed site for the hospital among a series of **city maps, ca. 1887–1919** (84 items, 1 in.). (Later records relating to the hospital are described in paragraph 48.34.)

48.16. A series of laws eventually involved the Department of the Interior in the matter of the suppression of the slave trade and the colonization of blacks in Africa. By an act of March 2, 1807, Congress prohibited the importation of slaves into the United States after January 1, 1808, and provided penalties for those engaged in the slave trade. In 1819 Congress attempted to implement this legislation by enacting stringent penalties for the crime of importing slaves and by appropriating $100,000 to enforce the law. It also made provisions for use of armed vessels to seize slave ships and for the return of recaptured persons to Africa. An act of June 16, 1860, authorized the President to negotiate contracts with persons or societies to receive recaptured slaves and to provide for their sustenance in Africa for one year.

48.17. Until 1861, responsibility for executing the slave trade laws was divided among several executive departments. U.S. marshals and attorneys, under the supervision of the Department of the Interior, undertook the apprehension and prosecution of persons engaged in the importation of slaves. On May 2, 1861, the President assigned to the Secretary of the Interior full responsibility for executing the slave trade laws.

48.18. A treaty with Great Britain of April 7, 1862, implemented by an act of Congress of July 11, 1862, granted mutual search rights to specially commissioned vessels of both governments. Vessels suspected of being slave ships were to be sent to one of the Mixed Courts of Justice established at New York, Sierra Leone, or the Cape of Good Hope. The courts, consisting of one judge and one arbitrator for each government, were to judge the facts without appeal. These courts not only tried the slavers but also negotiated the resettlement of the African captives.

48.19. There had been some effort to colonize recaptured slaves and free blacks in Liberia and other places since the establishment of the American Colonization Society in 1816. In 1862 Congress passed several acts to aid in the colonization of free blacks. On August 4, 1862, Rev. James Mitchell was appointed by the President as an agent to assist in the execution of these laws on colonization, and he used the title Commissioner of Emigration. Several projects were started for colonization in places such as Haiti, New Granada, British Honduras, and the British and Danish West Indies. None, however, was successful, and on July 2, 1864, Congress repealed the appropriations for colonization projects, except such money as was needed to meet previously incurred expenses and existing commitments.

48.20. The slave trade was almost entirely suppressed by the end of the Civil War, due to the efforts of the British and U.S. navies and the prosecution of slave traders by the Mixed Courts of Justice. In 1870 the Mixed Courts were abolished and the duties of the Department of the Interior relating to the suppression of the slave trade outside the territorial limits of the United States were transferred to the Department of State. In the same year the supervisory powers of the Secretary of the Interior over U.S. attorneys and marshals was transferred to the new Department of Justice, ending the responsibility of the Department of the Interior concerning the slave trade within the territorial limits of the United States. It was not for several years, however, that all unfinished business of the Department concerning the slave trade was concluded.

48.21. The Patents and Miscellaneous Division kept the records about the suppression of the slave trade and about colonization. These records have been reproduced as M160 and include **letters received, 1854–72** (2 ft.). The letters are arranged by subject or correspondent and thereunder chronologically. Subjects and correspondents include the President; several executive departments; Congress; U.S. attorneys, marshals, judges, and arbitrators of the Mixed Courts; slave and Navy ships; the Commissioner of Emigration; colonization schemes; and the American Colonization Society. There is a **register of the letters received, 1858–72** (1 vol., 2 in.), arranged alphabetically by initial letter of surname or position of writer and thereunder chronologically.

48.22. Other records about the slave trade and colonization include **letters sent, 1858–72** (1 vol., 2 in.), which are arranged chronologically and are indexed by addressee and partially by subject. They relate mainly to the capture of both slave ships and vessels being prepared for the slave trade; judicial proceedings against persons engaged in the slave trade; colonization attempts at Ile à Vâche, Haiti; projected colonization schemes in the Danish West Indies, the British West Indies, and British Honduras; and the delivery of recaptured Africans to Liberia. Some of these letters contain copies of contracts concerning the colonization of liberated Africans on the Isthmus of Chiriqui in the Republic of New Granada and on Ile à Vâche. **Press copies of letters sent, 1861–69** (3 vols., 3 in.), are arranged chronologically. The letters sent and the press copies are also part of M160.

48.23. Other series also relate to the slave trade and colonization. The U.S.S. *Atlanta* was involved in the suppression of the African slave trade in the Caribbean Sea area. Among the records of the Patents and Miscellaneous Division are the **steward's weekly returns of provisions for the ship, November 1858 to May 1859** (1 vol., ½ in.), which are arranged chronologically. The returns give the amounts of different kinds of food issued each day and information about the receipt and transfer of men, arrivals and sailings, and other matters. **Records concerning financial adjustments, 1861–65** (½ in.), are arranged by subject and thereunder chronologically. They consist chiefly of canceled requisitions of the Secretary of the Interior as well as Treasury Department certificates of examination and adjustment of accounts; they relate to other business, including the suppression of the slave trade and other subjects. **Letters sent concerning the judiciary, 1854–69** (42 vols., 3 ft.), are arranged chronologically in volumes numbered 1 to 47 (five volumes are missing). There are alphabetical indexes to addressees in each of the first five volumes. Letters about the suppression of the slave trade are among these records.

48.24. There are also records concerning the slave trade and colonization in other record groups in the National Archives, including RG 21, Records of District Courts of the United States; RG 45, Naval Records Collection of the Office of Naval Records and Library (not described in this guide); RG 59, General Records of the Department of State; RG 84, Records of the Foreign Service Posts of the Department of State; and RG 118, Records of U.S. Attorneys and Marshals (in the Archives Branch, Atlanta Federal Archives and Records Center).

48.25. The records of the U.S. Penitentiary for the District of Columbia are a part of the files of the Patents and Miscellaneous Division. These records include a **register of convicts, 1831–62** (3 vols. and unbound papers, totaling 4½ in.), arranged by number assigned in order of reception of prisoners. The information given for individual convicts is somewhat different in each volume; it usually includes name, number, date of reception, sex, color, crime for which convicted, term of sentence, occupation, and date and method of release. Two volumes are labeled "Journal of the Reception of Convicts," and, with some overlapping, have entries for all convicts. The third volume, labeled "Register of Convicts," has more detailed information concerning the first 341 convicts (those received before March 1844). The unbound records are preliminary versions of parts of the volumes.

Records of the Indian Division

48.26. The records of the Indian Division date from 1849, the year of the establishment of the Department of the Interior, although the Division itself was not formally set up until about 1870. The Indian Division was primarily a clerical unit for handling the correspondence of the Secretary and for maintaining records that related to Indian affairs. There is information relating to black history among the records of this Division because the Five Civilized Tribes held slaves and participated along with other Indians in the Civil War. During the war the Creeks and Seminoles had divided loyalties, but the Chickasaw and Choctaw and some of the Cherokee became Confederate allies. Some loyal Indians were forced to flee to Kansas. Many men of these and other Indian tribes were enlisted in Confederate and Union military forces and participated in campaigns in the Indian Territory. After the war the Government aided Indian refugees in Kansas to return to their homes in the Indian Territory, and punitive measures were imposed on the principal tribes that had remained there. As a result of treaties negotiated in 1866, the tribes were obliged to make numerous concessions, including the freeing of black slaves held by them, the extension of the rights enjoyed by the Indians to the freedmen, and the allotment to the freedmen of a share of the tribal lands. Government action in subsequent years to obtain for the freedmen their share of the land and Indian resistance to this provision in the treaties resulted in records that are valuable for genealogy and the history of slavery among the Indians at the time of the Civil War. (See also RG 75.)

48.27. The **miscellaneous records of the Indian Division, 1838–1905** (1 ft.), are arranged by subject. These files include records relating to legislation concerning persons of African descent in the Choctaw and Chickasaw Nations, 1866.

48.28. The **special files** relating to negotiations with Indians, land matters, investigations, and other subjects, **1848–1907** (5 ft.), are arranged by subject and thereunder in chronological order. There are files relating to Negro Seminoles, 1870–75, and to payments to Indian freedmen for land.

Records of the Indian Territory Division

48.29. This Division was established in July 1898 by an order of the Secretary of the Interior. It was placed in charge of "all business relating to the Indian Territory and the Five Civilized Tribes excepting such matters as more properly belong to the Appointment and Finance Divisions." Previously this work had been done by the Indian Division. The records of this Division also include records about former slaves of the Indians.

48.30. The **special files of the Indian Territory Division, 1898–1907** (34 ft.), are arranged by subject and thereunder chronologically. Interspersed among these files are records relating to Indian freedmen, particularly from the Choctaw, Chickasaw, and Cherokee tribes.

48.31. The records of this Division also include the **final rolls of the Five Civilized Tribes, 1899–1914** (20 vols. and unbound papers, totaling 2 ft.). The rolls are arranged by name of tribe and thereunder divided into rolls for citizens by blood, citizens by marriage, and freedmen. Besides the rolls for the Seminole, Cherokee, Chickasaw, Choctaw, and Creeks in Indian Territory, there are also rolls for the Mississippi Choctaw and the Delaware Cherokee. There are separate rolls for minor children and newborn babies in many of the groups.

48.32. The rolls were prepared by the Commissioner to the Five Civilized Tribes and were submitted to the Secretary of the Interior for approval as provided by several acts of Congress. Approval was based on the legitimacy of an individual's claim of being either an Indian or an Indian freedman. Because land or money from land claims was involved, many people claimed to be Indians or freedmen in order to share in the settlements. Many, however, could not prove their relationship to the tribes. Both approved and disapproved names are included. Most rolls give name, age, sex, degree of Indian blood, and roll and census card numbers of individuals. The final rolls, including only approved names and not including the supplements of 1914, were published by authority of Congress under the title *The Final Rolls of Citizens and Freedmen of the Five Civilized Tribes in Indian Territory.* A separate index volume was also published. These rolls have been reproduced as T529.

Post–1907 Records

48.33. The classified filing system started in 1907 provided for the maintenance of most records in one series. The **central classified files, 1907–53** (1,618 ft.), are arranged according to a numeric-subject classification system. Twenty-five major numerical classifications for "files" were established for records relating to activities of bureaus of the Department and for other important subject areas. Each of these files was divided into a number of secondary classifications.

48.34. There is a major subject file in the central classified files for "Freedmen's Hospital" (#14). Secondary subject classifications (14–1 to 14–49) for the hospital include application and admission for treatment; staff regulations and management; maps, blueprints, and tracings; expenditures; grounds; patients; annual reports; personnel; history of Freedmen's Hospital and its relationship to Howard University; nurses; interns and externs; and the employee quarters and the tuberculosis building. Another major file, "Eleemosynary Institutions" (#20), includes records for Howard University. Secondary subject classifications (20–1 to 20–22) include annual reports, supplies and materials, buildings and grounds, annual supplies, amending of charter, communistic activities, and history. Other file classifications that include administrative records for both Freedmen's Hospital and Howard University are monthly reports (#1–1), appropriations (1–16), special reports–comptroller (1–104), Public Works Administration allotments (1–264), and advertisements (13–18 for Howard and 13–23 for Freedmen's Hospital).

48.35. The major classification "Administrative" (#1) includes information about racial discrimination (1–280). The materials in this sub-file are varied. A few of the subjects are discrimination against the black industrial workers, protests from black political organizations, studies about blacks, segregated schools, training and employment of black workers, and restrictive covenant cases in the Supreme Court. This category also includes information about the relationship between blacks and the Department of the Interior. Harold L. Ickes, who was appointed Secretary of the Interior by President Franklin Roosevelt in 1933, agreed to the formation of the Interdepartmental Group Concerned with the Special Problems of the Negro Population. Records of this group include the minutes of the first meeting, which took place on February 7, 1934. Some of the participants were Robert C. Weaver, Associate Economic Advisor on the Status of the Negro at the Department of the Interior; Henry A. Hunt, an assistant administrator at the Farm Credit Administration; William H. Hastie, assistant solicitor, Department of the Interior; Forrester B. Washington, assistant national director of the Civil Works Administration; Eugene Kinckle Jones, Economic Advisor on Negro Affairs, Department of Commerce; and Robert L. Vann, assistant to the Attorney General, Department of Justice. Other minutes and reports of the Interdepartmental Group are also among the administrative records.

48.36. Under the major category "Office of Education" (#6) is the secondary subject classification Negro education (6–61). These records include a Department of the Interior publication entitled ***Fundamentals in the Education of Negroes,*** compiled and edited by Ambrose Caliver, Senior Specialist in the Education of Negroes (Bulletin No. 6, 1935). The records also include correspondence and reports by Caliver (see also RG 12). There is a mimeographed copy of "Abstracts of the Report to the Research Committee to the National Interracial Conference, 1928," by Charles S. Johnson.

48.37. Specific topics can often be located by using the **alphabetical card index to the central classified files, 1907–57** (364 ft.). There are many cards under "Negro," "Colored," and "Race" as well as under individual names of people and institutions. Many of these subjects are not included in the file classifications described above. Some of the cards indicate that there were a number of letters about a given topic. Others show that there were only a few letters. Below are some samples of subject headings: "Negro Americana at Howard University"; "Negro Business Institute"; "Negro Chamber of Commerce of Denison, Texas"; "Negro Chorus"; "Negro Colonization (Greater Liberia Act)"; "Conference on the Economic Status of the Negro"; "Negro Democratic Welfare Club of Rosewell, New Mexico"; "Negro Freedmen Cherokees"; "Negro Freedom Rally"; "Negro Golfers"; "Negroes in the Defense Program"; "Negro Industrial Workers"; "Negro Land Grant Colleges"; "Negro March on Washington Committee"; "Negro Murals"; "Negro Pageant Movement"; "Negro Professional Man and the Community (Carter G. Woodson and Guichard B. Parris)"; "Negro and the New Deal"; "Negroes in the Navy"; "Negroes, Recreational Areas for"; "Negro Skilled Labor"; "Negro Statistical Data"; and "Negro Welfare Association." Under "Colored" there are topics labeled "Colored Boys," "Colored Citizens Committee," "Colored Democratic Club," "Colored Druggists Association," "Colored High School (Cherokee)," "Colored Medical Center," "Colored National Democratic Division," "Colored Orphan Boarding School (Cherokee)," "Colored People (Creek)," "Colored People (Racial Discrimination in Parks)," "Colored Physicians," "Colored Schools," "Intimidation of Colored Settlers in Kansas," "Colored Soldiers," "Colored State Fair," "Colored Students," and "Colored Union Benevolent Association."

48.38. Another heading in the alphabetical index to the central classified files is "Racial Discrimination." Some subjects under this heading are racial discrimination of the National Park Service, racial discrimination in connection with homestead applications, racial discrimination in the cafeteria near the Department of Agriculture, and racial discrimination in the recreational system of the District of Columbia. There are a number of subject cards for Marian Anderson. When the Daughters of the American Revolution refused to permit Anderson, a black performer, to sing in Constitution Hall, Secretary Ickes invited her to give a recital on the steps of the Lincoln Memorial on Easter Sunday 1939. The concert was sponsored by Howard University. There is correspondence relating to the 1939 concert as well as to later ones, to a mural of Anderson in the Department of the Interior, and to various other matters relating to her.

48.39. The audiovisual records include sound recordings of the 1939 concert, including an address by Ickes on racial prejudice (#48–223). There are also recordings of her performances at the 1943 dedication of the Marian Anderson mural at the Department of the Interior commemorating the Easter Sunday concert (#48–654), at the dedication of the Hyde Park National Shrine (#48–541A), and at the Harold L. Ickes memorial service in 1952 (#48–708). There is a 5-minute sound recording by the Department entitled "Negro Workers in Defense" (48–532) and an 8-minute one with two parts entitled "John Henry" and "Nobody Knows" (#48–210).

48.40. A few films made by bureaus of the Department include footage of blacks. "Down Mobile Way" (#48–31), a 1935 film produced by the National Park Service, is about Alabama State parks. It depicts various cultural and commercial activities in the Mobile area. There are scenes of Civilian Conservation Corps (CCC) youths working in the State parks, including a brief dance by a black CCC youth. The National Park Service also produced a 1937 film about New Jersey State parks entitled "Outdoors in the Garden State" (#48–36). It includes a scene showing a black CCC jazz band. The Bureau of Reclamation produced a 1936 film entitled "Settlement on Reclamation Projects" (#48–44). There are views of various projects and of individuals who participated in them, including a family of black homesteaders.

48.41. Architectural drawings and plans relating to hospitals, schools, and charitable institutions, 1879–1933 (911 architectural and engineering drawings), are arranged alphabetically by State, thereunder by city, and thereunder by name of structure. Included are blueprint drawings, tracings, and specifications for buildings at Howard University and Freedmen's Hospital.

Record Group 49
Records of the Bureau of Land Management

49.1. The Offices of the Secretary and the Register of the Treasury at first handled the disposition of the public domain, but an act of April 25, 1812, established the General Land Office (GLO) as a bureau in the Department of the Treasury to administer all public land transactions except surveying and mapping work. In 1849 the GLO was transferred to the Department of the Interior. The GLO also administered the Homestead Act of 1862. This act provided that any citizen or intending citizen who was the head of a family and over 21 years of age could gain a legal title to 160 acres of surveyed public domain after 5 years of continuous residence and payment of registration fees ranging from $26 to $34. As an alternative, land under the act could be acquired after 6 months residence at $1.25 an acre.

49.2. A 1946 reorganization plan consolidated the GLO and the Grazing Service, also in the Department of the Interior, to form the Bureau of Land Management. The Bureau classifies, manages, and disposes of public lands and their resources. It also administers federally owned mineral resources on non-Federal lands.

49.3. There are public land records for black Americans, but to find them it is necessary to know the name of the individual, the county and State in which the land was located, and the full legal description of the land in terms of fractional section, section, township, range, and principal meridian. This information can be obtained from the recorder of deeds in the county in which the land is located. One of a number of townsites settled by blacks moving to the western public land States was Nicodemus, Kans. The file for Kirwin, Kans. (cash entry 4851, Headquarters Tract Book Volume 70), includes information about Nicodemus, including a plat for land in the NW[4], section 1, township 8 south, range 21 west in Graham County, Kans. This file is a part of the **land-entry papers of the GLO, 1796–1973,** with a few records dating as early as 1770 (8,927 ft.), which are arranged by State and thereunder by land office, type of entry, and final certificate.

Record Group 51
Records of the Office of Management and Budget

51.1. The Bureau of the Budget, under the immediate direction of the President, was established in the Department of the Treasury by an act of June 10, 1921. Reorganization Plan No. 1 of 1939 transferred the Bureau to the Executive Office of the President. The Bureau assisted the President in formulating Government fiscal programs, clearing legislative proposals from Federal agencies, and preparing the U.S. annual budget, Executive orders, and Presidential proclamations. It developed plans to improve the efficiency and administrative management of the Government and to improve, develop, and coordinate Federal and other statistical services; it also informed the President about the progress of activities in Government agencies. It inherited some functions of the President's Commission on Economy and Efficiency, the Bureau of Efficiency, the Central Statistical Board, the Central Statistical Committee, the Federal Board of Surveys and Maps, and the Federal Hospitalization Board. Some of the records relate to fiscal matters affecting black institutions or organizations, particularly those in Washington, D.C.

Records of the Bureau of the Budget

51.2. The **general subject files, 1921–38** (104 ft.), are arranged alphabetically. There are some folders with information about black history. Most of them include only a few documents. Some of the folder titles are "American Negro Exposition, 1936"; "District of Columbia–Industrial School for Colored, 1925"; "District of Columbia–National Training School for Girls"; "Interior Department–Freedmen's Hospital, 1926–38"; "Interior Department–Howard University, 1923–37"; and "Negro Labor Congress, 1925."

51.3. The **subject files of the Director of the Bureau of the Budget, 1939–68,** are arranged in four chronological periods (1939–46, 1947–52, 1953–60, 1961–68) and thereunder by subject or a subject-numeric classification scheme. This series constitutes the official correspondence file of the Bureau. It includes letters received and sent as well as memorandums and reports reflecting the policies and duties of the Director. The black history folders include only a few documents. There are files for Freedmen's Hospital and Howard University under the headings for both the Federal Security Agency and the Interior Department. There are also folders entitled "American Negro Exposition," "Employment–

Fair Practices,'' and ''Fair Employment Practice Committee–General.''

51.4. For the period 1947–52 there are folders for Howard University (⅛ in.) and for Freedmen's Hospital (⅛ in.). The period 1953–60 includes a few documents in folders entitled ''Civil Rights Privileges and Immunities,'' ''Civil Rights Commission,'' and ''Employee-Management Relations/Discriminatory Practices.'' There is also a folder for Howard University (½ in.). There is more black history material for the period 1961–68 (totaling about 3 in.). The folder titles are ''Commission on Civil Disorders,'' ''Civil Rights,'' ''President's Council on Equal Opportunity,'' ''Civil Rights Commission,'' and ''Office of Equal Opportunity.''

Records of the Bureau of Efficiency

51.5. An act of February 28, 1916, gave the Division of Efficiency, created in 1913 in the Civil Service Commission, independent agency status as the Bureau of Efficiency. The Bureau served the President and administrative agencies by studying and recommending solutions for problems in organization and business methods and made special surveys at the request of heads of agencies, congressional committees, and Members of Congress. It established a system of efficiency ratings for Federal employees.

51.6. The **general files, 1913–33** (210 ft.), are arranged according to a subject-numeric filing scheme. There is material about Freedmen's Hospital (#684, 5 in.) and Howard University (#685, ¼ in.).

Record Group 53

Records of the Bureau of the Public Debt

53.1. From 1776 to 1817, subscriptions to Government loans were handled by offices of the commissioners of loans established in the States under supervision of the Continental Congress and continued under the Federal Government. An act of March 3, 1817, abolished the loan offices and transferred their duties and records to the Second Bank of the United States. After the bank's charter expired in 1836, the loan office records and related records of the bank were transferred to the Office of the Register of the Treasury, which had been created in 1781 to keep accounts of the public money and the public debt and had been continued after 1789 within the Department of the Treasury. In 1919 the Register's Office, retaining only those functions relating to issuing securities, was placed under the Commissioner of the Public Debt. In 1921 the Public Debt Service was established, and in 1940 it was converted into the Bureau of the Public Debt. Some of these records relate to several black men who held the position of Register of the Treasury, and a small records series relates to the education of freed slaves.

53.2. The Bureau of the Public Debt generally conducts or directs transactions related to public debt issues of the United States, the former governments of Puerto Rico and the Philippine Islands, and Government-owned corporations for which the Treasury acts as agent. The Bureau supervises the manufacturing of distinctive paper used in printing public debt securities, the issuing and calling in of securities, and the examining and filing of redeemed bonds and other securities.

General Correspondence of the Office of the Register of the Treasury

53.3. Several black men served as Register of the Treasury: Blanche K. Bruce, former U.S. Senator, served from 1881 to 1885 and again for several months in 1898 until his second term was cut short by his death. Bruce also acted as Register at times between his official appointments as Register. Judson W. Lyons, a Georgia lawyer and politician, served from 1898 to 1905; William T. Vernon, a Missouri educator, served from 1906 to 1911; and James C. Napier, a Nashville, Tenn., political leader, served from 1911 to 1913. The records in this record group include correspondence and accounting ledgers handled by these men and their office staffs. The material itself pertains to financial matters rather than to aspects of black history. For example, included among the **miscellaneous letters received, 1865–85 and 1894–96** (94 vols., 15 ft.), arranged chronologically, are numerous letters addressed to Register Blanche K. Bruce from 1881 to 1885. Many of the records during Bruce's term are addressed to "The Register."

Miscellaneous Correspondence and Reports

53.4. After the Civil War, crops from some specified farm areas were to be sold to finance schools in the South Carolina Sea Island region. These farm areas were called school farmlands. Among the miscellaneous records are **accounts of interest paid on the South Carolina School Fund and related correspondence, 1869–1906** (2 in.). These records are arranged chronologically and include copies of enabling legislation; receipts from teachers; information about the sale of school farmlands; correspondence with O. O. Howard, the head of the Freedmen's Bureau, pertaining to the fund; receipts for deposits to the school fund; and an account book.

Record Group 54

Records of the Bureau of Plant Industry, Soils, and Agricultural Engineering

54.1. The Bureau of Plant Industry, Soils, and Agricultural Engineering was established February 13, 1943, in the Agricultural Research Administration. Government procurement, propagation, and distribution of seeds and plants began in the Agricultural Section established in the Patent Office in 1839. These activities were transferred to the Department of Agriculture Division of Gardens and Grounds in 1862 and to the Division of Seeds in 1868. As plant work became more specialized, Divisions of Botany, Pomology, Vegetable Physiology and Pathology, and Agrostology were established in the Department from 1869 to 1895. To coordinate and develop plant investigations conducted by these divisions,

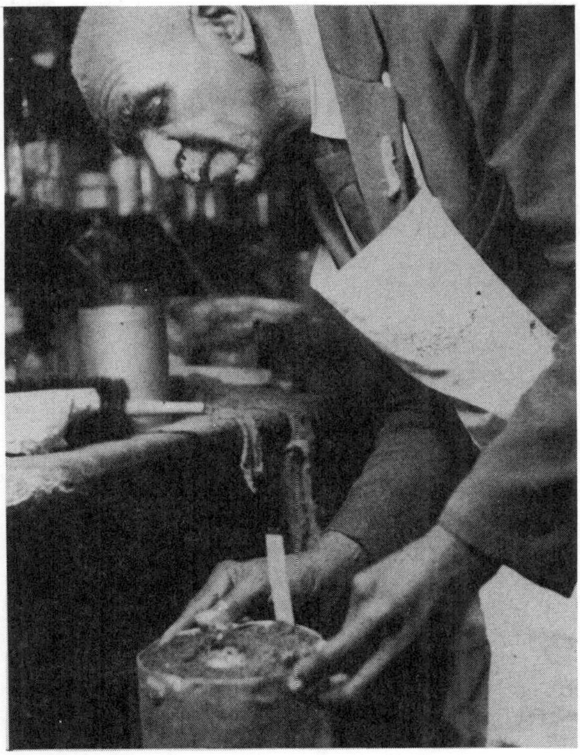

Photograph of George Washington Carver from the Harmon Foundation still picture collection. 1938. Photographer unknown. RG 200, National Archives Gift Collection. (200(s)-HS-6-200)

the Bureau of Plant Industry was established in 1901. In 1938 soil investigations were transferred to the Bureau. In 1943 engineering research was transferred from the Bureau of Agricultural Chemistry and Engineering to the newly designated Bureau of Plant Industry, Soils, and Agricultural Engineering. The Secretary of Agriculture abolished this Bureau on November 2, 1953, and transferred its functions to the Agricultural Research Service. These records include correspondence with the faculty of Tuskegee Institute.

54.2. The **general correspondence of the Office of the Chief of the Bureau of Plant Industry, 1908–39** (574 ft.), is arranged in numerical order by file numbers. File 6815 (½ in.) includes correspondence with George Washington Carver, Booker T. Washington, and Robert R. Moton—all of Tuskegee Institute in Alabama. Most of the correspondence is with Carver and pertains to technical aspects of plant cultivation. The Bureau sometimes distributed seeds for experimentation, and some of the correspondence from Tuskegee requests seeds for black farmers.

54.3. The **letters sent by the Office of the Chief, 1901–29** (475 vols., 75 ft.), arranged chronologically, include a number of letters sent to George Washington Carver concerning such topics as the cultivation of mulberry trees, silk culture, seed distribution, strawberry plants, and new varieties of seed. Most of the volumes are indexed by name of correspondent.

Record Group 55

Records of the Government of the Virgin Islands

55.1. The Danish West Indies (consisting of three main islands—St. Thomas, settled by the Danes in 1672; St. John, occupied in 1717; and St. Croix, purchased from the French in 1733—and many smaller, uninhabited islands) were administered by the Danish West India and Guinea Co. until they became Danish royal colonies in 1754. Except for a brief period of English rule, these islands remained under Danish rule until the United States purchased them in 1917. They were renamed the Virgin Islands of the United States and placed under the jurisdiction of the Navy Department. In 1931 they were transferred to the jurisdiction of the Interior Department. A Governor appointed by the President heads the local administration of the Islands. Some of these records were generated by black officials.

55.2. The records of the Office of the Governor and the Government Secretary include records for Governor William H. Hastie. Hastie, a black attorney, was appointed by President Franklin D. Roosevelt as the judge of the district court of the Islands in 1937. In 1946 President Truman appointed Hastie as the Governor of the Virgin Islands. Hastie's annual reports, which were submitted to the U.S. Secretary of the Interior, are included among the **annual reports of the Governor and subordinate offices in the Island administration 1917–49** (4 ft.), arranged by name of the official.

55.3. Miscellaneous correspondence of executive officials, 1920–50 (5 ft.), arranged by name of official, includes Hastie correspondence, 1946–49, on a wide variety of social, financial, judicial, and general administrative matters, as well as some personal matters.

55.4. In 1924 President Coolidge appointed a Federal commission of five black Americans to investigate conditions in the Virgin Islands. The information collected by the commission is among the Records of the U.S. Senate, RG 46 (#74A–F24).

Record Group 56

General Records of the Department of the Treasury

56.1. The Department of the Treasury was established by a 1789 act that directed the Secretary of the Treasury to prepare plans for improving and managing revenues and supporting public credit, to prepare and report revenue and expenditure estimates, to superintend the collection of revenues, to decide on forms for keeping and stating accounts and making returns, and to grant all warrants for money issued from the Treasury. This record group includes records of the Office of the Secretary and its subdivisions and those of units performing service functions for the entire Department. Some of these records relate to slavery, the slave trade, black activities during and after the Civil War, and blacks as employees of the Department.

Correspondence of the Office of the Secretary of the Treasury

56.2. The **correspondence of the Office of the Secretary of the Treasury, 1789–1917** (about 2,500 ft.), consists of two major series of letters sent and received, dating from 1789 to 1878 and from 1878 to 1917, together with related registers and indexes. Each major series includes several subseries, under which are sub-subseries or "sets" arranged according to the name of the office of the addressee or addressor or according to the function concerned. A letter of the alphabet was assigned to each sub-subseries for filing convenience. For example, in the subseries dating from 1833 to 1878 are letters to and from the President ("A" series), the heads of executive departments and Treasury bureaus ("B" series), and the Congress ("C," "D," and "E" series).

Letters Sent

56.3. Some correspondence concerning black history is included among the **letters sent 1789–1912.** The letters sent for this period are themselves divided into two chronological series—those dating chiefly from 1833 to 1878 and those from 1878 to 1912. For the earlier series (1833–78) there are **alphabetical name and subject indexes and registers** (67 vols., 13 ft.), which include entries pertaining to black history topics such as slavery and the slave trade, problems of foreign nationals who wished to visit or immigrate to the United States with their slaves, the shipment of goods and money from benevolent groups abroad for freedmen, land distribution policies of the Direct Tax Commission (see RG 58), and bounties to black veterans of the Civil War.

56.4. Some examples of this correspondence among the **letters sent to Cabinet officers and heads of bureaus ("B" series), 1833–60** (14 vols., 2 ft.), arranged chronologically, include information about a vessel fitted out in Cuba for a slaving voyage to Africa, 1859, and the cost of removing the cargo of the slaver *Orion,* 1860. The "Bc" series, **letters sent to Cabinet officers, 1861–66** (3 vols., 6 in.), arranged chronologically, contains information concerning the donation of goods, such as clothing and Bibles, from abroad for the freedmen; the alerting of the New York customs collector to ships being outfitted for the slave trade; the awarding of prize money for the capture of the slave ship *Nightingale;* the dispatching of a special agent to Haiti to provide relief and protection for freedmen there; and expenditures for freedmen by officers of the War Department.

56.5. There are several series of letters sent to customs collectors in various ports. These are indexed in part by the **abstracts of decisions relating to customs cases** ("Pierpont's index"), **1833–63** (2 vols., 4 in.), arranged alphabetically by subject. The volumes include at least 25 entries pertaining to correspondence about slavery and the slave trade.

Letters Received

56.6. Letters received, 1789–1912, include subseries with information about blacks. **Correspondence with customs collectors, 1789–1833** (45 vols., 8 ft.), is arranged by name of port and thereunder chronologically. Materials relating to blacks in this subseries can be found under Southern ports such as Key West and New Orleans. Most of the material relates to slaves coming into the United States on ships such as the Mexican brig *Bravo* and the British schooner *Trimble.* The question was

Children kneeling at worship service in Chicago, Ill. Date and photographer unknown. RG 208, Records of the Office of War Information. (208-PR-26A-3).

whether the blacks were being brought in in violation of the act of April 20, 1818, which prohibited slave importation from Africa, and just what was to be done with the blacks brought in.

56.7. The **letters received from the Navy Department, 1823–1909** (3 ft.), are arranged chronologically. There is material pertaining to the capture of slavers by U.S. Navy vessels, especially from 1860 to 1861. The ships involved include the slavers *Storm King, Erie, Bogota,* and *Wildfire.* Lists of the crews of the U.S. vessels are given along with some information about the number of Africans on each ship and the amount of bounty to be paid.

56.8. The **letters received relating to the direct tax, 1863–81** (5 in.), are arranged chronologically. Some of the material relates to the sale or leasing of land to blacks. By a Presidential order of September 16, 1863, a number of plantations that had been bought by the United States for delinquent taxes were divided up and made available to freedmen. The tracts of land in South Carolina were 10 acres each and sold for sums of 12-15 dollars. Some freedmen had already paid for the land and others were living on it in anticipation of buying when suddenly the transactions were halted. The agents disbursing the land wrote requesting permission to continue the sales. There also is material relating to islands such as Parry's Island and St. Helena Island and especially to Port Royal. Other materials relate to the problems of the freedmen in paying for the land because of poor cotton crops, problems with caterpillars, and a lack of mules.

56.9. The **letters received from the First through the Sixth Auditors, 1817–1910** (35 ft.), are arranged sequentially by name of office and thereunder chronologically. John R. Lynch, a black politician and former Congressman from Mississippi, was appointed by President Benjamin Harrison to be the Fourth Auditor of the Treasury (serving the Navy Department). He served from 1889 to 1893. Ralph W. Tyler, a black journalist and politician, was appointed Fourth Auditor by President Theodore Roosevelt and again by President William Taft; Tyler served from 1905 to 1913. This series includes letters, reports, and statements from Lynch (5 in.) and Tyler (4 in.) relating to the operation of the Auditor's offices. Among Lynch's correspondence is one note signed by Robert H. Terrell as "Chief of Division." Terrell, who was later appointed a judge of the municipal court of the District of Columbia, is also listed in the "Biography of Treasury Employees" (described in paragraph 56.16).

56.10. The **letters received from the Register of the Treasury, 1827–1910** (3 ft.), are arranged chronologically. Between 1881 and 1910, three black men served as Register of the Treasury: Blanche K. Bruce, Judson W. Lyons, and William T. Vernon (see RG 53). Included in these records are letters from Bruce (1 ft.), from Lyons (3 in.), and from Vernon (1 in.). Their records pertain to routine business matters. The Register was a position that was often awarded to black men when patronage jobs were allotted. The records of blacks who held the position at later dates are in other series.

56.11. Letters received from collectors of internal revenue, 1864–1908 (23 ft.), are arranged alphabetically by name of State or Territory, thereunder numerically by revenue district, and thereunder chronologically. Included are some records for Charles W. Anderson, a black businessman and politician who was appointed collector of internal revenue for the second and third districts of New York. Anderson was first appointed by President Theodore Roosevelt in 1905. He resigned in 1935, having served during most of this period with the exception of the Wilson years. Anderson's records (2 in.) consist of letters received relating to administrative matters.

Central Files

56.12. The **central files of the Office of the Secretary of the Treasury, 1917–32** (110 ft.), are arranged in three groups: general correspondence, correspondence concerning tax cases, and correspondence concerning individuals. Within each group the records are arranged alphabetically by subject or Treasury office, name of company, or name of individual. The general correspondence includes a folder entitled

"Personnel–Segregation of Treasury Department Employees," 1924–32 (¾ in.).

56.13. The **central files of the Office of the Secretary of the Treasury, 1933–56** (96 ft.), are arranged in three groups: general correspondence, correspondence concerning tax cases, and correspondence concerning individuals. Within each group the records are arranged alphabetically by subject, Treasury office, name of company, or name of individual. The general correspondence includes a file about the Fair Employment Practice Committee (1 in.) and one entitled "Personnel–Negro Employees" (1 in.), which includes some name lists of black employees for as early as 1911. There is a personnel file concerning segregation in the Treasury Department, 1933–35 (¼ in.). There are also a few letters from blacks in the correspondence from individuals. These can be located by using the **alphabetical name and subject index to the central files, 1933–56** (35 ft.).

Records of Various Divisions Within the Office of the Secretary of the Treasury

Records of the Division of Appointments

56.14. The Division of Appointments had supervision over all matters relating to appointments and other personnel changes in the Department's central and field services, such as handling correspondence with Members of Congress, the Civil Service Commission, and others; the preparation of nominations and commissions for all Treasury officials, when required; and the preparation and approval of the Department's payrolls in Washington, D.C.

56.15. The **applications for appointments as heads of Treasury offices, 1830–1910** (15 ft.), are arranged alphabetically by name of applicant. There are some applications from blacks. For instance, one file (1 in.) is for John R. Lynch, applying for a second term as Fourth Auditor of the Treasury, and one 1897 letter is from Ernest Lyon asking to be considered for Fourth Auditor or for a commissionership of the Land Office.

56.16. The **applications and recommendations for positions in the Washington, D.C., offices of the Treasury Department, 1830–1910** (276 ft.), are arranged alphabetically by name of applicant. The records consist of letters received relating to the appointment of clerks, printers, printers' assistants, Secret Service agents, messengers, laborers, watchmen, charwomen, and other Treasury employees. Unsuccessful applications are included. Applications from blacks are among these records. The **"Biography of Treasury Employees," 1835–1912** (15 vols., 4 ft.), arranged in rough chronological order and thereunder by administrative unit, can serve as a partial index to the applications and recommendations. For each employee, the biography gives position, grade, age, and date of appointment; the State and congressional district appointed from; contemporary legal residence; relatives in office; military service; the persons who submitted recommendations; and the dates and circumstances under which the position was vacated. The biography includes racial designations in some volumes in the form of a small letter "c" for colored, usually in red ink. Most information about black employees is from the post-Civil War period.

56.17. Personnel folders of notable Treasury employees, 1822–1940 (1 ft.), arranged alphabetically by name of individual, include the folders for at least three black men: Matthew A. Henson (¼ in.), Solomon Johnson (⅛ in.), and William Johnson (⅛ in.). Henson was an Arctic explorer, and he received an appointment as a messenger in the New York Customs Collector's Office. Both Solomon Johnson and William Johnson (unrelated) had served as barbers to Abraham Lincoln. They received appointments as laborers in the Treasury Department at the request of President Abraham Lincoln.

56.18. The **records of Presidential appointments, 1833–1945** (70 ft.), are arranged alphabetically by name of appointee or applicant. Most of the records are dated in the late 19th and the 20th centuries. The records consist of correspondence relating to appointments to major departmental positions that were made by the President and confirmed by the Senate. There are folders for the following black officials: for Register of the Treasury, James C. Napier (2 in.), William T. Vernon (1 in.), and Blanche K. Bruce (2 in.); for customs officials, P. B. S. Pinchback (½ in.), William D. Crum (2 in.), and Robert Smalls (1 in.); and for collectors of internal revenue, Charles W. Anderson (3 in.) and Joseph E. Lee (3 in.). Included in the files are recommendations, petitions, oaths of office, notices of promotions and dismissals, letters received and copies of letters sent relating to charges and investigations, and unsuccessful as well as successful applications.

56.19. Lists of major Treasury officers ("Presidential appointments"), **1806–1907** (8 vols., 1 ft.), are arranged by office and thereunder chronologically. Generally, each entry gives only the name and address of the appointee and the date of his appointment to office. Many of the black officials named in the previous paragraph, such as Bruce, Smalls, Pinchback, and Crum, are listed in these volumes.

56.20. Correspondence relating to political patronage, 1909–33 (8 in.), is arranged in rough alphabetical order by Treasury office and thereunder chronologically. One file (2½ in.) concerns a 1921 protest campaign against the appointment of a black man as Register. Many of the letters and petitions were from white females who worked in the Register's Office. One letter mentioned that four black men had been appointed Register in the past.

56.21. The **records relating to customhouse nominations, 1849–1910** (210 ft.), are arranged alphabetically by State or Territory, thereunder by port or district, and thereunder chronologically. The letters, received mainly from customs collectors, concern the subordinate officers in the Customs Service. There are records for black officials such as Pinchback (1 in.); John H. Deveaux, a collector at the ports of Brunswick (2 in.) and Savannah, Ga. (8 in.); Henry M. Turner, customs inspector at Savannah (¼ in.); and Christopher C. Wimbish, surveyor of the port of Atlanta (1 in.).

56.22. Applications for appointments as Customs Service officers, 1833–1910 (165 ft.), are arranged by office, thereunder alphabetically by State or Territory, thereunder by name of port, and thereunder alphabetically by surname of applicant. The series consists of letters received from Treasury Department officials, Members of Congress, Government employees, officeseekers and their friends, politicians, and other persons. There are files for some black customs collectors: for example, John C. Dancy, collector at Wilmington, N.C. (6 in.); James B. Dudley, also a collector at Wilmington (2 in.); and Robert Smalls, collector of customs for the port of Beaufort, S.C. (6 in.).

56.23. Applications for positions as internal revenue collectors and assessors, 1863–1910 (100 ft.), are arranged by officer, thereunder alphabetically by State and Territory, thereunder numerically by district, and thereunder alphabetically by name of applicant. Included are records for black men such as H. A. Rucker, who served as the collector of internal revenue in Atlanta (1 ft.); Col. J. E. Bryant, an applicant for collector in Georgia (½ in.); a controversial applicant in Mississippi named James Hill (1 in.); and Mifflin W. Gibbs, receiver of monies at Little Rock, Ark. (¼ in.). Some black men also applied for positions as assessors; for example, Francis E. Dumas in Louisiana (⅛ in.), Blanc F. Joubert in Louisiana (⅛ in.), and Edwin Belcher in Georgia (½ in.). The records consist of letters received from Treasury officers, politicians, applicants, friends of applicants, Government employees, and other persons. Information in the records relates to the removal as well as the appointment of collectors and assessors of internal revenue.

56.24. Applications for positions as charwomen, laborers, and messengers, 1890–1902 (2 ft.), are arranged alphabetically by name of applicant. In some of the letters, applicants describe themselves as colored or Negro. The records consist of letters and applications received concerning the appointment, removal, and resignation of charwomen, laborers, messengers, carpenters, painters, and other persons employed in Treasury Department buildings in Washington, D.C.

Records of the Division of Bookkeeping and Warrants

56.25. The **miscellaneous records of the Division of Bookkeeping and Warrants, 1793–1922,** with gaps (9 ft.), are arranged by subject. The series consists of lists, abstracts, and fiscal documents relating to the many functions of the Division. There are records pertaining to an investigation of the accounts of the Freedmen's Bureau in 1874 (2½ in.) by the Secretary of War. The investigation resulted in charges of fraud and embezzlement on the part of the disbursing officers.

Records of the Division of Captured Property, Claims, and Land

56.26. The **letters received** by this Division, **1863–87** (24 ft.), are arranged chronologicaly and thereunder alphabetically by name or office or writer. The records contain letters received from collectors, surveyors, and other officers of the Customs Service; special agents of the Treasury Department; Members of Congress; the Secretary of War, the Adjutant General, and Army officers; the Secretary of the Navy and Navy officers; merchants; importers; manufacturers; and other persons. The records relate to the leasing of plantations and other business matters in the South. Because of the nature of the records, there is information about freedmen, the Freedmen's Bureau, and plantation life after the Civil War interspersed throughout the records.

56.27. An act of Congress, dated March 3, 1871, authorized the President to nominate three commissioners of the Southern Claims Commission to determine the validity of the claims of southerners loyal to the U.S. Government during the Civil War for stores or supplies taken by or furnished to the Army of the United States. The **letters received by the Southern Claims Commission, 1871–80** (2 ft.), are arranged chronologically. The letters consist of inquiries from officials and individuals relating to the Commission's criteria for "loyalty," methods of taking testimony, the use of Treasury and Justice Department records, statements from informants on the loyalty of claimants, the appointment of special commissioners to hear and collect testimony in various parts of the South, applications for positions with the Commission, and the closing of the Commission. One agent, W. B. Figures, mentioned in a July 26, 1871, letter that "Many of the claimants are colored citizens." Many of the questions that he raised in his letter about the status of blacks during the Civil War are also raised in other letters in this series. M. F. Plesants, a special commissioner in Richmond, Va., wrote on November 30, 1871, that "I can only say in reference to these claims and the claims of colored men generally, that I have not seen an instance of what appeared to me as fraud." Some agents listed claim numbers for blacks that can be used to find additional information about whether or not the claims were allowed or disallowed. Usually "col'd" for colored is beside the names of black applicants. This series also includes a letter from Hiram R. Revels, the black Reconstruction Senator from Mississippi, dated January 11, 1873, recommending a gentleman to be a claims agent.

Records of the Office of the Chief Clerk

General Records

56.28. The **records of the Office of the Chief Clerk, 1913–49** (6 ft.), arranged according to a numeric classification scheme, include a folder entitled "Negroes, 1921–34." It consists of minutes and correspondence of the Interdepartmental Group Concerned with the Special Problems of Negroes and the report of the agricultural committee of that group, May 1934. The folder includes information about segregation in the Treasury Department. Among the records is also the file "Messengers and Laborers" (2 in.), which includes some information about black employees, and the file "Ku Klux Klan," which consists of several documents relating to the protection of Treasury buildings during the 1925 Klan parade.

Records Relating to Expositions, 1867–1941

56.29. The Jamestown Tercentennial Exposition was held at Norfolk, Va., from April 26 through November 30, 1907, to celebrate the first permanent settlement of English-speaking people in the Western Hemisphere. The Jamestown Exposition Co., incorporated by the General Assembly of Virginia on March 10, 1902, was responsible for the preliminary planning of the exposition and for raising the money for it. There was also a Negro Development and Exposition Co., which was responsible for the separate Negro exhibition.

56.30. The **correspondence concerning the Negro exhibition, 1906–9** (1 ft.), is arranged alphabetically by name of writer or subject. The series contains letters and telegrams received and copies of letters sent relating to the Negro exhibition at the Jamestown Tercentennial Exposition. Included are letters relating to the liabilities of the commissioners, the construction and decoration of the Government building housing the Negro exhibits, the regulation governing the maintenance of the restaurant and other concessions, and a contract for the purchase and removal of the building by the Negro Development and Exposition Co.

56.31. Letters received by the special disbursing agent, 1906–8 (1 ft.), arranged chronologically, consist of letters and reports received from the Secretary and Assistant Secretary of the Treasury, the president and other officers of the Negro Development and Exposition Co., and various claimants. The letters relate to corrections and changes in disbursement abstracts; notifications of the acceptance of construction proposals and authorizations for the payment of contractors' vouchers; authorizations for special expenditures by Government agents and inspectors; and the settlement of claims against the Government.

56.32. Some of the printed materials among these series mention that blacks exhibited in the World's Industrial and Cotton Centennial Exposition in New Orleans, 1884–85; the Cotton States and International Exposition in Atlanta, 1895; the Tennessee Centennial Exposition in Nashville, 1897; the Paris Exposition, 1900; and the South Carolina Interstate and West Indian Exposition in Charleston, 1901–2. This record group includes no records at all for the Paris Exposition. There are no separate series for the black exhibits in the other expositions even though they may be mentioned in disbursement records or from time to time in correspondence.

Cartographic Records

56.33. There are two **manuscript maps of Government farms for freedmen in southeastern Virginia, ca. 1866–70** (2 items), which show the locations of farms for freedmen and list the acreage of individual farms. One map shows the First District, Negro Affairs, Department of Virginia and North Carolina, which covered the peninsula between the York and James Rivers southeast of Williamsburg, Va. The other map shows the Second District, covering the area from Norfolk, Va., south to the Great Dismal Swamp.

Record Group 58

Records of the Internal Revenue Service

58.1. The Office of the Commissioner of Internal Revenue was established in the Treasury Department in 1862 to help finance the Civil War. The agency under the Office was known as the Bureau of Internal Revenue until 1953, and thereafter as the Internal Revenue Service. During the periods 1791–1802 and 1813–17 the Treasury Department collected internal revenue taxes through an office headed by the Commissioner of the Revenue. In 1866 the Commissioner of Internal Revenue was given responsibility for terminating the work of the commissions that had been created to collect direct taxes in the States declared to be in insurrection. Wartime taxes were gradually abolished or reduced until only taxes on liquor and tobacco existed in 1883. From that time until 1913 the Bureau was chiefly concerned with the collection of taxes on these two commodities, although other tax and regulatory activities were occasionally assigned to it. With the adoption of the 16th amendment in 1913, the collection of income taxes became one of the Bureau's principal functions. From 1919 to 1927 it enforced Prohibition laws. Today the Service is responsible for the administration, assessment, and collection of all internal revenue taxes and the administration of laws relating to alcohol, alcoholic beverages, tobacco, and firearms. Black history materials in these records primarily relate to U.S. Government relations with freedmen after the Civil War, but there are also some records pertaining to slavery and to black appointees to the Service.

Records for the Period 1803–61

58.2. Assessment lists, 1815–16 (53 vols., 3 ft.), are arranged by State, thereunder by collection district, and thereunder alphabetically by name of the property holder. Many of the assessment lists are on microfilm. The lists for Pennsylvania are nearly complete. Each entry shows the name of the property holder; a description of the land, buildings, slaves, furniture, jewelry, and watches held; and amount of tax. Because of the Gradual Abolition Act of 1780, there were few slaves left in Pennsylvania by the dates of these lists.

Records for the Civil War Period

58.3. To obtain money to carry on the Civil War, new taxes were levied on many articles, and the Office of the Commissioner of Internal Revenue was established to collect them. An act of August 5, 1861, provided for a direct tax and an income tax, with a Commissioner to supervise their collection and a principal collector and assessor in each of the collection districts into which the several States and Territories were divided. Each State could assess, collect, and pay its quota of the direct tax. The last collection under this act was not made until 1888. By an act of March 2, 1891, the moneys collected were returned to the States. Many of the records of or relating to the Direct Tax Commissions in the States in rebellion are in the National Archives. The most complete are those for South Carolina. The South Carolina records give details about the transition of blacks in the Beaufort area from slavery to freedom.

58.4. In the Beaufort region, blacks constituted virtually the entire population. Consequently, the records for the South Carolina Direct Tax Commission for this period largely concern the former slaves, their acquisition of abandoned lands in the Sea Islands, and related aspects of their lives, such as education, farming, and legal, military, and political activities.

58.5. General correspondence relating to the South Carolina Direct Tax Commission, 1862–93 (3 ft.), is arranged by subject and concerns the appointment of tax commissioners and clerks, Lincoln's instructions to the commissioners outlining the scope of the Commission's activities, a list of lands sold for direct taxes, redemption applications and claims, and school reports and notices from the Department of Justice of the judgments rendered by the U.S. Court of Claims. Information about former slaves is interspersed throughout the records because the commissioners were ordered to reserve some land for charitable, educational, or police purposes. Some of the land reserved for charitable purposes was sold to the black population.

58.6. Certificates for land sold to heads of families, 1863–72 (13 vols., 3 ft.), are arranged numerically. The certificates are made out to "heads of families of the African race" or "colored citizens." Some land was leased rather than sold. There are also certificates for lands leased to "heads of families of the African race," 1866–86 (5 in.). These certificates are also arranged numerically. The records indicate the date of the deed, the name of the buyer, the purchase price, and the location of the land.

58.7. There are **applications to purchase land by preemption, 1864** (10 in.), arranged in rough chronological order, filed in response to a circular issued by Gen. Rufus Saxton to freedmen of South Carolina, authorizing freedmen to locate on land set aside for them. The records indicate the name of the claimant, the subject of the claim, and the final judgment.

58.8. The crops from some specified farms were to be sold to finance schools in the Sea Island region. These were called school farmlands. **Correspondence relating to school farmlands, 1866–99** (2 vols., 10 in.), is arranged by subject. Information includes name of original owner of the land, its location and size, receipts, and correspondence concerning land ownership and the disposition of proceeds from the land.

58.9. Some of the lands sold during this period were later claimed again by their antebellum owners. **Applications to redeem real estate sold for direct taxes, 1872–99** (2 ft.), are arranged alphabetically by name of applicant. The records include letters of application, petitions, and correspondence. There are various other series that relate to these and other claims.

58.10. There are several maps among the South Carolina records. There is a **plat of lands owned near the mouth of the Ocmulgee River, ca. 1866–67** (1 sheet), which shows the holder of each plot and the amount of land held. A **manuscript map of St. Helena's Parish, S.C., ca. 1865** (5 ft.), details the rectangular land subdivisions carried out in the area. Included are field notebooks of surveyors, which contain the data from which the map was constructed. There are also **manuscript, annotated, and printed maps relating to St. Helena's Parish and part of St. Luke's Parish, 1855–95** (6 in.).

Records of the Post-Civil War Period

58.11. Among the personnel records are **lists of collectors, 1876–1907** (16 vols., 6 in.), and **lists of collectors and assessors, 1862–83** (5 vols., 3 in.). The entries are arranged by collection district and give the name and some information about each collector, assessor, or agent. Included among these lists are names of blacks such as Henry W. Purvis of South Carolina, James C. Napier of Tennessee, and P. B. S. Pinchback of Louisiana.

58.12. Records of the organization of the offices of collectors, 1822–1911 (42 vols., 6 ft.), are arranged by collection district and thereunder chronologically. There are entries for some black collectors, such as Henry A. Rucker, appointed in 1897 in Atlanta, Ga.; Joseph E. Lee, appointed in 1898 in Jacksonville, Fla.; Dr. J. E. Shephard, appointed in 1899 in Raleigh, N.C.; and Charles W. Anderson, appointed in 1905 in New York City. The records show the duties of each official, his name, date of appointment, and information about other employees in the office.

58.13. Some of the correspondence sent to these collectors from the Office of the Commissioner of Internal Revenue is interspersed among the **letters sent to collectors, 1863–1915** (1,052 vols., 175 ft.). These letters are arranged chronologically and relate to administrative and personnel matters.

58.14. See also RG 56, Records of the Department of the Treasury, and RG 366, Records of Civil War Special Agencies of the Treasury Department.

Record Group 59

General Records of the Department of State

59.1. A Department of Foreign Affairs, whose Secretary was empowered to commission and direct the activities of U.S. ministers and consuls, negotiate with ministers of foreign states, and conduct any other matters relating to foreign affairs assigned by the President, was established by an act of July 1789. By an act of September 1789 it was designated the Department of State, and its Secretary was given such additional functions as preserving and publishing laws and treaties, keeping the seal of the United States and affixing it to certain documents signed by the President, and serving as custodian of the records of the United States previously held by the Secretary of Congress. Other domestic functions were eventually assigned to the Department, but with the expansion of the Government most of these were passed to other agencies. Many of the State Department records described below are reproduced on microfilm. These records relate to many aspects of black history, particularly to black individuals or organizations concerned with African or other international issues.

Records of the Period 1789–1906

Diplomatic Correspondence

59.2. The **diplomatic correspondence of the Department of State, 1785–1906,** is for the most part arranged in the following four main series of letters: instructions sent by the Department to U.S. diplomatic officers in foreign countries, their despatches to the Department, notes from the Department of State to diplomatic representatives of foreign governments in the United States, and notes from such representatives to the Department. The correspondence in each of these series of records is generally bound separately for each country. When these series are taken as a whole for any given country, they contain information on all phases of U.S. diplomatic relations with that country. The instructions, despatches, and notes to and from foreign missions relate to such matters as the negotiation of treaties; international conferences, commissions, and expositions; claims of U.S. citizens against foreign countries and of citizens of foreign countries against the United States; immigration to the United States; the extradition of fugitives from justice; the protection of U.S. citizens in foreign countries and of foreign nationals in the United States; admiralty prize cases; awards to seamen for lifesaving service; and ceremonial matters. The instructions and despatches also contain information on the general administration of diplomatic posts.

59.3. Black history records among the diplomatic correspondence are mostly those created by black diplomats. It is believed that Ebenezer D. Bassett, who became Minister Resident and Consul General in Haiti in 1869, was the first black diplomat. Haiti and Liberia were recognized by the U.S. Government during the Civil War. From this time formal diplomatic representatives to these nations were usually black Americans. James Milton Turner, Henry Highland Garnet, Ernest Lyon, and William Henry Heard are a few of those who served as Minister Resident and Consul General to Liberia. Well-known blacks who served in Haiti are Frederick Douglass and John Mercer Langston. Black diplomats also served in Sierra Leone, the Malagasy Republic, Senegal, Portugal, France, India, Russia, Paraguay, the West Indies, Nicaragua, and Venezuela. It is generally possible to identify black diplomats through the appointment records (described in paragraphs 59.28–59.31). (See also RG 84.) After identifying the name of the representative, his post, and the date of his tenure, it is possible to locate instructions sent by the Department of State to him and original despatches and reports received by the Department from him.

59.4. The **diplomatic instructions, 1785–1906** (214 vols., 43 ft.), are arranged chronologically from 1791 to 1833; after 1833 they are arranged by country and thereunder chronologically. The instructions were sent by the Continental Congress and the Department of State to its diplomatic officers in foreign countries, pertain to all phases of U.S. rela-

Jesse Owens (1913-80). Jesse Owens made history in track events during his 4 years at Ohio State University. At the Big Ten Championships in Ann Arbor, Mich., in 1935, Owens tied the world record for the 100-yard dash and surpassed the world record for five other events. This outstanding athlete won four gold medals at the Berlin Olympics in 1936. Photographer unknown. RG 208, Records of the Office of War Information. (208-N-S 6470).

tions with foreign governments, and relate to the general administration of diplomatic posts. Instructions to black diplomats are interspersed throughout the records after the Civil War period. There is a **register of diplomatic instructions and of notes to foreign missions, 1870–1906** (8 vols., 4 ft.). The entries in each volume are arranged alphabetically by country and thereunder chronologically. The register shows the dates and names of persons to whom instructions were sent, gives brief digests of the instructions and notes, and in most cases refers to the volumes and page numbers where the instructions and notes may be found.

59.5. Despatches from diplomatic officers, 1789–1906 (2,202 vols., 610 ft.), arranged alphabetically by country and thereunder chronologically, consist of original despatches and reports, with related enclosures, received by the Department of State from its diplomatic officers in foreign countries. They relate to all phases of U.S. diplomatic relations with foreign countries and to the administration of U.S. legations and embassies. Among the related enclosures are newspaper clippings, copies of notes to and from the countries' foreign offices, copies of death notices and of marriage certificates, publications, and ceremonial letters.

Despatches from black diplomats are scattered throughout the post-Civil War despatches. There is a **register of despatches from U.S. diplomatic officers and of notes from foreign missions, 1870–1906** (10 vols., 4 ft.). The entries in each register volume are arranged alphabetically by country, thereunder as despatches or notes, and thereunder chronologically. The register gives the name of the sender of the despatch or note, the date, the number of the despatch, and a brief digest of the note or despatch.

59.6. Haiti and Liberia are important for the study of black history not only because of the number of black diplomats who served there but also because the history of American blacks is closely connected with these nations, especially through colonization projects. Notes to the foreign missions of Haiti and Liberia in the United States are included among the voluminous series of **notes to foreign missions, 1793–1906** (137 vols., 24 ft.), arranged alphabetically by country and thereunder chronologically. These notes relate to many phases of U.S. relations with foreign countries. There are two volumes for Haiti, 1850–1905, and one for Liberia, 1862–1903. The first volume for Haiti contains some notes to the legations of the Dominican Republic, Hawaii, and Liberia. The notes to foreign missions for the post-1780 period are entered in the eight-volume register that also lists the diplomatic instructions (see paragraph 59.4.).

59.7. Notes from foreign missions in the United States, 1789–1906 (871 vols., 144 ft.), arranged alphabetically by country, include original communications and related enclosures received by the Department of State from foreign legations and embassies in the United States. The subjects of these communications are similar to those of the notes to foreign missions (described in paragraph 59.6). The inclusive dates for Haiti are 1861–1906 (1 vol.) and for Liberia, 1862–1906 (1 vol.).

59.8. Notes from the British Legation in the United States to the Department of State, 1791–1906 (147 vols.), reflect two issues of concern to the British Government in its dealing with the United States: the suppression of the slave trade and, in the period 1822–60, the Negro Seamen's Acts, which circumscribed the activities of black seamen at various southern ports in the United States.

Records of Special Agents, Missions, and Commissions

59.9. The President of the United States and the Secretary of State have sent special agents and missions to many parts of the world on many different tasks and have appointed special commissioners to undertake specific duties for the Department. During the early years of U.S. history, naval officers entering the ports of countries with which the United States had no formal relations were sometimes given special diplomatic missions in addition to their regular duties. The assignments of these special agents, missions, and commissioners have included negotiating and ratifying treaties, collecting information, delivering ceremonial letters, and investigating the slave trade. The main series of records concerning special agents and missions, 1789–1906, are the **instructions to special agents, 1823–1906** (4 vols., 8 in.), and the **despatches from special agents, 1794–1906** (56 vols., 10 ft.). The instructions are arranged chronologically and are indexed by name of agent or commission; the despatches are arranged in rough chronological order by mission and thereunder chronologically.

59.10. A *List of Documents Relating to Special Agents of the Department of State, 1789–1906* (National Archives: Special List No. 7, 1951; compiled by Natalia Summers) serves as a guide to State Department correspondence with these agents. Subjects pertaining to black history mentioned in the *List* are a 1791 mission to Florida to arrange for the return of fugitive slaves; an 1815 mission to recover from Bermuda, Halifax, and the British West Indies the slaves captured and sold there by the British during the War of 1812 and to arrange for the return of those willing to go back to their former owners; an 1816 and an 1846 mission to observe and report conditions in Santo Domingo and to guard the personal and commercial rights of U.S. citizens there; an 1840 mission to investigate the slave trade in Cuba; an 1849 mission to procure information regarding the capacity of the government and people of Liberia to assume the responsibilities of an independent state; and an 1878 mission to extend U.S. influence along the coasts of Africa and Asia and among the islands of the Indian Ocean.

Consular Correspondence

59.11. There are consular records for Grand Bassa and Monrovia in Liberia and for Aux Cayes, Cap-Haïtien, Port-au-Prince, and St. Marc in Haiti. The earliest records for Liberia are 1852; for Haiti, 1797. The **consular correspondence of the Department of State, 1785–1906,** is for the most part arranged in the following four main series of letters: instructions sent by the Department to U.S. consular officers in foreign countries, the consular despatches to the Department, notes to foreign consuls in the United States from the Department, and notes from foreign consuls to the Department. The instructions and despatches concern such matters as the protection of U.S. citizens, including the issuance of passports and the settlement of estates of citizens dying abroad; the relief and protection of U.S. seamen in foreign ports; commercial matters, including inspections of vessels, certifications of cargo manifests and the value of goods, and other information for customs officials; and the administration of consulates, including appointments, leaves of absence, equipment and supplies, and funds and expenditures. The despatches also report on foreign economic, political, and social conditions. Many of the despatches are accompanied by such enclosures as copies of correspondence (between consuls and local government officials, U.S. diplomatic representatives, other consuls, and U.S. naval officers commanding naval units in foreign waters), newspaper clippings, publications, notices of death of U.S. citizens, and lists of U.S. citizens residing in consular districts. The notes relate to the protection of citizens of foreign countries in the United States.

59.12. The **copies of instructions sent by the Department of State to U.S. consular officers regarding their official duties, 1800–1906** (201 vols., 42 ft.), are arranged chronologically without regard to post except that for the years 1835–74 they are arranged geographically and thereunder chronologically. There are several **registers of instructions to consuls, 1800–17** and **1833–74** (16 vols., 3 ft.), and **1870–1906** (12 vols., 5 ft.). The earliest register is arranged alphabetically by name of consul, the next is arranged by consular post and thereunder chronologically, and the later one is arranged alphabetically by consulate and thereunder chronologically.

59.13. Despatches from consular officers, 1789–1906 (3,528 vols., 843 ft.), arranged alphabetically by consulate and thereunder chronologically, give the replies to consular instructions and report on a wide range of subjects; besides routine matters, they deal with economic, political, and social conditions abroad. There are **registers of consular despatches, 1828–70** (38 vols., 6 ft.) and **1870–1906** (14 vols., 5 ft.). The earlier register is arranged by consulate and thereunder chronologically; the latter is arranged alphabetically by country, thereunder alphabetically by name of consulate, and thereunder chronologically.

59.14. Notes to foreign consuls in the United States, 1853–1906 (4 vols., 1 ft.), are arranged chronologically and relate to many phases of consular duties. **Notes from foreign consuls, 1789–1906** (17 vols., 3 ft.), are arranged chronologically and consist of communications received in the Department of State from foreign consuls in the United States, including those of Haiti and Liberia.

Miscellaneous Correspondence

59.15. The miscellaneous correspondence of the Department of State includes correspondence with persons other than diplomatic and consular officers of the United States and of foreign countries. Much of this correspondence was with individuals, firms, and Federal and State officials in the United States, but it includes a number of letters to and from persons in foreign countries and in the U.S. Territories. The **miscellaneous letters (letters received), 1789–1906** (1,533 vols. and unbound papers, totaling 422 ft.), include some letters concerning the slave trade: the capture of a brig with 270 Africans on board by the revenue cutter *Dallas* and the disposition of the slaves, 1820, and the case of the ship *Panther,* captured as a slaver, 1846. There are letters from the American Colonization Society, such as an 1843 letter relating to the difficulties between the colony of Liberia and British traders. The records include several aids for finding the subjects for the miscellaneous letters. These are a **calendar, 1789–1825** (3 vols. and index slips, totaling 3 ft.), arranged alphabetically by name of writer; a **register of and index to miscellaneous letters, 1817–60** (34 vols., 5 ft.), arranged chronologically and alphabetically; and **indexes to miscellaneous letters, 1837–1906** (46 vols., 5 ft.), each volume of which is arranged alphabetically by the first letter of the writer's surname and thereunder chronologically.

59.16. Another series under miscellaneous correspondence that contains information pertinent to black history is the series of **reports of the Secretary of State to the President and Congress, 1790–1906** (22 vols., 5 ft.). The materials are arranged chronologically. Each volume of reports before June 1870 contains a subject index; reports after 1870 are entered in the index to domestic letters, 1840–1906. Interspersed in several volumes are letters that relate to matters concerned with the slave trade, the U.S. African Coast Squadron, and the case of the Spanish schooner *Amistad* (a slaver taken over by the slaves on board and eventually brought to Connecticut for adjudication); there are also communications between the United States and Great Britain relating to Liberia.

59.17. Also included among these records are **petitions for the recognition of Liberia, 1849–50** (1 in.). The petitions are from private citizens in eight Northern and four Southern States and the District of Columbia. They are arranged chronologically.

59.18. There are three **proclamations by antislavery societies in London addressed to President Lincoln, 1862–64** (¼ in.). The proclamations were enclosures to despatches from the U.S. Minister at London. They are arranged chronologically. There is an address to President Andrew Johnson by the British and Foreign Antislavery Society, September 1865, which was also an enclosure to a despatch from the U.S. Minister at London, dated September 19, 1865.

Records of the Post–1906 Period

Numerical File, 1906–1910

59.19. The records that made up the central files of the Department of State from 1789 to 1906 were divided into several series on the basis of origin and type of record—instructions, despatches, miscellaneous records, and so forth. On August 15, 1906, the Bureau of Indexes and Archives discontinued these series, and after that date it filed most of the records according to subject in one main series: the numerical file. As new subjects arose they were designated by case numbers, which were assigned sequentially. The **numerical file, 1906–10** (1,172 vols., 372 ft.), consists of general correspondence with U.S. consular and diplomatic officers;

foreign missions; delegates to international conferences, commissions, and expositions; other Government agencies and departments; private organizations and firms; and individuals. The records are arranged sequentially by subject case number.

59.20. There is a **card index to the numerical files, 1906–10** (200 ft.), which gives the name of sender or addressee, the date, and a brief summary of the message. It is arranged alphabetically (by subject, by individual name, by Foreign Service post or country, and by Government department), thereunder as "to" or "from," and thereunder chronologically. There are several cards on colonization of blacks in Africa, particularly Liberia; a card entitled "Colored Farmers' Cotton Business Co-operative Union"; cards under "Negro" and "Negroes," with subtopics such as colonization, black Americans in foreign countries, restrictions against immigration of blacks to Australia, and black American workers in Chile; a card on consular service; and cards for Booker T. Washington and his secretary Emmett J. Scott, who was later treasurer of Howard University, pertaining mostly to Liberia.

59.21. Among the records in the numerical file are a file containing correspondence and despatches relating to the refusal of British authorities of South Africa to admit Rev. J. Albert Johnson, a black American bishop, to Transvaal, Orange River Colony, and Natal and reports of the Department of Native Affairs of Cape Colony on the conduct of the African Methodist Episcopal bishop in South Africa (#18495). (The African Methodist Episcopal Church was founded by black Americans in Philadelphia, Pa., in the late 18th century.)

59.22. The Liberian records in the numerical file include various despatches and reports from black American diplomats. In 1907, for instance, U.S. Minister to Liberia Ernest Lyon submitted a report on his visit to Grand Cess; he described the geographic area, customs of the people, and attempts of the government to enforce customs regulations at that port (#5570). In 1908 the Liberian Legislature authorized the appointment of a commission to visit the United States in search of diplomatic and financial assistance. Despatches and reports relating to the commission are included in case file 12083. While the envoys were in the United States, they asked Booker T. Washington of Tuskegee Institute to take the position of Chargé d' Affaires for Liberia in the United States. In this file are Washington's letter to Secretary of State Elihu Root about this offer and his requests to be furnished with reports on Liberian matters. In 1908, Henry F. Downing, former U.S. Consul at Loanda, urged President Theodore Roosevelt to appoint a commission of experts to visit Liberia and report on the country and its resources. The American Commission to Liberia sailed from New York in April 1909 and included Roland Post Faulkner of Washington, D.C., Chairman; George Sale, superintendent of education of the Baptist Home Mission of Negro Schools; and Emmett J. Scott, private secretary to Booker T. Washington (#12083). In this same file is an 87-page report on Liberian colonization prepared by Frank Abial Flower, attaché to the American Commission, which includes information on aid to emigrants, on Liberian land laws, and on taxes. In numerical file 3523, there is correspondence that relates to the proposed work of the Americo-Industrial Co. of Oklahoma, which was interested in the emigration of black Americans to Liberia.

59.23. Because the numerical file did not meet the recordkeeping demands of the Department of State (at the time the file was discontinued the Bureau had had to establish 25,892 separate cases), a new and more comprehensive filing system was adopted in mid-1910: the decimal file.

Decimal File, 1910–49

59.24. This system is basically a subject file with predetermined subjects designated by a decimal code. The **decimal file, 1910–49** (13,620 ft.), consists of correspondence of the Department of State with its diplomatic and consular officers, other Government agencies, foreign governments, Congress, the President, and the public; the correspondence deals with practically all activities of the Department except those relating to appointments, passports, publications, accounts, and a few other subjects. The decimal file is divided into four time periods: 1910–29, 1930–39, 1940–44, and 1945–49. The classification scheme, however, is continued with only minor changes through these periods. There is an **index to communications sent and received, 1910–49** (5,287 ft.). The index cards are arranged alphabetically—in part by country, in part by name of Foreign Service post, and in part by Government agency; thereunder as "to" or "from"; and thereunder chronologically. Most of the index cards refer to despatches from Foreign Service posts (embassies, legations, and consulates) and to instructions sent them by the Department. Some cards refer to internal memorandums and to communications between the Department of State and other Government agencies. Each card gives the name of sender, the date, the document's decimal file classification, a summary of the message, and the number of the despatch or instruction. There is also a **name index, 1940–49** (3,157 ft.), arranged alphabetically by name and thereunder chronologically. Each card gives the subject and date of document, the names of sender and addressee, the decimal file classification, and a summary of the message.

59.25. Some of the entries pertaining to black history from the name index are listed below to demonstrate the wealth of sources available among the records of the Department of State. For the period 1910–29 there are cards pertaining to Marcus Garvey and his wife Amy A. Garvey; the Black Star Line; the *Negro World* and the [Universal] Negro Improvement Association; the *Afro-American* newspaper of Baltimore, Md.;

W.E.B. DuBois and Liberian affairs, Haitian affairs, the Second Pan African Congress, and his nomination for various assignments; Negroes and African colonization, the National Half-Century Anniversary of Negro Freedom Exposition, Haitian colonization, black Americans in foreign countries, and policies of foreign countries toward black Americans; the Associated Negro Press; correspondence of Robert R. Moton, president of Tuskegee Institute, about Haitian and Liberian Affairs; the Negro Foreign Born Citizens Alliance, Inc.; the National Negro Education Congress; Booker T. Washington's correspondence about Liberia, his European trip, and a proposed Conference on the Negro; Emmett J. Scott's correspondence about Liberian and Haitian affairs; land claims of the American Colonization Society; and rights of U.S. nationals to hold or acquire real property in Liberia.

59.26. Name index cards for the period 1930–39 cover such subjects as the Afro-American Club; the *Afro-American* newspaper company; Afro-American Legions for black veterans; the Afro-American Navigation Association about emmigration to Liberia; the political activities of Langston Hughes and James W. Ford, *Afro-American* correspondents; the Afro-Asian League, founded by a Japanese who was reported to be organizing blacks in Pittsburgh, Pa.; W. E. B. DuBois' concern with Liberia and Ethiopia; Rabbi Josiah A. Ford's immigration plans for black Americans to Ethiopia; Marcus Garvey and the activities of his Universal Negro Improvement Association; Howard University's concerns about affairs in Liberia, Ethiopia, and Haiti; Fisk University; the NAACP's publicity about anti-lynching legislation, about political issues affecting blacks in Haiti, Mexico, Liberia, and Ethiopia, and about the Scottsboro trial, which resulted in the death sentence for eight blacks in Alabama; the Negro Afro-American Club; the Negro Association of London; the Negro Building at the Texas Centennial Exposition; the Negro Congress; the Negro Mechanic's and Farmer's Association; Negro musicians in Europe; the Negro Nationalist Society of America; the Negro Peoples Committee; the Negro Volunteers of America of New York City; the Negro Welfare Association of Great Britain; the Negro World Alliance and its plans for immigration to Liberia; the Negro worker; the *Negro World,* which was the journal of Garvey's Universal Negro Improvement Association; Negroes in the Federal Government, particularly in consular positions; and the boxer Joe Louis.

59.27. Subjects appearing in the name index for the period 1940–44 include international activities of Baltimore *Afro-American* news correspondents; the African Churches' Mission of Liverpool, England, requesting financial assistance for the Booker T. Washington Children's Home; the African Methodist Episcopal Church's endeavors to obtain visas for aliens; the African Nationalist Pioneering Movement's efforts to combat racial discrimination; "Private Joe Louis—American," an article appearing in *The African Nationalist*; the Council on African Affairs; Colored

Orphan Asylum, Riverdale, N.Y.; W. E. B. Dubois' trip to Haiti; NAACP officials' (such as Walter White and Thurgood Marshall) concern about discrimination and blacks in the World War II effort; Ethiopian and Haitian affairs; Negro Actors Guild of America; National Congress of Negro Citizens; 1940 Negro Exposition in Chicago commemorating the 75th anniversary of freedom of blacks from slavery; *Negro Handbook*; Negro Labor Victory Committee; Negro land-grant colleges; Negro Nationalist Appeal; Negro Newspaper Publishers Association; the Negro Pageant Movement in Los Angeles; the Negro Welfare Cultural and Social Association of Havana; the Negro German Front in Venezuela; and "Negroes Also Have Feelings," a clipping on ". . . Hollywood's Gross Misrepresentation of Negro Life."

59.28. Some of the cards pertaining to black history from the name index for 1945–49 are the Afro-American Life Insurance Co. of Jacksonville, Fla.; Afro-American National Economical Society of Milwaukee, Wis.; *Afro-American* newspaper; Afro-American Steamship Co. of New York regarding the vessel *Toussaint L'Ouverture*; Afro-World Fellowship's effort to establish a film production center in Jamaica; *Pittsburgh Courier*

Joe Louis and Lena Horne. Chicago, Ill. The world's heavyweight champion, Joe Louis, joined Lena Horne at the piano in a Chicago nightclub. Lena Horne has been successful in almost every form of entertainment—movies, musical comedy, cabaret, television, and recordings. Joe Louis, the "brown bomber," held his championship title more than 11 years and defended it more often than any of his predecessors. Date unknown. Source, Wide World Photos. RG 208. Records of the Office of War Information. (208-PR-27-20H).

publishing company; the American Negro Theater; the *Amsterdam News'* request for information about a mission to Liberia under the auspices of the U.S. Public Health Service; *Color Line* of Mt. Vernon, N.Y., a paper with the purpose of bringing about better racial relations; W. E. B. Dubois' request to travel to London for the fifth Pan African Congress and references to the World Conference of Partisans of Peace in Paris and other international meetings; Negro Chamber of Commerce; Negro Labor Victory Committee; Negro Newspaper Publishers Association trip to West Africa; *Negro Notes;* the Negro Welfare Cultural and Social Association of Port of Spain, Trinidad; NAACP's concerns about black soldiers in Europe, colonialism, peace negotiations, the San Francisco Conference, representation in the United Nations, Liberian affairs, arrangements for dark-skinned delegates to the World Monetary Conference to stay in private homes in Savannah, Haitian affairs, human rights, black Americans abroad, and the presentation of the Spingard Medal to Ralph Bunche; National Association Against Racial Discrimination; National Council of Negro Democrats; National Council of Negro Women; the travels of Paul Robeson; Ralph Bunche's opinions about peace negotiations; Congressman Adam Clayton Powell, Jr., and his wife Hazel Scott; Howard University; Joe Louis' boxing matches; the National Joint Conference Committee of the Community Progressive Negro Painters Union, Inc.; and the New Harlem Tenants League's concern about Ethiopian affairs, racism, and lack of representation of blacks in government.

Appointment Records

59.29. By an act of September 1789, the Secretary of State was designated to keep the Great Seal of the United States and was required to make out and record all civil commissions of U.S. officials appointed by the President and to affix the seal to such documents. Beginning in 1874, the responsibility for preparing, recording, and sealing some civil commissions was transferred by successive laws from the Department of State to the executive departments that had jurisdiction over the appointees. The Department of State's records relating to the appointment and commissioning of departmental and Foreign Service personnel and other Federal officials have usually been kept by the departmental unit having custody of the Great Seal of the United States.

59.30. The **applications and recommendations for public office, 1797–1901** (350 ft.), are arranged in chronological periods, roughly by Presidential administrations. The records consist of letters received by or forwarded to the Department of State from applicants for positions in the Government and from persons recommending them. The first black diplomat, Ebenezer D. Bassett, was appointed to serve in Haiti in 1869. The chronological segments that include records about black diplomats are 1869–77, 1877–85, 1885–93, 1893–97, and 1897–1901. Within each group the applications and recommendations are arranged alphabetically by name of applicant. There is a microfilm publication (M968) for the records of the Grant administration, 1869–77. President Grant received many requests for appointments to positions in the Territorial Governments, the judiciary, and the diplomatic and consular services. Many of the applicants were veterans of the Union Army who hoped to receive special consideration from their former commander. There were a number of applications from blacks for positions in the post-Civil War period. Some of those who applied under Grant were Ebenezer D. Bassett, George T. Downing, Frederick Douglass, Martin R. Delany, James Milton Turner, and Henry M. Turner.

59.31. After 1901 only the applications and recommendations for appointment to the Foreign Service were retained out of all the applications for diplomatic service. These **case files, 1901–24** (120 ft.), arranged alphabetically by name of applicant, contain letters of application and recommendation, birth certificates, statements of personal history, notices of examination, newspaper clippings, photographs, and other pertinent papers. Black applicants to posts in Haiti, Liberia, and other places are included. For example, two black applicants for posts in Liberia were Owen L. W. Smith and Ernest Lyon.

59.32. Other black diplomats can be identified by using the **list of U.S. diplomatic officers by country, 1789–1939** (n.d., 3 vols.), and the **list of U.S. consular officers by post, 1789–1939** (n.d., 21 vols.). The list of U.S. diplomatic officers is arranged alphabetically by country in which the diplomatic post was located, thereunder by class of officer, and thereunder chronologically by date of appointment. It names the officers for each post, showing name, title or grade, nationality (sometimes race), place of birth, residence when appointed, date of appointment, and, occasionally, date of death, retirement, termination of service, or transfer to another post. The list of U.S. consular officers by post is arranged alphabetically by consular post, thereunder by class of consular officer, and thereunder chronologically by date of appointment. It shows name, title or grade, nationality (sometimes race), place of birth, residence when appointed, date of appointment, and, occasionally, the date of death, termination of service, retirement, or transfer to another post.

Foreign Service Inspection Records

59.33. Inspection reports on U.S. consulates, 1896–1902 (3 vols., 9 in.), arranged chronologically, cover such subjects as personnel, quarters, office hours, Government property, accounts and returns, summaries of business, estimates and allotments, trade and economic work, political reporting, visa and immigration work, citizenship and passport work, and other consular business. Each volume contains an index to the posts inspected and an index to the names of persons mentioned in the reports, some of whom were black diplomats. There are also **inspection reports on Foreign Service posts, 1906–39** (74 ft.), arranged alphabetically by the name of the city where the post was located. These contain information similar to the inspection reports on U.S. consulates and include references to the work of black diplomats, especially at Liberian and Haitian posts.

Records of the Office of the Counselor

59.34. The Office of the Counselor of the Department of State was established in 1909. The duties of the Counselor embraced the study and treatment of legal and other questions referred to him. The **general records, 1916–28** (80 ft.), are arranged according to a decimal classification scheme and relate to congresses of the Communist International, to revolutionary organizations and subversive individuals in foreign countries and in the United States, to trade with the U.S.S.R., to activities of foreign diplomatic and consular officers, to political and economic conditions in foreign countries, and to duties and personnel of the Office of the Counselor. The records are indexed alphabetically by name and subject (21 rolls, 16mm microfilm). Some of the references in the index include Marcus Garvey; the Universal Negro Improvement Association, its organ the *Negro World,* and those who joined with Garvey; Negro anarchists; the *Negro Champion,* "a communistic Negro newspaper published in connection with the American Negro Labor Congress"; the Negro Labor Congress; the Negro labor question in Panama; the Negro question referred to by the Third International of Moscow; Negro troops in Germany; Negro troubles—race war, 1919; and Negro work.

Records of the Passport Division and of Field Offices

59.35. Since 1789, the Department of State has issued passports to U.S. citizens traveling abroad. **Passport applications, 1795–1812, 1830–31, and 1833–1905** (1,084 vols., 255 ft.), arranged chronologically, include both letters and form applications. Included with a typical application are supporting letters and affidavits from friends and relatives concerning the applicants' citizenship, residence, and character. A typical letter or application also contains information regarding the applicant's immediate family, his date and place of birth and (if foreign-born) of naturalization, his occupation or business, and his physical characteristics. These records include scattered applications from black Americans. For instance, the July 22, 1863, application for John Valentine, a "free man of color," was granted for use in traveling to and from New York. In the post-Civil War period there are applications from some black diplomats and their families.

Records of the Visa Division

59.36. Before World War I, aliens did not need visaed passports in order to enter the United States, except for a brief time during the Civil War. The **visa case files, 1914–40** (367 ft.), are arranged in three chronological groupings—1914–23, 1924–32, and 1933–40—and thereunder alphabetically. (Visa case files for 1914–23 and 1924–32 have been destroyed except for precedent cases and case files that contain policy material or relate to significant individuals.) The files consist of correspondence of the Department of State with applicants for visas, their relatives and attorneys, Members of Congress, Foreign Service officers, organizations, and firms regarding the granting of visas for individual aliens to enter the United States. Information about black foreigners who applied for visas can possibly be found in the name index to the decimal file (described in paragraph 59.23). For example, there are cards referring to visas for Marcus Garvey (1929); Kadalie Clements, contributing editor to the *Negro Champion* (1927); and Annabell O'Neal, for whom a visa was requested by the African Methodist Episcopal Church (1940).

Audio-Visual Records

59.37. There is available a Spanish-language version of the motion picture "Henry Brown, Farmer," 1943 (#59-53), produced by the Department of Agriculture and narrated by black actor Canada Lee. The film attempts to depict the daily existence of a southern black farmer and his contribution to the war effort through food production.

Record Group 60

General Records of the Department of Justice

60.1. The Department of Justice was established by an act of 1870 that continued and expanded the legal and administrative duties of the Attorney General (provided for by an act of 1789) to conduct suits in the Supreme Court, give opinions on questions of law at the request of the President or heads of departments, and make recommendations to the President on appointments and pardons. The duties of the Department include providing means for the enforcement of Federal laws, representing the Government in any court, supervising Federal penal institutions, detecting violations of Federal laws, except those assigned to other agencies, and administering immigration and naturalization laws and registration of aliens. The records relate to a number of legal issues that affected blacks.

Records of the Attorney General's Office

60.2. Opinions on legal questions, 1790–1870 (7 ft.), are arranged chronologically by date of opinion. Originals, copies, and drafts of opinions on legal questions furnished to the President and heads of departments by the Attorney General include information about slavery and the slave trade, citizenship status of free black people, service of black men in the Armed Forces, treatment of black sailors in various ports, black servants' legal status, petitions of black prisoners for pardons, American Colonization Society activities, testimony of blacks in court, right of black persons to own property, and Freedmen's Bureau affairs.

60.3. The **letters received, 1813–70** (60 ft.), are arranged by source of letter and thereunder chronologically. These letters were received by the Attorney General from the President, heads of departments, other Federal officials, and private citizens. The letters concern such subjects as the African slave trade, domestic slavery, the Civil War, and Reconstruction. The African slave trade was declared illegal after 1807, but many ships continued to engage in the trade. One of the most famous slavers was the *Amistad,* a Spanish schooner that was commandeered in 1839 by the Africans on board, who ordered the crew to steer the schooner for Africa. Instead, they steered it to the vicinity of Long Island, where it was seized by a U.S. brig. Records relating to the *Amistad* and other slavers—such as the *Antelope,* captured in 1819; the *Wildflower,* 1860; the *Susan,* 1861; the *Emily and Caroline,* 1814; the *Panther,* 1848; the ketch *Brothers,* 1850; the brig *Echo,* 1859; and the *Nicaragua,* 1858—are among the letters received.

60.4. Letters received concerning domestic slavery include information about the illegal importation of blacks, the legality of blacks testifying against whites in court, the Fugitive Slave Act, and the legal status of slaves. Interspersed throughout the records is information about blacks during the Civil War and Reconstruction periods, such as the confiscation of slaves during the war, the employment of freed slaves, racial violence and riots, the right of blacks to own land, political rights, the Enforcement Act, the Civil Rights Act of 1866, suffrage, whites attempting to reclaim ownership of former slaves by force, the Freedmen's Bureau, and nonprosecution of whites for crimes against blacks.

60.5. There is no formal index to the letters received, 1813–70, but there are several **registers, 1809–63** (6 vols., 1 ft.), which are arranged chronologically and show the name of the writer; subject and, sometimes, the date received; action taken; and, occasionally, remarks.

60.6. The corresponding letters sent are in **general letter books, 1818–60** (14 vols., 3 ft.). They are arranged chronologically, and the subject matter is similar to that of the letters received (described in paragraphs 60.3 and 60.4).

Records of the Department of Justice

General Records

60.7. The **opinion books, 1870–1934** (76 vols., 11 ft.), are arranged chronologically by date of opinion. These are copies of opinions on legal questions given by the Attorney General to the President and heads of departments. Some of the opinions relate to black history and concern topics such as Freedmen's Hospital and Asylum, the 50th anniversary of the Emancipation Proclamation, operations of the Freedmen's Bureau and the Freedman's Savings and Trust Co., and bounty claims of black soldiers. There are indexes to the opinions in the volumes.

60.8. The **letters received, 1871–84** (312 ft.), are called the source-chronological files. They are arranged by source (President, departments, Congress, and judicial districts) and thereunder chronologically. The files include letters received from the President; executive departments; Congress; Federal judges, attorneys, and marshals; State officials; and the general public. Included is material relating to Reconstruction in the South. There is information, especially for the Southern States, about election outrages and riots, race riots, the rise of white terrorist organizations such as the Ku Klux Klan, the administration of the 14th amendment, the Enforcement Act, the civil rights acts, arrests without due process, taxation of black people, intermarriage of blacks and whites, Indians and freedmen, abduction of black people, bounty frauds in cases of black troops, and education. There is also information about the Freedmen's Bureau, the Freedman's Bank, Howard University, employment of black workers in the Department of Justice, and black reaction to Reconstruction violence. In some instances these matters became formal cases. Of special interest is a group of reports on the activities of the Ku Klux Klan, 1871–72 (3 in.), prepared by Secret Service agent H. C. Whitley, who infiltrated the group in order to make the report.

60.9. There is a **subject index to letters received in the source-chronological files, 1870–84** (10 vols., 2 ft.). Entries are arranged alphabetically by subject of the letters in the upper half of the pages and by name of correspondent in the lower half. There are also **registers of letters received in the source-chronological files, 1871–84** (87 vols., 18 ft.); the registers are arranged (1) chronologically by date of letter in volumes 1–23 and (2) by source and thereunder chronologically by date of letter in the remaining 64 volumes.

60.10. The **year files, 1884–1903** (649 ft.), are arranged by an intricate annual numbering system. File 7202/1888 (9 in.), which pertains to an election case in Florida, includes documents dating from 1888 to 1892; file 4728/1889 (10 in.), which is about election frauds in western Tennessee, includes documents from 1889 and 1890. Files pertaining to black history within this series generally concern election frauds and violence, racial violence, and peonage. The files may include petitions, affidavits, newspaper clippings, transcripts of hearings, and accounts as well as correspondence. Problems that black Americans encountered in the post-Civil War South are well documented in this series.

60.11. The **index to letters received, 1884–1908** (49 vols., 14 ft.), is arranged (1) alphabetically by name of writer, subject, and State of writer and thereunder chronologically by receipt of letter and, (2) beginning about 1891, by type of correspondent (generally "Executive," "Departments," "Attorneys and Marshals," "States and Territories," and "Miscellaneous") and thereunder alphabetically by name or title of writer. Shown are name, date, and purport of letter and the file number in either the year files or the straight numerical files. Volume 1904–5 for attorneys and marshals contains file numbers for cases pertaining to peonage and violence in Southern States. There are also several miscellaneous indexes, one of which is entitled "Index to the Year Files by State." Under Southern States, entries pertaining to election laws or election frauds give file numbers for cases that involved blacks being denied the right to vote.

60.12. The corresponding outgoing letters for this period are included among the **general and miscellaneous letter books, 1870–1913** (654 vols., 74 ft.), and are arranged chronologically by the date of the letter. Most of the volumes are indexed alphabetically by name or office of addressee. Outgoing letters to U.S. attorneys and marshals instructing them in the performance of their official duties are arranged chronologically in the **instruction books, 1870–1904** (230 vols., 59 ft.), and the individual volumes are indexed alphabetically by name or office of addressee.

60.13. The **straight numerical files, 1904–37** (2,689 ft.), are arranged by a straight numerical filing system beginning with the number 25013. Each case or subject, when the first papers on it were filed, was given a consecutive number with no distinction as to class, nature, or subject. These are general correspondence files that consist of letters both received and sent. Among the records for black history in this series is file 158260 (7½ ft.). This file contains correspondence, newspaper clippings, pamphlets, and petitions related to lynching of blacks, mob violence, and racial discrimination. The letters come from small groups and private citizens as well as from large organizations such as the NAACP. Much of the correspondence urges the adoption of anti-lynching legislation, such as the Dyer and the Constigan-Wagner bills. Some of the correspondence relates to individual lynchings in various parts of the country, alleged peonage, unlawful search and seizure, and discrimination in education. This file also includes information about the inequitable distribution of relief to blacks after the 1912 Mississippi flood; the Elaine, Ark., and Chicago, Ill., race riots of 1919; acts of violence against black brakemen on several southern railroad lines; and some cases of job discrimination.

60.14. File 198589 (10 in.) consists of information about the Ku Klux Klan. There are reports that contain information about Justice Department investigations of the group, letters that contain questions from the public about the organization and allegations of important public officials being members of the Klan, and newspaper articles about the activities of the group. Materials about Marcus Garvey and his Universal Negro Improvement Association are included in file 198940 (4 in.). A peonage case that went to the Supreme Court involved a black man named Alonzo Bailey; file 143691 (3 in.) contains information about the case of *Alonzo Bailey* v. *The State of Alabama.* File 164211 (2 in.) relates to Jack Johnson, a black boxer who was prosecuted for violations of the Mann Act. Other files include information on the Brownsville riot of 1906, the Houston riot of 1917, the Black Legion, election frauds, racial violence, and labor discrimination. One index to the straight numerical files is described in paragraph 60.11. There is also a **card index to letters received and sent, 1908–10** (77 ft.), arranged by type of document (letters received and letters, orders, and circulars sent), thereunder by source or addressee, and thereunder chronologically. The **card index to general department files, ca. 1910–20** (85 ft.), is arranged alphabetically by name of person or firm. **Record slips, 1910–67** (3,623 ft.), are arranged in chronological periods, thereunder, through 1946, by source of letters received or addressee of letters sent, and thereunder chronologically by date of letter. Beginning with 1947, the slips are arranged by year, thereunder by classification system, thereunder by source or addressee, and thereunder chronologically. Before 1939, slips for letters received and letters sent were filed separately; thereafter they were interfiled.

60.15. Classified subject files, 1914–41 and 1945–49 (13,822 ft.), are arranged by a subject-numeric system that uses a numerical file designation. The primary classes usually represent a Federal law or an administrative subject. The primary class number is usually followed by a standard secondary number that represents the judicial district in which the case arose. Three important primary classes with some information about black history are 50, "Peonage" (10 ft.); 72 "Election Frauds, Hatch Act, Corrupt Practices and Anti-Lobbying" (15 ft.); and 144 "Civil Rights" (15 ft.). Most information about blacks is in the files for southern judicial districts. Peonage cases primarily involve blacks, but there are some that involve immigrants or other minorities. Election fraud cases include information about blacks being barred from the polls, often by violent means; denial of the right to register to vote; late opening or early closing of polls; vote bribes; insufficient number of ballots on voting day; and payment of whites to keep black voters from the polls. The civil rights files concern lynching and other forms of racial violence, denial of due process to black citizens, denial of the right of suffrage, job discrimination, and labor unionism.

60.16. There are other classified subject files that concern Marcus Garvey, alleged radical black publications during World War I, the Ku Klux Klan, and other topics. Indexes and record slips to these files are described in paragraph 60.14.

Miscellaneous Records

60.17. The **Glasser file, 1938** (6 ft.), arranged by type of material, was collected during the course of a study for the Department by Abraham Glasser, an attorney in the Lands Division, and other attorneys. The study was about the use of military force by the Federal Government in strikes, race riots, and other internal disturbances. There is some material (about 3 in.) relating to black history on topics such as the unionization of black workers by the International Workers of the World and the American Federation of Labor and information about race riots between 1917 and 1920 in Little Rock, Helena, and Elaine, Ark.; Lexington, Ky.; Omaha, Nebr.; Washington, D.C.; Winston-Salem, N.C.; Chicago and East St. Louis, Ill.; and other locales.

Record Group 62

Records of the Council of National Defense

62.1. The Council of National Defense was established in 1916 to coordinate resources and industries for national security and welfare. The Council, which consisted of six Cabinet members and was assisted by an advisory commission, directed investigations and made recommendations concerning mobilization of resources for defense and sought to create conditions that would permit immediate concentration and utilization of resources in time of need. In 1918 the Council was concerned mainly with stimulating civilian morale, coordinating the work of State and local defense councils and women's committees, and studying problems of postwar readjustment and reconstruction. The Council's activities were suspended in 1921.

62.2. The Reconstruction Research Division gathered information on the subject of industrial demobilization and studied postwar readjustment problems with which the country was faced after World War I. This Division collected relevant **newspaper clippings on economic and social problems in the United States, 1918–19** (6 ft.). They are arranged by subject. One folder is entitled "Negroes" (1 in.), and other clippings pertaining to black history are in other folders throughout the series. Some of the subjects covered are the migration of blacks to the North, extension work among black farmers, treatment of soldiers in France and after their return to the United States, the work of Robert R. Moton and Tuskegee Institute, the postwar situation for blacks, education, labor, the Pan African Congress, and the growth and development of black communities.

62.3. Some of the records of the Council relate to the participation of black women in the domestic war effort. The Committee on Women's Defense Work, more commonly referred to as the Woman's Committee, was appointed by the Council of National Defense on April 21, 1917, to coordinate and centralize the organized and unorganized forces of women throughout the country for patriotic work. There were divisions of the committee in each State, and many of the Southern States had a separate committee for black women. Both the white and black committeewomen concerned themselves with child welfare, food production, home economics, health and recreation of soldiers, home and foreign relief, Liberty Loan campaigns, the Women's Land Army, and women in industry.

62.4. The **abstracts of the work of the State divisions, 1917–18** (4 ft., #13B D1)—arranged in 6-month segments, thereunder alphabetically by subject, and thereunder alphabetically by State—include information about "colored women's committees" under the subject heading "Organization" for various States. For example, the abstract entitled "Organization–Negroes," states, "the work of the colored women was for some months under our direction, but the Governor then appointed a colored women's commission, and we serve now only in an advisory capacity." The black women's work in Maryland was carried on by black clubs and organizations and included different types of war emergency work, such as entertaining black soldiers at Fort Meade, working on the Liberty Loan drive, working with the Red Cross, assisting in the war savings campaign, and raising $500 for a sun parlor at the hospital for black soldiers.

Record Group 63

Records of the Committee on Public Information

63.1. The Committee on Public Information (1917–19) was created to release Government news during World War I, sustain morale, and administer voluntary press censorship. Authors, artists, professors, and volunteer speakers (the "four minute men") contributed their services.

Commissioners were stationed at major foreign capitals to represent the Committee.

63.2. The records include the **general correspondence of George Creel, Chairman, 1917–19** (10 ft.), which is arranged alphabetically by name or subject. One folder is entitled "Emmett J. Scott" (¼ in.). As a special assistant to the Secretary of War, Scott's specific duty was "to maintain the morale of the colored population of the United States." The **correspondence of Carl Byoir, Associate Chairman,** with Government agencies and divisions of the Committee, **1917–18** (2 ft.), is arranged alphabetically by name and subject. One file, "Negroes" (1 in.), includes correspondence with Scott and other black leaders. Both files include reports, correspondence, clippings, and press releases that contain information about the problems of blacks in America, especially lynching, and the attitude of black newspapers. The records also include a card file for Washington, D.C., "listing colored churches, meeting dates of fraternal organizations, names of four minute men and theaters open to speakers" (3 in.).

Record Group 65

Records of the Federal Bureau of Investigation*

65.1. The Federal Bureau of Investigation (FBI) inherited the functions of the Chief Examiner for the Department of Justice (appointed in 1907), the Bureau of Investigation established under the Chief Examiner in 1908–9, the Bureau of Criminal Identification established in 1907, and the Bureau of Prohibition. It was designated the Federal Bureau of Investigation by Executive order in 1933.

65.2. The FBI investigates Federal law violations within the jurisdiction of the Justice Department, operates a technical laboratory and a national police academy, and gathers, classifies, preserves, and exchanges criminal identification records. Some of the records relate to investigations of black activists.

65.3. The *Investigative Case Files of the Bureau of Investigation, 1908–1922,* M1085 (955 rolls, 16mm microfilm), include investigative reports, correspondence, memorandums, and other documents complied by the Bureau, 1908–22. Some records are dated as late as 1924. This publication includes four series of investigative case files: general investigative records ("miscellaneous files"), 1908–22, arranged by file number; investigative records relating to German aliens ("old German files"), 1915–20, arranged by file number; investigative records relating to Mexican neutrality violations ("Mexican files"), 1909–21, arranged numerically; and investigative records transferred from the Department of Justice ("Bureau section files"), 1920–21, arranged in two groups and thereunder by number.

65.4. The microfilm publication includes an index to the records (111 rolls). The index includes a number of entries under "Negro." Some major headings with many entries are "Negro Activities" and "Negro Agitation." Each entry indicates the State involved and the file number. There are a number of cross-references. Some other headings for black history are "Negro Agitation by Japanese," "Negro American Alliance," "Negro and the New Social Order," "Negro Church," "Negro Congress," "Negro World" (five index cards), "Negro Deserters," "Negro Exodus," "Negro Factories Corporation," "Negro Helpers," "Negro IWW Activities," "Negroes and the Great War," "Negro International Congress," "Negro Movement," "Negro Population Uprising," "Negro Press Association," "Negro Publications," "Negro Question," and "Negro Urban League." Each index card has one or more entries.

65.5. The records also include a closed series of **investigative files relating to civil rights leader Martin Luther King, Jr., 1963–77** (57 ft.), arranged by FBI field office and thereunder in rough chronological order, and some tapes (83 items) arranged chronologically.

* *Restrictions may apply to this Record Group. Consult NARS staff.*

Record Group 66

Records of the Commission of Fine Arts

66.1. The Commission of Fine Arts was established as an independent agency by an act of May 17, 1910. It is composed of "seven well-qualified judges of the fine arts" appointed by the President, each of whom serves a 4-year term or until a successor is appointed. The Commission's duties include advising, at the request of the President or any congressional committee, on all matters of art with which the Federal Government is concerned. Specifically, it advises on the location of statues, fountains, and monuments in the District of Columbia; the plans and designs for public structures and parks in the District; the selection of artists and models for statues, fountains, and monuments erected by the United States; and the design and execution of medals, insignia, and coins. Since 1944, expenditures for the Commission have been administered by the Department of the Interior.

66.2. The **microfilm copy of minutes of the Commission, 1910–67** (16 rolls, 2½ ft. of accessioned films), are arranged chronolog-

Portrait of Marian Anderson, contralto. She was born in Philadelphia. 1950. Source, RCA-Victor. RG 306, Records of the U.S. Information Agency. (306-PS-50-11597).

ically. These official minutes and accompanying exhibits include information about a number of projects, monuments, and memorials relating to blacks. By using the following records, material relating to black history projects can be located.

66.3. The **general files, 1910–54** (36 ft.), are arranged alphabetically by project and include folders for several black history projects. There is one folder about a proposed memorial for Frederick Douglass, and another folder containing a number of letters, some legislation, and some photographs for a proposed memorial statue for the "faithful colored mammies of the South" (½ in.). The folder entitled "Slum Clearance" contains mostly copies of legislation and a few clippings (2 in.). One clipping mentions the role of Hilyard R. Robinson, a black architect, in the slum clearance project. There is a file folder for another black architect, Albert I. Cassell, who designed several of the buildings at Howard University.

66.4. The **central files, 1902–68** (30 ft.), are arranged by a subject classification scheme. The records of public buildings in the District of Columbia include information about various schools, some of which served the black community. For example, there are records for the Charles H. Houston Elementary School (2 in.), which was "named for the Negro attorney who pioneered legislation for school desegregation and the abolition of restrictive housing covenants.'' The records relating to Federal public buildings include material relating to Howard University (6 in.), such as correspondence, drawings, blueprints, reports, and clippings.

66.5. The **project files, 1910–52** (93 ft.), are arranged alphabetically by subject. These are case files concerning individual projects considered by the Commission, usually containing memorandums and correspondence with artists, Government officials, and other persons; newspaper and magazine clippings; pamphlets, bulletins, copies of legislation, reports, and other Government documents; and maps, drawings, plans, sketches, blueprints, and photographs. A number of projects involved black Americans, and many of the projects, especially in Washington, D.C., give information about segregationist policies. Some of the black history projects were a mural of Marian Anderson in the Department of the Interior building, a proposed memorial for Crispus Attucks, a bathing beach for blacks at Potomac Park Tidal Basin in the District of Columbia, buildings at Freedmen's Hospital and Howard University, a ''Negroes' Contribution to America Memorial,'' and a Booker T. Washington memorial half dollar (the Washington records include some information about George Washington Carver). A file folder entitled ''Dormitories for Women—World War II'' includes material about the Colored Women's Hotel in Washington, D.C., and a drawing of the building by Hilyard R. Robinson, associate architect.

Record Group 68

Records of the U.S. Coal Commission

68.1. The U.S. Coal Commission was created in 1922 to aid Congress in framing legislation by gathering data regarding commerce in coal and the coal industry. The Commission expired by statutory limitation one year later, after conducting a broad investigation of the coal industry and its problems.

68.2. These records include **Public Health Service sanitary surveys of coal communities, 1923** (1 ft.), arranged by State. These are narrative surveys about the living conditions in these communities. The surveys generally give the racial composition of each mining area. Blacks were largely concentrated in West Virginia and Alabama mining communities.

68.3. Racial information is also provided in the completed **mining community ''A'' schedules, 1922–24** (8 ft.), which are arranged for the most part by geographic area. These schedules were prepared by the

Living Conditions Section of the Division of Investigation of Labor Facts. These schedules were used for company-controlled communities and included questions about wage rates, intermittency of employment, labor turnover, earnings, costs of living, and retail prices. Information about race is under the heading "Prevailing Nationalities."

Record Group 69

Records of the Work Projects Administration

69.1. The Work Projects Administration (WPA, known as the Works Progress Administration until July 1, 1939) was established May 6, 1935, with responsibility for the Government's work relief program. It succeeded the Federal Emergency Relief Administration (FERA) and the Civil Works Administration (CWA), both established in 1933. On July 1, 1939, the WPA was made part of the Federal Works Agency (see RG 162), and the National Youth Administration was separated from the WPA and placed in the Federal Security Agency (see RG 119). When the WPA was officially abolished June 30, 1943, the Division of Liquidation of the Work Projects Administration was set up in the Federal Works Agency and functioned until June 30, 1944.

69.2. The WPA operated at four organizational levels—the central administration at Washington, regional offices, State administrations, and district offices. Except for certain federally sponsored projects, State and local governments helped finance and supervise WPA work projects. Because of the close administrative and chronological relationship between the FERA, CWA, and WPA, and because of numerous changes in their organization, some of the records described below are interrelated and overlapping. There are central and State correspondence files for each of the Federal relief agencies. Blacks were involved in many of these work relief projects.

Central Files of CWA, FERA, and WPA

69.3. The **CWA central files, 1933–34** (32 ft., 6 in.), arranged alphabetically by name of correspondent or subject, include a folder entitled "Interracial Correspondence" (1in.). Most of the correspondence pertains to the employment of blacks on CWA projects. Forrester B. Washington, black social worker from Atlanta, was appointed Director of Negro Work in the CWA in 1934. There are a few letters and a clipping in this folder pertaining to members of the "Black Cabinet," such as Robert C. Weaver and William H. Hastie in the Department of the Interior, Eugene

Eddie "Rochester" Anderson clowning during the filming of Metro-Goldwyn-Mayer's film, "For Better, For Worse." Date and photographer unknown. RG 208, Records of the Office of War Information. (208-PU-164M-1).

Kinckle Jones in the Department of Commerce, Henry A. Hunt at the U.S. Farm Credit Administration, and Robert L. Vann at the Department of Justice. The records concern alleged CWA discrimination against blacks on its projects, inequitable salaries for whites and blacks, and recommendations for the integration of blacks into CWA programs.

69.4. The **FERA old subject files, 1932–35** (34 ft., 7 in.), are arranged alphabetically by subject. There are folders labeled "Interracial Correspondence" (2 in.), which include letters to and from Forrester B. Washington concerning personal requests for relief, wages, minimum pay, and problems of skilled and white-collar black workers. Some of the correspondents are Alfred Edgar Smith of the WPA, Roy Wilkins of the NAACP, John P. Davis of the Joint Committee on National Recovery, and Lawrence A. Oxley of the Division of Negro Labor in the Department of Labor. There are also some accomplishment reports written by Washington. The reports contain information about complaints against the FERA, integration of blacks into the FERA program, interpretation of the FERA mission to the black public, and other subjects.

69.5. The **FERA new subject files, 1935–36** (38 ft., 4 in.), are arranged according to a subject-numeric classification scheme. The file for interracial relations (#060, ¼ in.) includes some correspondence with the

NAACP about discrimination against blacks on relief rolls and a "1935 Report—Summary—Negro Clients of Federal Unemployment Relief," by Alfred Edgar Smith, dated December 31, 1935.

69.6. The **WPA general subject series, 1935–44** (309 ft.), is arranged according to a decimal classification scheme. The public relations records (#102, 1 ft.) include a few reports from Alfred Edgar Smith; the reports are located mainly in the folders for 1936 to 1938. The reports are generally entitled "Reports of Activities," and each gives an overview of the activities of Smith's office for one month. The reports include surveys of black participation in WPA projects, reports about field trips, information about the general employment status of blacks, statistics about the type of correspondence received, and information on public relations activities within the black community. The monthly reports are for 1936–38 but may not be filed in the folder that corresponds to the month for which the report was submitted. For example, the reports for December 1936 and February, April, and May of 1937 are filed in the folder for "Jan. 1, 1937."

69.7. Other reports in the public relations files relating to black history are "Negro Project Workers—An Annual Report of Matters Incident to the Administration of Race Relations in the Federal Unemployment Relief Program—for the year 1936," by Alfred Edgar Smith, and various weekly "Negro Press Digests," which summarize articles pertinent to Government programs. A May 7, 1937, report by Smith gives highlights of his field trip to several States to survey black participation in WPA projects.

69.8. The WPA general subject files also include correspondence for black educator James A. Atkins, who served as the WPA Specialist in Negro Education. The files for the education program (#211.4) include four folders (3 in.) for Atkins; the folders refer to the education of black adults, blacks and the defense program, conferences with educational and recreational leaders, training projects for blacks, and suggestions for educational programs for blacks in various States. The folder "Negro Education" (#214.2, ⅛ in.) contains a list of materials needed for an "Adult School for the Negro Blind" erected by the WPA, information about the special problems of black youths in educational areas, and publications about the education of blacks.

69.9. "Negro Recreation" (#216.51, ¼ in.) includes information about facilities in various States that could be used by blacks for recreational purposes, training programs and projects concerning black recreation, and black community centers.

69.10. The **WPA State series, 1935–44** (870 ft.), is arranged alphabetically by State and Territory and thereunder according to a decimal filing scheme. There is a file entitled "Negro Education" (#651.346). The amount of material in this category varies by State, from no records to a few reports and some correspondence. For example, the file for Mississippi

(⅛ in.) includes a few pieces of correspondence with Atkins about a black history week exhibit, while there is no file for Iowa.

Microfilm Copies of Central Office and State FERA, CWA, and WPA Records

69.11. These **State microfilm records, 1933–45** (approximately 15,980 rolls), include project files, statistical data, financial and accounting records, Presidential letters, and miscellaneous records of various offices and divisions; there are also card indexes to some project files and miscellaneous indexes to central office and State files. These records generally have no racial information, and it is necessary to know the State, county, and project number to use them. Occasionally there is some indication in the title of the project that yields some information for black history. For example, a project file for Raeford City, Fayetteville, North Carolina District (#O.P. 65–32–515, W. P. 695), gives the following project description: "Demolition of two abandoned school buildings and repairing and painting of the following school buildings: Laurel Hill, Peachmont, Friendship, Raeford, Fryes Mission, Piney Bay, Antioch, Raeford Colored and New Hope."

Records of the FERA Transient Division

69.12. The Transient Division was established to supervise grants to States for the relief of indigent persons who could not qualify under State laws requiring that only residents could be recipients of relief. Most of the administrative correspondence of the Division was placed in the central files. The separately maintained records consist largely of periodic statistical reports, surveys of camp facilities, and policy records on the establishment of work camps and on the WPA reorganization of the transient program.

69.13. The **1934 statistical reports** (9 ft.), arranged alphabetically by State, give some information about the race of those aided by the Division. The **reports on shelters and camps, 1935** (3 ft.), arranged alphabetically by State, include racial information because many of the shelters and camps were segregated. There are lists of facilities available to the transients and some descriptive information about the facilities. For example, some of the facilities for blacks in Florida included a "colored infirmary" in Jacksonville, which housed about 20 persons; a "colored transient camp" in Duval County for 70 persons; and "Veterans Camp #2" in Petersburg, which could maintain about 100 black veterans.

Records of the FERA Sectional Economic Research Project

69.14. Included are administrative records and some research material created in studies of the United States by economic sections under the **"four phases of sectional economy—industrial, agricultural, political, and social," 1934–37** (13 ft.), arranged by type of material.

Many of the tables and much of the statistical information include information about black laborers, professionals, and farmers and about the income level and living conditions of blacks. Some of the narrative reports also give information about the economic status of blacks. The studies of the Maryland Eastern Shore canning industry state that the laborers were "over fifty percent Negro." The report particularly stressed how those who worked in the canning industry were affected by the Depression.

Records of the FERA and WPA Emergency Education Program

69.15. This program supervised State and local projects for adult education in arts and crafts, vocational training, parent education, and child care; provided literacy classes for blacks and others and assistance to nursery and rural schools; and supervised the college student aid program. The records consist of Washington office reports, memorandums, correspondence, and some teaching materials. After 1939 the records of this program were incorporated in the WPA central files.

69.16. Much of the correspondence in these files relating to educational programs for blacks consists of records sent or maintained by James A. Atkins, the WPA Specialist in Negro Education. The **alphabetical State series, 1933–35** (10 ft.), includes reports about school systems, applications for aid, and general correspondence. Some of the correspondence and reports give information about segregated school systems, such as the number of black and white students and teachers and the differences in pay of black and white teachers.

69.17. College student aid affidavits, 1934–35 (3½ ft.), arranged alphabetically by State, include applications from black colleges for money to pay work-study students.

69.18. The **subject series, 1937–38** (7 ft.), arranged according to a decimal filing scheme and thereunder by year, includes a file entitled "Negro Education" (#321). The folder for 1937 includes a few letters concerning educational projects for blacks, and the file for 1938 (¼ in.) includes some correspondence with Atkins and a copy of the WPA publication *A Selected Bibliography of Free and Inexpensive Materials on Negro Education,* 1938 (6 pp.).

69.19. The **decimal State series, 1933–39** (33 ft.), is arranged alphabetically by State and thereunder by a decimal filing scheme. "Negro Education" (#436) gives information about jobs for black educators, educational programs for blacks, requests for aid from various schools, and the work of Atkins and his travel to various meetings and conferences to work with black educators. Much of the correspondence consists of letters of appreciation to Atkins for his help and guidance. The size of the file "Negro Education" varies for each State.

Records of the WPA Federal Project Number One

69.20. The Federal arts program was approved as WPA-sponsored Federal Project Number One on September 12, 1935, to provide employment for qualified artists, musicians, actors, and authors on local relief rolls. It superseded all art projects operating under FERA or WPA State administrations and consisted of the Federal Art, Music, Theater, and Writers' Projects, including the Historical Records Survey until October 1936, when the Survey was made an independent unit. Federal Project Number One was terminated June 30, 1939. With the exception of the Federal Theater Project, which was abolished in July 1939, the arts programs continued as State projects.

Records of the Federal Art Project

69.21. The Federal Art Project provided employment for qualified artists on local relief rolls. Some black artists became involved in the project, but there are few segregated records about their participation. There is some correspondence with black artists interspersed among the **correspondence with State and regional offices, 1935–40** (17 ft.), arranged by chronological periods—1935–36, 1937, and 1938–40—and thereunder alphabetically by State. The files for New York City include correspondence with black artist Charles Alston. Artists such as Alston, Georgette Seabrooke, Allan Rohan Crite, Sam Brown, and Charles Seebree exhibited at traveling shows called Negro Extension Galleries; they also taught drawing, painting, and sculpture to the public at various art centers.

69.22. The **general records of the Federal Art Project program in Ohio, 1934–42** (6 in.), are arranged by type of record and thereunder chronologically. The records indicate how the Ohio WPA art program functioned. The reports for the project include summaries of Federal Art Project work in Ohio and statements about black artists in these projects.

Records of the Federal Music Project

69.23. The **monthly educational reports for the Federal Music Project, June and December 1936 and January 1937 to April 1940** (7 in.), arranged chronologically, give statistical information about State music programs and information about black participation. The information for the reports was compiled in the central office.

69.24. Research notes describing current musical festivals, 1935–36 (6 in.), arranged alphabetically by State, contain information about black participation in these festivals. For example, the May 1935 report for New York includes a description of Westchester County's Fifth Annual Negro Jubilee, which was held on May 7 under the auspices of the county recreation commission. The Westchester Negro Choral Union, composed of 350 voices, sang spirituals and works by Bach and Handel under the direction of Alston Burleigh, the son of Harry T. Burleigh, a black composer.

69.25. Records relating to music research, 1935–36 (4 in.), arranged alphabetically by subject, include a folder relating to Negro spirituals (¼ in.) and one entitled "Negro" (¼ in.). Both folders include research reports and materials copied from books about black music. The folder "Negro" includes information about different types of black music, such as folk songs, blues, work songs, "bad man ballads," and songs dealing with romance and conflict between the sexes.

Records of the Federal Theater Project

69.26. Included in these records are records of Washington and New York City national offices, the National Service Bureau in New York, regional service bureaus, and State offices. The records consist of correspondence, including files of the national director; narrative and statistical reports on productions; newspaper clippings, press releases, and other publicity; research material, monographs, and histories of the theater; and playscripts, play catalogs, and production bulletins. There were all-black theater groups in some cities, and there is information about the operation and performances of these groups. Blacks were organized into drama groups, vaudeville troops, puppeteers, and various types of musical production groups.

69.27. The **general correspondence of the national office, 1935–39,** arranged alphabetically by subject, includes several folders (3 in.) relating to Negro theater. The materials in these folders give an overview of black participation in the Federal Theater Project. There are lists and descriptions of the plays performed by black troops, WPA project numbers, names and addresses of troop leaders, and correspondence along with reviews and comments. There are also letters pertaining to discrimination in WPA, the treatment of black actors and actresses, racial comments in some plays, salaries of black performers, and the locations of black theater groups. There is correspondence from the NAACP, the Urban League, the National Council of Negro Women, and black newspaper editors.

69.28. The **correspondence of Hallie Flanagan, the National Director of the Federal Theater Project, 1937–39** (1 ft.), is arranged chronologically. Although Flanagan's headquarters were in New York City, these records were maintained in the Washington office. The correspondence relates to play selection, production, and personnel. The activities of black theater projects are discussed in some of the correspondence.

69.29. The **lists of plays produced by the Federal Theater Project, 1935–39** (3 in.), arranged by type of play, include plays put on by black groups. Some of the lists give play, author, city of performance, and opening date.

69.30. Press releases ("Daily Press Bulletins"), 1936–39 (8 in.), arranged chronologically by date of issuance, were prepared by the Department of Information in New York City. The press releases include information relating to the activities of the black theater groups.

69.31. The **records relating to Civilian Conservation Corps entertainment, 1936–39** (1 ft.), arranged alphabetically by subject, include a folder entitled "Negro Unit for Entertainment at CCC Camps." It contains a few documents relating to requests for a black unit to entertain at a CCC camp.

69.32. The **Vassar College collection of press clippings relating to personnel and activities of the Federal Theater Project, 1936–39** (3 ft.), arranged alphabetically by subject and thereunder by date of clipping, includes a folder of mounted clippings under "Negro" (1 in.). The folder contains reviews of various plays and clippings relating to various other aspects of community responses to these productions.

69.33. Typewritten copies of newspaper clippings collected at Vassar College, 1936 (10 in.), arranged alphabetically by subject, include the folder "Negro Theater" (2 in.), with articles giving reviews and comments on productions by black theater groups.

69.34. The **Vassar College collection of programs and promotional materials, 1935–39** (7 ft.), arranged alphabetically by name of production, includes information about black productions such as "African Vineyard," "Black Empire," "The Black and White Musical Review," "The Emperor Jones," "Haiti," "Harlem Bound," "John Henry," "Little Black Sambo," "Swanee Minstrels," "Walk Together Chillun," "MacBeth," and others. The files include theater programs, press information sheets, announcements, tickets, press releases, handbills, posters, photographs, floor plans for notes, costume sketches, and other items.

69.35. Blueprints for stages of Federal Theater Project productions or related processes, 1938–39 (2 in.), arranged by subject, include the blueprint with the floor plans for a production of "Othello."

69.36. The **National Service Bureau general subject file, 1935–39** (5 ft.), arranged alphabetically by subject, includes correspondence relating to research about the black theater, invitations for original manuscripts relating to blacks, and a list of black little theaters. Information about blacks is interspersed throughout the records, but there are also several folders under "Negro" (2½ in.).

69.37. The **general correspondence of the National Service Bureau Exhibit and Speech Department, 1937–39** (3 ft.), arranged alphabetically by subject, relates to exhibits that were prepared about the

Federal Theater Project for display at colleges and universities, art institutions and museums, and other locations. There are folders for Dillard University, the NAACP, and Negro universities, all of which contain only a few documents. The NAACP correspondence relates to the disparagement of black people in Federal Theater Project plays.

69.38. The **correspondence and reports of the National Service Bureau Research Department, 1936–39** (6 in.), arranged alphabetically by subject, include the report "Negro Theater in the West" and information about the participation of blacks in various minstrel shows and plays.

69.39. The **general correspondence of the Eastern Regional Office** ("general subject file"), **1937–39** (2 ft.), arranged alphabetically by subject, includes records relating to Federal Theater Project activities in Connecticut, New York, Pennsylvania, New Jersey, Massachusetts, Maine, and New Hampshire. The records include a folder relating to the production of the play "Haiti" in Boston (¼ in.).

69.40. The **correspondence of the Eastern Regional Office with State offices, 1936–39** (6 ft.), arranged alphabetically by State and thereunder alphabetically by subject, includes folders relating to black theater units and to various plays put on by them. For example, for Massachusetts there is a folder entitled "Negro Unit" (½ in.) and one about minstrel shows (⅛ in.). For New Jersey there are files labeled "Little Sambo" (¼ in.), "Mississippi Rainbow" (¼ in.), and "Negro Unit and Scripts" (¼ in.).

69.41. The **general correspondence of the Federal Theater Project Eastern Regional Research Department, 1935–39** (8 ft.), is arranged alphabetically by subject. Major research was conducted by this department on the contributions of various races and ethnic groups to American drama, with a special emphasis on New York City. The contributions of blacks to the American theater were researched by this department, and the records include synopses of plays about blacks. The records about the black theater (10 in.) include folder titles such as "Negro Contributions to the American Theater," "Negro Drama–Correspondence," "Negro Research–Originals," "The Negro in American Drama–H. J. Lawson," "Negro Plays Rejected," "One Act Negro Plays," "Full Length Negro Plays," "Plays and Pageants from Negro Life," and "Negro Plays—A–Z."

69.42. The **records relating to research assignments of staff members of the Eastern Regional Research Department** ("assignment file"), **1938–39** (1 ft.), are arranged alphabetically by the name of employee. The files include research assignments, research reports, memorandums, outlines, notes, bibliographies, clippings, and other materials relating to various aspects of the staff's research work. Some of the documents in the assignment file relate to black Americans.

69.43. Play lists, 1936–38 (3 ft.), arranged by subject, list the royalty and nonroyalty plays suitable for production by the Federal Theater Project. The lists generally give a synopsis of each play, production notes, and name and address of the publisher of the play script. Each list deals with a specific subject, and one list is entitled "Negro Plays."

69.44. The Federal Theater Project Radio Division records include **radio scripts of the New York City Federal Theater Project, 1936–39** (16 ft.), arranged alphabetically by title of the series of playscripts. Some of the scripts that relate to black history are "When 'Uncle Tom's Cabin' Made History," "John Brown," "The Underground Railroad," "Negro Art Singers," and "Negro Melody Singers." The Radio Division had **scripts received from various sources, 1936–39** (2 ft.), arranged alphabetically by the title of the script. The scripts were prepared by units of the Federal Theater Project, the Federal Writers' Project, and others. A few of the titles of scripts for productions relating to black history are "Black Empire," "Eli Whitney and the Cotton Gin," and "When 'Uncle Tom's Cabin' Made History." The Radio Division also received **plays and scripts from the Buffalo unit of the Federal Theater Project, 1937–39** (5 in.), arranged alphabetically by subject. Some of the productions by or relating to blacks were "Invention of the Cotton Gin," "Jubilee Singers," and "Uncle Tom's Cabin." The **radio scripts of the Los Angeles Federal Theater Project, 1937–39** (8 ft.), arranged alphabetically by title of series or playscript, include black productions such as "A Capella In Bronze."

69.45. Federal Theater Project **bound production bulletins, 1936–39** (21 ft.), arranged alphabetically by the title of the production, contain material relating to the planning and production of Federal Theater Project plays. For each play, a bulletin includes a synopsis, director's notes, technical director's report, designs for costumes and stage plans, notes on music, press notices and publicity, program, a statement of royalty paid, photographs, plans for sets, costume notes and samples of fabrics, a statement of audience reaction, and a prop list. Not all production bulletins include all these items of information. Some of the production bulletins for plays with either part-black or all-black casts are "African Vineyard," "All-American Minstrels," "Bassa Moona," "Black Empire," "The Black and White Revue," "Brer Rabbit," "The Emperor Jones," "An Evening with Dunbar," "Little Black Sambo," "Noah," "The Octroon or Life in Louisiana," "Porgy," and "Trilogy in Black."

69.46. There are also Federal Theater Project **unbound production bulletins, 1936–39** (4 ft., 2 in.), arranged alphabetically by the title of the production. Information for these bulletins was required under nine regular headings: synopsis, director's report, technical director's report, designs for costumes and stage plans, photographs, press notices, audience reaction, programs, and cost of production. Many of the black plays previously named are also a part of this series. In addition are "Run Little Children" and "Swanee Minstrels."

69.47. The Federal Theater Project for New York City had an active black theater unit. The city's **community drama staff's weekly meeting minutes, 1935–39** (5 in.), arranged alphabetically by borough and thereunder chronologically, include minutes for Harlem for the period 1937 to 1939 (1 in.). The **New York City Community Drama Center weekly reports, 1934–39** (2 ft., 1 in.), arranged alphabetically by borough and thereunder chronologically, also include information about Harlem (1 in.) and relate to various aspects of theater activity there. **Correspondence of the New York City Office of the Federal Theater Project, 1935–39** (4 ft., 2 in.), arranged alphabetically by subject, includes a folder entitled "Negro Theater" (1 in.) and one entitled "Negro Vaudeville" (¼ in.). **Press releases of the New York City Department of Information, 1936–39** (2 ft.), are arranged alphabetically by type of production and thereunder by subject or title of production. The records filed under "Negro" (3 in.) include reports on the establishment of the Negro Theater, a survey of the WPA black theater in New York City, and biographical statements relating to individuals connected with the black theater. Folder titles include "Negro–38," "Negro–37," "Swing It," and "Swing Mikado." **New York City Department of Information press books and feature material, 1937–38** (10 in.), are arranged in two subseries: alphabetically by specific play and alphabetically by general type of production. Some of the plays performed by the black theater unit are "Haiti" (1 in.), "Swing Mikado" (½ in.), and "Androcles and the Lion" (½ in.). There is also a folder entitled "Negro Publications" (⅛ in.). The **general correspondence of the New York City Radio Division, 1936–39** (3 ft.), arranged alphabetically by subject, includes correspondence, reports, memorandums, press releases, press clippings, radio addresses, and other records relating to the business of the Division. There is a folder labeled "Negro Radio" (¼ in.), which includes several scripts for radio programs.

69.48. The Federal Theater Project Living Newspaper was a series of plays based on historical facts. **Living Newspaper research materials relating to specific topics, 1936–39** (16 ft.), are arranged by title of specific topic and thereunder by subject. The records for one topic—"Negro" (11 in.)—include excerpts from published books, resumes of printed materials, magazine articles, newspaper clippings, speeches, interviews, pamphlets, various publications, and other materials. There are materials about Africa; biographies of famous blacks; and information about the black codes, discrimination, education, the Freedmen's Bureau, the

Ku Klux Klan, legislation, lynching, race riots, Reconstruction, slavery, songs, statistics, and the status of blacks in America. Some of the other records in this series also include information for black history. For example, under "Youth Problems" there is a subheading "Negro Education." **Living Newspaper research materials, 1936–39** (8 ft.), arranged alphabetically by subject, include folders with parts of the script for "Ethiopia" (3 in.), several folders on lynching (3 in.), a "Negro Living Newspaper Playfolder No. 1 (Esp. Civilian Research)" (1 in.), and "Negroes, Harlem–Housing" (⅛ in.). The Living Newspaper research materials for "Injunction Granted," "One Third of a Nation," and "Medicine," 1936–38 (10 in.), arranged by name of play, include a brief script about the black codes.

69.49. The Federal Theater Project files include **reports from the California project, 1935–39** (2 ft.), arranged by type of report and thereunder chronologically by date of report. "Negro Unit Weekly Reports," 1938–39, are included in this series. The **reports of the Federal Theater Project in Connecticut, 1936–39** (5 in.), are arranged alphabetically by type of report and thereunder chronologically by date of document. This series includes a report on the history of the Connecticut Federal Theater Project, 1935 –39, and weekly, semi-monthly, or annual reports of the various project units or the State director, including reports from the black theater unit and the children's unit. **Correspondence with Connecticut, national, and other Federal Theater Project and WPA personnel, 1937–39** (10 in.), is arranged alphabetically by name of individual. This series consists mainly of correspondence, memorandums, and telegrams dealing with the activities of the Connecticut Federal Theater Project. One of the correspondents is Michael Adrian, the supervisor of the black theater unit in Connecticut. The **general correspondence of the Connecticut Federal Theater Project** ("alphabetical subject file"), **1936–39** (2 ft.), arranged alphabetically by subject, includes correspondence, reports, memorandums, contracts, and essays. There is a folder labeled "The Hartford Negro Unit" (½ in.) and one entitled "Living Newspaper–Negro" (½ in.) as well as production materials for some black plays, including "Emperor Jones" and "Noah." The **Federal Theater Project files for Iowa, 1936–38** (5 in.), arranged alphabetically by subject, include records relating to minstrel scripts (1 in.). **Correspondence of the Massachusetts Federal Theater Project with the national office, 1936–39** (5 in.), is arranged alphabetically by name of national office official and thereunder chronologically by the date of the correspondence. The correspondence of J. Howard Miller, who was the national office deputy director, includes a memorandum about black personnel employed on the Federal Theater Project of Massachusetts as of February 25, 1939. The **records relating to special units of the**

Massachusetts Federal Theater Project, 1936–39 (8 in.), are arranged by type of unit and thereunder chronologically. Some of the units represented are the Negro unit, the English unit, and the Italian and Yiddish units. The folder relating to the Negro unit (1½ in.) includes correspondence with Ralf Coleman, Director, Negro Drama.

69.50. Federal Theater Project press clippings, 1936–39 (210 looseleaf binders, 28 ft.), are arranged alphabetically by State. Some of the clippings relate to black theater productions. At the end of the series is an alphabetical subject listing. Under the heading "Negro" is a list of productions by the black theater units.

Records of the Federal Writers' Project

69.51. The Federal Writers' Project was organized by the WPA in the fall of 1935 as one of the projects designed to utilize the skills of the so-called white-collar unemployed. A Section of Negro Affairs, with Sterling A. Brown as editor, was set up in the fall of 1935 to supervise the employment of qualified black writers and to superintend the collection of available material for the guide on the history of black Americans. In addition to assisting with the editorial work on black folklore and making plans for a book to be entitled "The Negro as an American," this Section produced a number of additional serious studies on black Americans. Richard Wright, who was on the staff on the Federal Writers' Project, won recognition for his story "The Ethics of Jim Crow," which was published in *American Stuff,* an anthology of creative writing prepared by staff members in their off-duty time.

69.52. The records of Brown's staff include **correspondence pertaining to ex-slave studies, 1936–40** (5 in.), arranged alphabetically by State. The materials include correspondence and editorial reports relating to the slave narrative collection compiled by the Federal Writers' Project in 1936–39 and edited by the members of the Library of Congress project in 1940.

69.53. There are also **reports and miscellaneous records pertaining to black studies, 1936–40** (8 in.), arranged alphabetically by State. The records include editorial and weekly progress reports and miscellaneous records on employment, work status, and black history; "Negro Press Digests" and other news releases; bibliographies; manuscripts and related correspondence; and office files of Sterling A. Brown.

Records of the Historical Records Survey (HRS)

69.54. The HRS records include reports from regional and field supervisors, general and editorial correspondence, manuals, and an incomplete set of HRS publications. Most of the records concern the inspection, listing, and inventorying of archival and other materials in libraries, historical societies, city and county offices, churches, and other non-Federal depositories. The administrative records relating to most of the surveys of non-Federal records are among these files, but the published surveys generally are not.

69.55. Some of the surveys of non-Federal records include information for black history. Church surveys sometimes include information about black churches, and county records surveys give racial information along with vital statistics. Non-Federal records from local depositories also yield some information for black history, but the amount and type varies by State. The administrative correspondence in these files provides information about the types of surveys that include black history information.

69.56. The **general project correspondence, 1936–42** (53 ft.), arranged alphabetically by State and thereunder chronologically, includes scattered materials for black history. For example, the January–August 1936 file of Alabama State Director Myrtle Miles includes a transcript of Lowndesboro Presbyterian Church records. The church, which was located in Lowndes County, Ala., served a congregation of whites but did occasional baptisms for black children and adults. The names of those blacks, and sometimes brief information about them, are included in the transcript.

69.57. The general project correspondence for the District of Columbia includes some correspondence with Carter G. Woodson, the founder and director of the Association for the Study of Negro Life and History. In a March 6, 1936, letter from Luther H. Evans, the National Supervisor of HRS, to Woodson, Evans states, "We have requested twenty workers to collect information on non-Governmental records. Included in this number of workers are four Negroes, who will devote their time and energies to the securing of information as to the records of Negro history, which are to be found in the District of Columbia." Evans went on to say that these workers would concentrate on the records of black churches and manuscript collections relating to black history. He also requested Woodson's aid with the project. The District of Columbia records also include a few other Woodson letters. The general project correspondence for the District of Columbia for 1940 and 1941 includes some information about an "Index to Negro Spirituals" project, a "Survey of Membership Records and Social Welfare Programs of Negro Churches," and an index to the *Norfolk Journal and Guide* for the years 1936 and 1937. There is also a copy of a list of the "Writings of Frederick Douglass in the Douglass Memorial Home" in Anacostia, District of Columbia. The general project correspondence includes information about black history projects in other States, but there are generally no separate folders relating to them. The District of Columbia records described above are just an example of the types of records that are available for black history in this series.

69.58. The HRS **field and regional supervisors reports, 1936–39** (10 ft.), arranged alphabetically by State and thereunder chronologically, also include some black history materials. For example, the records for the District of Columbia include a "Report of Accomplishments and Objectives of the Historical Records Survey, District of Columbia, Bessie F. Clay, Director, March 14, 1938 to September 14, 1939." The report mentions a survey of manuscripts at Howard University and work done at the Frederick Douglass Memorial Home, including the arrangement of the library and the indexing and arrangement of files.

69.59. HRS **correspondence relating to church archives inventories, 1938–41** (5 ft.), is arranged alphabetically by State and thereunder chronologically. Information about black churches is often mentioned. For example, in a folder entitled "Church Editorial–Florida, 1938" there is a report about the organization of local churches; the report includes information about the black National Baptist Convention, Inc. There were studies of black churches done in Michigan, Virginia, Illinois, and other States.

Records of the Division of Professional and Service Projects

69.60. This unit was known successively as the Division of Professional and Service Projects, 1935–41, the Division of Community Service Programs, 1941–42, and the Service Division, 1942–43. Its general function was to supervise federally sponsored white-collar work relief projects. Projects included some studies of black history topics, such as the Reconstruction period in Tennessee and ex-slaves in Kentucky. Other projects related to race relations, blacks in industry, studies of black farmers, housing, income, education, politics, health, youth employment, children, welfare, recreation, and welfare agencies. The records in this series pertain to administrative matters and must be located by project number. However, some of the completed studies are available among the records of the WPA Research and Records Library (see paragraph 69.82).

69.61. Scrapbooks of "This Work Pays Your Community Week," 1940–41 (63 ft.), are arranged by State and size. Large scrapbooks, many with decorated covers, were submitted by State division offices to document "This Work Pays Your Community Week," May 20–25, 1940. The contents of the scrapbooks vary from State to State, but some of them include pictures of workers and participants on all-black and integrated projects; sometimes additional information is given about these projects.

69.62. The records of the Division of Women's and Professional Projects include some **records for the household workers training program, 1934–37** (4 ft.), arranged by subject. Both black and white women were part of household service training projects, but most of the records do not give racial breakdowns of participants. However, in a folder entitled "Household Service Training—Courses of Study" there is an outline of a training program for household workers that was submitted by Florida Agricultural and Mechanical University, a university that served the black community. The Division of Women's and Professional Projects was later absorbed by the Division of Professional and Service Projects.

Records of the WPA Division of Statistics

69.63. The Division—known also as the Division of Social Research and as the Division of Research, Records, and Statistics—was responsible for assembling and analyzing statistical information for WPA use. The records include general administrative correspondence, statistical tabulations, and materials used at appropriation hearings. Most of the publications of this Division are included in the WPA Research and Records Library (see paragraph 69.82).

69.64. The **records relating to surveys of sewing projects for women, 1936–39** (8 in.), are arranged by type of record. Although most of the records relate to a survey in Pittsburgh in 1939, there are reports, publications, instructions to surveyors, statistical tables, working papers, and other materials for other studies, 1936–39. The surveys include information about age, race, family responsibility, and possibility of employment for the women on WPA sewing projects.

69.65. The **surveys of WPA separations, 1936–37** (3 ft.), arranged by type of record, give information about the general separation policies of WPA and their effects on various kinds of persons, including blacks. There is a table of the "Industry of Usual Employment of Separated Workers, Classified by Industry of Private Employment after Separation," with information by race and sex.

69.66. Labor shortage studies, 1937 (2 ft.), arranged by location, include folders about the shortage of domestic servants in Boston and New York City (½ in.).

69.67. Records relating to employment on WPA projects, 1941–42 (2 ft.), arranged by subject, include a number of racial statistics. Some of them give the number of blacks who worked on individual projects or in nationwide projects, such as the household workers training projects.

Records of the WPA National Research Project

69.68. The National Research Project on Reemployment and Recent Changes in Industrial Techniques analyzed and augmented existing information with field surveys to determine "the extent of recent changes in industrial techniques and to evaluate the effects of these changes on the volume of employment and unemployment." Most of its records were turned over to the Bureau of Labor Statistics and the Bureau of Agricultural

Economics, but included here are reports, memorandums, and correspondence relating to the organization and administration of the project and its relations with other Government agencies and private institutions. Much of the statistical information among these records gives racial data. **Labor market studies for selected communities, 1936–38** (11 ft.), arranged by type of record, include information about black laborers in various communities as well as information about facilities for blacks, such as nurseries and schools.

Records of the WPA Division of Information

69.69. This Division's records include interoffice memorandums, speeches and publicity materials, community improvement appraisal committee reports, correspondence, newspaper and magazine clippings concerning the national WPA program, and radio scripts.

69.70. The **"Negro Press Digest" and related clippings, 1936–42** (7 in.), arranged chronologically, consist of weekly digests of news stories concerning blacks and their relationship with the Federal Government as well as some clippings used in preparing the digests for the period August through December 1939. The first digest covers the week ending November 4, 1936, and the last is for the week ending January 31, 1942. The set of digests is relatively complete through 1939, but there are only a few for 1940 and 1941.

69.71. Press clippings concerning black affairs, 1936–40 (1 ft., 3 in.), arranged alphabetically by subject, chiefly include clippings from black newspapers that pertain to blacks and to the WPA and other relief agencies. There is a small quantity of correspondence interfiled. The clippings are filed under 27 subject headings and relate to such specific programs as art, drama, the Federal Theater, education, health, home relief, social work, women's work, and the Federal Writers' Project. They also relate to such general topics as discrimination, comments on WPA, politics, and labor reductions and dismissals. There are also files for the Civilian Conservation Corps, the National Youth Administration, and the Public Works Administration. Many of the clippings are inadequately identified as to date and source.

69.72. The **office file of Dutton Ferguson, 1938–39** (5 in.), is arranged in part chronologically by date of report and in part chronologically by year and thereunder alphabetically by surname of correspondent. The records consist mostly of weekly activity reports, letters received, and letters sent by Ferguson, who was the special assistant in charge of relations with the black press. The reports, which cover the period June 4, 1938, through December 29, 1939, summarize Ferguson's activities during the preceeding week. The letters received by Ferguson are identified as "Letters From" and cover the years 1938–39. His replies, called "Letters To,'' cover only the year 1939. A few newspaper clippings are included with the incoming letters.

69.73. The **general publications file of the Division of Information, 1936–41** (8 in.), is arranged in alphabetical order by title of publication or subject. The file consists chiefly of pamphlets, leaflets, and brochures relating to the WPA and its programs; there are also reprints of sections of WPA publications. Included is a copy of a pamphlet issued by the WPA and New York State entitled ''WPA and the Negro.''

69.74. The **information service** (''primary'') **file, 1936–42** (43 ft.), arranged according to a numeric classification system, includes press releases, excerpts from reports, memorandums, photographs, periodicals, and correspondence relating to the activities and the administration of the WPA. In file classification 983 (5 in.) the following folders relate to blacks: ''Negroes Benefited by WPA—Alabama to Missouri and Montana thru Wyoming'' and ''Negroes Benefited by WPA,'' not by States. There is also a copy of ''Occupational Characteristics of White Collar and Skilled Negro Workers,'' prepared by the WPA of Georgia (110 pp., administrative project 165–34–6069).

69.75. Photographs and biographical information about WPA officials, 1933–42 (1 ft.), arranged alphabetically by name, include folders for Mary McLeod Bethune and T. Arnold Hill.

69.76. Scripts for motion pictures produced by WPA, n.d. (1 binder, 1 in.), include the script for ''We Work Again,'' written by Alfred Edgar Smith. **Correspondence with WPA film depositories, 1937–42** (1 ft.), is arranged by type of depository, thereunder alphabetically by the name of the depository, and thereunder chronologically. The correspondence relates to the distribution of WPA films by depositories holding copies of them. There is information about the film ''We Work Again,'' which demonstrates the activities of blacks under the Federal Work Program.

69.77. Records relating to State emergency relief programs under the FERA, 1933–36 (2 ft.), are arranged alphabetically by State, thereunder by type of record, and thereunder chronologically. The records for Georgia include ''Statistics relating to FERA Teachers in Georgia, January 22, 1935,'' and also a report entitled ''Negro Nursery Schools.''

69.78. Records of FERA assembled by the Division of Information relating to FERA programs (''FERA subject file''), **1933–35** (2 ft.), arranged alphabetically by subject, include several files entitled ''Negro'' (totaling ½ in.). The materials in these files include copies of the Urban League periodical *Opportunity, Journal of Negro Life* for November and December 1934; photographs and a brief narrative about the Negro Work Center in Charlotte, N.C.; information on projects for black women; a press release with a biography of James A. Atkins, dated September 22,

1934; and a list by State of white-collar projects by and about blacks.

69.79. General correspondence of the Radio Section ("radio correspondence by name"), **1936–42** (4 ft.), arranged alphabetically by name of person or subject of correspondence, includes folders entitled "Negro Activities," "Negro Spiritual Hour, Philadelphia, Pa.," and "William Grant Still" (totaling ⅛ in.). William Still, a namesake of the abolitionist, was a black composer. **Radio scripts for State and local broadcasts, 1936 and 1939–42** (5 ft.), are arranged alphabetically by State and thereunder chronologically. The records for Delaware, September–December 1940, include an address by Ethelena M. Haynes, Supervisor, WPA Nursery School for Negroes. The records for Massachusetts include a series of plays entitled "History on Parade." One of the plays is based on the life of the abolitionist William Lloyd Garrison. The program of events for the New York City WPA music project features the Negro Chorus.

69.80. The Catalogue of Electrical Transcriptions, 1936–42 (1 vol., ½ in.), is arranged by program series and thereunder numerically by program number. The catalogue lists WPA musical groups and musical selections recorded by the RCA Manufacturing Co. and other companies. The musical groups featured include the Negro Melody Singers and the Los Angeles Choir. **Program notes for recordings of musical programs in California, 1941** (1½ in.), are arranged in two subseries: Southern California program notes and Northern California program notes, and thereunder numerically by record number. There are notes for the Southern California WPA Negro Chorus, the Southern California WPA Negro Dance Band, the Northern California Negro Chorus, and the Northern California Colored Women's Choir. **Scripts and related correspondence for recorded talks of prominent persons used on electrical transcriptions** ("radio guest talks on WPA"), **1939–42** (1 ft.), are arranged alphabetically by initial letter of the individual's surname. There is a folder for Paul Robeson (⅛ in.), who was invited to sing at a WPA program. Robeson's wife wrote to decline the request.

Records of the WPA Division of Investigation

69.81. These records consist primarily of investigation reports on fraud, embezzlement, the misappropriation of funds, inefficiency, and disloyalty. They include FERA, CWA, and WPA investigation case files, Division Reference and Office of Deputy Commissioner case files, and FBI investigative reports. There are name indexes available for the investigation reports.

Records of the WPA Research and Records Library

69.82. The **WPA Research and Records Library, 1933–45** (450 ft.), arranged by the Dewey Decimal System, includes a number of publications pertaining to black history, many of which were products of WPA projects. There is a card index to the records. Some of the subjects under "Negro" are relief, agriculture, unemployment, Alfred Edgar Smith, Forrester B. Washington, Ambrose Caliver, education, artists, housing, public service, commerce, newspapers, poetry, health, skilled workers, literature, religion, moral and social conditions, recreation, and domestic. There are studies relating to blacks in Baltimore; Birmingham; Dallas County, Ala.; Edgefield, S.C.; Spokane, Wash.; Atlanta; Chicago; and the States of Massachusetts, Arkansas, North Carolina, Virginia, Nebraska, Mississippi, and others. There is information about the library collections at Howard University and Hampton Institute. Some of the publications relate to the treatment of blacks and their participation in National Youth Administration, Federal Works Agency, and various WPA programs.

WPA Audiovisual Records

69.83. Approximately 100 items in the still picture files relate to blacks. Blacks are shown in a wide variety of projects, including theater, music, art, scientific research, and construction. In addition, there are many photographs of facilities erected by the WPA to provide welfare, child care, and educational services for black children. The WPA is described as a source of hope for blacks during the Depression years in the film "We Work Again," 1937 (#69.6), and blacks are shown participating in music, art, and theater projects. Among the recordings of the Federal Music Project are many performances by black musical groups during the period 1937–39. Program content of these radio broadcasts was usually devoted to renditions of traditional black folksongs, blues, and spirituals. In the series "What Good Is Art," there is a 1939 dramatization on the legend of John Henry, produced by the WPA Graphic Arts Division of the Federal Art Project and the Federal Theater Radio Division (#69-224). This program was based on the Fred Becker woodcuts portraying John Henry.

Record Group 75

Records of the Bureau of Indian Affairs*

75.1. The Bureau of Indian Affairs was established in 1824 within the War Department, which from the establishment of the Federal Government had exercised jurisdiction over Indian affairs in their civilian as well as military aspects. Known as the Office of Indian Affairs until 1947, when it was officially designated the Bureau of Indian Affairs, it operated informally within the War Department from 1824 until 1832, when Congress authorized appointment of a Commissioner of Indian Affairs. In 1849 the

Bureau was transferred from the War Department to the newly created Department of the Interior.

75.2. The Bureau of Indian Affairs is responsible for most of the Federal Government's relations with Indians, including their economic development, education, and legal rights. The Bureau's responsibility has, however, never extended to all Indians, but only to Indians living on reservations or maintaining their tribal affiliation in some manner. In 1824 the Bureau inherited a well-established system of Indian superintendencies and agencies, and the basic organizational structure has remained unchanged. The Bureau now consists of the central office, area offices, and field installations that include Indian agencies, boarding schools, and irrigation projects. The records relate to blacks who were held as slaves by Indians and the relations of these blacks with the Indians after emancipation.

Records of the Office of the Secretary of War Relating to Indian Affairs

75.3. Records of the Office of the Secretary of War for the period before the establishment of the Bureau of Indian Affairs in 1824 include **letters received relating to Indian affairs, 1800–23** (2 ft.), arranged by year and thereunder alphabetically by name of writer. The letters came to the Department mostly from Indian superintendents and agents, factors of trading posts, Territorial and State Governors, military commanders, Indians, and missionaries. The letters mainly concern Indians in the southern part of the United States. Some of the letters pertain to black slavery in Indian country. The letters received have been reproduced as M271. **Letters sent relating to Indian affairs, 1800–24** (6 vols., 1 ft.), are arranged chronologically. Each volume is indexed alphabetically. These volumes have been reproduced as M15.

Records of the Bureau of Indian Affairs

75.4. With the advance of white settlement, there was an increasing demand to remove the Indians in the East to an Indian territory west of the Mississippi River. Indian removal became an explicit policy of the Bureau during the administration of President Andrew Jackson. A number of treaties were negotiated in which tribes agreed to give up their lands in the East and move west.

75.5. The Creek removal records include a **census roll, 1833** (1 vol., 1 in.), arranged by name of town and thereunder by name of head of family. The census gives the names of the heads of families and the number of males, females, and slaves in each family. There is an **alphabetical index to Creek reserves, n.d.** (1 vol., 1 in.), which serves as an index to the census rolls. The Cherokee removal records include the **Eastern Cherokee census rolls, 1835–84** (19 vols. and unbound papers, totaling 2 ft.). Most of the rolls are arranged by geographic location of residence. They list the heads of families and give information concerning each family and its property, including slaves.

Records of the Land Division

75.6. The records of this Division relating to land sales and leases include reports on the appraisal of improvements made by persons who were regarded by the Cherokee as intruders on their land. The appraisement was performed by a board of appraisers. The members of the board submitted a final report with many enclosures. The enclosures—which constitute most of the records—consist of narrative reports of findings in specific cases, with transcripts of testimony. The reports for individual cases are divided into two sets, one concerning freedmen and one concerning other intruders. The reports within each set are arranged by a number that was assigned on the date each report was received.

75.7. Among the enrollment records of the Land Division are records relating to Cherokee citizenship. The Cherokee citizenship of many ex-slaves of the Cherokee of Indian Territory and of some of the Shawnee and Delaware Indians who claimed Cherokee citizenship was disputed by the Cherokee. The establishment of their status was important in determining their right to live on Cherokee land and to share in certain annuity and other payments, including a special $75,000 award voted by Congress in 1888. A series of investigations was conducted in order to compile rolls of Cherokee freedmen and of Shawnee and Delaware Cherokee. There are records concerning payments to Cherokee freedmen among the records of the Finance Division (see paragraphs 75.16 and 75.17). The **letters received relating to Cherokee citizenship, 1875–89** (1 ft.), are arranged by year and thereunder by file number. Many of the letters relate to individual claims, but some of them are of a more general nature. Some pertain to freedmen and other "intruders" on Cherokee lands.

75.8. Affidavits, 1889–90 (3 ft.), submitted to Commissioner John W. Wallace by applicants for enrollment as Cherokee citizens and by witnesses are arranged in part by number assigned in rough alphabetical order and in part in alphabetical order by initial letter of surname of applicant. The affidavits are divided into the following groups: admitted Shawnee, rejected Shawnee, deceased Shawnee, admitted Delaware, rejected Delaware, "free Negroes" (freed at the beginning of the Civil War), admitted Cherokee freedmen, authenticated Cherokee freedmen, and rejected Cherokee freedmen. (Admitted freedmen were persons who had not previously been recognized as Cherokee citizens but who were now so recognized. Authenticated freedmen had been recognized previously, and most of their affidavits were intended to secure the enrollment of young children or to establish their identity as persons who were recognized as citizens.) **Affidavits of questioned Cherokee freedmen, 1889–91** (2 in.), are arranged alphabetically by initial letter of surname of applicant. These are affidavits submitted by applicants about whom there was some doubt. The affidavits were given by Wallace to agent Leo E. Bennett for further investigation. The agent returned them with his report in 1891, and he included some further evidence with some of the affidavits. **Affidavits, 1891–92** (6 in.), were submitted to Bennett by persons whose applications were rejected by Wallace or who did not apply to Wallace. There are affidavits of the applicants themselves and of witnesses. Most of the affidavits were enclosures to incoming letters of the Bureau. They are divided into several parts—for Delaware, Shawnee, accepted freedmen, and rejected freedmen. **Affidavits, 1893** (3 in.), were submitted to Special Commissioner Marcus D. Shelby by applicants for enrollment as Cherokee freedmen. The affidavits are in two groups—those for admitted applicants and those for rejected applicants. In each group the affidavits are arranged numerically by number assigned in alphabetical order by initial letter of surname of applicant. Some evidence from former investigations is included with these affidavits.

75.9. The **"Wallace rolls," 1890** (5 in.), were compiled by Wallace as a result of his investigations and were submitted with his final report. In general, the individual rolls are arranged alphabetically by initial letter of surname of head of family. There are rolls for authenticated, admitted, and rejected freedmen; free Negroes; admitted and rejected Shawnee and Delaware; and special groups, mainly children and deceased persons. Individual entries give name, age, sex, residence, and other pertinent information. **Revised copies of the Wallace rolls, ca. 1890–96** (6 vols., 6 in.), are generally arranged alphabetically by initial letter of surname of head of family. The revisions were prepared in the Bureau. There are rolls for authenticated and admitted freedmen, for Shawnee, and for Delaware. Individual entries give name, age, sex, residence, and other pertinent information. Some of the volumes include name indexes.

75.10. The **roll of Cherokee freedmen, 1896–97** (1 vol. and unbound papers, totaling 2 in.), is divided into sections for authenticated and contesting (admitted) freedmen and their descendants. Thereunder family groups are listed together, but there is no apparent pattern to the order of listing. The roll gives an individual's name, position in family, age, sex, district of residence, and sometimes other information. Many letters and reports relating to Cherokee freedmen are among the Bureau's **letters received, 1881–1907** (1,559 ft.), which are arranged chronologically by year and thereunder by file number.

75.11. Other records relating to enrollment of the Five Civilized Tribes—the Cherokee, Creek, Choctaw, Chickasaw, and Seminole—include **letters received relating to Choctaw freedmen and other freedmen, 1878–84** (1 in.). The letters are arranged by file number assigned by date of receipt of the letter in the Bureau. These are the letters designated

Woman feeding her poultry. Putnam County, Ga. She raised enough poultry and eggs to supply the family needs with surplus to sell. Her husband was the only black landowner in the Harmony community. May 1941. Irving Rusinow, photographer. RG 83, Records of the Bureau of Agricultural Economics. (83-G-41031-BAE).

"Freedmen in Indian Territory," which were segregated by the Bureau from the main series of incoming correspondence. Most of the letters relate to the citizenship status and land rights of ex-slaves of the Choctaw.

75.12. The **rolls of Choctaw freedmen, 1885** (1 vol., 1 in.), are arranged by district and thereunder by family group; family groups are entered together, but there is no apparent pattern to the order in which they are listed. The rolls were submitted to the Bureau by the National Secretary of the Choctaw Nation. They consist primarily of rolls of freedmen who were admitted to citizenship, but included are lists of those whose status was considered doubtful and also some unbound lists of those who had elected to leave the Choctaw Nation. Entries for individuals give name, position in family, nationality of parents, name of former master, acreage of cultivated land, amount of livestock, and other pertinent information.

75.13. Miscellaneous records and reference materials of the Land Division include printed matter concerning **attorneys' claims against the Old Settler Cherokee, 1888–95** (3 in.), arranged by subject. This material relates chiefly to claims of attorneys for fees for prosecuting claims of the Old Settler Cherokee against the United States. Included are a few documents relating to claims of Cherokee freedmen.

Records of the Civilization Division

75.14. The records relating to **Civil War claims of loyal Creeks, 1869–70** (1 ft.), are arranged by claim number. The records consist of affidavits of claimants and witnesses and of the joint findings of the Creek agent and the southern superintendent. These records relate to individual claims of Creek Indians and freedmen who were loyal to the Union during the Civil War.

Records of the Education Division

75.15. Attendance books for Choctaw and Chickasaw neighborhood schools in Indian Territory, 1900–1901 and 1906–7 (1 vol., 1 in.), are arranged in rough alphabetical order by name of school and thereunder chronologically. Entries for individual schools give name of teacher, number of days in session, and information concerning enrollment and attendance of Indian, white, and Negro children. There is an alphabetical index to the names of schools and teachers. **Attendance statistics for Cherokee day schools in Indian Territory, 1906** (1 vol., 1 in.), arranged alphabetically by name of school or agency, include entries for individual schools and give name of teacher, number of days in session, and figures for enrollment and attendance of Indian, white, and Negro children.

Records of the Finance Division

75.16. This Division was responsible for the administrative examination of accounts, appropriations, remittances, stock investments, settlement of claims, and, generally, all matters involving the expenditure of money for or on account of Indians. Records concerning tribal and individual moneys and payments to Indians include the **Cherokee freedmen payment roll, 1897** (1 vol., 2 in.), arranged by family group with names of individuals numbered in order. This is a roll of Cherokee freedmen who were entitled to participate in an award by the U.S. Court of Claims. This roll is a duplicate copy used by agent Dew M. Wisdom, who completed the work of making payments that was begun by special agent James G. Dickson. Entries for individuals give various identification numbers, name, age, sex, amount due, and sometimes other information. For each person who had been paid by Dickson, the amount paid, claimant's signature, date of receipt, and signatures of witnesses are also given. For persons who had not been paid by Dickson, there is an indication of the action taken, usually a reference to the supplemental roll for those paid by Wisdom. There is an **alphabetical index to the Cherokee freedmen payment roll, 1879** (1 vol., ½ in.).

75.17. There is also a **supplemental payment roll for Cherokee freedmen, 1897** (1 vol., ½ in.), arranged by family groups with names of individuals numbered in order. This is a roll of Cherokee freedmen who were entitled to participate in an award by the U.S. Court of Claims, most of whom were paid by Wisdom. The persons listed on this roll were those who had not been paid by Dickson, who began the work but did not complete it. Included are names of some persons who were not paid by Wisdom (in most cases, persons who appeared on the rolls more than once). Entries for individuals give various identification numbers, name, age, sex, amount due, and, sometimes, other information. For each person who was paid, the amount paid, address, signature, date of receipt, check number, and signatures of witnesses are also given. There are also references to the affidavits and other records submitted as exhibits. There is an **alphabetical index to the supplemental payment roll for Cherokee freedmen, 1897** (1 vol., ¼ in.). **Exhibits for Cherokee freedmen payment rolls, 1897** (9 vols., 10 in.), are arranged by numbers assigned in rough chronological order. The exhibits include affidavits, with some letters of administration and guardianship, submitted by persons claiming a share in payments made to Cherokee freedmen by Dickson and Wisdom; the exhibits were transmitted to the Bureau with the rolls. Affidavits submitted to Dickson are separated from those submitted to Wisdom.

General Records of the Five Civilized Tribes Agency

75.18. The records described below are in the Archives Branch, Fort Worth Federal Archives and Records Center.

Records of the Commissioner to the Five Civilized Tribes

75.19. The Federal Government adopted the policy of dividing tribal lands among individual Indians with the General Allotment Act of 1887. In 1893 Congress authorized the establishment of a commission to negotiate agreements with the Five Civilized Tribes that would provide for the dissolution of the tribal governments and the allotment of land to individual tribal members. Senator Henry L. Dawes of Massachusetts was appointed chairman of the Commission to the Five Civilized Tribes on November 1, 1893, and it was generally referred to as the Dawes Commission. In order to allot land to individual Indians, it was necessary for the Dawes Commission to determine the membership of each tribe. Before 1896 the tribal governments exercised sole jurisdiction over tribal citizenship. An act of Congress of June 10, 1896, authorized the Dawes Commission to receive applications for citizenship and to add names to existing tribal rolls. More than 7,500 applications were received under the 1896 act, and the Commission enrolled over 2,000 persons. The Commission enrolled individuals in the following categories: citizens by blood, citizens by marriage, newborn citizens by blood, minor citizens by blood, freedmen (former slaves of tribal members), newborn freedmen, and minor freedmen. The records relating to enrollment include enrollment cards, the final rolls, and an index to the final rolls. **Enrollment cards** ("census cards"),

1899–1907 (144 ft.), are arranged by tribe and thereunder by enrollment category. Within each category there are generally three groups: straight (persons who were enrolled), doubtful, and rejected. Within each group the cards are arranged numerically by a number assigned by the Commission. For each tribe the cards relating to applicants as "Freedmen" contain the name of the person who owned the applicant as a slave and the owner of the applicant's parents. Entries in the final roll of those enrolled as eligible to participate are arranged by tribe, thereunder by enrollment category, and thereunder numerically by the enrollment number assigned by the Dawes Commission. Entries in the index are also arranged by tribe and thereunder by enrollment category, and within each category they are arranged alphabetically by the first two letters of the enrollee's surname. Therefore it is possible to determine the enrollment number from the index. The roll itself provides each enrollee's name, enrollment number, age, sex, degree of Indian blood, and enrollment card number. The cards, the index, and the rolls have been reproduced as M1186.

75.20. In addition to the general records for all of the Five Civilized Tribes, there are records for each tribe. Records relating to Cherokee citizenship indicate that tribal officials strongly opposed the enrollment of freedmen and secured a court injunction in 1903 that halted the enrollment process for months. Many freedmen were excluded from the Cherokee rolls that the tribal officials submitted to the Dawes Commission. These rolls document claims for participation in the award. However, the U.S. Court of Claims made a separate award to the excluded freedmen in the case of *Moses Whitmire, Trustee* vs. *the Cherokee Nation.* In 1912, the U.S. Supreme Court reversed the *Moses Whitmire* decision, and the excluded freedmen were forced to relinquish the allotments they had selected.

75.21. Applications for enrollment as freedmen, 1897 (2 ft.), are arranged numerically by exhibit number assigned in rough chronological order by date of application. These are notarized applications prepared on printed forms submitted by persons claiming a share of a payment made to Cherokee freedmen. These notarized applications show the applicant's name, age, and district of residence in the Cherokee Nation as well as the names and ages of other family members. There are some letters from claimants and officials of the Cherokee tribal government included with the application forms. **Lists of freedmen applicants, 1897** (½ in.), are arranged in rough alphabetical order by initial letter of applicant's surname. A typewritten list includes each applicant's name, roll number from the 1880 Cherokee census, roll number from the Wallace rolls (see paragraph 75.9), exhibit number from the 1897 application, district of residence within the Cherokee Nation, and, occasionally, remarks about other enrollments. There is also a handwritten list of freedmen applicants that provides only a reference to the exhibit number. These lists were submitted as evidence to the Dawes Commission by the Cherokee National Council in enrollment proceedings.

75.22. There are two **dockets to rejected and doubtful Cherokee applications, 1904–5** (2 vols., 3 in.). One docket is for Cherokee freedmen. Within the docket there are separate sections for doubtful and rejected applications. Within each section, entries are arranged numerically by case number assigned chronologically by the date the case was opened. The docket contains an index to names of applicants. The information for each application includes the names of the applicant and the attorneys, the decision of the Commission, date prepared, date forwarded to the Commissioner of Indian Affairs, and date approved by the Secretary of the Interior. Many doubtful and some rejected applications were eventually enrolled, and there are often references to enrollment card numbers. **Rejected and doubtful applications for enrollment, 1898–1907** (44 ft.), are arranged by enrollment category and thereunder numerically by application number assigned chronologically by date of application. There are numerous gaps between the numbers. These are original applications for enrollment with supporting evidence submitted to the Dawes Commission. The records include carbon copies of the testimony taken at hearings held by the Commission, notices and letters sent to the applicants and the attorneys for both the applicants and the Cherokee tribe, correspondence with the Secretary of the Interior about the applications, and copies of the Commission's decisions. The applications are for the following categories: doubtful citizens by blood, rejected citizens by blood, doubtful freedmen, rejected freedmen, and newborn freedmen.

75.23. Records relating to Choctaw and Chickasaw citizenship include handwritten **indexes to applications for enrollment, 1900–1906** (11 vols., 6 in.). Arranged by type of application, entries within each index are alphabetical by surname. These indexes include references to the applications of the Choctaw and Chickasaw freedmen who testified at Atoka and Colbert between June 4 and June 16, 1900. There are separate **lists of pending applications, 1902–5** (1 in.), for Choctaw freedmen and Chickasaw freedmen. Within each list the names are arranged numerically by enrollment card number. **Dockets of special enrollment cases, 1905–7** (3 vols., 6 in.), are arranged numerically by case number assigned chronologically by the date the case was opened. They include "Joe and Dillard Perry Cases" involving freedmen who wished to be enrolled as citizens by blood. **Case files of freedmen seeking transfer from Chickasaw freedmen status to Chickasaw by blood enrollment, 1905–6** (2 in.), are arranged numerically by case number assigned chronologically by the date the case was opened; there are many gaps in the case numbers. In the case files are applications, carbon copies of letters from the Commisssion to applicants and their attorneys, and summaries of the actions taken on the applications. All of the applications were denied.

75.24. Records relating to Creek citizenship include **miscellaneous handwritten indexes, 1902–6** (10 vols., 1 ft.), to applications in various enrollment categories, including freedmen. The indexes, arranged alphabetically by surname of enrollee, generally provide only the individual's enrollment number or enrollment card number. The **Creek original enrollment cards** ("old series cards"), **1898** (7 ft.), arranged numerically by card number, were prepared from the authenticated 1895 Creek census. Each card contains the names of the members of a family group and each person's age, sex, degree of Indian blood, post office address, district or town of residence, 1895 payroll number, and relationship to the head of the family group. There is an **alphabetical index to the enrollment cards for freedmen, 1898** (1 vol., 1 in.).

75.25. The records relating to Seminole citizenship include **enrollment schedules, 1900** (2 in.), arranged numerically by enrollment card number. The handwritten schedules, prepared on printed forms, contain the names of persons enrolled as Seminole citizens by blood and as Seminole freedmen. The information given for each person includes age, sex, band name, post office address, and parents' names and 1897 enrollment numbers.

75.26. The Dawes Commission allotted more than 15 million acres of land to the persons it enrolled as members of the Five Civilized Tribes. The **applications for allotment** ("allotment jackets"), **1899–1907** (1,500 ft.), are arranged by tribe, thereunder by enrollment category (including freedmen), and thereunder by enrollment number assigned chronologically by date of enrollment. Along with the original applications for allotment submitted on printed forms, there are transcripts of hearings held by the Commission pertaining to the selection of tracts, printed plat maps annotated to show the location of tracts selected, notices of contested allotment selections, and some related correspondence.

75.27. Records relating to allotments made to Cherokees, n.d. (40 pp.), include a typed alphabetical index to the names of persons who filed allotment selections on land that had previously been selected by freedmen whose enrollment had been denied after the Supreme Court's *Moses Whitmire* decision. The information given for each entry includes name, Dawes' enrollment number, name of the freedman who had first selected the land, and the legal description of the land. The **index to rejected Cherokee freedmen, n.d.** (50 pp.), is arranged alphabetically by surname. There are two typed alphabetical **indexes to the applications of Cherokee freedmen who made allotment selections but were subsequently denied enrollment, n.d.** (50 pp.). The information given for each freedman includes Dawes' enrollment number, allotment application number, and allotment card number. Allotment application numbers match those assigned to **denied allotment applications, 1902–7** (33 ft.), which are arranged numerically by application number assigned chronologically by date of application. These are original allotment applications submitted on printed forms, transcripts of hearings held by the Commission, printed plat maps annotated to show the location of tracts selected, applications to relinquish or cancel selections, notices of contested allotments, and some correspondence relating to selections. The **records of Cherokee allotments** ("final record"), **1903–14** (31 vols., 10 ft.), are arranged by enrollment number, with numerous gaps. Among those to whom allotments were made were freedmen and newborn freedmen. The information for each allottee includes enrollment number, the legal description of the tracts allotted, the area of each tract, its appraised value, and the deed number.

75.28. The records relating to allotments to Choctaws include allotments to Choctaws, Chickasaws, and Mississippi Choctaws. **Allotment ledgers, 1903–10** (38 vols., 10 ft.), arranged by enrollment category, were prepared on printed forms and give for each allottee the name of the tribe, enrollment number, and information about each tract. There are **indexes to the allotment ledgers, n.d.** (3 vols., 6 in.), including one for Choctaw and Chickasaw freedmen. Within each index, the names are arranged alphabetically by the first two letters of the surname. The **records of allotments for Choctaws and Chickasaws within the Choctaw Nation, 1903–8** (8 vols., 3 ft.), are arranged by enrollment category and thereunder in rough numerical order by certificate number assigned chronologically by date issued. The information given for each allotment includes the allottee's name and enrollment number and information about the land. The **index to the record of allotments, n.d.** (3 vols., 6 in.), is separated into the following enrollment categories: citizens by blood or marriage, freedmen, and Mississippi Choctaws. Within each volume, entries are alphabetical by the first two letters of the allottee's surname. **Press copies of letters sent relating to deeds and patents for Choctaws and Chickasaws, 1903–9** (18 vols.,1 ft.), are arranged by type of deed and thereunder chronologically by date sent. The letters were sent by the Chairman of the Commission to the Secretary of the Interior to transmit deeds or patents for allotments to several Choctaw and Chickasaw groups and to Choctaw and Chickasaw freedmen. The transmittal letter generally lists the name and enrollment number of each allottee and the legal description of the land allotted.

75.29. Records of delivery of patents, 1905–17 (4 vols., 8 in.), are divided into the following enrollment categories: Choctaws by blood, newborn and minor Choctaws, Choctaw freedmen, and Mississippi Choctaws. Within each volume, entries are arranged numerically by enrollment number. The information given for each allotee includes name and enrollment number, homestead and surplus patent number, date of delivery, method of delivery, and the name of the person to whom the patents were delivered. **Records of patents, 1904–14** (14 vols., 1 ft.), for allotments made to Choctaws and Chickasaws, including Choctaw and Chickasaw freedmen, are arranged by type of patent and thereunder by enrollment category. Within each volume, entries are arranged numerically by patent number assigned in chronological order by date issued. The records give information about each patent, such as number, name of allottee, and date prepared.

75.30. Records relating to allotments to Chickasaws include **lists of pending applications for enrollment, 1902–5** (1 in.). There are separate typed lists for Choctaw and Chickasaw freedmen whose applications for enrollment were pending at the time allotment began. Each list is arranged numerically by enrollment card number and gives each applicant's name, age, sex, and enrollment card number. The **record of allotment to Choctaws and Chickasaws within the Chickasaw Nation, 1903–8** (9 vols., 3 ft.), is arranged by enrollment category and thereunder in rough numerical order by allotment certificate number assigned chronologically by date issued. There is an **index to the record of allotment, n.d.** (3 vols., 6 in.), with categories for citizens by blood and marriage, freedmen, and Mississippi Choctaws. The **record of selection certificates mailed, 1904–14** (11 vols., 1 ft.), to Choctaws and Chickasaws by blood, Choctaw and Chickasaw freedmen, and Mississippi Choctaws are arranged by type of certificate and thereunder by enrollment category. Within each volume, entries are arranged numerically by certificate number assigned chronologically by date issued. The original **letters received by the Chickasaw Land Office from the Chairman of the Commission transmitting patents to land allotted to citizens by blood and freedmen, 1904–5** (1 ft.), are arranged by type of patent and thereunder numerically by patent number assigned chronologically by date issued.

75.31. The records relating to allotments to Creeks include **allotment ledgers, 1900–14** (15 vols., 1 ft.), arranged by enrollment category and thereunder numerically by enrollment number. The ledgers were prepared on printed forms and list lands allotted to Creeks by blood, minor Creeks, newborn Creeks, Creek freedmen, and newborn Creek freedmen. There are separate **indexes to the allotment ledgers, n.d.** (2 vols., 2 in.), for Creeks by blood and for Creek freedmen. Within each volume, entries are arranged alphabetically by the first two letters of the allottee's surname. The **record of allotment, 1899–1914** (18 vols., 3 ft.), is arranged by enrollment category and thereunder numerically by enrollment number. It includes original and some duplicate and triplicate copies of records of land allotted to Creeks and Creek freedmen. The records include a legal description of the tracts allotted.

75.32. Tract books, 1900–14 (4 vols., 1 ft.), prepared on printed forms and listing land allotted to Creeks and Creek freedmen, are arranged numerically by selection certificate number assigned chronologically by date issued. In the **indexes to the tract books, n.d.** (7 vols., 6 in.), entries within each enrollment category are arranged alphabetically by the first two letters of the allottee's surname. The **record of deeds issued to Creek and Creek freedmen allottees** ("file books"), **1902–8** (3 vols., 6 in.), is arranged numerically by deed number assigned chronologically by date issued. The **index to the record of deeds, n.d.** (1 vol., 2 in.), is arranged alphabetically by the first two letters of the allottee's surname.

75.33. The records relating to allotments to Seminoles include **approved allotment schedules, 1901–6** (½ in.), which are typewritten lists arranged numerically by selection certificate number assigned chronologically by date issued. They include allotments to Seminole freedmen. The **record of allotment, 1901–6** (3 vols., 1 ft.), arranged numerically by enrollment number, includes an original, duplicate, and triplicate copy of a record, prepared on printed forms, of land allotted to Seminoles and Seminole freedmen. The information given for each allottee includes name and enrollment number, the legal descriptions of the tracts allotted, area and appraised value of each tract, and certificates and deed numbers. The **record of homestead certificates mailed, 1902–8** (1 vol., 1 in.), to Seminoles, Seminole freedmen, and newborn Seminoles is arranged by enrollment category and thereunder numerically by certificate number assigned chronologically by date issued. The information given for each certificate includes number, allottee's name and post office address, and date mailed. The **record of patents issued, n.d.** (1 vol., ½ in.), to Seminoles, newborn Seminoles, and newborn Seminole freedmen is arranged by enrollment category and thereunder numerically by patent number assigned chronologically by date issued. It is indexed by name of allottee. The information given for each patent includes number, allottee's name and enrollment number, and date issued. The **record of deeds delivered, 1902–8** (6 vols., 6 in.), includes separate volumes for each enrollment category, including Seminole freedmen and newborn freedmen. Within each volume, entries are arranged numerically by enrollment number. The information given includes allottee's name and enrollment number, deed number, date prepared, and dates executed and delivered.

Office Files of the Five Civilized Tribes Agency

75.34. Prior to allotment, each of the tribal governments allowed non-Indians to live and work within the tribal territory under a permit system that required the payment of fees and taxes. The superintendent of the

Union Agency was responsible for enforcing the rules established by the tribal governments and for removing persons who were considered "intruders" by the tribes. By 1900 there were more than three times as many non-Indians as Indians in the Indian Territory, and the superintendent of the agency complained frequently to the Commissioner of Indian Affairs about the difficulty of identifying and removing "intruders." In 1906 an Intruder Division was established within the agency to place allottees in possession of their land and to investigate leases to determine whether they had been obtained by fraud.

75.35. The records relating to intruders include **lists of intruders in the Cherokee Nation, n.d.** (18 pp.). The names in each list are arranged by a claim number or roll number. Each list is a typed schedule of persons considered to be intruders by the Cherokee tribal government. These alleged "intruders" filed claims for compensation for improvements made to their land under an act of Congress of March 1893. There are lists of persons on the Wallace rolls of freedman who were reported to the agency as intruders by the tribal government. The lists of freedmen contain only the person's name and number from the Wallace rolls.

75.36. The records relating to Choctaw and Chickasaw segregated coal and asphalt land include **schedules of improvements on segregated land, 1905** (3 in.), arranged numerically by a schedule number. There are numerous gaps in the numbers. These are handwritten copies of "Schedule of Improvements of Indian Citizens and Freedmen on Segregated Coal and Asphalt Lands in the Choctaw and Chickasaw Nation, Indian Territory as Appraised by Cyrus Beede, U.S. Indian Inspector Under Direction of the Department of the Interior."

75.37. Rolls of persons claiming ownership of improvements, 1908–9 (½ in.), are arranged chronologically by date compiled. Entries within the rolls are alphabetical by the first letter of the claimant's name or numerical by claim number. These are the original supplemental rolls of "citizens and freedmen of the Choctaw and Chickasaw Nations" who claimed improvements located on segregated coal and asphalt land. Information given for each claimant includes a description of the improvements.

75.38. An act of Congress of April 1904 removed all restrictions from land allotted as "surplus" to "adult whites and Negroes" and authorized the Secretary of the Interior to approve applications for removal of restrictions from individual allottees. By 1907 more than 6,000 applications had been approved. Arranged chronologically, letters relating to sales under the April 1904 act include **press copies of letters relating to the sale of land allotted to Creeks sent by the agency to the Commissioner of Indian Affairs, 1905–7** (1 vol., 1 in.). The volume is indexed by names of "grantees" and "grantors" mentioned in the letters. The letters include information about the competency of individual allottees and the appraised value of land to be sold. The **record of applications for the removal of restrictions as provided by the April 1904 law, 1904–6** (1 vol., 1 in.,), is arranged in rough chronological order by date of receipt of the application. The information given for each application includes the date received, the applicant's name and enrollment number (the enrollment number indicates whether the applicant was a freedman), address, and, sometimes, remarks about actions taken. The **applications, 1904–11** (101 ft.), are arranged numerically by application number assigned chronologically by date of receipt. These are original petitions submitted by allottees or their heirs, transcripts of testimony, correspondence between the agency and applicants or their attorneys, and copies of the agency's recommendations to the Secretary of the Interior. The information given in a petition includes the applicant's name, age, education, business experience, property owned, description of the land to be sold, and reason for wanting to sell.

75.39. An act of Congress of May 27, 1908, removed all restrictions from whites, freedmen, and mixed-bloods who were less than one-half Indian; the act also provided that mixed-bloods who were more than one-half but less than three-quarters Indian could sell some lands. **Case files on requests for removal of restrictions based on the May 1908 law, 1908–42** (350 ft.), are arranged numerically by application number assigned chronologically by date received. There are original applications, reports of field employees, appraisals, summaries of title searches, orders for the removal of restrictions, correspondence, and various forms relating to the collection and distribution of the proceeds of sales and the payment of taxes. The **orders for removal of restrictions under the May 1908 law, 1908–13** (11 vols., 2 ft.), are arranged in rough chronological order by the date the order was filed. These are printed forms issued by the Secretary of the Interior to remove restrictions on allotted lands. The information contained in the order includes the applicant's name, tribe, enrollment number, and degree of Indian blood as well as the legal description of the land. There is an **index to the orders for removal of restrictions, n.d.** (1 vol., ½ in.), arranged alphabetically by the first two letters of the applicant's surname.

75.40. Records relating to the Tullahassee Boarding School, 1910–14 (2 vols., 1 ft.), are arranged by type of record and thereunder in rough chronological order. This school was operated by the Creek tribal government for black children. The records include correspondence, enrollment lists, vouchers, abstracts of disbursements, property returns, and physician's statements. The bulk of the correspondence is between the superintendent of the school and the supervisor of Indian schools.

75.41. Many of the other records of the Five Civilized Tribes Agency give information about the participation of the freedmen and their descendants in various areas of Indian life. Records pertaining to legal disputes between Indians and freedmen as well as to the presence of mineral deposits on freedmen's lands are interspersed among the files.

75.42. See also RG 48, Record of the Office of the Secretary of the Interior, and RG 279, Records of the Indian Claims Commission. Other records relating to blacks among the Five Civilized Tribes are among the holdings of the Oklahoma Historical Society, Oklahoma City, Okla.

** Restrictions may apply to this Record Group. Consult NARS staff.*

Record Group 76

Records of Boundary and Claims Commissions and Arbitrations

76.1. This collective record group was established from segregated files relating to international boundaries, claims, and arbitrations received from the Department of State and international commissions. Claims of U.S. citizens against foreign governments and claims of foreign nationals against the Government of the United States have usually been settled according to terms of treaties, conventions, or other international acts by claims commissions, arbitration, or outright award. Most of the claims commissions have been international commissions created by two or more countries, but domestic claims commissions have also been established to distribute to claimant citizens lump-sum indemnities received from foreign countries following diplomatic negotiations.

76.2. Following the War of 1812, the United States was a party in a dispute with Great Britain over property and slaves lost during the war. Some of the slaves were voluntary fugitives, while others were taken by force. Some of the provisions of the Treaty of Ghent, signed on December 24, 1814, called for restoration of "all territory, places and possessions." A dispute arose as to how these provisions should apply to slaves. The dispute was referred to the Emperor of Russia for arbitration in accordance with article V of the convention signed on October 20, 1818. His decision, given on April 22, 1822, was in favor of the United States, and so a mixed claims commission was established on June 30, 1822, to determine the average amount to be paid as compensation for each slave and to determine the validity of property claims. This mixed commission consisted of two members each from the United States and from England, a commissioner, and an arbitrator. On November 13, 1826, a new convention was signed in which Great Britain agreed to pay $1,204,960 in satisfaction of all claims under award of the Emperor of Russia, and a domestic claims commission was established by an act of 1827 to determine the amount of award, if any, individual claimants should receive. The domestic commission met in Washington, D.C., and decided on 1,060 claims between July 10, 1827, and August 31, 1828, when it adjourned.

Records of the Mixed Claims Commission

76.3. The **minutes of the mixed claims commission, August 25, 1823, to March 26, 1827** (1 vol., 2 in.), are arranged by date of meeting. The volume is a journal of the meetings of the commission established under the convention of June 30, 1822, to determine the value of slaves and the validity of property claims. The minutes consist of a brief account of the business transacted at each session. The **miscellaneous records of the mixed claims commission, 1814–28** (7 vols.), are arranged by type of record in folders numbered from 1 to 82. There is an **index, n.d.** (3 in.), to the records, which is arranged alphabetically by subject. Records in the folders include documents in support of the claims of some individuals, ca. 1822–23; correspondence and reports about slaves and property carried away by the British, 1822–23; papers regarding the sale of slaves carried off by the British, 1814–15; depositions and other documents regarding the value of slaves in Louisiana in 1815; a list of slaveowners, showing place of residence, n.d.; a list of Negroes said to be free, n.d.; letters sent by U.S. commissioners, 1824–25; a list of refugee slaves in Nova Scotia, 1815–18 (Halifax list); and a name index to commission minutes described above. The volumes include a printed copy of a congressional report containing information about slaves and property carried away by British forces; a document furnished by the British Government entitled "Bayly's List of Slaves," including slaves remaining in Tangiers and on board British vessels; a receipt book in four volumes documenting payments made to claimants, 1827–28; and a volume labeled "Indemnity for Slaves," containing handwritten copies of arguments, memorandums, and extracts of commission minutes, ca. 1824. The records of the mixed claims commission also include copies of **letters sent, 1823–25** (1 vol.), arranged by date of letter; a **docket of eight claims scheduled for hearing by the commission, 1825–26** (1 vol.), arranged by date of hearing, which gives the names of slaves; and **records relating to detained U.S. vessels, ca. 1812–19** (7 ft.), generally arranged by type of record.

Records of the Domestic Claims Commission

76.4. The **case files of the domestic claims commission, ca. 1814–28** (3½ ft.), are arranged by claim numbers 1–1060 and thereunder principally by name of State of origin; there is an index arranged alphabetically by name of claimant. The **index, n.d.** (16 in.), gives the name of claimant and claim number. The case files consist of documentary evidence submitted by claimants in support of their claims. Most of the cases concern slave claims. The number of records for each claim is small; the records usually consist of depositions, letters, and other documents that show the number of slaves carried away by British forces, State and county where claim originated, and name, age, and value of slaves. Frequently there is a statement of whether the claim was allowed or rejected and the amount of award, if any. There is also a **list (docket) of claims, 1826** (1 vol.), arranged by claim numbers. The **minutes of the domestic claims commission, 1827–28** (3 vols.), are arranged by date of meeting and consist of a brief account of business transacted at each session, information about commission organization, and rules and regulations adopted for the conduct of business. There is also a **list of awards, 1827–28** (1 vol.), arranged by date of award, and a **definitive list of slaves and property, n.d.** (1 vol.), arranged by name of State and thereunder alphabetically by name of claimant. The list of slaves is for eight States and the District of Columbia and contains the names of 3,608 slaves valued at $1,190,610 and a list of property valued at $306,956.27. It usually gives the following information about each claim: name of claimant, names of slaves, estimated value, and description of documents submitted as proof. Slave lists are in two, small, bound volumes, n.d. One, labeled "British Documents," contains a list of slaves (black men, women, and children) on board a British vessel. The other volume, labeled "Index and List," contains a list of slave claims, giving for each the name of the claimant, claim number, and amount of award.

Other Records

76.5. The **case files of claims of U.S. citizens settled under the Claims Convention of 1853 between the United States and Great Britain, 1853–55** (2 ft.), include documents relating to the alleged seizure and detention of U.S. vessels and their cargoes, 1812–52. These records are arranged by claim (docket) number (1–40). There is a name index. Some of the claims relate to vessels allegedly engaged in the slave trade, such as the brig *Cyrus*, seized by the British in June 1844; the barque *Jones,* seized at St. Helena in 1840 by a British man-of-war on the charge of being engaged in the slave trade; and the brigantine *Volusia,* seized in July 1850 off the west coast of Africa for engaging in the slave trade.

76.6. Among the **miscellaneous claims cases involving Great Britain, 1815–53** (10 in.), arranged alphabetically by name of vessel, are claims relating to vessels charged with being in the slave trade. These were the *Louisa Beaton,* detained in 1850, and the barque *Peytona,* seized in Mauritius, 1853. Papers relating to the slave schooner *Euphrates,* detained in 1839 off the west coast of Africa, include an extract of a letter on the slave trade from Liberia.

76.7. The **miscellaneous claims against Great Britain, ca. 1860** (1 in.), arranged by type of record, include papers relating to the case of the American brig *Jehossee,* seized by H.M.S. *Falcon* for attempting to ship slaves from Adaffi, West Africa, January 1860.

Record Group 83

Records of the Bureau of Agricultural Economics

83.1. The Bureau of Agricultural Economics was established in the Department of Agriculture in 1922. Until 1939 the Bureau conducted studies and disseminated information relating to agricultural production, crop estimates, marketing, finance, labor, and other agricultural problems and administered several regulatory statutes. The Bureau was reorganized in 1939, after which it supervised and coordinated economic and statistical research in the Department through four assistant chiefs who were in charge of agricultural statistics, income and distribution research, production research, and program analysis and rural life research. In 1953 the Bureau was abolished and its functions were transferred to the Agricultural Research Service and the Agricultural Marketing Service. Some of these records relate to black farmers and to black agricultural colleges.

General Records of the Bureau of Agricultural Economics

83.2. General correspondence, 1922–23 (72 ft.), is arranged by numbers assigned to incoming correspondence. There are many gaps in the numbering sequence caused by the bringing together of related correspondence under one number and by the retention of correspondence in divisional files. Included with the correspondence are reports and minutes of meetings reflecting the organization of the Bureau and its work in estimating crops, preparing market news reports, and conducting studies relating to rural credit, marketing, and related subjects.

83.3. A **record of letters received, 1922–23** (105 ft.), for the general correspondence described above, consists of 3½- by 6-inch slips on which are recorded the subject and date of each item of correspondence, the date of its receipt, the name of the correspondent, and the division or office to which it was referred. Arranged alphabetically by subject or name of correspondent, these record slips demonstrate that there were a number of letters pertaining to the study of black history. However, the cited letters are very difficult to find in the correspondence. The index entries do give some information about the content of each letter. Some of the many subjects addressed were the activities of Tuskegee and Hampton Institutes pertaining to studies of rural blacks, field trips in black communities, job applications, farm techniques, crop standards, black migration, the National Agricultural Congress, the Committee on Negro Farm Problems, and speeches and seminars on agricultural topics. Under the heading "Negroes" are entries about letters pertaining to the Negro Agricultural and Technical College of North Carolina, Thomas M. Campbell of Tuskegee Institute, the amount of money expended on blacks in agriculture by the Federal Government, black migration, statistics and studies on black farm laborers, the National Negro Educational Congress, technical agricultural information on grades and standards, and the employment of blacks in the U.S. Department of Agriculture.

83.4. General correspondence, 1923–46 (1,846 ft.), is divided into three chronological subgroups (1923–35, 1936–40, and 1941–46) and is arranged thereunder alphabetically by name of correspondent or by subject. There is an **alphabetical subject index to the correspondence, 1923–45** (5 ft.), but it is only a partial index. There are a number of files, relating to black history. In each chronological segment of the records it is possible to find correspondence with black schools. There are, for example, folders for Tuskegee and Hampton Institutes in each segment, with materials pertaining to a wide variety of subjects. The records include requests for publications, speakers, and agricultural information. There are statistics about black farmers, black extension agents, black migration, agricultural courses of study, land use projects, agricultural workshops and conferences, and farm management. For the 1923–35 period there is a folder for William S. Scarborough (⅛ in.), who, although born a slave in Georgia, rose to become the president of Wilberforce University in Ohio. He was hired for a brief term by the U.S. Department of Agriculture to do a study on farms owned and operated by black farmers in various agricultural regions of the United States. The study was published by the Bureau of Agricultural Economics in 1926 with the title *Tenancy and Ownership among Negro Farmers in Southampton County, Virginia* (27 pp.). (A copy of the report is not in the folder but is included among the publications in RG 287.) For the 1936–40 period there is a folder entitled "Afro-American National Congress" (½ in.). Most of the correspondence in the folder is for the year 1940 and pertains to the Department of Agriculture exhibit at the American Negro Exposition in Chicago, Ill. The plans for the Department's exhibit indicate that it was to be a graphic presentation of land use planning among blacks at Boley, Okfuskee County, Okla. The 1936–40 segment of the general correspondence also includes a folder, "Negro in America" (½ in.), that contains correspondence with the members of the Carnegie Study of the Negro in America, which was directed by Gunnar Myrdal. There is information about agricultural train-

Farmer in Harmony Community, Putnam County, Ga. Harmony was one of six communities studied by the Bureau of Agricultural Economics from 1930 to 1940 to determine the elements of farm community stability or lack of it. May 1941. Irving Rusinow, photographer. RG 83, Records of the Bureau of Agricultural Economics. (83-G-41062).

ing for black leaders held in Atlanta and Nashville and at Tuskegee Institute; migration of black farmers; the displacement of black workers; adult education for blacks; black extension agents and their work; agricultural education; and the work and influence of rural pastors. Some black schools other than Tuskegee and Hampton appear under the heading "Schools." For example, among the records for the 1941–46 period there is a file "Schools–Texas (Prairie View)" (1 in.). The records primarily concern training programs sponsored by the Department of Agriculture for the benefit of black farmers and farm workers. There was a School of Philosophy for the Negro Vocational Agriculture Teachers of Texas held at Prairie View in 1940 or 1941. There is information about other educational programs at Prairie View and about the speakers who were invited to participate. The 1941–46 records also include a file entitled "Defense Program–Negroes" (filed under "Negroes"), which contains only three letters. Two of them pertain to a Conference on the Negro in National Defense in November 1940, and one concerns the improvement of the War Food Administration's services to black farmers. **General correspondence, 1946–53** (119 ft.), arranged by a subject-numeric filing system, includes under the category labeled

"Associations" folders for Tuskegee and Hampton Institutes. The folders contain only a few letters, most of which relate to agricultural education.

83.5. Correspondence relating to regional activities, 1939–46 (79 ft.), arranged alphabetically by name of region and thereunder by name of State or by subject, includes scattered information about black farmers, migratory laborers, and the organization of black communities. For the south-central region there is information about a proposed Negro leadership study. The proposed study was to examine the organization of rural black communities and their members' interrelations with leaders such as pastors and professional people.

83.6. Dr. Foster F. Elliot was an associate chief of the Bureau of Agricultural Economics. The **office and reference file of Dr. Elliot, 1934–56** (6 ft.), is arranged alphabetically by subject under various major topics. Several of the reports among his records include some information about blacks. Two of them are *Economic Conditions in the South* (64 pp.), prepared for the President by the National Emergency Council in 1938, and *Migrant Labor* (58 pp.), prepared by the Federal Interagency Committee on Migrant Labor and published in 1947 by the Department of Labor.

83.7. The **"comments" on special surveys, 1916–49** (19 ft.), arranged in two parts alphabetically by subject, include narrative reports, correspondence, and statistical tabulations concerning special reports made by field and state representatives. Under "Miscellaneous" there is a folder entitled "Population Movements (Negroes), 1923" (½ in.), which includes information about the northern and urban migration of southern blacks.

83.8. The **general correspondence of the Division of Agricultural Finance, 1920–39** (7 ft.), is arranged alphabetically by subject. There is a folder entitled "Plans for Financing Negro and White Tenant Farmers in the South" (⅛ in.), which includes loan specifications based on the size of the farm, form of repayment, crop system, and farm management.

83.9. Reports, speeches, and articles relating to farm management, 1902–20 (36 ft.), are arranged alphabetically by name of author or agency or by subject. There is some information about black farmers in various reports, especially those for the South. The following reports specifically pertain to blacks: "Report on the West Virginia Colored Institute Farm Near Charleston, West Virginia," 1911 (15 pp.), and "Cost of Tile Drainage at West Virginia Colored Institute," 1912 (1 p.), both by J. H. Arnold; "Report of the West Virginia Colored Institute Farm," 1913 (5 pp.), by A. W. Curtis; and "Report on (Negro) Labor Situation at Pittsburgh, Cincinnati, and Louisville," 1917 (6 pp.), by Frank Montgomery.

83.10. Research reports, 1937–42 (3 ft.), arranged alphabetically by name of State, include the "experimental farming report on Heard County, Georgia," a study of low income farmers. Ten farmers cooperated in the program, which was designed to increase income and promote conservation. One of the 10 was a black man named McKinley Philpot.

83.11. The **manuscript file of the Division of Farm Population, 1917–35** (4 ft.), arranged alphabetically by subject, includes some reports that give information about the black farm population. For example, the study on rural-urban migration in North Carolina includes information about the race of those who migrated.

83.12. The **project files of the Division of Land Economics, 1934–43** (11 ft.), arranged alphabetically by subject, include scattered information about black sharecroppers and tenants among the various tenancy studies.

83.13. The **project files of the Division of Program Surveys, 1940–45** (5 ft.), are arranged alphabetically by title of project. These records include the folder "Negro–Rationing," 1942 (¼ in.). The records include interviews with blacks in Chicago on the subject of rationing. The project files also include a folder entitled "Special Reports re Negroes" (½ in.). The reports pertain to black farmers who worked as day laborers and sharecroppers, to the problems of peonage and mistreatment of blacks in the South, to racism and the antidiscrimination campaign of the Congress of Industrial Organizations (CIO), and to racial problems in various cities, such as Detroit and Chicago. Another folder, "Negro Study" (½ in.), contains drafts of a study based on interviews with black youths living on farms in six southern counties. There is also a study of black Americans' reactions to World War II.

83.14. The audiovisual records of the Bureau of Agricultural Economics include approximately 70 photographs of black farmers and tenant workers shown at various agricultural activities and in their homes. The photographs date from 1906 to 1941 and were taken in Southern States.

Record Group 84

Records of the Foreign Service Posts of the Department of State

84.1. The Continental Congress sent diplomatic agents on missions to European courts early in the Revolutionary War. The first permanent diplomatic representative was appointed in 1778 and the first consul in 1780. Diplomats frequently served also in a consular capacity until Congress established an independent consular service in 1792. In 1924 the diplomatic and consular services were combined into a single Foreign Service.

84.2. Most of the Ministers Resident and Consuls General to Haiti from 1869 until 1913 were black diplomats. Ebenezer D. Bassett served in the post from 1869 to 1877 and was succeeded by John Mercer Langston (1877–85). Frederick Douglass served as Minister Resident to Haiti from June 1889 to July 1891. Henry W. Furniss was appointed Envoy Extraordinary and Minister Plenipotentiary in November 1905 and served until 1913. Several black diplomats also served as consuls at Cap-Haitien. One who served an especially long term was Dr. Lemuel W. Livingston, who served in that post from January 1894 until December 1919. Some black diplomats also served in the Dominican Republic. Campbell L. Maxwell served as Consul to Santo Domingo from January 1892 until he was appointed Consul General in April 1898. He served in that position until July 1904. Archibald H. Grimké also served as Consul to Santo Domingo from 1894 to 1898.

84.3. Duties of a diplomatic officer, a minister or ambassador, have included sending to the Department of State reports on the policies of the government to which he was accredited and other information relating to the government, finances, commerce, arts, sciences, and condition of the host nation that might be considered useful to the United States. Duties of a consular officer have included receiving marine protests and declarations involving a U.S. interest, settling the estates of U.S. citizens who died within the consular district, taking measures for the conservation of wrecked U.S. vessels and their cargoes, ensuring that masters of U.S. vessels comply with legal requirements respecting the custody of ship papers and the discharge of U.S. seamen, providing for the relief and repatriation of destitute U.S. citizens, and certifying invoices of goods shipped to the United States.

84.4. The records of many posts, especially for the early years, are incomplete. Some officers, upon leaving their posts, took the correspondence, regarding it as personal property; other records were destroyed by fires, earthquakes, insects, and adverse climatic conditions. Among post records, the instructions received from the Department of State and the copies of despatches to the Department are largely duplicated by records maintained by the Department (see RG 59). The Department's records are more complete, and the finding aids for them are more comprehensive, than are those for this record group. In 1938 the posts began to send all records created before 1913 directly to the National Archives. In 1948 posts began to transfer all records through 1935, and periodic transfers continue. The National Archives has also received a considerable quantity of records from closed posts, several in politically unstable areas dated later than 1935, and now has records of more than 60 diplomatic and 850 consular posts.

Records of Diplomatic Posts

84.5. These records consist of embassy and legation records of the following types that have been bound into volumes: original signed instructions and copies of despatches; notes from the government of the country in which the post was located and copies of notes to it; copies of instructions and communications to subordinate consulates and despatches and reports from them; miscellaneous correspondence; passport records; records of births, marriages, and deaths of U.S. citizens; listings of important events; notes of administrative changes; and inventories of consular property. There are also registers and some card indexes. The records dated before 1912 are generally bound by series and thereunder chronologically; after 1912 they are arranged by year and thereunder by subject according to the decimal classification scheme of the Foreign Service.

84.6. There are **records for Haiti, 1860–1935** (77 ft.), arranged according to a decimal filing scheme, which include those generated by the many black diplomats who served there. The records for the black diplomats in the **Dominican Republic** are interspersed among the **post records, 1883–1935** (57 ft.), arranged according to a decimal filing scheme.

84.7. The records of diplomatic posts also include scattered references to Afro-American citizens abroad. Some 1930 correspondence from the Ethiopian Legation includes information about a black American held by French Somaliland authorities on a murder charge. There is some 1932 correspondence with the Legation relating to the detention of Afro-American Dr. Reuben S. Young, Public Health Officer at Dire Daoua, and reports on the influence of Josiah A. Ford, a British West Indian rabbi who was the inspiration for the immigration of many Afro-Americans to Ethiopa. Correspondence and despatches for 1934 report the prosecution by a special tribunal of various Ethiopians for a criminal attack upon two black Americans.

84.8. Most of the **records for the Liberian Legation, 1856–1941** (28 ft.), were created by black diplomats, especially in the post-1871 period. The despatches received are arranged in chronological periods and thereunder by class of correspondent. The volumes contain despatches received from the U.S. Department of State (diplomatic and consular), letters from the Liberian State Department, and miscellaneous letters received. Some of the volumes are labeled with the name of the U.S. diplomatic representative who received the correspondence, including James Milton Turner, 1871–78; John H. Smyth, 1878–87; Charles H. J. Taylor, 1887–88; Ezekiel E. Smith, 1888–90; Alexander Clark, 1890–91; William D. McCoy, 1892–95; William Henry Heard, 1895–98; Owen L. W. Smith, 1898–1902; John R. A. Crossland, 1902–3; and Ernest Lyon, 1906–10. All of these diplomats were black Americans. Subjects of the correspondence include economic conditions, internal problems, agriculture, the slave trade, assistance to seamen, crops, and boundary problems. The general correspondence for the Liberian Legation includes some information on black Americans. There is 1912 correspondence and a report of Maj. Charles Young, military attaché, Liberian Frontier Forces; 1921 correspondence includes papers relating to the activities of the Universal Negro Improvement Association in Liberia; 1927 correspondence contains papers relating to U.S. emigration to Liberia; and 1930 correspondence includes (1) a copy of a lease for the land located on Saint Paul River (belonging to the New York State Colonization Society) by the African Methodist Episcopal Zion Church and (2) papers relating to Charles S. Johnson, U.S. representative on the International Commission of Inquiry that investigated forced labor, slavery, and maltreatment of local people by the Liberian Government. Some additional correspondence of Maj. Charles Young, 1911–21 (5 in.), is arranged chronologically and concerns various expeditions and general conditions in the interior.

Records of Consular Posts

84.9. As distinguished from records maintained by the Department of State relating to various posts, the entries below cover material that was maintained by consular posts as their records and that was transferred to the National Archives. In general, this material consists of original signed despatches and reports to the Department; correspondence between supervising consulates and consular agencies under their jurisdiction; miscellaneous correspondence received and sent; records of fees received for notarial, shipping, and other services; records of passports issued or visaed; records of births, marriages, and deaths of U.S. citizens; records regarding the disposal of property; records of the settlement of estates of and the protection of U.S. citizens; certifications of merchandise shipped from or received in the consular district; lists of important events; notes on administrative changes; inventories of consular property; and court records of certain posts where ministers and consuls exercised judicial authority over U.S. citizens. Most of the material is in bound volumes.

84.10. As mentioned above, some black diplomats served in diplomatic positions in Haiti, Liberia, and the Dominican Republic. Other black diplomats served in consular posts. James G. Carter was appointed Consul at Tamatave, Madagascar, in 1906. He served in that post until the consulate was transferred to Tananarive, Madagascar, in 1916. He served as Consul at Tananarive from July 1916 until March 1927, when he was offered the post of Minister Resident and Consul General to Liberia. He declined that post and instead was assigned as Consul at Calais, France. He served there until the consulate was closed in June 1940. After a brief tour as Consul at Bordeaux, he was once again assigned as Consul at Tananarive, Madagascar, in 1940. In January 1941 he was promoted to Consul General and served in that rank until his retirement in 1942.

84.11. Richard T. Greener served as Consul at Bombay, India, from January until May 1898, when he was appointed Consul (later commercial agent) at Vladivostok, Russia. William H. Hunt served as a consular officer for 33 years. He was appointed vice consul at Tamatave, Madagascar, in March 1899 and was promoted to Consul in August 1901. In 1906 he was transferred as Consul to St. Étienne, France, where he served until his transfer in 1926 to Guadeloupe, French West Indies. He served from 1929 to 1931 as Consul at St. Michael, Azores, and then as Consul at Monrovia, Liberia, until his retirement in 1932.

84.12. George H. Jackson served as Consul at La Rochelle, France, from 1899 until his transfer to Cognac in 1908. James W. Johnson began his service as Consul in 1906 at Puerto Cabello, Venezuela. In 1907 he became Consul at Gorée-Dakar, French West Africa, and from June 1908 to January 1909 he served as Consul at Corinto, Nicaragua. Christopher H. Payne served as Consul at St. Thomas, Danish West Indies, from 1903 to 1917. J. N. Ruffin served as Consul at Asunciòn, Paraguay, from 1897 to 1907. Mahlon B. Van Horn preceded Christopher Payne as Consul at St. Thomas, serving from 1897 to 1903. John T. Williams served as Consul to Sierra Leone, British Africa, from 1898 to 1906.

84.13. Herbert R. Wright served as Consul at Utilla, Honduras, from 1905 until he was transferred to Puerto Cabello, Venezuela, in 1908, where he served until 1917. William J. Yerby served as Consul for over 25 years in Sierra Leone; Gorée-Dakar, French West Africa; Oporto, Portugal; and La Rochelle and Nantes, France from 1906 to 1932.

84.14. Records pertaining to these and other diplomats as well as to black Americans abroad can be found among the records for consular posts.

Record Group 85

Records of the Immigration and Naturalization Service

85.1. Between 1882 and 1891 the Secretary of the Treasury had general supervision over immigration. The Office of the Superintendent of Immigration of the Department of the Treasury was established by an act of 1891 and was designated a bureau in 1895. In 1903 the Bureau of Immigration became part of the Department of Commerce and Labor. Functions relating to naturalization previously not centralized were assigned to the Bureau in 1906, and its name was changed at the same time to the Bureau of Immigration and Naturalization. It was transferred to the Department of Labor in 1913 as the Bureau of Immigration and the Bureau of Naturalization. In 1933 an Executive order reunited those Bureaus to form the Immigration and Naturalization Service, which was transferred in 1940 to the Department of Justice. The Service administers laws relating to the admission, exclusion, deportation, and naturalization of aliens; investigates alleged violations of those laws; patrols U.S. borders to prevent unlawful entry of aliens; supervises naturalization work in designated courts; cooperates with public schools to provide citizenship textbooks and other services that prepare candidates for naturalization; and registers and fingerprints aliens in the United States.

85.2. A **subject correspondence file of the central office, 1906–32** (107 ft.), is arranged according to a numeric classification scheme. There is an **alphabetical name and subject index to the correspondence, 1903–52** (31 rolls). The index includes some cards under the heading "Negroes (Africans)" that pertain to subjects such as employment of blacks by the Bureau, discrimination and mob violence against blacks, colonization schemes, Japanese and German propaganda among blacks, citizenship status of blacks, status of former slaves, travel of blacks outside of the country, foreign wives and children of black soldiers, problems between black and alien laborers, and questions about racial designations.

Record Group 86

Records of the Women's Bureau

86.1. The Women's Bureau, established in the Department of Labor in 1920, succeeded the Woman-In-Industry Service, a war emergency agency authorized in 1918 to ensure effective employment of women while serving their health and welfare. Many of the records of the Woman-In-Industry Service were destroyed by fire in 1930. The Women's Bureau develops standards, policies, and programs to promote the welfare of working women, increase their efficiency, improve their working conditions, and advance their opportunities for profitable employment. It publishes reports on trends in the employment of women and the characteristics of the female working force; women's employment opportunities, wages, and conditions of work in occupations and industries; the dual role of women as workers and homemakers; and factors affecting women's income, financial responsibilities, and needs. The Bureau analyzes and makes recommendations concerning existing and proposed labor laws and regulations applicable to women and laws affecting their civil and political status. In cooperation with other Labor Department bureaus, it assists in coordinating activities of the Department for wider implementation of programs affecting all workers. The Bureau also plans programs of study and observation for women community leaders, provides technical materials to international agencies, and advises U.S. delegates attending international conferences concerned with women's status in political, social, economic, legal, and educational fields. Black women are a large and important segment of the female work force, and many of these records relate to them.

Records of the Office of the Director

86.2. The Director of the Women's Bureau exercises general supervision over all the work of the Bureau and is responsible to the Secretary of Labor for carrying out the provisions of the organic act. All the work of the Bureau is planned and directed in the Office of the Director, including correspondence and general administrative activities. From 1918 to 1947 the correspondence files were divided into major subject categories. The following categories include records about black women: correspondence with unions; correspondence with women's organizations; correspondence–miscellaneous subjects and organizations; and correspondence–household (domestic) file.

86.3. Correspondence with unions, 1918–47 (2 ft.), is arranged alphabetically by the type of union. Among the records is one folder on railroad brotherhoods that includes several pieces of correspondence from the Brotherhood of Sleeping Car Porters and from its Ladies Auxiliary. There are also a few letters from the Protective Order of Dining Car Waiters, Local 465 of Los Angeles, asking for information about work opportunities for black women. The letters generally concern requests for information about women, various meetings and conferences about organized labor, and union membership for women.

86.4. Correspondence with women's organizations, 1918–47 (9 ft.), is arranged alphabetically by name or type of organization. One folder is entitled "Negro Women's Organizations" (1 in.) and contains information dating from 1934 to 1946. Most of the correspondence is with the National Council of Negro Women, the National Association of Colored Women, Inc., and the Chicago Federation of Colored Women's Clubs. The correspondence concerns employment for black women, their legal and economic status, meetings and conferences in which Women's Bureau staff played a part, and requests for publications and information.

86.5. Correspondence–miscellaneous subjects and organizations, 1918–47 (10 ft.), is arranged alphabetically by subject or organization. One folder is entitled "Negro Organizations–Miscellaneous" (1 in.). It consists of correspondence with the NAACP; the Urban League; the Bureau of Negro Welfare and Statistics in Charleston, W. Va.; the Southern Negro Youth Congress in Birmingham, Ala.; the New Jersey Negro Welfare Commission on the Condition of the Urban Population; the Julius Rosenwald Fund; and other organizations. The correspondence pertains to black women's employment, the employment of a black woman in the Women's Bureau, the National Negro Congress, and the 1945 Conference on Post-War Employment. There is also a folder for the Negro Welfare Survey Committee of Richmond, Va., with a November 1928 report by that committee concerning social conditions for blacks in Richmond. Two folders pertain to the National Interracial Conference of 1928 (2 in.). They include abstracts of the research committee of the conference; the committee's purpose was "to construct a reasonably faithful contemporary picture of Negro life and the status of race relations." The abstracts give a number of population and health statistics. The folder for the Urban League (1 in.) includes correspondence from local branches of the organization in Springfield, Ill.; Richmond, Va.; Pittsburgh, Pa.; Atlanta, Ga.; Baltimore, Md.; and Washington, D.C. Much of the correspondence is about the employment status of black women, training opportunities for them, and occupations open to them.

86.6. Correspondence–household (domestic) file, 1919–47 (2 ft.), is in two parts, one arranged chronologically and one by subject. The records concern household workers and contain substantial information about black women is scattered throughout. There is information (sometimes including statistics) about wages, hours, working conditions, meetings and conferences on household employment, the effect of the Depression, protests against exclusion from both the National Recovery Administration codes and Social Security benefits, education and training, and legislation that affected domestic workers. There are also publications, pamphlets, and reports on the subject of domestic work.

86.7. The **general correspondence files, 1948–56,** are arranged according to a subject-numeric classification scheme. There is an alphabetical card index to this series. It contains references to correspondence with black organizations such as the Urban League, the National Council of Negro Women, and the National Association of Colored Women as well as the NAACP, the Associated Negro Press, Alpha Kappa Alpha and Delta Sigma Theta Sororities, and the National Scholarship Fund for Negro Students. Most of this correspondence pertains to meetings and conferences or to the employment status of and opportunities for black women.

Division of Investigations

86.8. The Division of Investigations conducts all the Bureau's original investigations, the greater part of its work being done in the field. The studies done by this Division were later published as numbered bulletins. There is a series of **correspondence relating to bulletins, 1918–41** (9 ft.), arranged by bulletin number. There are correspondence files relating to wages, hours, and working conditions for women in various States. The

Religious service. Date and photographer unknown. RG 208, Records of the Office of War Information. (208-PR-26A10).

wage information, particularly for the Southern States, is sometimes separated under categories for white or black women. There is also information about black women in household employment; in laundries; as hairdressers, cotton and textile workers, and tobacco workers; and as a segment of the unemployed during the Depression. Most of the information for the bulletins was compiled from onsite surveys or from census statistics.

Division of Statistics and Division of Reports and Exhibits

86.9. The Division of Statistics compiles all the statistical data from field agents' schedules and from other sources that are incorporated in the publications and in the files of the Bureau. The Division of Reports and Exhibits prepares and edits the bulletins and all the other publications of the Bureau. These records include **bulletin numbers 1 through 260, 1918–56** (2 ft.), arranged in numerical sequence (see also RG 287). A few of the bulletins pertain specifically to black women. For example, Bulletin 70 is entitled *Negro Women in Industry in 15 States;* 165, *The Negro Woman Worker;* and 205, *Negro Women War Workers.* There is also pertinent information in bulletins about household employment, women as breadwinners, work in power laundries, the relief and unemployment situation during the Depression, the condition of employment among migrant workers, and work in canning, tobacco, and lumber industries. Most of the information pertaining to black women workers, however, is incorporated into bulletins on occupations or regional work conditions for women. There is a separate bulletin on women in the industries of nearly every State. Such bulletins discuss wages, hours, and working conditions. For many States, particularly the southern ones, there is specific information about black women. Most of this information concerns wages, but sometimes occupations or working conditions, especially segregated facilities, are discussed.

Division of Research

86.10. The duty of this Division is to search out existing material relating to various investigations and studies undertaken by the Bureau that may be used in its reports and recommendations or that may be needed to answer inquiries made by organizations and individuals throughout the country. The Division keeps track of legislative enactments and prepares and keeps up-to-date maps and charts showing State legislation for women workers. These records include a series of **articles and speeches, 1918–42** (9½ ft.), that were prepared for periodicals, radio shows, meetings, and conferences. Each article or speech was assigned a number, and they are arranged accordingly. Some specifically relate to black women's occupational opportunities, especially as industrial and household workers. For example, there is a May 1935 speech entitled "The Plight of Negro Domestic Labor" that was presented by Women's Bureau Director Mary Anderson to a meeting at Howard University in Washington, D.C., on the Position of the Negro in Our National Economic Crisis; a 1934 radio script entitled "The Domestic Worker of Today"; and a 1936 article by Jean Collier Brown entitled "The Negro Woman Worker," which was submitted to the *American Federationist* for publication.

86.11. The Research Division files also include **correspondence about household employment, 1930–47** (2 ft.), with special emphasis on the postwar period, arranged by subject and thereunder chronologically. There is also **material relating to two Women's Bureau conferences 1956–65** (5 in.), arranged by type of records, pertaining to private household work. The conference records include a transcript of the 1964 conference, questionnaires prepared to help establish "Suggested Guidelines for Surveying Private Household Workers and Their Employers," and information on the National Committee on Household Employment. This committee was founded in 1965 to act as a clearinghouse and coordinator of efforts to upgrade the status of private household employees, promote the expansion of job opportunities, and develop standards for the work. The Women's Bureau invited representatives from organizations such as the Urban League, the National Council of Negro Women, and the National Association of Colored Women's Clubs to participate in these meetings.

86.12. Also among the records for this Division is a series of **survey materials, 1920–55** (29 ft.), arranged by subject. There are three folders that relate to black women (totaling about 1 in.). They are entitled "Negro Women," "Employment," and "Negro Women–National Council of Negro Women Study." They include reports and studies concerning the occupations of black women in various cities and employment opportunities available to them. There is also a study done by the National Council of Negro Women; the study is about the council's program activities in local areas in 1952.

Division of Legislation and Standards

86.13. This Division monitored the activities of State and national lawmakers in the area of women's rights and worked to promote equal rights for women. The Division also studied court decisions that affected women. Among the **records relating to legislation, 1933–67** (19 ft.), arranged by subject, is one folder on civil rights bills (2 in.). The folder includes copies of proposed and enacted civil rights laws from both the U.S. House of Representatives and the U.S. Senate for the period 1964–66. The legislation pertains to antidiscrimination laws, proposals for the establishment of an agency similar to the Fair Employment Practice Committee, jury duty, voting, poll taxes, and voter registration.

86.14. The audiovisual records include pictures of black women working in heavy industry, sewing factories, and canteens and cafeterias (11 items). About half of the photographs are undated, the rest are dated 1919. Some include the names of the factories in which the women were employed.

Record Group 87

Records of the U.S. Secret Service

87.1. The U.S. Secret Service was organized in July 1865 as a division in the Office of the Solicitor of the Treasury. The Service had responsibility for detecting and bringing to trial persons involved in the counterfeiting of treasury notes, bonds, and other securities of the United States. Occasionally after 1893 and regularly since the assassination of President McKinley, the Service has provided protection to the President. This service has been expanded to include members of the President's immediate family, the President-elect, the Vice President or other official next in succession to the office of President, the Vice-President-elect, and candidates for the offices of President and Vice President. Protection is also provided for former Presidents, for the widow of a President during her lifetime, and for a deceased President's minor children until age 16, unless such protection is declined. Some of the records relate to the activities of black civic and political groups.

87.2. *Daily Reports of United States Secret Service Agents, 1875–1936* (T95, 843 rolls), contain some records relating to black history. There is no index; however, knowledge of the date of a President's speech to a black group might uncover data. For example, on October 12, 13, and 16, 1911, agents reported circumstances relating to a speech by President Taft to the Afro-American League in Los Angeles (roll 530).

Record Group 88

Records of the Food and Drug Administration

88.1. The Food and Drug Administration (FDA) was designated by the Agricultural Appropriation Act of 1931 to continue the regulatory functions performed by the Bureau of Chemistry, the Board of Food and Drug Inspection, and the Food, Drug, and Insecticide Administration—all of which had been established under the Food and Drugs Act of 1906. The FDA and most of its functions were transferred in 1940 from the Department of Agriculture to the Federal Security Agency, which became the Department of Health, Education, and Welfare in 1953. The Administration enforces the Federal Food, Drug, and Cosmetic Act; the Tea Importation Act; the Import Milk Act; the Caustic Poison Act; the Hazardous Substances Labeling Act; the Filled Milk Act; and other acts. It is responsible for promoting purity, standard potency, and honest and informative labeling of consumer products covered by these acts.

88.2. The FDA records include photograhs, 1906–35 (3,800 items), relating to chemical analysis of products and fraudulent labeling of drugs; inspection of milk, fish, and other foods; the seizure and destruction of contaminated foods; and the manufacture of sugar candy, liquors, and other commodities. Photographs of onsite inspections often depict employees, some of whom are black. Pictures of oyster houses in Washington, D.C., and Baltimore, Md., show black workers, as do photographs of banana boats, fish and produce markets, and other businesses such as an ice cream plant, a bakery, and a poultry packer.

Record Group 90
Records of the Public Health Service

90.1. The Public Health Service (PHS), originally called the Marine Hospital Service, has its origin in an act of 1798 that authorized hospitals for the care of sick and disabled U.S. merchant seamen. Subsequent legislation greatly broadened the scope of its activities. Its name was changed to Public Health and Marine Hospital Service in 1902 and to Public Health Service in 1912. The PHS was under the jurisdiction of the Treasury Department from 1798 to 1939, when it was placed in the newly created Federal Security Agency, which became in 1953 the Department of Health, Education, and Welfare. The PHS, under the direction of the Surgeon General, is responsible for providing medical care to personnel of the Coast Guard, the Coast and Geodetic Survey, and the merchant marine; providing health services to American Indians; preventing the spread of disease; researching the cause, prevention, and control of disease; extending and improving State and local health services through technical assistance and financial aid; collaborating with foreign governments and international organizations in world health activities; supervising manufacture of biologic products; collecting, analyzing, and publishing vital and health statistics; and disseminating health information.

90.2. The **central file of the general correspondence of the PHS, 1897–1946** (514 ft.), is arranged in three chronological segments (1897–1923, 1924–35, and 1936–46) and thereunder by a subject-numeric filing scheme in the 1897–1923 segment; for the two later segments, thereunder by class of correspondent. The central files include correspondence, reports, memorandums, and other records about medical officers, foreign ports, boards of officers, disease drugs, serums and vaccines, public health education, hygiene and sanitation, inspection of immigrants, and cooperation with State and local agencies. Interspersed among the records of the State boards of health is some information about the health of the black population. File 1950, "Societies and Organizations," includes some folders (about 4 in.) for black organizations. The folders generally include only a few documents, and most are from the period 1924–46. Below are a few examples of the types of health work reported to PHS by black organizations.

90.3. The Negro Organization Society of Hampton Institute, Va., worked for better schools, health, homes, and farms. The organization sponsored a 1936 conference on venereal disease control. The Urban

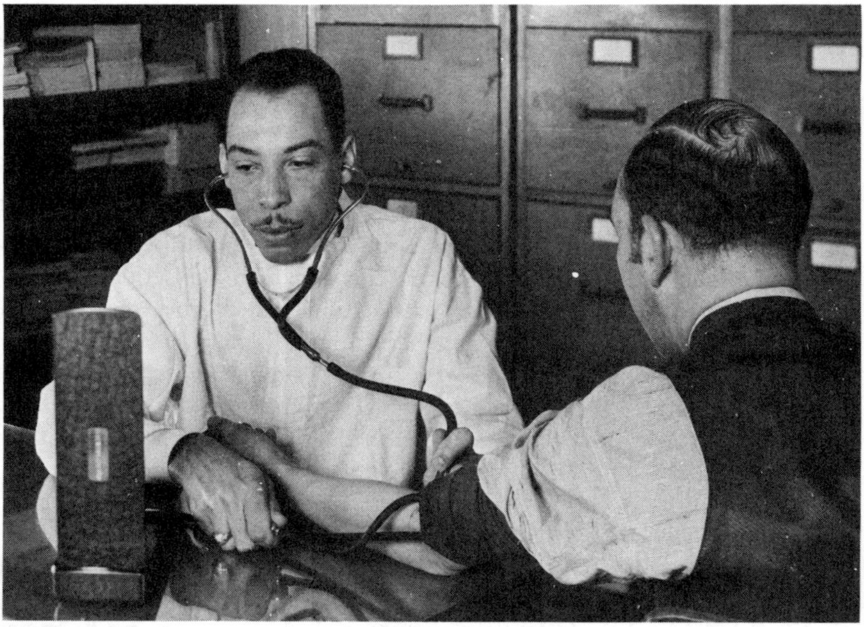

Dr. Harold Whitted. Date and photographer unknown. RG 208, Records of the Office of War Information. (208-N-S-4264-5).

League, the Negro Medical Association, and the Negro Wartime Health Committee were also concerned with venereal disease control and education, especially among enlisted men in the Armed Forces. The Negro Welfare Survey Committee studied the health problems of blacks in Richmond, Va. The National Association of Colored Graduate Nurses, Inc., based in New York City, was concerned with discrimination against black nurses. A letter from that organization dated June 13, 1944, states that "according to our records, 15 Negro public health nurses have been appointed during the past three years." The Southern Negro Youth Congress wrote about the "Negro Health Week" of the PHS. A folder labeled "Negro in America" has information pertaining to a study of syphilis in Tuskegee, Ala., in the 1940's. Health matters were a part of the National Youth Administration-sponsored "Negro Exposition of Progress in Alabama" and of the "Negro Life in America" exposition in Chicago in 1940.

90.4. There are photographs made by the graphics unit of the Office of Health Information of the Division of Public Health Methods relating to the effects of communicable diseases on blacks during the period 1898–1934. Black patients are numerous in photographs depicting diseases caused by dietary deficiencies, social dislocation, and substandard sanitary and housing conditions. Blacks also appear in the roles of health officers and medical personnel and as participants in the National Negro Health

"National Negro Health Week." Date and artist unknown. RG 90, Records of the Public Health Service. (90-G-3420).

Week movement. There is a recording of a radio broadcast during the week of July 5–12, 1942, celebrating the 28th observance of National Negro Health Week begun at Tuskegee Institute in 1915 by Booker T. Washington. The theme of the program is black community preparedness in health and defense.

90.5. Earlier PHS records are available only on M753, *Letters Received by the National Board of Health, 1879–84* (59 rolls). The letters were registered and sorted into subject categories. The first three rolls of the microfilm publication contain these registers. Some of the letters, especially the State reports (18 rolls), contain information about the health of the black population, including mortality rates, incidence of diseases, treatment records, and demographic information. For example, letter 1370 for Norfolk, Va., is a "Health and Mortality Report" or blacks in the fourth ward and in parts of the first and third wards, 1878–79.

90.6. The **general records of the Venereal Disease Division, 1918–36** (149 ft.), are arranged according to a decimal classification scheme. The first segment (100–199) consists of statistical and narrative reports on the incidence of venereal disease, treatment clinics, prostitution, and related matters for each State, 1919–20. Most of the printed forms have separate columns for statistics for blacks and whites under the headings "W" for whites and "C" for colored. The general records also include a study of "Untreated Syphilis in Negroes in Macon County, Alabama," 1932–33 (#417, 4 in.).

90.7. A campaign to combat syphilis among blacks in Georgia is the subject of the film "Three Counties Against Syphilis" (#90–12), produced by the Department of Agriculture in 1938. Mobile clinics manned by employees of the U.S. Public Health Service and the State Public Health Service are shown as part of the fight against the disease in Camden, Glynn, and McIntosh Counties.

Record Group 96

Records of the Farmers Home Administration

96.1. The Farmers Home Administration (FHA) was established in the Department of Agriculture by an act of August 14, 1946, to succeed the Farm Security Administration (FSA). The FSA was established in 1937 in the Department of Agriculture to succeed the Resettlement Administration, which had been established in 1935 to administer rural rehabilitation and land programs begun in 1933 under the Subsistence Homesteads Division of the Department of the Interior and the Federal Emergency Relief Administration. The FHA provides small farmers with credit to construct or repair homes and farm buildings, improve farming operations, or become farmowners; it also gives individual guidance in farm and home management.

96.2. Part of FSA was moved to Cincinnati, Ohio, in 1942. The **general correspondence maintained in the Cincinnati office, 1935–42** (122 ft.), is arranged according to a subject-numeric classification scheme. One classification (#130–02) relates to FSA personnel matters, such as discrimination against blacks and aliens and veterans preference. Materials about blacks (5 in.) are included in one general folder entitled "Negroes" and in folders for black personnel in most of the FSA regional offices. The records include lists of black employees, lists of black candidates for appointments, information about the salaries of black personnel, memorandums on FSA integration policies, and some correspondence with black officials, such as Mary McLeod Bethune of the National Youth Administration, Maj. Campbell C. Johnson of the Selective Service System, and Alfred Edgar Smith of the Work Projects Administration. The files also include correspondence of black FSA employees George S. Mitchell, Assistant Administrator; Joseph A. B. Evans, race relations specialist; and Constance E. H. Daniel, senior administrative assistant. A letter dated October 27, 1931, from Mitchell to Major Johnson describes Daniel's work: "Mrs. Daniel is responsible to the administrator of the FSA for frequent field inquiry as to the application of our program to the needs of low-income Negro families eligible for our rehabilitation programs." She was also to report the problems of black occupants of defense housing projects under the management of FSA, advise the FSA Administrator on the use of black personnel within the agency, and tend to public relations matters involving the black community.

96.3. Correspondence with the general public to which individual replies were made, 1933–35 (19 ft.), arranged alphabetically by name of correspondent, consists mostly of requests of individuals asking to be located on a homestead project or proposals for establishing such projects. Some of the letters are from individuals who identified themselves as black Americans. For example, a January 26, 1934, letter from Peter Johnson of Dothan, Ala., to the Department of the Interior asks, "will you please send me full particulars of your plan to help colored people and settle them upon their own little homes. My people are in dire need of economic aid in this section of our beloved country."

96.4. The **general correspondence of the Resettlement Division, 1935–42** (38 ft.), arranged according to a classification scheme, includes a folder on blacks (#130–02). Most of the information in the folder pertains to black personnel in the Division, but there is some information about farm projects and migratory labor camps.

96.5. Correspondence concerning migratory labor camps, 1935–43 (12 ft.), arranged according to a classification scheme, includes interspersed material about black migratory workers, especially in the South. The records relate chiefly to the establishment of and details of the operation of the migratory labor camps, but there is also information about housing, health, employment, and general conditions of the migrants.

96.6. The records of field offices generally include **farm ownership case files, 1937–46** (Regions 1 to 11, 414 ft.), which are generally arranged alphabetically by the name of the borrower. Each case file usually includes the loan application, appraisal reports and data concerning the prospective borrower, loan and variable payment agreements, loan analysis, mortgage, farm and home plans, and insurance policies. The loan application and some of the other forms in each case file indicate the race of the applicant. The borrowers were visited periodically by farm management and home management supervisors who were sent out by FHA to monitor the progress of the farmer and his wife in carrying out the farm plan and the home plan. The supervisors' reports are in the case files.

96.7. Soil conservation project records, 1935–40 (209 ft.), arranged alphabetically by State and thereunder by project number, include a file for the Tuskegee, Ala., project (½ in.). The records include some historical information about the development of this all-black project. (See also RG 114.)

Record Group 97

Records of the Bureau of Agricultural and Industrial Chemistry

97.1. The Bureau of Agricultural and Industrial Chemistry was established in 1943 as the successor agency of several units in the Department of Agriculture, beginning with the Division of Chemistry established in 1862. This Division was succeeded by the Bureau of Chemistry in 1901, the Bureau of Chemistry and Soils in 1927, and the Bureau of Agricultural Chemistry and Engineering in 1938. The Bureau of Agricultural and Industrial Chemistry and its predecessors were engaged in chemical and technological research on the use of agricultural commodities. The work involved soil analysis and the enforcement of the Food and Drugs Act. The Bureau was abolished in 1953.

97.2. The **general correspondence, 1907–18** (820 ft.), arranged by year and thereunder by a numerical filing scheme, includes correspondence with members of the staff and faculty of Tuskegee Institute, such as George Washington Carver, J. H. Washington, and E. T. Atwell. There are only a few letters from blacks (1908, #18386; 1910, #3568; and 1911, #8222), and they are requests for technical information (about such matters as canning regulations and pure food laws) and for publications.

Record Group 100

Records of the Occupational Safety and Health Administration

100.1. The Occupational Safety and Health Administration was established in May 1971 in the Department of Labor, succeeding the Bureau of Labor Standards. Established as the Division of Labor Standards in November 1934 and renamed in 1948, the Bureau promoted industrial safety and health and gave technical advice to State labor departments, labor unions, and trade associations. It developed national standards for labor legislation and labor law administration and assisted the Bureau of International Labor Affairs in implementing international labor standards. Through agreements negotiated between Federal and State agencies, it coordinated enforcement of laws concerning wage rates, work hours, industrial homework, child labor, and safety and health. The Bureau served as an adviser on conditions and programs in the area of child labor and youth employment standards and prepared publications and exhibits for public information.

100.2. The **classified general files of the Bureau of Labor Standards, 1934–49** (162 ft.), arranged according to a subject-numeric classification scheme, include some letters relating to black history. The **alphabetical index to the classified general files** (144 ft.) includes correspondence under the headings "NAACP," "Negro Labor Victory Committee," "Committee on Negro Organization," "Colored Trainmen," "National Association of Colored Women," and "Southern Negro Council." The index seems more complete than the records themselves.

Record Group 101

Records of the Office of the Comptroller of the Currency

101.1. The Office of the Comptroller of the Currency was created in the Department of the Treasury in 1863 to administer the National Banking System. The Comptroller executes laws relating to the supervision of national banks and trust companies in the District of Columbia. The Office redeems national bank notes and supervises the issuance of Federal Reserve notes. The comptroller's approval is needed for organizing new national banks, consolidating national banks, converting State-chartered banks to national banks, and establishing branches (including foreign branches) of national banks. The Office's functions also included liquidating the Freedman's Savings and Trust Co. (1881–1920).

101.2. The Freedman's Savings and Trust Co. (F.S.&T. Co.) was a banking institution chartered by the U.S. Government under an act approved March 3, 1865, for the benefit of freed slaves. By its charter, the company was managed by a board of 50 trustees, of whom 9, including the president and vice president of the bank, constituted a quorum for the transaction of business at any regular or special meeting of the board, except that 10 affirmative votes were required to elect a trustee. The military savings banks at Beaufort, S.C., and at Norfolk, Va., were transferred to the company soon after its establishment. In the period 1865–70, a total of 33 branch offices were established, including one in New York City in 1866. In 1874 the trustees were authorized to select, with the approval of the Secretary of the Treasury, three commissioners to take charge of the effects of the company and to report on its financial state to the Secretary of the Treasury. This arrangement was altered by an act of Congress approved February 21, 1882, in which the Secretary of the Treasury was authorized and directed to appoint the Comptroller of the Currency to administer the affairs of the company. Thus the Comptroller of the Currency was made Commissioner ex officio and in that capacity liquidated the affairs of the company. Reports were submitted by the Comptroller to Congress on the first of December every year. The final report on the trust was submitted in 1930.

101.3. Letters received by the Commissioners of the F.S.&T. Co. and by the Comptroller of the Currency as ex officio Commissioner, 1870–1914 (27 ft.), arranged by subject, include legal papers, dividend checks, payrolls, expense checks, and passbooks.

101.4. Letters sent by the Commissioners of the F.S.&T. Co. and by the Comptroller of the Currency as ex officio Commissioner, 1874–1913 (34 vols., 4 ft.), are arranged chronologically and consist of press copy books of letters sent to depositors and others. There is an index in each volume.

101.5. The board of trustees met regularly on the second Thursday of each month at the Washington office, the principal office of the company. The journal of minutes of these meetings and of committee meetings are arranged chronologically by the date of the meetings. The **minutes and journals, 1865–74** (7 vols., 7 in.), have been reproduced as M874, *Journal of the Board of Trustees and Minutes of Committees and Inspectors of the Freedman's Savings and Trust Company, 1865–74* (2 rolls).

101.6. Printed copies of annual reports of the Commissioners of the F.S.&T. Co. and of the Comptroller of the Currency as ex officio Commissioner, 1881–1919 (2 in.), are arranged chronologically. Reports for 1883–88 and 1913 are missing. A copy of *The Charter and By-Laws* (1872) is filed with these reports.

101.7. The **signature books, n.d.** (53 vols., 8 ft.), include the registered signatures and personal identification data of depositors. They are arranged by name of city in which the branch of the F.S.&T. Co. was located and thereunder by account number. There is an index in each volume. These records have been reproduced as M816, *Registers of Signatures of Depositors in Branches of the Freedman's Savings and Trust Company, 1865–74.* The information contained in many of the registers is as follows: account number; name of depositor; date of entry; place born; place brought up; residence; age; complexion; name of employer or occupation; names of wife or husband, children, father, mother, brothers, and sisters; remarks; and signature. The early books sometimes also contain the name of the former master or mistress and the name of the plantation. In many entries not all the requested information is given. Copies of death certificates have been pinned to some of the entries, and each certificate has been filmed immediately after the page that shows the registration of the person's signature.

101.8. The records also include **loan and real estate ledgers and journals, 1870–1916** (14 vols., 3 ft.), arranged roughly chronologically; **mail register and abstract of letters, 1872–84** (2 vols.), arranged chronologically; and the **dividend payment record, 1882–89** (16 vols., 2 ft.), arranged by name of city in which the branch of the F.S.&T. Co. was located and thereunder by number of depositor's account (volumes 7, 9, and 11 are missing).

101.9. The **indexes to deposit ledgers, 1865–74** (46 vols., 2 ft.), are arranged alphabetically by name of State and thereunder by name of city in which the branch was located. The names are indexed alphabetically by first letter of surname and thereunder by sound. The indexes list the names of depositors in 26 branches of the F.S.&T. Co. and include the depositors' names and account numbers, or, in some cases, what appear to be the page numbers of the deposit ledgers. In a few volumes the amount of the deposit is also given. In several volumes parts of the alphabet are missing, and some volumes are missing. These records have been reproduced as M817, *Indexes to Deposit Ledgers in the Branches of the Freedman's Savings and Trust Company, 1865–74* (5 rolls).

101.10. There is one **volume of proceedings of the attorney for the F.S.&T. Co., n.d.** (1 vol., 1 in.), entitled "Exchange, Atlanta Branch, F.S.&T. Co." **Miscellaneous finance and accounting records, 1870–98** (1 ft.), are arranged by subject and include a **cash blotter, 1882–99** (1 vol.); a **register of U.S. bonds owned by F.S.&T. Co., n.d.** (1 vol.); **statements of disbursing accounts, 1884–1906,** arranged roughly by name of Comptroller of the Currency (as Commissioner of F.S.&T. Co.) and thereunder chronologically; an **interest book, 1871–73** (1 vol.); a **journal 1872–74** (1 vol.); **paid dividend checks for fourth and final dividends, 1882–83; Commissioners' ledger balances, 1877–90** (1 vol.); **inspectors' ledger balances, 1870–74** (1 vol.); a **record of accounts barred by acts of Congress, 1881–85** (1 vol.); a **record of bonds filed for lost passbooks, 1875–85** (1 vol.); and an **itemized statement of receipts and expenditures, 1875–78** (1 vol.).

101.11. The **bank organization and liquidation files, 1863–1970** (290 ft.), arranged by bank charter number, include information about other black banks that had closed. For example, the Douglass National Bank of Chicago (#12227, 1 in.) was lauded as the "first U.S. bank directed by Negroes" *(The Daily News,* April 27, 1921; this clipping is in the file). The records include lists of officers and shareholders, publicity materials, and correspondence.

Record Group 102

Records of the Children's Bureau

102.1. The Children's Bureau was established as part of the Department of Commerce and Labor in 1912 and was transferred to the newly created Department of Labor the following year. In 1946 the Bureau, exclusive of the child labor functions centered in its Industrial Division, was transferred to the Social Security Administration of the Federal Security Agency. When the Agency was abolished in 1953, its functions and units, including the Social Security Administration and the Children's Bureau, were transferred to the newly created Department of Health, Education, and Welfare. The Children's Bureau compiles reports on all matters relating to childhood and implements programs to promote child health and welfare, especially those relating to infant and maternal mortality, working mothers, the birth rate, orphanages, juvenile delinquency, desertion, dangerous occupations, accidents, child diseases, employment, and State and community measures for the protection and care of children. It administers Federal aid to State agencies for child welfare, maternal and child health, and crippled children. It also plans with public and voluntary national, State, and local organizations and agencies for the development and extension of services for children and youth. Some of these records relate to black children and to organizations interested in their welfare.

102.2. The **central file, 1912–40** (450 ft.) is arranged in six chronological segments—1912–20, 1921–24, 1925–28, 1929–32, 1933–36, and 1937–40—and thereunder according to the Bureau's subject-numeric filing system. The records consist mainly of correspondence, memorandums, and reports of Bureau chiefs and staff members of the Bureau's constituent divisions. Several headings relate to race: "Race Relations" (#0–2–9) contains the subheading "Negro race," under which there are records for education, morals, crime, delinquency, economic condition, dependency, industrial condition, political rights, and health; "Special Advisory Committee on Service for Negro Children" (#1–2–0–4–16); "Infant Mortality Among Colored" (#11-121); and "Study of the Negro Situation in Baltimore," (#11–548), 1915–22. The numbers in parentheses are the index numbers (see paragraph 102.3) to series in which there is information specifically on blacks; however, there are some other file categories that contain statistical data or other information about black youths.

102.3. There is an **index to the central file, 1914–40** (158 ft.), which is arranged in chronological segments corresponding to those of the central file and thereunder alphabetically by surname of correspondent. The index is on 3- by 5-inch cards; each card shows the correspondent's name and address, the date of the letter, the date of the Bureau's reply, and the file number. Some index entries pertinent to black history are "Association of Colored Women's Clubs"; "National Urban League"; "National Association of Colored Graduate Nurses"; "National Conference of Colored Parents of Atlanta, Ga."; "National Congress of Colored Parents and Teachers, Louisville, Ky."; "National Federation of Colored Women's Clubs, Capahosic, Va."; "American Negro Exposition, Chicago"; "Colored Emergency Relief Bureau, Jacksonville, Fla."; "Colored Orphan Asylum, New York City"; "National Association of Teachers in Colored Schools"; "NAACP"; and "Association for the Protection of Colored Women." For most of the organizations there are only a few pieces of correspondence in the central file. However, there is more correspondence (about ½ in.) for each of the following: the "Urban League"; "Negro in America, New York City"; "Journal of Negro Education, Howard University, Washington, D.C."; and "Associated Negro Press, Washington, D.C."

102.4. State plans for the maternal and child health program, 1936–45 (90 ft.), are arranged chronologically by year and thereunder alphabetically by name of State. The plans for Southern States often include information about programs for black children or about areas of the State in which the population was principally black. Records for the maternal and child health program document the functions, policies, procedures, and operations of the Bureau under title V of the Social Security Act and provide information on the development of health services for mothers and children. Title V also provided for the development of welfare services for crippled children. **State plans for programs for crippled children, 1936–47** (82 ft.), are arranged chronologically by year and thereunder alphabetically by name of State. **State plans for the programs of child welfare services, 1936-49** (44 ft.), are arranged by year and thereunder alphabetically by name of State. These plans are for the administration of title IV of the Social Security Act, which provided for the development of child welfare services. These services included adoption, foster-family care, and care for unmarried mothers, for children of working mothers, and for juvenile delinquents. The records for all three programs document the functions, policies, procedures, and operations of the Bureau under the act and give information on the development of welfare services for children, the role of the Federal Government, and the relationship between Federal and State Governments in these fields. Included are annual plans of operation and budget estimates that the States submitted to the Bureau for approval, budget amendments and supplements, and related analyses, recommendations, authorizations, reports of expenditures, and correspondence. Some of the records include information about services to black children.

Record Group 106

Records of the Smithsonian Institution

106.1. The Smithsonian Institution was created by an act of August 10, 1846, under terms of the will of James Smithson of London, as an establishment for the "increase and diffusion of knowledge among men." The Institution performs fundamental research; publishes the results of studies, explorations, and investigations; preserves for study and reference millions of scientific, cultural, and historical items; maintains exhibits of the arts, American history, aeronautics and space exploration, technology, and natural history; participates in the international exchange of learned publications; and engages in national and international cooperative research and training programs.

106.2. Among the audiovisual records of the Smithsonian Institution is a sound recording dramatizing the theme of racial equality (#106–153). The program, the 13th and final segment of the series "Let Freedom Ring," was produced in 1937 by the Office of Education and the Smithsonian to celebrate the 150th anniversary of the Constitution. The program is based on the concept of freedom and human rights.

Record Group 114

Records of the Soil Conservation Service

114.1. The Soil Conservation Service (SCS) was established in the Department of Agriculture by an act of April 27, 1935, to provide a permanent program for preventing and controlling soil erosion. Its predecessor, the Soil Erosion Service, created in the Department of the Interior by the National Industrial Recovery Act of 1933, had been transferred in March 1935 to the Department of Agriculture. The SCS, which inherited many functions from other Government agencies, began in 1937 to provide technical and other assistance to farmers in soil conservation districts organized under State laws. The SCS was given responsibility for assisting in water conservation programs in 1944 and was authorized to assume the soil survey program of the Bureau of Plant Industry, Soils, and Agricultural Engineering in 1952. Duties of the SCS include conducting soil and snow surveys, erosion control activities, river basin surveys, and investigations to promote agricultural stability in the Great Plains area; assisting local groups in planning and developing land and water resources in multiple county areas; and giving technical help to landowners and operators who participate in the Department's agricultural conservation, cropland conversion, and cropland adjustment programs.

114.2. Three major phases of land utilization projects included the purchase of land generally unsuited to farming, the conversion of the purchased land to a use beneficial to the people of the United States, and the permanent rehabilitation of the people living on purchased land. Some of these projects involved black farmers. The files on **approved projects, 1934–39** (228 ft.), arranged by State and thereunder by project number, include files for the all-black Tuskegee land utilization project (project A1–8, 2 ft.). The Tuskegee material includes proposals, preliminary plans, final plans, photographs, maps, exhibits, publications, and general correspondence. A report about the personnel on the Tuskegee project indicates that all of the employees except the appraisers were black. There were over 450 families involved in the project, and the families were almost evenly divided between owner-operators and tenants. A majority of the families were on relief. The records include a 1933 Tuskegee Institute publication entitled *Economic Aspects of the Farm Situation of Negro Farmers in Macon County, Alabama, 1931,* by J. R. Otis (42 pp.).

114.3. See also RG 96, Records of the Farmer's Home Administration.

Record Group 115

Records of the Bureau of Reclamation

115.1. The Bureau of Reclamation, first known as the Reclamation Service, was created under the Reclamation or Newlands Act of 1902, which established a reclamation fund from the sale of public lands to finance the location, construction, and maintenance of irrigation works that would store, divert, and develop waters for reclaiming arid and semiarid lands in the States and Territories. The act gave responsibility for administering the fund to the Secretary of the Interior, who established the Reclamation Service to exercise that function under the jurisdiction of, but not as a part of, the Geological Survey. In 1907 the Service was separated from the Survey and was made directly responsible to the

The caption of this photograph reads, "A Negro shanty in Pender County, N.C. Fortunately this type of rural home is rapidly disappearing." Date and photographer unknown. RG 115, Records of the Bureau of Reclamation. (115-SM-3NC).

Secretary. It was renamed the Bureau of Reclamation in 1923. The Bureau plans, constructs, and operates irrigation works in 17 contiguous Western States and Hawaii and builds and operates hydroelectric powerplants.

115.2. The audiovisual records of the Bureau include photographs of towns, agricultural activities, industries, roads, bridges, and drought conditions in some Southern States. Approximately 20 of the photographs available from the Bureau's files show black farmers and their agricultural activities during the period 1902–40, with emphasis on tobacco cultivation in Georgia, South Carolina, and Alabama in 1927.

Record Group 118

Records of U.S. Attorneys and Marshals*

118.1. Provision for U.S. attorneys and marshals was made by the Judiciary Act of 1789. Under authority of the act of 1870 that created the Department of Justice, the Attorney General exercises general supervision over U.S. attorneys and marshals, who are appointed by the President for each judicial district. U.S. attorneys investigate violations of Federal criminal laws, present evidence to grand juries, prosecute Federal criminal cases, and serve as the Government's attorney in civil litigation in which the United States is involved or has an interest. U.S. marshals execute and serve writs, processes, and orders issued by U.S. courts and U.S. commissioners and commissions; notify the Department of Justice of defiance of Federal authority; and serve as local disbursing officers for salaries and expenses of U.S. attorneys, marshals, and Federal courts within their districts. Since the establishment of the Administrative Office of the U.S. Courts in 1939, marshals have disbursed funds appropriated for Federal courts only at the discretion of that Office.

118.2. The **records of U.S. attorneys and marshals, 1853–71,** with a few records earlier and later than these dates (about 600 ft., located in the regional archives branches), include materials relating to black history such as election fraud cases, particularly during the Reconstruction period, and cases relating to racial violence and civil rights. The amount of black history material for each region varies; however, material from the Southeastern States, 1824–1975 (about 150 ft., in the Archives Branch, Atlanta Federal Archives and Records Center), provides a sample of the type of records available. Black history materials are interspersed throughout the records for this region, but most are related to peonage cases at the turn of the 20th century and to civil rights activities, such as the desegregation of schools and public accommodations and the activities of the Ku Klux Klan in the 1950's and 1960's. The records include grand jury reports, U.S. attorneys' case files, and U.S. attorneys' and marshals' correspondence files.

118.3. The records for the Southeastern States also contain information about the prosecution of landowners and others accused of holding blacks in slavery in southern Alabama, 1907–12, and grand jury investigations of Ku Klux Klan activities in northern Georgia, 1949–50. The records include material relating to the desegregation of the University of Mississippi at Oxford by a black student named James Meredith in October 1962 (4 ft.), arranged by type of material. The Meredith case records consist of copies of reports about interviews conducted by FBI agents throughout the United States with Department of Justice attorneys, U.S. military personnel, U.S. deputy marshals, University of Mississippi students and faculty, and media personnel. The records concerning the Meredith case also include FBI laboratory investigation reports, statements given to FBI agents, and photographs taken by or surrendered to the FBI.

118.4. See also RG 60, Records of the Department of Justice, and RG 48, Records of the Secretary of the Interior.

* *Restrictions may apply to this Record Group. Consult NARS staff.*

Record Group 119
Records of the National Youth Administration

119.1. The National Youth Administration (NYA) was established within the Works Progress (later the Work Projects) Administration (WPA) in 1935. In 1939 the NYA was transferred to the Federal Security Agency and in 1942 to the War Manpower Commission. The NYA remained in existence until the end of 1944. The NYA conducted two major programs for needy young people between the ages of 16 and 24: an out-of-school work program (which provided employment and vocational training on public industrial, manual, construction, professional, and clerical projects to unemployed youth who had left school) and a student work program (which furnished part-time employment on projects devised by school authorities to high school, college, and graduate students who otherwise would have been unable to continue their education). After December 1941 both programs were reoriented to serve the needs of national defense—particularly the out-of-school work program, which in 1942 became the war production training program.

119.2. The NYA conducted many programs specifically for black youths, including aviation and other defense training, health programs, and school and college programs in cooperation with black organizations. To advise the NYA, the President created the NYA National Advisory Committee of 32 leaders in education, business, finance, labor, agriculture, church, welfare, and youth groups. Two black representatives were appointed to the Committee: Mary McLeod Bethune, president of Bethune-Cookman College, and Mordecai Johnson, president of Howard University.

Division of Negro Affairs

119.3. NYA recognized the specific needs of black youth by establishing a Division of Negro Affairs, whose staff members participated in the policy decisions of the agency. Mary McLeod Bethune was appointed Director. The Division was responsible for the coordination of NYA activities affecting black youths and the development of projects to afford employment opportunities to them. It investigated complaints of discrimination against blacks and cooperated with other NYA divisions and offices in the development of research in black affairs. The Division was also responsible for getting black administrative staff in other NYA units. From the period 1935–42, State supervisors of Negro Affairs functioned in 27 States; in 1942, when programs began to be administered on a regional basis, regional Negro Affairs representatives served in 9 of 11 regional structures. Negro Project Supervisors were used throughout the country. By 1943, when the NYA program was coming to an end, blacks made up approximately 10 percent of the total staff engaged in administrative, supervisory, technical, clerical, and other functions of the agency.

119.4. There are six series of Bethune records. The **general subject file of the Director, 1936–41** (1 ft.), arranged alphabetically by subject, concerns subjects such as applications for jobs within the Division, addresses and speeches, press releases, aviation training, proposed Negro projects, the New England Conference of Colored Youth, publications about Negro youth, Negro college aid, and bibliographies of research materials concerning black youths. The file of **early "inactive" correspondence, 1935–38** (5 in.), arranged by subject, includes information under headings such as "Adult Education," "Community Organizations," "Unemployed Women," "Meetings with Negro Leaders," and "Federal Arts Program." The Division submitted its **final report** in **1943** (2 in). It is arranged in two parts: part I, Historical Background of Negro Youths, 1930–40, and part II, the National Youth Administration. Part II gives the history of the Division, and the final chapter, "Evaluation of the NYA Program for Negroes," assesses its accomplishments. The **Director's file of correspondence and reports on Negro conferences, 1935–41** (1 ft.), arranged by subject, consists of material on a variety of subjects. There is information about the February 1937 NYA Conference for Negro State Administrative Assistants and Members of State Advisory Committees, with related background materials. There is also correspondence about the Second National Conference on the Problems of the Negro and Negro Youth. National defense meetings were frequent, and the Division collected data pertaining to black participation in the war effort. There are also several folders of reference materials on projects for black youths as well as some tables and bar graphs of statistics about them, which were used in exhibits. The **miscellaneous file of research and publicity materials, 1935–41** (5 in.), arranged by subject, includes press releases, publications about black youths (some of the publications were prepared by the Division), and correspondence and reports from which information was gathered for publications. The **Director's file of reports of State directors of Negro affairs, 1936–39** (2 ft.), is arranged in three chronological segments—1936–37, 1937–38, and 1938–39—and thereunder alphabetically by State. The reports include information about staff and other administrative matters, projects for black youths, and other State-related matters.

Records of the Deputy Executive Director and the Deputy Administrator

119.5. Several series among the records of Deputy Executive Director Richard Brown and the Deputy Administrator include information about black history. For example, **Brown's miscellaneous alphabetic-name correspondence, 1935–41** (40 ft.), arranged by subject, contains a folder labeled "Dr. Harvey," the contents of which include an April 8, 1936, memorandum entitled "Negro Representation on Relief," and other memorandums and reports scattered throughout the series contain additional information. The series of **correspondence with NYA State directors concerning projects, 1935–38** (13 ft.), and the **administrative reports received from NYA State offices, 1935–38** (24 ft.), both arranged alphabetically by State, include information about black personnel in State offices and about projects conducted for black youths. Also among the records are the **working and data files of an NYA history project, 1935–43** (33 ft.). The records are arranged by subject. One subject is the "Negro Program" (1½ ft.). The records gathered for the history of this program are mostly publications, some of which were published by NYA, and correspondence and reports that relate principally to NYA projects for black youths and black personnel in the Administration.

Records of the Office of Information

119.6. The information section of this Office presented the NYA program to the public. The picture files (approximately 300 items) depict the activities of black youth in various projects, such as shop, domestic, and scientific training. Several films were produced to support and encourage participation in the agency's programs. In the "National Youth Administration and Negro Youth," 1940 (#119.11), many blacks formerly on relief are shown receiving training and assistance in NYA projects in Dorchester, Ga., and at Georgia State College. Another film, "Youth-Building at Wilberforce," 1939 (#119.13), shows Mary McLeod Bethune approving Wilberforce University as a resident project center and students at various occupational tasks.

Other Records

119.7. Other offices at NYA also include information pertinent to black history. Among the records of the Student Project Planning Section of the Division of Student Works are **tables summarizing data concerning black applicants for NYA student aid, 1937** (2 ft.), arranged alphabetically by State. The **records summarizing allocations of funds to student-aid programs, 1935–43** (10 in.), arranged chronologically and thereunder by State, include statistics in most of the reports about student-aid programs for black youths. Some records pertaining to black history are scattered among the records of the regional offices. For example, several folders entitled "National Negro Affairs" (totaling ¼ in.) are among the **correspondence of the Region 3 Youth Administrator, 1942–43** (3 ft.), arranged alphabetically by subject.

119.8. Among the **NYA publications file, 1935–42 (82 ft.),** arranged alphabetically by State, are the "Proceedings of the Second National Conference on the Problems of the Negro and Negro Youth," January 1939 (123 pp.), and reports and pamphlets about black youths in Florida, Georgia, Illinois, Indiana, Louisiana, New Jersey, North Carolina, Ohio, South Carolina, Texas, and West Virginia. A few of the titles are "Job Opportunities for Negro Youth in Columbus Ohio," by Chester J. Gray, June 1938 (87 pp.); "Achievements by Negro Youth of South Carolina," by A. Cecile Johnson, n.d. (21 pp.); and "The Atlanta Negro . . .," by Joseph A. Pierce, June 1940 (136 pp.). The Georgia publications include eight bulletins that were published by the "Colored Division" of the State NYA.

119.9. Among the records created during the liquidation of the NYA are **final reports of 46 State NYA offices dating to July 1943** (3 ft.), arranged alphabetically by State. Many of these give descriptions of projects for black youths or including black youths. Some give information about black personnel.

Record Group 121

Records of the Public Buildings Service

121.1. The Public Buildings Service (PBS) designs, constructs, manages, maintains, and protects most federally owned and leased buildings. It is also responsible for the acquisition, utilization, and custody of General Services Administration real and related personal property. The still pictures, 1855–1966 (120,000 items), include photographs of the hundreds of murals painted for Government buildings by artists commissioned by the PBS, largely during the Depression years, some of which deal with various aspects of black history. A great percentage are repetitious, usually following the format of stylized depictions of working black fieldhands, but some are genuinely valuable artworks on phases of the black experience in the United States. A few of the artworks are by black artists.

This post office in Monroe, La., was built near the end of the 19th century. Date and photographer unknown. RG 121, Records of the Public Buildings Service. (121-C-13J-2).

Record Group 123
Records of the U.S. Court of Claims

123.1. The U.S. Court of Claims was established by an act of February 24, 1855, to hear claims against the United States based on any law of Congress, regulation of an executive department, or contract with the Government, express or implied, including all claims referred to the court by Congress. Under this act the court was only a factfinding agency, and its conclusions were submitted to Congress for approval and for the granting of awards. In 1863 Congress enlarged the court's jurisdiction and gave it authority to render judgments against the Government, with the right of appeal to the Supreme Court. An act of 1925 abolished appeals from the Court of Claims to the Supreme Court and substituted writs of certiorari. Litigation before the court arises under legislation that confers to it either permanent or temporary jurisdiction. The court has permanent jurisdiction in general jurisdiction cases, which concern claims brought directly by claimants under general provisions of law, and in congressional and departmental cases, which concern claims referred by Congress or by executive departments. It has had temporary jurisdiction in District of Columbia cases, French spoliation cases, and Indian depredation cases. Some blacks brought cases before this court.

123.2. Predominant among cases referred to this court by Congress were those growing out of the Civil War. These concern claims resulting from the seizure of stores, supplies, and cotton by Union forces during the war; claims resulting from the occupation of and damages to real estate by Union forces; claims for differences of pay between that of grade in which military service was rendered and that of grade in which pay was received; claims of Indian freedmen; and claims for unpaid balances of bounties for military service. These case files include claims by or about black people. The claims made by blacks generally have "Col'd" after the name. Many of the cases filed by southerners include information about slavery and plantation life during and after the Civil War. The **case files, 1884–1952** (722 ft.), arranged by case number, may contain letters of reference from congressional committees to the Court of Claims transmitting petitions for investigation and determination of facts, with accompanying copies of congressional bills and resolutions, memorials, and other pertinent papers; orders referring claims to the commissioners; and petitions, answers, and other pleadings, motions, briefs (a great many on loyalty), depositions, affidavits, interrogatories, orders (including those remanding cases), findings on loyalty, findings of facts and opinions of the court, and summary reports of Commissioners.

123.3. Records of the Court of Claims Section (Justice), RG 205, include material relating to the defense by the United States of the claims described in paragraph 123.2. See also records of the Southern Claims Commission in RG 217, Records of the U.S. General Accounting Office.

Record Group 126

Records of the Office of Territories

126.1. The Office of Territories was established in 1950 by administrative order of the Secretary of the Interior to carry out certain of his responsibilities pertaining to areas under U.S. jurisdiction but noncontiguous to the United States. The Office is concerned with the development of the economic, social, and political life of the Territories and with the advancement of international peace and security through the close coordination of Territorial affairs with the defense and foreign policies of the United States. Before 1873, it was a function of the Secretary of State to serve as the channel through which officers of the Territorial governments communicated with the Government in Washington, but in 1873 these powers and duties were transferred to the Secretary of the Interior.

126.2. The **central classified files, 1907–51** (608 ft.), arranged according to a file classification scheme, include scattered materials relating to black history. The files for Alaska contain proposals by the United Congo Improvement Association to set up a colony in Alaska for black families on relief in the late 1930's. The president of the association was Joe T. Thomas, who was based in Cleveland, Ohio. He proposed that the colony be established on the Kenai Peninsula. The folder for the United Congo Improvement Association (#9–1–60, 1 in.) includes a petition supporting the establishment of the colony signed by hundreds of people, maps that probably were drawn by Thomas, and correspondence relating to the project.

126.3. The records relating to the Virgin Islands (#9–11) include some correspondence and reports of William H. Hastie, a black judge who was appointed Governor of the Virgin Islands by President Harry S Truman in 1946. Hastie served until 1949.

Record Group 128

Records of Joint Committees of Congress

128.1. Joint standing committees are created infrequently by the two Houses of Congress; select joint committees are created more frequently, sometimes for investigative or ceremonial purposes. The records of joint committees are similar to those of standing and select committees of the Senate and of the House of Representatives and consist, in general, of correspondence of chairmen, correspondence and memorandums of staff members, transcripts of hearings, exhibits, committee reports, and petitions and memorials.

128.2. Some of the joint committees, particularly those that were established during the Civil War period, include information about slavery and the condition of freedmen. During the 38th and 39th Congresses (1863–67) there was a Joint Committee on the Conduct of the War. From the 39th through the 41st Congresses (1865–71) some members met in the Joint Committee on Reconstruction. **Joint Committees To Inquire into the Condition of the States Which Formed the So-Called Confederated States of America** (the Insurrectionary States) were formed **during the 39th (1865–67) and 42d (1871–73) Congresses.** The records for each of these joint committees (totaling about 6 in.) include reports, correspondence, and petitions. They describe some of the war conditions and the resulting problems between blacks and whites. There are petitions asking for equal legal and political rights for all Americans regardless of color. The joint committees made recommendations for various types of legislation, including provisions for the protection of freedmen in general and black voters in particular.

Record Group 129

Records of the Bureau of Prisons

129.1. The Bureau of Prisons was established in the Department of Justice by an act of May 14, 1930. To it were transferred the personnel, records, and duties of the Superintendent of Prisons, who had been responsible for Federal prison matters since 1907. The Bureau is responsible for the administration of Federal penal and correctional institutions and for Federal prisoners in non-Federal institutions. A central Board of Parole, also established in 1930 with authority in parole matters over all Federal prisoners, succeeded separate boards of parole for each institution housing Federal prisoners. Records about black prisoners are scattered throughout the records, although there were some institutions that primarily housed blacks and some that had segregated cell blocks for black prisoners.

129.2. The administrative files of the Bureau of Prisons were originally part of the classified subject files of the Department of Justice central files. After their transfer to the Bureau of Prisons, the records were continued under their original filing system until the adoption of a new system in 1938. Included among the **administrative files** is **Class 4 (prison matters), 1930–37** (570 ft.), arranged according to a file classification scheme. There is an alphabetical **name index** to the files, **1930–38** (8 ft.). On each card is a brief statement about the content of the letter. Few cards specifically mention blacks. One institution that primarily served blacks was the National Training School for Girls in Washington, D.C. (#4–7–9–2, ¼ in.). In 1926 this institution held 98 girls: 83 black girls, 3 black infants, and 12 white girls. Attempts were being made to send the white girls to another institution.

129.3. Jail inspection reports from Indiana, Massachusetts, Oregon, and South Carolina, 1931–46 (4 ft.), are arranged by State. The standard form for the report includes a question about whether the prisoners of different races were segregated. The reports for South Carolina include some narrative statements about the care of black prisoners.

Record Group 130
Records of the White House Office

130.1. The White House Office was established by an Executive order in 1939 as one of the five divisions of the Executive Office of the President. In addition to serving the President by performing many detailed activities, it maintains communication with Congress, individual Members of Congress, heads of executive agencies, the press, and the general public. In addition to records of the White House Office, this record group includes records maintained by various White House offices and officials before 1939 that were not regarded as personal papers of the Presidents.

130.2. The records include various appointment registers that give information about black appointees. It is necessary to know the name of the appointee. For example, the **registers of appointments made by the President to the States, 1857–1912** (11 vols., 4 ft.), arranged chronologically, include an entry for March 4, 1869, stating that John Mercer Langston of the District of Columbia had been appointed a member of the Board of Public Health. He was nominated March 2, 1871, and commissioned March 15, 1871. The **registers of appointments made by the President to diplomatic and military positions, 1861–1912** (11 vols., 4 ft.), include a March 4, 1877, entry stating that Langston had been appointed Minister Resident and Consul General to Haiti. He was nominated October 16, 1877, and commissioned October 30, 1877.

130.3. Among the audio documents of the White House Office is President Harry S Truman's address at the commencement exercise at Howard University on June 13, 1952 (#130.30). Truman devoted a substantial part of his speech to a detailed review of his administration's visions, programs, and accomplishments in the civil rights field during the period 1947–52.

Record Group 134
Records of the Interstate Commerce Commission*

134.1. The Interstate Commerce Commission (ICC) was created in 1887 to regulate, in the public interest, common carriers engaged in transportation, interstate commerce, and foreign commerce to the extent that it takes place within the United States. It is now responsible for promoting safe, adequate, economical, and efficient service in all modes of transportation subject to its authority; encouraging the establishment and maintenance of reasonable charges for transportation services, without unjust discriminations or unfair competitive practices; requiring carriers and freight forwarders to file and publish rates, rules, and regulations concerning interstate traffic; and fostering the development, coordination, and preservation of a national transportation system adequate for postal service, the national defense, and U.S. commerce.

134.2. The **formal case files, 1887–1924** (5,456 ft.), are arranged by assigned docket number and indexed alphabetically by name of carrier, subject, or correspondent. The case files relate to conditions on common carriers, rates charged for services, and matters involving complaint and answer proceedings, ex parte proceedings of the Commission, and proceedings based on carrier applications for relief under provisions of the various interstate commerce acts. A typical case file includes a complaint containing the name of the parties at dispute and the nature of the controversy, a motion of the Commission for investigation or a petition of a carrier for relief, a statement of facts, exhibits, official transcripts of testimony, reports, correspondence, telegrams, other legal documents and papers, and the order of decision of the Commission. The **alphabetical card index to the case files, 1887–1950** (300 ft.), includes entries under "Colored Passengers" and "Negroes." Most of these relate to separate but equal train facilities and Jim Crow cars. Two examples are an 1887 discrimination case (3 in.) brought against the Western and Atlantic Railroad Co. by William H. Councill and a 1909 discrimination case (6 in.) brought by Wesley J. Gaines et al. against the Seaboard Air Line Railway Co.

134.3. The **general correspondence of the Operating Division, 1887–1906** (110 ft.), is arranged according to a numeric system in which a common number was assigned to each incoming letter, its reply, and attachments. In the **alphabetical subject index** to this correspondence, **1887–1906** (11 ft.), arranged alphabetically by name of carrier, subject, or correspondent, are several entries under "Colored Passengers."

134.4. Among the records of the Bureau of Enforcement (or its predecessor) is a series of **closed cases on racial discrimination by motor carriers in interstate commerce and investigation reports by ICC field representatives, 1961–70** (15 ft.), arranged by assigned number. The case files are numbered RD–0 through RD–310. These cases grew out of alleged racial discrimination on buses and in depot waiting rooms, washrooms, and restaurants, The complaints were usually made to ICC field representatives by blacks in the South, including the "Freedom Riders," some as early as 1958. The complaints were forwarded to the Bureau of Enforcement in Washington, where the files were maintained. In many instances the matter was referred to the Department of Justice for appropriate action. However, these investigative report case files consist of complaints that the Commission chose not to prosecute. The files consist of correspondence, reports, legal briefs, photographs, diagrams, and press clips.

* *Restrictions may apply to this Record Group. Consult NARS staff.*

Record Group 135
Records of the Public Works Administration

135.1. The Public Works Administration (PWA), established originally as the Federal Emergency Administration of Public Works by the National Industrial Recovery Act of 1933, was created to prepare and help construct and finance a comprehensive public works program. In 1939 PWA became a part of the Federal Works Agency (see RG 162), and in 1943 PWA powers and functions were transferred for liquidation to the Office of the Federal Works Administrator. Most of the general classified correspondence before 1941 and some divisional records were destroyed in 1943.

135.2. Although a number of issues about black labor and housing were raised with the PWA, records regarding these matters are difficult to find. Individual work projects can be located by geographical site and date. Some of the housing projects for blacks can be identified because they were named after famous figures in black history. One useful file is among **Division of Investigation case files, 1933–41** (11 ft.), which are arranged in numerical order by the number assigned to each case file. File A. F. 375 (1 in.) is entitled "Discrimination against Negro Workers on Certain PWA Projects in Illinois." The evidence in the case chiefly consists of affidavits of black union bricklayers who were denied jobs on PWA projects on the grounds that no blacks were wanted or that there were no jobs available at the time. The report gives several project numbers for the Chicago metropolitan area and discusses the attitude toward blacks held by the employers on these projects and the policies of the unions. The case file includes a September 23, 1933, letter from Harold L. Ickes, Administrator of PWA, to the State engineers for the PWA. In it he states that on work projects there should be "no discrimination exercised against any person because of color or religious affiliation." File A. F. 375 includes lengthy statements of the complaints, conclusions, recommendations, and signed statements by blacks who attempted to obtain work on various PWA projects in the Chicago area.

135.3. For the period 1933–39 there are approximately 10 items in the PWA photographic files that document housing developments for blacks in Birmingham and Miami as well as schools constructed for black children in Independence, Mo., and Chattanooga and Memphis.

135.4. See also RG 48, Records of the Office of the Secretary of the Interior; RG 183, Records of the Bureau of Employment Security; and RG 196, Records of the Public Housing Administration.

Record Group 144

Records of the Temporary National Economic Committee*

144.1. The Temporary National Economic Committee (TNEC) was created by a joint resolution of Congress in June 1938 to study monopoly and concentration of economic power and to make recommendations for legislation. The TNEC was composed of Members of both Houses of Congress and representatives of several executive departments and commissions. Information was obtained largely from hearings and special studies that were conducted by participating agencies or by the TNEC staff. Extensive investigations of insurance, investment banking, and corporate practices were conducted by the Securities and Exchange Commission, one of the participating agencies. The Committee was abolished in April 1941.

144.2. There is some information about black businesses interspersed among these records. For example, the **preliminary questionnaires sent to legal reserve life insurance companies by the Securities and Exchange Commission, 1938–41** (102 ft.), arranged alphabetically, include information about some black insurance companies, such as the Afro-American Life Insurance Co. and the North Carolina Mutual Life Insurance Co. Each file includes a questionnaire, exhibits, the annual statement for 1937, and some correspondence.

* *Restrictions may apply to this Record Group. Consult NARS staff.*

Record Group 145

Records of the Agricultural Stabilization and Conservation Service

145.1. The Agricultural Stabilization and Conservation Service had its beginnings in the Agricultural Adjustment Administration (AAA), established in the Department of Agriculture under the Agricultural Adjustment Act of May 12, 1933. The AAA administered aid to farmers through programs and parity payments designed to conserve soil resources, stabilize

Billie and wife Caroline McKenzie arrive in Miami and await transportation to Belle Glade, where they will work in harvest fields. April 11, 1943. Pace, photographer. RG 145, Records of the Agricultural Stabilization and Conservation Service. (145-AAA-8492).

market prices of farm products, and bring about an equitable relationship between incomes of farmers and nonfarm groups. In 1943 the AAA was transferred to the War Food Administration. The Production and Marketing Administration, established in 1945, assumed most functions of the War Food Administration. In 1953 the Production and Marketing Administration was designated the Commodity Stabilization Service, which was renamed the Agricultural Stabilization and Conservation Service on June 5, 1961. Many black farmers were very interested in the assistance programs administered by these agencies. The records described below document the relationship between the AAA and black farmers.

145.2. The general records of the AAA include **central correspondence files, 1933–47** (1,400 ft.), arranged in chronological periods and thereunder alphabetically by initial letter of surname of correspondent. The records for the 1933–35 period include folders entitled "Negro" (¼ in.) and "Tuskegee Institute" (⅛ in.). The correspondence pertains to the participation of the black population in the AAA program and to various other agricultural matters. There is a Tuskegee Institute publication entitled *Tuskegee's Service in National Recovery* (18 pp.).

145.3. The 1936–38 period of the central correspondence files includes folders labeled "Tuskegee" (½ in.), "Associated Negro Press" (¼ in.), and "Negro" (½ in.); there are also individual folders for three black field officers in the Southern Division of the AAA—Jennie B. Moton (1 in.), Albon L. Holsey (3 in.), and James P. Davis (5 in.). These files relate to a wide variety of subjects, such as the education of black farmers and black extension agents. The files include speeches and information about conferences and meetings with black farmers. There is also correspondence with several black AAA officials, including the three field officers named above, Frederick D. Patterson of Tuskegee Institute, and Claude A. Barnett of the Associated Negro Press, who also worked with AAA. These records pertain to their daily activities as liaisons with black farmers, to studies of landlord-tenant issues and blacks, and to the effects of the agricultural conservation program on cooperating black farmers. There are some materials relating to the film "The Negro Farmer."

145.4. A 1939–42 folder in the central correspondence files for the Associated Negro Press (¼ in.) contains correspondence with Claude A. Barnett about the production of the film "Henry Brown, Farmer" (#16–665), information about the American Negro Exposition in Chicago in 1940, and materials used for speeches and publicity about the effectiveness of AAA programs among black farmers.

145.5. The **subject correspondence files, 1933–38** (91 ft.), are arranged in chronological periods and thereunder alphabetically by subject. For the 1933–35 period there is a file folder entitled "Negro" (¼ in.) that contains material pertaining to the participation of the black population in Depression-recovery programs, with special emphasis on the work of the AAA. There is also a folder "Negro" (½ in.) for the 1936–38 period. It contains material pertaining to AAA public relations with the black community; black employees of AAA, such as Albon L. Holsey and James P. Davis; the travel of AAA employees to disseminate information about the AAA; meetings and conferences with black farmers; and the soil conservation program and black farm owners.

Record Group 146

Records of Federal Civil Service Agencies

146.1. The U.S. Civil Service Commission was created in 1871 as the Advisory Board of the Civil Service. The Commission was authorized to establish a merit system under which selections for Government service appointments would be based on applicants' demonstrated relative fitness. It examined applicants for Federal positions; supplied personnel officials with qualified candidates' names; established standards for reinstating, promoting, and transferring Federal employees; conducted investigations to enforce Civil Service laws and regulations; studied the administration of the Government security program; and administered the Veterans Preference Act of 1944, the Classification Act of 1949, the Government Employees Incentive Awards Act, the Civil Service Retirement Act, the Voting Rights Act of 1965, and the statutory provisions and Civil Service regulations that restrict Federal employee political activity. In 1979 many of the functions of the Civil Service Commission were transferred to the Office of Personnel Management.

146.2. The **records relating to the 1965 Voting Rights Act, 1965–72** (40 ft.), are arranged by subject. The Commission was given the responsibility of overseeing voter registration in key political subdivisions in the South. Many of the registrants were black. The records include statistical reports of examiners, who were usually Federal employees in the affected State and who had been appointed by the Commission to examine applicants and list those eligible to vote. The lists indicate whether the voter was white or black and literate or illiterate. Some of the records are reports of observers who watched newly registered voters casting their ballots.

Record Group 151

Records of the Bureau of Foreign and Domestic Commerce and Successor Agencies

151.1. The Bureau of Foreign and Domestic Commerce was created in the Department of Commerce and Labor in 1912 to promote the development of U.S. commerce and industry by compiling and distributing information on domestic and foreign trade, manufacturing, and markets. Five major offices were formed within the Bureau in 1945: the Offices of International Trade, Small Business, Domestic Commerce, Business Economics, and Field Service.

151.2. Most of the records compose the **central file, 1914–58** (847 ft.), arranged primarily by topics, commodities, and geographic areas by use of a decimal classification system. The major category labeled "Negro, 1927–50" (#402.10, 3 in.) gives information about black business conference arrangements, business education, and the services of the

Bureau to black business; hotel availability, insurance policies, and theater accommodations for blacks; and general economic conditions for the black community. Much of this material is for the years 1927 and 1928. There are indexes to the central file.

151.3. The Negro Affairs Division was established November 1, 1933, to collect and disseminate factual material on black businesses, make special studies on black businesses and economic subjects, contact black groups, and issue bulletins and economic publications bearing on commerce and trade affecting the black population. Correspondence in the file labeled "Negro Affairs Division," 1937–40 (#160.2, ⅛ in.), deals with administrative changes and appointments within the Division.

151.4. See also RG 40, General Records of the Department of Commerce.

Record Group 155

Records of the Wage and Hour and Public Contracts Divisions

155.1. The Wage and Hour Division was established in the Department of Labor to administer the wage and hour provisions of the Fair Labor Standards Act of 1938. The act establishes minimum wage, overtime compensation, equal pay, and child labor standards for persons employed in interstate or foreign commerce, in the production of goods for such commerce, and for certain other activities. The Public Contracts Division was created in the Labor Department to administer the Walsh-Healey Public Contracts Act of 1936, which required Government supply contracts exceeding $10,000 to stipulate minimum wage, overtime pay, nonemployment of child and convict labor, and safety and health standards. The two Divisions were consolidated into the Wage and Hour and Public Contracts Division in 1942. In 1971 the organization was placed under the newly created Employment Standards Administration and was renamed the Wage and Hour Division.

155.2. Among the **records of the Wage and Hour Division, 1938–42** (80 ft.), arranged by type of industry, are the files of 41 industry committees, including the Puerto Rico Industry Committee. The files contain transcripts of hearings, briefs, exhibits, and recommendations on minimum wages and maximum hours, 1938–42. Economic information about black workers is included in the records of the tobacco, gray-iron jobbing foundry, clay products, bus and train, and pulp and primary paper industries. Other industries that were investigated in which blacks were

Man working in the foundry of a large midwest machine tool plant. Massive chains like this were used for handling heavy flasks and finished castings. January 1942. Palmer, photographer. RG 208, Records of the Office of War Information. (208-NP-3A-1).

employed in large numbers were rubber products manufacturing, lumber and timber products, Puerto Rican needle-work, and fabric and leather industries. There are also hearings on regulations governing the employers of "Red Caps" (railroad station porters).

Record Group 157

Records of the Maritime Labor Board

157.1. The Maritime Labor Board (1938–42) was established to strengthen the development of the U.S. merchant marine by improving labor relations in the maritime industry. Included among the records is some information about the effects of segregation and discrimination on black workers in the maritime industry and about disputes arising out of the unwillingness of white seamen to work with blacks. Some reports discuss the condition of black maritime workers, especially longshoremen in Southern States.

157.2. The **classified general file, 1938–42** (56 ft.), is arranged according to a decimal classification scheme. Category 095, "Company Files," arranged alphabetically by name of company, includes copies of collective bargaining agreements and the official record of any Board mediation cases in which the company was involved. Scattered throughout the company files is information about black workers. For example, the collective bargaining agreement of the Merchants and Stevedores Association of Pensacola, Fla., stipulates that "the work shall be divided equally between white and colored associations on a 50/50 basis." Several other companies with such agreements were Norton, Lilly and Co. of New Orleans, La.; Clyde Wallog of Galveston, Tex.; and Luchenback Gulf of Texas and Lake Charles. Among the records are 82 unpublished studies and reports, some of which give specific information about black workers. For example, study 58, "Operation of the NMU Hiring-Hall in New York City" (14 pp.), provides information about the difference in hiring practices for black and white workers.

Record Group 162

General Records of the Federal Works Agency

162.1. The Federal Works Agency was created by the President's Reorganization Plan No. 1 of 1939, which transferred to it the Public Buildings Administration, the Public Roads Administration, the Public Works Administration, the Work Projects Administration, and the U.S. Housing Authority (USHA). The Federal Works Agency was abolished by an act of 1949, and most of its functions were transferred to the General Services Administration.

162.2. The general records of the Federal Works Agency include **correspondence of John Carmody, the Administrator of the Agency, 1939–41** (5 ft.), arranged alphabetically by name of correspondent. His files include a few letters under "NAACP" and "Walter White" pertaining to NAACP charges of "gross discrimination" in housing projects, discrimination in the cafeterias in public buildings, and other matters.

162.3. The **correspondence of Administrators with smaller Federal agencies, 1939–42** (1 ft.), arranged by name of agency, includes a folder entitled "National Housing Agency—Federal Public Housing Authority (Formerly USHA Sojourner Truth Project)" (2 in.). The folder includes letters and telegrams, reports, and a few clippings about the controversial Sojourner Truth Housing project in Detroit, Mich. Because there was a ban on tearing down houses during the war period, the only space available for this housing project for black defense workers was near a Polish Catholic community. The white community began to oppose the anticipated movement of blacks into the community as the housing project neared its completion. The materials in this file represent both sides of the controversy and include some handwritten letters.

162.4. The **correspondence of Administrator Phillip B. Fleming, 1942–45** (7 ft.), arranged alphabetically by subject or name of correspondent, also includes a folder on the Sojourner Truth Housing project (½ in.). This folder contains the transcript of a meeting between Federal Works Agency officials and a black-led delegation of Detroit activists on February 11, 1942. There is some correspondence with Eleanor Roosevelt. She wrote from the White House on January 24, 1942: "The colored people originally protested this site and the Housing Authority concurred. What has happened to make it more suitable since that decision?" She also asked why the whites were "so slow" in registering their protests. Acting Administrator Baird Snyder replied on January 31, 1942, that the black defense workers felt that "they were in a class of colored society above that of the slum clearance dweller," and the whites were slow in stating their protests because the use of the site "was rather played down" by the USHA.

Record Group 164

Records of the Office of Experiment Stations

164.1. The Office of Experiment Stations was established in the Department of Agriculture on October 1, 1888, to popularize the results of agricultural experiments and to disseminate scientific information among experiment stations created under the Hatch Act of 1887. The Office also promoted agricultural education, administered experiment stations in Alaska and the insular possessions, and conducted investigations concerning irrigation, nutrition, and drainage. In 1915 the Office was combined with other offices carrying out extension and home economics work to form the States Relations Service. When that Service was abolished in 1923, the Office of Experiment Stations resumed its separate identity.

164.2. The **general correspondence with State experiment stations and agricultural colleges, 1888–1937** (29 ft.), is arranged alphabetically by State and thereunder alphabetically by name of correspondent. The correspondence for Alabama includes some letters to and from George Washington Carver, the director of the Agriculture and Experiment Station at Tuskegee Normal and Industrial Institute.

Record Group 171

Records of the Office of Civilian Defense

171.1. The Office of Civilian Defense (OCD) was established in the Office for Emergency Management by an Executive order of May 20, 1941, to coordinate Federal, State, and local defense relationships regarding the protection of civilians during air raids and other emergencies and to facilitate civilian participation in war programs. The nine regional offices that coordinated the work of State and local defense organizations were closed in 1944, and an Executive order terminated the OCD in 1945.

171.2. The **central file of OCD, 1941–42 (55 ft.),** arranged by a numeric filing scheme, includes a folder entitled "Negroes in Defense" (#280, 3 in.). Many of the records in this folder were generated by Crystal Bird Fauset, a black woman who had served in the Pennsylvania Legislature but came to Washington, D.C., to be Director of the Racial Relations Division of OCD from 1941 to 1944. The records include telegrams and correspondence about the 1941 march on Washington proposed by black labor leader A. Philip Randolph, the establishment of the Committee on Fair Employment Practice (FEPC), and civil defense training for black youths. There is correspondence with Walter H. White of the NAACP; A. Philip Randolph, who was the head of the Negro March on Washington Committee; President Roosevelt; Eleanor Roosevelt; members of the Black Cabinet, such as Frank S. Horne at the U.S. Housing Authority, Robert C. Weaver at the Office of Production Management, and William J. Trent of the Federal Works Agency; and black aviatrix Willa Brown. There are numerous applications for jobs in Government defense agencies, and many invitations for Fauset to speak. Other materials pertain to housing for single black men and women who were working with Government defense agencies and to recreational facilities for black soldiers. There are a number of form letters sent out by William Alexander, who worked as an information specialist in the Racial Relations Division. There were racial relations officers in some of the regional offices of OCD. In an April 13, 1942, memorandum from Jonathan Daniels to Fauset, Daniels reported that $120,000 in salaries was paid for OCD "Race Advisors."

171.3. Much of the correspondence between Fauset and the regional racial relations officers is included in the **regional file, 1941–42** (32 ft.), arranged by region, thereunder by States, and thereunder by decimal filing system. For each region where there was a racial relations officer, there is a file on blacks (#280, totaling for all regions about 8 in.). The records pertain to local civil defense training, political matters, blacks and the war effort, community problems, and public reaction to OCD's policies.

171.4. The **OCD central file, 1942–45** (73 ft.), arranged alphabetically, includes folders entitled "Racial Relations" (4 in.), which contain the correspondence of Fauset, Alexander, and others pertaining to the development of local protection programs, such as air raid shelters, fire protection, and the mobilization of volunteers for war activities as well as numerous other subjects.

171.5. The **miscellaneous records of the Division of Federal-State Cooperation, 1941–44** (10 in.), arranged by subject, include reports to the Racial Relations Division from Pauline Redmond (½ in.). Redmond was a racial relations specialist and Associate Director, Division of Youth Activities. These are field reports prepared by Redmond after traveling to various parts of the country to attend conferences held by blacks or to give speeches about OCD concerns.

171.6. The Division of Federal-State Cooperation prepared **war-impact area studies, 1943–44** (2 ft.). They are arranged alphabetically by State. These reports include information about the history of the community, reports about congested production and racial tension areas, and data pertaining to employment, housing, health care, population, and war contracts.

171.7. Newspaper clippings collected by the Public Counsel Division, 1942–44 (13 ft.), arranged numerically, include a folder on race relations (#14G, ¼ in.). The folder contains clippings that give some information about the black community's response to OCD and that report about various race riots and other local community problems.

171.8. The records of OCD include sound recordings pertaining to black Americans. Black attitudes toward World War II is the subject of a radio program in the series "You and the War" (#171.45), presented by the Fifth Region Civilian Defense Headquarters at Columbus, Ohio, which was broadcast to the Ohio, Kentucky, Indiana, and West Virginia areas on March 29, 1942. In addition, there is a dramatization of the life of Booker T. Washington (#171.53) that uses dramatic sketches and musical excerpts to provide a sound portrait of the educator's lifework.

Record Group 173

Records of the Federal Communications Commission

173.1. The Federal Communications Commission (FCC) was established by the Communications Act of 1934 to regulate radio broadcasting and interstate and foreign communications by radio and wire. Under the creating act, the FCC succeeded the Federal Radio Commission, established in 1927, and also acquired functions of the Postmaster General in fixing rates for Government use of wire facilities and certain regulatory functions of the Interstate Commerce Commission. At present the FCC supervises the charges and operating practices of common carriers engaged in interstate or foreign communications, issues broadcasting licenses, assigns broadcast frequencies, classifies radio and television stations and prescribes the nature of their services, and enforces radio requirements for some classes of vessels.

173.2. The FCC records include complaints and cases pertaining to racial issues on radio and television, but they are difficult to find because subject access to the records is limited. There are a few racial complaints that can be located in the **general correspondence file, 1927–71** (about 500 cubic feet), arranged in chronological segments according to a subject-numeric classification scheme. An alphabetical complaints file (#44–3), which is a part of the general correspondence file, includes folders on the "Amos and Andy" show (¼ in.) and a folder about the "Jack Benny" show (2 in.) for the period 1947–56. Both of these folders include some correspondence about racial attitudes.

Record Group 174

General Records of the Department of Labor

174.1. The present Department of Labor was created in 1913 as one of the successor agencies of the Department of Commerce and Labor. Although a Department of Labor had previously existed, it was without Cabinet rank and was the predecessor agency of the Bureau of Labor Statistics. The Department has jurisdiction over matters relating to the welfare of U.S. wage earners, including the improvement of their working conditions and the advancement of profitable employment opportunities. Some of the records relate to the Department's policies toward blacks in the labor force.

General Records

174.2. The **chief clerk's files, 1907–42** (112 ft.), arranged by a subject-numeric filing scheme, contain several folders that relate to black history (#8/102 to #8/102G, #16/38, #150, #20/458, #20/659, and #46/11—totaling about 6 in.). Most of these records relate to the Division of Negro Economics. Secretary of Labor William B. Wilson established this

Division as an emergency wartime office in 1918 to advise him on matters affecting black workers and to outline and direct plans for greater production by black workers for the war effort. The records include numerous letters proposing the establishment of an office such as the Division of Negro Economics and about the appointment of George E. Haynes, a professor at Fisk University, as Director of Negro Economics. Giles B. Jackson, a black attorney from Richmond, Va., was also appointed by Wilson in 1918 to be Chief of the Negro Division of the U.S. Employment Service (USES). There is also information about blacks migrating to the North, race riots, black soldiers' employment after World War I, job discrimination, defense work, and relations between black workers and the Department of Labor.

174.3. The **records of the Division of Negro Economics, 1918–21** (6 in.), arranged alphabetically by name and subject, are incomplete. The records include correspondence and reports about the activities of the Division, conditions of black workers, and race relations. Two major reports were published by the Division: *The Negro Migration, 1916–17,* and *The Negro at Work During the World War and During Reconstruction.* These reports are among the publications of the U.S. Government (see RG 287), but the Division's files do contain some background information for them. Some of the records for the Division were generated by Karl F. Phillips, Haynes' assistant.

Records of the Secretaries of Labor and Their Principal Assistants

174.4. The records of most of the Secretaries of Labor have some information about black history. Information about particular subjects is available in a subject-coded card index that is in the Historian's Office at the Department of Labor in Washington, D.C. The index is arranged by Secretary and thereunder chronologically. Color codes indicate subject. The index begins with the first Secretary and has been consistently updated. Records of some of the earlier Secretaries, which are generally less voluminous than the more recent ones, tend to be indexed in greater detail.

174.5. The **office files of Secretary William B. Wilson, 1913–21** (2 ft.), are arranged according to the same filing scheme as the chief clerk's files. One folder, "Race Riots in East St. Louis," 1917 (#13/65, ¼ in.), includes correspondence with Illinois officials about the riot and the brief *Report by the Illinois State Council of Defense on the Riots at East St. Louis by Its Committee on Labor,* June 30, 1917 (4 pp.).

174.6. The **subject file of Secretary Frances Perkins, 1933–44** (39 ft.), is arranged alphabetically in two parts—1933–40 and 1940–44. The later segment includes three folders entitled "Negro" (totaling 3 in.), which contain correspondence and reports pertaining to various employment problems for blacks, such as job discrimination, organized labor, and defense employment. There is also information about blacks and the National Recovery Administration, housing, the New York World's Fair, the 1940 Negro Exposition in Chicago, meetings with black organizations, black women workers, and blacks in the building trades. Perkins appointed Lawrence A. Oxley as Chief of the newly established Division of Negro Labor in 1934. Some reports and correspondence from Oxley are among these records. The **records of Secretary Perkins relating to the U.S. Employment Service, 1934–39** (2 ft.), arranged chronologically and thereunder alphabetically, include a folder entitled "Lawrence A. Oxley, Special Report, May 23, 1939" (1 in.). This report documents the activities of the Division of Negro Labor for almost 5 years. It contains annual reports, weekly reports, and lists of State Conferences on Employment Problems of the Negro, including some programs, agenda, and related newspaper clippings, papers, and speeches from the conferences. Perkins' materials also include records relating to the War Manpower Commission, 1942–45 (1 ft.), arranged in two parts—one chronologically and the other alphabetically by subject. There is one folder entitled "Negro" (⅛ in.).

174.7. Among the **records of Secretary James P. Mitchell, 1953–60** (100 ft.), arranged by subject, are materials pertaining to minority groups conferences in 1955, 1956, and 1957; the President's Committee on Government Contracts; civil rights and equal rights issues and proposed legislation concerning them; discrimination; segregated Bureau of Employment Security offices; employment policies; the economic status of blacks; the Urban League; unemployment; and Roberta Church, minority groups consultant.

174.8. Among the **records of Secretary Arthur J. Goldberg, 1961–62** (130 ft.), arranged by subject, is information concerning the President's Committee on Equal Opportunity in Employment; discrimination in the areas of recruitment, hiring, training, apprenticeship, promotion, union membership, and youth employment; unemployment; civil rights and antidiscrimination legislation; Government contracts; the 1962 Urban League conference; demographic reports about the black population; black Congressman Adam Clayton Powell, Jr.; and Richard Chapin, minority groups consultant.

174.9. Among the **records of Secretary W. Willard Wirtz, 1962–69** (175 ft.), arranged by subject, are some relating to the President's Committee on Equal Employment Opportunity; employment services to minority groups; discrimination; unemployment; the anniversary of the Emancipation Proclamation; the NAACP National Conference on Negro Employment; military training; youth employment; picketing and demonstrations; civil rights and antidiscrimination legislation and the

This laborer is warehousing cotton in Coosa Valley, Ala. May 1941. Irving Rusinow, photographer. RG 83, Records of the Bureau of Agricultural Economics. (83-A-44419).

passage of the Civil Rights Act of 1964; and Richard Chapin, minority groups consultant.

174.10. The records of **Secretaries George P. Shultz, 1969–70** (89 ft.), **James D. Hodgson, 1970–73** (63 ft.), **Peter J. Brennan, 1973–75** (116 ft.), and **John T. Dunlop, 1975–76** (72 ft.)—all arranged by subject—include material about such black history topics as integration, voting rights, the black family, the Poor People's Campaign, the Equal Employment Opportunity Commission, the Interagency Committee on Minority Enterprise, the National Advisory Commission on Civil Disorders, Government contract compliance, training and apprenticeship, and black elected officials.

174.11. Some of the records of members of the Secretaries' staffs also include information about black history. John J. Gilhooley was an Assistant Secretary of Labor from 1957 to 1960. Some of Gilhooley's records relate to the **International Labor Organization Conference in Geneva, Switzerland,** in **1957** (1 ft.), arranged chronologically; these records include reports relating to discrimination in employment. Gilhooley also collected **records relating to the President's Committee on Government Contracts, 1957–60** (2 ft.), arranged chronologically. This Committee was charged with supervising enforcement of the clause in all Government contracts that prohibited racial discrimination in employment. Secretary of Labor James P. Mitchell was a member of the Committee. These materials include minutes, agenda, staff papers, subcommittee reports, information about cases to be reviewed by the Committee, Committee publications, a published report entitled *Five Years of Progress, 1953–58, A Report to President Eisenhower by the President's Committee on Government Contracts, A Reproduction of Clippings* (which contains a section of clippings from black newspapers), and information about conferences with minority group leaders.

174.12. Millard Cass was a special assistant to the Secretary of Labor in 1953 and Deputy Under Secretary from 1954 to 1960. **Cass' subject files, 1953–60** (35 ft.), arranged alphabetically, include information about blacks under headings such as "Migratory Labor," "Rural Poverty," "Farm Labor," "Nondiscrimination," "Civil Rights," "Civil Disorders," "Demonstrations," "Manpower," and "Construction Work" (particularly the Philadelphia plan for the employment of a quota of black construction workers).

174.13. There are some sound recordings of speeches or interviews given by the Secretaries that include information about black history. A June 12, 1956, press conference with Secretary Mitchell (#174–3) includes information about civil rights legislation and employment of black workers in the Federal Government. Secretary Wirtz gave a press conference on January 31, 1966 (#174–68), which included information about civil rights legislation, and he gave a speech on May 18, 1966 (#174–70), to the Conference of the NAACP Legal Defense and Educational Fund. An excerpt of Wirtz's speech, dated December 5, 1968 (#174–92), gives information about discriminatory employment practices. There is also a recording of the ceremony at the signing of the on-the-job training contract with the Urban League on September 18, 1969, at which both Secretary Wirtz and Whitney M. Young, Jr., of the Urban League were participants (#174–87).

Record Group 176

Records of the Bureau of Human Nutrition and Home Economics

176.1. The Bureau of Human Nutrition and Home Economics began as the Office of Home Economics, established in 1915 when the States Relations Service was organized in the Department of Agriculture. Created to carry out certain provisions of the Smith-Lever Act of 1914 and to continue nutrition studies conducted since 1894 in the Office of Experiment

Stations, the Office was given bureau status in 1923. Its name was changed in 1943 to the Bureau of Human Nutrition and Home Economics. The Bureau conducted research on food, fiber, and other agricultural products; housing and household buying; textiles and clothing; use of income; and household management and equipment. It disseminated information through publications, correspondence, and cooperation with other agencies. On November 2, 1953, the Bureau was abolished and its functions were transferred to the Agricultural Research Service.

176.2. The **general correspondence of the Bureau of Human Nutrition and Home Economics and its predecessors, 1917–39** (171 ft.), arranged in chronological segments and thereunder alphabetically by name or organization of correspondent, includes interspersed materials for black history. For example, the correspondence for 1939 contains some letters from researchers for Gunnar Myrdal's "Negro in America" study pertaining to food consumption of black farm families; correspondence with Ralph Bunche at Howard University, who also worked with the Negro In America study group; and correspondence with Tuskegee and Hampton Institute faculty and students, mostly concerning the schools' requests for publications.

Record Group 183

Records of the Bureau of Employment Security

183.1. The Bureau of Employment Security of the Social Security Board was created in 1939 by merging the U.S. Employment Service (USES), an outgrowth of the job placement function of the Division of Information of the Bureau of Immigration and Naturalization, with the Bureau of Unemployment Compensation, which had been established as an independent agency by the Social Security Act of 1935 to administer the unemployment insurance program. In 1949 the Bureau of Employment Security was transferred to the Department of Labor and was given responsibility for administering veterans' and farm placement services and manpower development and training projects. The Bureau was abolished in 1969 and its functions were assigned to the Office of the Assistant Secretary for Manpower in the Department of Labor.

183.2. Among USES records, those of most importance for black history relate to the work of Lawrence A. Oxley and Karl F. Phillips. Oxley served as Chief of the Division of Negro Labor, 1934–39, and as a field representative of USES, 1937–39. Phillips served as Assistant Director of the Labor Department's Division of Negro Economics, 1918–21 (see RG 174), and as a Commissioner of Conciliation, 1921-33. Oxley also served as a Commissioner of Conciliation in the 1930's. As Commissioners, Phillips and Oxley aided in the adjustment of labor disputes involving black workers. Records of Oxley's and Phillips' activities in all these capacities are filed together in USES records.

183.3. Phillips' alphabetical correspondence file, 1918–33 (1 ft.), pertains mostly to labor disputes, employment problems, and political issues in the black community. Of special interest is his correspondence with Congressman Oscar DePriest of Illinois, who was the first black congressman from a Northern State. Phillips' records include correspondence with A. Philip Randolph of the Brotherhood of Sleeping Car Porters, a newsclipping collection relating to black workers, a report on black immigrants from Latin America, and information about back-to-Africa movements and about the activities of black organizations, such as the Urban League.

183.4. The Division of Negro Labor was created by Secretary of Labor Frances Perkins in 1934 to advise the Department on all matters relating to the black wage earner. **Oxley's correspondence with Government agencies, 1934–38** (2 ft.), arranged by name of agency, includes letters from a group known unofficially as the Black Cabinet. There is correspondence with Alfred Edgar Smith at the Work Projects Administration; Ambrose Caliver of the Office of Education; Eugene Kinckle Jones at the Commerce Department; Robert C. Weaver, who worked for the Federal Coordinator of Transportation; other black Government officials; the Public Works Administration (PWA); the Housing Administration; and other agencies. The correspondence gives information about the impact of the various New Deal programs on blacks.

183.5. Oxley's general correspondence files, 1934–39 (3 ft.), arranged chronologically and thereunder alphabetically by name, include letters from businesses, organizations, and individuals requesting information about Federal Government employment or about Government programs and publications. There are also complaints of discrimination from black applicants for Federal Government employment, questions and complaints about Civil Service examinations, and applications and recommendations for various jobs.

183.6. On July 1, 1937, Oxley's Division was transferred to the USES and he was appointed a field representative, although he also retained his title as Chief of the Division of Negro Labor until 1939. Oxley's duties as field representative were to visit State Employment Service (SES) offices and advise State and local staffs on the placement of black workers, to organize State conferences on the employment problems of black workers, and to handle personnel problems of black employees of SES. **Oxley's**

USES reports file, 1936–39 (2 ft.), arranged alphabetically by State, includes background material for the area in which each SES office was located. The material contains information on housing, employment, availability of work, and the impact of the Depression. The file also includes "Reports on the Availability of the Services of the State Employment Service Offices to Negro Applicants."

183.7. In 1939, when USES was transferred to the Social Security Board, Oxley was appointed Chief of the Negro Placement Service. The **general records of the Negro Placement Service, 1941–42** (5 in.), arranged by subject, consist of surveys of defense training opportunities for black workers and the placement of black workers in defense industries.

183.8. During World War II, when information about manpower availability was essential for defense production, the USES along with the War Manpower Commission (see RG 211) prepared **periodic labor market area reports, 1941–49** (60 ft.), arranged alphabetically by State. The reports include information about the black population, such as size, employment rate, employer discrimination, and conversion to a peacetime economy. In areas where segregation was present, folders sometimes contain separate narrative and statistical reports about the black population. For example, there is a report for Maryland entitled "Utilization of Negro Labor in Baltimore Defense Industries" (4 pp.).

Record Group 185

Records of the Panama Canal

185.1. The Panama Canal—the name of the organization that maintained and operated the canal, including the Government of the Canal Zone from 1914 to 1950—had its beginning in 1895 when the Nicaragua Canal Board was appointed by the President to study the feasibility of completing the Nicaragua Ship Canal begun by the Maritime Canal Company of Nicaragua. Several other boards and commissions made further studies. Under the supervision of the Secretary of War, the second Isthmian Canal Commission directed construction work for the canal and governed the Canal Zone. After several reorganizations, the Commission was abolished in 1914 and its functions and records were transferred to the permanent organization, the Panama Canal. An act of September 26, 1950, changed the name of the organization to the Canal Zone Government and limited its functions to maintaining civil government. Operation and maintenance of the canal were assigned to the Panama Canal Company, which replaced the Panama Railroad Company organized in 1849 to construct and operate a railroad across the isthmus.

185.2. The **general correspondence of the second Isthmian Canal Commission, 1905–14** (186 ft.), arranged according to an alphanumeric classification scheme, includes some records about the employment of black U.S. workers in the building of the canal. The file "Employment of Colored American Citizens" (#2–C–55, ½ in.) includes correspondence pertaining to the salaries of black employees, to questions of whether black employees should be paid in gold or silver, to conflicts between black employees and white or Jamaican workers, to the numbers of blacks employed, and to other employment difficulties. One memorandum indicates that in 1912 there were 44 black Americans with a total salary of $32,520 employed by the Commission and 25 black Americans with a total salary of $24,000 employed by the McClintick-Marshall contractors.

Record Group 188

Records of the Office of Price Administration

188.1. The Office of Price Administration (OPA) became an independent agency in 1942 and was charged with stabilizing wartime prices and rents. It established maximum prices for commodities (except agricultural commodities actually controlled by the Secretary of Agriculture) and maximum rents for defense areas, rationed scarce essential commodities, and authorized subsidies for production of some of the scarce commodities. Most of the price and rationing controls were lifted between August 1945 and November 1946.

Records of the Office of Racial Relations Adviser

188.2. This Office was established in 1943 to encourage participation of minority racial groups in OPA programs and to recommend appropriate action to responsible agency officers. Functions of the Office were transferred in 1944 to other units of the agency, but the special assistant to the Administrator on racial relations was retained in the Administrator's office. T. Arnold Hill was appointed to the position of special assistant in 1943. Frances Williams worked with Hill but had had the title of special assistant as early as 1941.

188.3. The records pertain to monitoring and encouraging the utilization of black workers in OPA as employees and as volunteer members of rationing boards throughout the country. The Office received complaints about disproportionately high prices in black neighborhoods and inequitable administration of rationing. It investigated these complaints and also maintained contact with black organizations and businesses. The

alphabetic subject files, 1941–44 (3 ft.), include such topics as the Methodist Church, NAACP, Urban League, National Association of Colored Graduate Nurses, National Association of Colored Women, and *Chicago Defender*.

188.4. The **regional files, 1941–44** (6 in.), arranged numerically by region, give specific information about price situations in black communities and statistics pertaining to the number of black members on rationing boards or employed by OPA. **T. Arnold Hill's office files, 1941–44** (10 in.), arranged alphabetically by subject, include statistical tables about black employment in OPA with State breakdowns, office memorandums, job descriptions, and information about OPA policies toward blacks in the areas of employment, prices, and rents.

Records of Administrative Management Offices

188.5. Functions of budget, administrative services, and personnel were assigned in 1942 to the Office of General Services, which was divided in November 1942 into the Professional Services Department and the Administrative Management Department, which comprised the Budget and Finance, Personnel, Business Services, and Organization and Planning Divisions.

188.6. The **general records of the office of the Director of Personnel, 1942–47** (7 in.), arranged alphabetically by subject, include a folder on race relations (2 in.). The Director of Personnel was responsible for developing and administering the personnel policy and programs of the agency and for keeping the Administrator advised on the many aspects of personnel management. The folder on race relations includes specific testimony and lists of witnesses for hearings on discrimination against black workers. The **directors memorandums, 1943–44** (3 in.), arranged chronologically, include a report on black housing in Washington, D.C., and a few pieces of correspondence pertaining to discrimination complaints.

188.7. The Program Planning and Administrative Branch was responsible for studying the overall needs of the agency for personnel service and management, supervising the development of programs to meet these needs, evaluating current programs and activities, providing administrative services to the director, and handling personnel matters not clearly a responsibility of the other branches. The **general records, 1942–47** (3 ft.), arranged by subject, include folders pertaining to blacks (3 in.) entitled "FEPC Report," "Negroes–Survey," and "Negro Employment." The Committee on Fair Employment Practice (FEPC) required all Government departments and agencies to make periodic reports as to the number and status of blacks employed within their jurisdictions for presentation to the President. The FEPC file gives detailed information about blacks in OPA, including names and grade classifications. The other two files contain similar information.

188.8. The Training Branch was established in June 1942 to integrate OPA training programs, plans, and policies. The **general records, 1941–47** (17 ft.), arranged by subject, include a folder on race relations (¼ in.). In it, the report "Analysis of Reports on Negro Participation in the Work of the War Price and Rationing Boards, April 30, 1945" documents the participation of 687 blacks on war price and rationing boards. The other materials in the folder consist of policy statements and statistical reports.

188.9. The **general records of the Placement Branch, 1942–46** (1 ft.), arranged by subject, include three folders (¼ in.) about blacks. This Branch was responsible for developing policies, procedures, and techniques for the administration of the placement program; for meeting the personnel requirements of the national and field offices; and for ensuring efficient utilization of OPA personnel procedures. These folders only include a few documents, mostly policy statements and statistical reports pertaining to blacks.

188.10. The Employee Relations Branch, made up of the Health and Employee Services Sections, was responsible for planning and developing employee relations programs in the national office and in the field, formulating and implementing policies that would guarantee maximum participation of employees in matters affecting them individually and collectively, and advising the supervisory staff and individual employees on specific employee-supervisor problems. The **general records, 1941–46** (1 ft.), arranged by subject, include folders entitled "Fair Employment Practice Committee" and "Racial Relations" (totaling about 3 in.). The FEPC folder contains information about specific discrimination complaints, primarily correspondence from the field. The racial relations file includes general correspondence about relationships with the black community and with black employees within OPA. There is a large chart entitled "Distribution of Employees in the Printing and Distribution Branch by Race and Salary Grade, August, 1942 and December 1942–January 1943."

Records of the Information Department

188.11. In cooperation with the operating divisions, this Department formulated and implemented OPA public information and educational policies. It consisted of the Office of the Deputy Administrator for Information, the Field Division, the Program Planning Division, the Editorial Division, and the Community Services Division.

188.12. The Field Division was established on November 2, 1943. In 1944 the *OPA Manual* provided that the Division consist of two branches—the Circulation Planning and Control Branch and the Community Service Branch. The Division was to plan the organization and basic procedures of the information staffs in the field and to develop systems of instruction, reporting, communication, and control. The **records relating to programs, 1943–46** (3 ft.), arranged alphabetically by subject, include the file "Negro" (1 in.), which contains the information program for the black community, clippings from black newspapers, and information about Frances Williams in the Racial Relations Adviser's office. The **regional survey reports, 1945–46** (2 in.), arranged alphabetically by subject, contain information concerning the attitude of the black press toward OPA.

188.13. The Editorial Division was responsible for the preparation, editing, and clearance of all written, printed, and visual materials produced by the Information Department and for the approval of special information materials prepared by the program departments of the OPA and designed for general distribution to the trade. **Newspaper clippings from black newspapers, 1944–45** (5 in.), are arranged according to the following subjects: rent, prices, veterans, local boards, enforcement, personnel, and rationing.

188.14. Among the records of the Men's Section of the Community Services Division are **records relating to black organizations, 1942–45** (3 in.), arranged by subject. These consist of interoffice memorandums, copies of outgoing letters, weekly activity reports of the Section, reports of field trips, and copies of articles submitted to magazines. They are concerned with the scope and effectiveness of the information programs designed for civic, social, and professional groups. **Correspondence with black associations, 1943–46** (2 in.), arranged alphabetically by name of association, relates to national activities of black business, educational, and civic groups in support of OPA wartime control programs.

188.15. The records of the Women's Section of the Community Services Division also include **records relating to black organizations, 1942–46** (3 in.), arranged alphabetically by name of organization. These records are similar to those described for the men's organizations, but also contain information about staff meetings. The files generated by Frances Williams, a black woman, consist of **general correspondence and progress reports, 1943–44** (2 in.). Ann Mason, also black, generated correspondence and reports (1 in.) filed in the records of the Group Services Branch. Some of the organizations contacted by Williams and Mason were Alpha Kappa Alpha Sorority; Ladies Auxiliary to the Brotherhood of Sleeping Car Porters; the *Chicago Defender* Forum; Liberty Park Housing Project, Norfolk, Va.; Delta Sigma Theta Sorority; Joint Council of Dining Car Employees; American Federation of Labor; National Congress of Colored Parents and Teachers; and National Council of Negro Women. There are also some regional reports of OPA activities in black communities throughout the United States.

188.16. Among the OPA publications are **"N" press releases, 1941–44** (1 in.), arranged by release number. These are releases to the black press issued by the OPA through the Office of Emergency Management and the Office of War Information that contain information about black individual and group participation in OPA projects and consumer news. **"OPA–N" releases, 1945–56** (1 in.), arranged numerically from 1 to 52, is a similar series.

188.17. Included among **informational and procedural issuances, 1940–47** (5 ft.), are folders entitled "Negro Leaflets" (½ in.) and "National Organizations Cooperating with Group Services Branch" (¼ in.). The former includes OPA pamphlets such as *A Negro Community Works in Behalf of Its Families,* and the latter has a list of black organizations that cooperated with OPA.

188.18. Among still pictures is a folder entitled "Regional Negro Activity," 1945 (11 items), which depicts black consumers engaged in various activities. There are also some photographs of a Cost of Living conference, n.d. (6 items), at North Carolina Agricultural and Technical College in Greensboro.

Records of Field Offices

188.19. Region V was composed of Texas, Kansas, Oklahoma, Missouri, Louisiana, and Arkansas; regional headquarters were in Dallas. For the region there is a series of **records relating to activities with black organizations and associations, 1944–46** (3 in.), arranged by type of material. The series includes press and interoffice memorandums; narrative progress reports of specialists of the group and educational services branches; newspaper coverage reports; agenda of educational institutes; speeches; and mailing lists. These records are available in the Archives Branch, Fort Worth Federal Archives and Records Center.

Record Group 195

Records of the Federal Home Loan Bank System

195.1. The Federal Home Loan Bank Board (FHLBB) was established by an act of July 1932 to provide credit reserves for savings and home financing institutions. The FHLBB governs the Federal Home Loan Bank System, which consists of 12 regional Federal Home Loan Banks and other member institutions; supervises the operations of the Federal Savings and Loan System established under provisions of the Home Owners Loan Act of 1933; and serves as the Board of Trustees for the Federal Savings and Loan Insurance Corporation, established by the National Housing Act of 1934 to insure accounts in thrift and home financing institutions in the System. Surveys of local housing situations include information about black residents. The Home Owners Loan Act of 1933 also established the Home Owners Loan Corporation (HOLC). The purpose of the Corporation was to grant long-term mortgage loans at low interest rates to financially distressed homeowners who were unable to procure financing through normal channels.

195.2. The **HOLC city survey file, 1935–40** (70 ft.), is arranged alphabetically by State and thereunder alphabetically by city. Some cities were resurveyed, so the file is in two parts. The file consists of reports, maps, questionnaires, transcripts of interviews, and workpapers relating to a survey and a partial resurvey of cities with a population of more than 40,000. The purpose of the surveys was to determine current and future values of real estate. HOLC assigned the project to its Mortgagee Rehabilitation Committee and later to the Research and Statistics Division. The survey reports and accompanying maps include information about the black population. Each survey report includes a history of the city; analyses of economic, social, and demographic trends; and an explanation of and a description of the mortgage market. Most of the maps were prepared from published maps by superimposing delineations of several classes of residential areas, such as commercial and industrial districts, percentage of foreign and black groups within the city, and locations of resources and major facilities.

Record Group 196

Records of the Public Housing Administration

196.1. The Public Housing Administration (PHA) was a successor to the U.S. Housing Authority (USHA), established to administer the U.S. Housing Act of 1937.This act authorized a system of loans, grants, and subsidies to help local housing authorities develop low-rent housing projects. In 1942 USHA functions were consolidated with other public housing units into the Federal Public Housing Authority (FPHA) under the National Housing Agency. During World War II the FPHA chiefly provided housing for workers in war industries under such legislation as the Lanham Act. In 1947 the FPHA was succeeded by PHA under the Housing and Home Finance

Agency. The PHA resumed public housing functions authorized by the 1937 act, liquidated properties constructed under the Lanham Act, converted barracks into temporary housing for World War II veterans, and, during Korean hostilities, performed defense housing activities under the Defense Housing and Community Facilities and Services Act of 1951. The PHA lapsed when the functions, powers, and duties of the Housing and Home Finance Agency were transferred to the Department of Housing and Urban Development in 1965.

Records of Predecessor Agencies

196.2. The **limited dividend applications, 1932–34** (58 ft.), arranged in numeric sequence, are among the records of the Housing Division of the Federal Emergency Administration of Public Works. These are chiefly applications received by the Division but also included are some applications received by the Reconstruction Finance Corporation during 1932 and 1933. These applications were for financial assistance for private development of low-rent housing projects, many in slum areas. Related correspondence, reports, surveys, and other records deal with an analysis of the limited dividend program and of housing conditions in many localities. The records incorporate information about the areas in which the projects were to be built, such as land values, construction costs, and the ethnic or racial makeup of the neighborhoods. Information about black housing is scattered among these records.

196.3. The **Federal program project files, 1933–44** (176 ft.), arranged by project number, K–1000 through H–127000, include correspondence, reports, surveys, and other records documenting the applications by cities for Federal aid, the construction of approved projects, and the transfer of completed projects to local housing authorities. These project files contain information on the merits of proposed projects, the acquisition of titles to land, the conflict of local interests, public relations, race relations, and finances.

196.4. Among the **orders of the Administrator, 1937–42** (2 ft.), arranged numerically, are six orders pertaining to housing for blacks. In 1938 Robert C. Weaver was appointed Special Assistant on Race Relations, and later an Office of Race Relations was established. The Office staff was to act as consultant on all questions arising from the application of the U.S. Housing Act of 1937. The orders that pertain to the Race Relations Office and to the handling of project applications concerning blacks are 96, 105, 195, 196, 200, and 201 (½ in.).

Public Housing Administration

196.5. The **historical files of PHA, 1934–48** (40 ft.), arranged by subject, consist of material assembled from various divisions and branches of the PHA for the purpose of preparing a history of PHA. The files contain correspondence, procedures, reports, publications, minutes of staff meetings, and other related material. These records include a general file on racial relations, 1944–48 (2 in.), which is a collection of materials pertaining to PHA racial policies. The records about site selection during the war housing program, 1943–44 (3 in.), contain special reports, correspondence, and work notes; they include information about problems of racial relations, the reaction of various individuals and groups to the proposed location of black housing projects in or near their communities, and the housing needs of urban blacks.

196.6. Records of the Intergroup Relations Branch, 1936–63 (12 ft.), arranged by subject, are principally those of the Special Assistant for Racial Relations. The records include directives and memorandums relating to agency policies and procedures concerning racial relations; reports and drafts of special studies, including "A History of Negroes in Public Housing, 1933–53"; a collection of Robert C. Weaver's speeches and papers for the 1930's and 1940's (see RG 207); and correspondence and other records that document the Branch's reviews of local housing authorities' policies on the hiring of minorities.

Record Group 200

National Archives Gift Collection

200.1. This record group includes personal papers, historical manuscripts, and cartographic and audiovisual material donated to the National Archives and Records Service. Although these materials are not official records of the U.S. Government, the National Archives Act of June 18, 1934, authorized their acceptance as gifts if they relate to and illustrate historical activities of the United States. The Federal Property and Administrative Services Act of 1949, as amended (44 U.S.C., 2107(2)), which superseded the 1934 act, authorized the acceptance from private sources of gifts that are appropriate for preservation by the Government as evidence of its organization, functions, policies, decisions, procedures, and transactions. The materials allocated to this record group have been donated by a wide range of business and cultural organizations and institutions and by many individuals. There is a wide variety of black history materials among these records.

Personal Papers and Historical Manuscripts

Joint Commission on Mental Health of Children, Inc.

200.2. In 1965 the 89th Congress amended the Social Security Act (79 Stat. 360) to authorize appropriations for a grant to an organization "composed of representatives of leading national medical, welfare, educational, and other professional associations, organizations, and agencies active in the field of mental health of children" to make a major study of the mental health of infants, children, and adolescents in the United States. As a result, 13 associations concerned with child mental health formed the Joint Commission on Mental Health of Children, Inc., to receive this grant. Forty-six associations eventually sponsored the joint commission. Among them were the NAACP, the National Council of Negro Women, and the Urban League. The **records of the joint commission, 1966–72** (50 ft.), consist of several series with various arrangements. Among them are program files with information about Head Start and the 1970 White House Conference on Children; meeting and membership records, including transcripts of proceedings of meetings of the board of directors and reports of the joint commission to Congress; and its published papers.

Records of the National Conference on Citizenship

200.3. During World War II a program was begun to naturalize millions of aliens who lived in the United States. The Federal Bar Association aided in this effort through the work of its Committee on American Citizenship. Near the end of the war there were discussions on the best ways to continue citizenship education, and these discussions resulted in the establishment of an annual meeting for discussing and promoting citizenship. The National Education Association agreed to serve as the sponsoring agency of the annual meetings, with the Immigration and Naturalization Service of the Department of Justice providing assistance. The first National Conference on Citizenship took place in Philadelphia on May 18 and 19, 1946, with representatives of about 100 civic organizations participating. The National Conference on Citizenship was incorporated by an act of Congress in 1953. One of the objectives of the organization was to hold an annual conference on citizenship.

200.4. The **staff reference file for the 24th annual National Conference on Citizenship, 1968** (2½ ft.), arranged by subject, includes some records that relate to black history. During the 1968 conference there was a climate of violence and civil unrest in the country. For that year the conference materials cover topics such as alienated youth, hippies, dropouts, and drug use and abuse as well as black history and philosophy, the education of blacks, the black community, and social and political problems affecting blacks. There is also some information about black students on college campuses.

Records of the American National Red Cross

200.5. The American Red Cross, organized in 1881, was chartered by Congress in 1905 to help carry out the obligations assumed by the United States under certain international treaties known as the Geneva or Red

Cross Conventions. Specifically, its congressional charter gives the American Red Cross the responsibility of acting as the medium of voluntary relief and communication between the American people and their Armed Forces and to carry on a system of national and international relief to prevent and mitigate suffering caused by disasters. Nationally and locally the American Red Cross is governed by volunteers; most of its duties are performed by volunteers; and it is largely financed by voluntary contributions.

200.6. The **general records of the Red Cross, 1881–1946** (900 ft.), are arranged according to a numeric filing scheme and are divided into three chronological segments—1881–1916, 1917–34, and 1935–46. Materials relating to black history are scattered throughout the records. However, there are some files relating solely to black history. Some examples are "Mississippi River Valley Flood/Negro Relations, 3/20/27" (#224.91, 2 in.); "Race and Racial Matters," 1917–34 and 1935–46 (#003, 2½ in.); "Negro Nurses," 1935–46 (#300.1, ½ in.); "Negro Blood," 1935–46 (#505109, 3 in.); and "Classes for Negroes," 1935–46 (#538 and #548, ⅛ in.). Many of these records concern the provision of segregated services to black servicemen and disaster victims, relations with the black community and the black press, use of blood from black donors to aid white patients, employment of black medical professionals, and employment of black personnel at Red Cross offices.

200.7. Some of the World War II records pertaining to blood programs include information about Charles Drew, a black physician who pioneered the work with blood plasma. He is mentioned, for example, among the records of the blood for Britain project (#303.02, 1 in.). Some records about his work are housed at the Red Cross archives in the American Red Cross Building, Washington, D.C.

200.8. Records dated later than 1946 are interfiled with the1935–46 files. A report issued by the Red Cross Administrative History Unit in 1950 is entitled "The History of the American National Red Cross" and includes a volume entitled "Group Relations: Negro" (#492.2, 1 in.).

Social Science Research Council Committee on Public Administration's Study of the Administration of the Federal Work Relief Program

200.9. The Committee on Public Administration of the Social Science Research Council was established in 1935 to appraise the administration of the Federal work relief program. The committee was to record the administrative development of this nationwide program. It was the committee's belief that the solution of the organizational problems of this multiple program, centering in the Presidency and involving many agencies, would throw light on the administrative problems of future national emergency efforts. These records include reports about a number of agencies, such as the Federal Emergency Relief Administration, the Civilian Conservation Corps, and the National Youth Administration.

200.10. Records of the National Youth Administration (NYA) program, 1934–36 (2 ft.), arranged alphabetically by subject, include a folder entitled "Negro Problems" (½ in.). The folder contains only NYA press releases about black youths or about other matters involving black Americans. There is one release containing a speech delivered by Frank S. Horne, Assistant Director, Division of Negro Affairs, NYA. The speech was delivered in Petersburg, Va., on November 12, 1936, and was entitled "Problems in Guiding Negro Youth" (14 pp.).

Audiovisual Records in the National Archives Gift Collection

Records Relating to Blacks in the Harmon Foundation Collection

200.11. The Harmon Foundation began its activities under the direction of William E. Harmon in 1922 with two specific projects: to fund parks and playgrounds in growing communities and to provide loans for students. By the time the foundation terminated its activities in 1967, a division of social research and experimentation had been added, along with a division of awards for constructive and creative achievement and an association for the advancement of nursing. The scope of the Harmon Foundation's work had grown to include experimental projects in recreation, social service, and education. In 1967, the foundation donated its textual records to the Library of Congress and its photographic materials—both still and motion pictures—and its sound recordings to the National Archives.

200.12. Because William E. Harmon had a special interest in black Americans, many of the foundation's audiovisual records deal with black life and culture both in the United States and in Africa. The still picture collection includes about 7,000 black-and-white prints, glass plates, and color slides divided topically into nine series. Most of these document the foundation's effort to support, mainly through exhibits and publicity, black American and African artists. As an innovator in this endeavor, the foundation exhibited artworks by black Americans in the early 1930's, at a time when blacks could neither attend art exhibits nor participate in them. The series **artworks by Negro artists, 1922–67,** contains 1,400 different black-and-white photographs of paintings, sculpture, and prints by 130 artists. The artists themselves are shown in photographic portraits at work in their studios or attending exhibits.

Left: William Edward Burghardt DuBois (1868–1963). Date and photographer unknown. RG 200, National Archives Gift Collection. (200(s)–HS–6–70). Right: Mary McLeod Bethune (1875–1955). Instrumental in establishing Bethune–Cookman College in Daytona Beach, Fla., Mary McLeod Bethune was known for her lifelong dedication to the welfare of young people. Her many achievements include the founding of the National Council of Negro Women, about 1936. Kenneth F. Space, photographer. RG 200, National Archives Gift Collection. (200–HS–6–47).

200.13. An accompanying file of 700 color slides duplicates many of the black-and-white items. Among the artists represented are Richmond Barthé, Palmer Hayden, Marvin Gray Johnson, Jacob Lawrence, and Hale Woodruff. The artworks in the **portraits of outstanding Americans of Negro origin, 1922–67,** series were painted by Betsy Graves Reyneau and Laura Wheeler Waring. Marian Anderson, W. E. B. DuBois, Ralph Bunche, and Thurgood Marshall are among the 85 black Americans represented. Half of the slides of the portraits are available in color. Photographs that show artworks on display, visitors viewing exhibits, artists explaining and demonstrating techniques, and artworks done during foundation-sponsored workshops are grouped in the series **Negro art exhibits, workshops, and demonstrations, 1927–47,** which includes over 550 black-and-white prints and glass slides.

200.14. In addition to the extensive coverage of Afro-American art, the Harmon still picture collection includes photographs taken on the campuses of the following black colleges and universities: Atlanta, Calhoun, Dillard, Fisk, Howard, Shaw, Talladega, Tuskegee, Virginia Union, and Xavier. The series includes 1,000 black-and-white prints made in 1936 and

1937. Students are shown in social, educational, and athletic activities.

200.15. Of the hundreds of motion picture films in the Harmon collection, 12 are related to blacks in the United States. All but one of these films relate to black educational institutions, blacks, and art. Those about education describe student life and academic programs at Hampton Institute, Xavier University, and the Calhoun School. Footage showing art classes at several black colleges, the 1931 exhibit work of black artists, and demonstrations by Palmer Hayden, Richmond Barthé, and several other artists are included in the five films on black artists. One other film deals with recreational activities at the Harlem Young Women's Christian Association.

Motion Pictures in the National Archives Gift Collection

200.16. The National Archives has over the years accepted for deposit films from private sources that are pertinent to the history of the United States. Although film subjects in the Gift Collection are quite diverse, ranging from newsreels to even a few feature films produced by Hollywood studios, many of them relate to black history.

200.17. The largest series relating to black history are the newsreels. The Paramount News films, which begin with August 29, 1940, include footage of blacks in military service during World War II, Jackie Robinson testifying before the House Un-American Activities Committee on the loyalty of U.S. blacks, Vice President Henry Wallace speaking on racial prejudice, and President Truman in 1947 and President Eisenhower in 1954 addressing NAACP leaders. Other black-related newsreel items are in the Universal News films, 1929–67, including coverage of black baptisms, revival meetings, and evangelists such as Father Divine, Elder Michaux, and Black Billy Sunday during the 1930's; race riots in Harlem and Chicago, 1935; the 1940 American Negro Art Exposition in Chicago; black soldiers and paratroopers during World War II; Ralph Bunche at the United Nations in 1950; Ben Davis, a black Communist, 1951; the Korean war; and Althea Gibson and other prominent black athletes and sports figures in the 1950's. For the 1960's there is footage on James Meredith and riots at the University of Mississippi in 1962; enrollment of blacks at the University of Alabama; the 1963 March on Washington; the signing of the Civil Rights Act of 1964; the civil rights march from Selma to Montgomery, Ala.; the riots in Los Angeles in 1965; Secretary of Housing and Urban Development Robert C. Weaver; the 1967 Newark and Detroit riots; and U.S. Supreme Court Justice Thurgood Marshall.

200.18. There are also black history materials in the MGM-Hearst Metrotone "News of the Day" newsreels and the Fox-Movietone newsreels. The "March of Times" was not a newsreel but was more like a documentary film that focused on issues of the day. Some of the black history scenes in "March of Times" films include the blues singer Leadbelly, black religious leader Father Divine, a depiction of black and white farmers in a segment called "King Cotton's Slaves," and a short on voodoo and the occult entitled "Harlem's Black Magic."

200.19. Other motion pictures in the Gift Collection that reflect racial attitudes include several feature films by Hollywood studios, such as the controversial 1915 film "Birth of a Nation" and the 1939 Civil War epic "Gone With the Wind." In the Thomas Edison film collection there is some miscellaneous footage showing "Negro chicken thieves" and black troops debarking in 1897 and 1898. The Ford film collection includes scenes of black farmers, workers, stevedores, shrimp pickers, and road gangs during the period 1919–32. A 1942 film scene depicts George Washington Carver with Henry and Edsel Ford at the Ford Motor Co.

200.20. Of importance also is the 1944 film "Let My People Live," produced by the National Tuberculosis Association, the Urban League, and the Veterans Administration, and a 1959 NBC news special "The Second Agony of Atlanta," which examines the attitudes of white and black Georgians during the integration of public schools. A three-part film produced by the National Council of Churches is entitled "Crisis in the Nation: White Racism." The film includes interviews with Whitney M. Young, Jr., of the Urban League and James Baldwin, a black author. There is a 1968 film produced by David Loeb Weiss Films, Inc., "No Vietnamese Ever Called Me Nigger," and a series of interviews from the "Ladies of the Press" television series with black personalities and activists, such as Cassius Clay (later called Muhammad Ali), James Meredith, Sammy Davis, Jr., Adam Clayton Powell, Jr., Mrs. Medgar Evers, Floyd Patterson, and Martin Luther King, Jr.

Sound Recordings in the National Archives Gift Collection

200.21. Recordings in the Gift Collection encompass a wide variety of subject matter for the study of black history. There is a 1906 recording of the 1895 Atlanta Exposition address by Booker T. Washington entitled "The American Negro." Of particular importance are several speeches by former Presidents, including a 1936 address by Franklin D. Roosevelt at the dedication of a new chemistry building at Howard University and an address at the 38th Annual Conference of the NAACP on June 29, 1947, by Harry S Truman. There are also recordings of the "Amos and Andy" radio program, a dramatization of the life of George Washington Carver along with a personal interview made in 1939, a 1936 recording of the prayer of a rural Georgia Negro minister and the response of his congregation, remarks made by Jesse Owens at the 1936 Olympic games, and a part of the 1938 Max Schmeling vs. Joe Louis fight. In addition, recordings are available of William C. Handy performing his "St. Louis Blues" at the 1940 Cavalcade of Music concert in San Francisco, Duke Ellington and his Jump for Joy Choir, the 1948 testimony of Paul Robeson about alleged communist sympathies during the Mundt bill hearings before the U.S. Senate, an interview in 1951 between Eleanor Roosevelt and Jackie Robinson, a debate over the civil rights plank in the party platform at the 1960 Democratic Convention in Los Angeles, and an interview with Martin Luther King, Jr., as he led marchers in Chicago to the 1960 Republican National Convention. The sound recordings also include a 1960 address by W. E. B. DuBois in Madison, Wis., entitled "Socialism and the American Negro" and an address by Malcolm X to a United Black Front rally in Harlem in 1963. During the 1960's and 1970's there are interviews with black personalities and activists such as Eldridge Cleaver, H. "Rap" Brown, Stokely Carmichael, Clarence Norris (the last of the "Scottsboro Boys"), Elijah Muhammad, Martin Luther King, Jr., James Meredith, A. Philip Randolph, Dick Gregory, Adam Clayton Powell, Jr., and Cassius Clay (Muhammad Ali).

200.22. Sound recordings from programs on National Public Radio include a number of black history topics for the 1970's. The subjects of these programs include the Black Caucus, blacks on welfare, black economic power, racism in the military, school busing, mass media and the black community, racial equality and civil rights, a memorial service for Martin Luther King, Jr., black politics, black life, Jesse Owens, Gordon Parks, Charles Drew, Mahalia Jackson, John H. Johnson, Carl Stokes, Kenneth Clark, Jesse Jackson, black Americans slave and free, and black women in contemporary America.

200.23. There are name and subject indexes to the audiovisual materials in the Gift Collection.

Record Group 202

Records of the National War Labor Board (*World War II*)

202.1. The National War Labor Board (NWLB), 1942–45, was established in the Office of Emergency Management to succeed the National Defense Mediation Board, created in 1941. The NWLB was to act as final arbiter of wartime labor disputes and to pass on adjustments in certain wages and salaries. It established 12 regional war labor boards and a territorial war labor board for Hawaii. For key industries, it created commissions and panels authorized to settle all but the most important dispute and wage stabilization cases.

202.2. The headquarters case records include **dispute case files, 1942–45** (243 ft.), which consist of major cases of industry-wide, policy-making significance. The files relating to cases that came to the Board on appeal from the regional boards or industry commissions were usually returned to them and consequently have a different arrangement. The headquarters case files are arranged numerically by case number. The **regional files, 1942–45** (1,365 ft.), are arranged by region and thereunder by case number.

202.3. There is a collection of published decisions and an index to NWLB case files, 28 vols. (Washington, D.C.: Bureau of National Affairs, 1946). Under the index heading "Discrimination" is the subheading "Racial Discrimination," and under the heading "Wage Differentials" is the subheading "Racial Differential." A wage differential is a different pay scale based on sex, race, or geographic location for the performance of the same job. There are at least 10 cases listed under these subheadings. For example, in a case brought against the Pittsburgh Plate Glass Co. et al., dated May 25, 1944 (#III-7360–D, 5 in.), the issues were wage differentials based on sex and race. There are several statements within the file pertaining to the NWLB application of Executive Order 8802 pertaining to fair employment practices. Another case involving the Western Electric Co. and the Point Breeze Employees Association pertains to separate facilities for black and white employees and to problems caused by integration within the plant, December 1943 (#III–4773–D, 1½ in.). A typical case file includes a final agreement, analytical reports, a transcript, findings and recommendations, correspondence with the disputants and interested parties, and hearing exhibits.

Record Group 204

Records of the Office of the Pardon Attorney

204.1. The Office of the Pardon Attorney was established in the Attorney General's office by an act of 1891. This office inherited the functions of a pardon clerk, a position that had been established in 1866. Before 1865, responsibility for recommending action on Federal pardon applications to the President had been shared by the Attorney General and the Secretary of State. The Office currently receives all requests for Executive clemency except in military cases; conducts all appropriate correspondence; receives reports from U.S. attorneys, trial judges, and others; and submits recommendations to the Attorney General and the President.

204.2. The **pardon case files, 1853–1946** (936 ft.), arranged numerically, include information such as the application for Executive clemency; letters of recommendation for pardon, including character affidavits; and correspondence with Members of Congress, Governors, State officials, White House officials, and private attorneys. Among these records is a case file for the Jamaican-born leader of the Universal Negro Improvement Association, Marcus Garvey (#42–793, 2 ft.). There are indexes to the files, but black persons have to be known by name.

Record Group 206
Records of the Solicitor of the Treasury

206.1. The Office of the Solicitor of the Treasury (1830–1934) was created in the Department of the Treasury to supervise all legal proceedings involving the collection of debts due the United States. The Solicitor directed, instructed, and required reports from all U.S. attorneys, marshals, and clerks of courts in matters relating to suits and proceedings for recovering debts due the United States; established regulations to guide customs collectors and required reports from the collectors concerning suits; issued distress warrants to direct proceedings against delinquent revenue collectors or receivers of public moneys; customarily examined all Treasury officers' official bonds, contracts, contractor bonds, and related legal documents; served as the Treasury Department law officer, which included advising Department officials on any legal question not involving the Constitution; and administered lands acquired by the United States in payment of debts and, with the approval of the Secretary of the Treasury, leased and sold such lands. Some of these records relate to the slave trade.

206.2. The **letters received by the Solicitor of the Treasury from U.S. district attorneys, marshals, and clerk of court, 1801–98** (51 ft.), are arranged alphabetically by name of State, thereunder by name of judicial district, and thereunder chronologically. This series includes letters (2 ft.) pertaining to suits for the forfeiture of vessels engaged in the slave trade and for related matters. Some of the letters received from officials in Massachusetts relate to the brig *Glamorgan,* a captured slaver, 1854. Letters from officials in the southern district of New York concern the capture of the *Ann D. Richardson* by the U.S. brig *Perry* at Rio de Janiero, 1849, and include several enclosures of reports of the U.S. consul at Rio de Janiero on the extent of the slave trade with Brazil. There are letters from New York officials about the barque *Laurens,* seized for violation of laws prohibiting the slave trade, 1848, and about the brig *Susan,* seized on the same charge in 1849.

206.3. Suits filed in Virginia courts for slave trade violations include those against the brig *Independence,* 1849; the brig *Excellent,* 1851; the *R. P. Brown,* 1853 and 1856; the *William G. Lewis,* 1858–59; the *Julia*

Deane, 1859; the *Storm King,* 1860; and the *Triton,* 1861.

206.4. The **letters received by the Solicitor of the Treasury from the Navy Department, 1815–95** (6 in.), are arranged chronologically and contain a few letters relating to the cost of labor for removing cargo from the slaver *Orion,* 1860, and letters relating to prize money due U.S. naval vessels for captured slavers, 1860–61.

206.5. Letters received by the Solicitor of the Treasury from the State Department, 1821–95 (1 ft.), arranged chronologically, include some letters (1 in.) containing reports of the outfitting of vessels for the slave trade and of violations of the slave trade acts. There are letters, 1845, pertaining to the request of the district attorney at Baltimore for a Presidential pardon for some of the crew of the *Montevideo* so that they could be used as witnesses against the captain and mate, who were indicted for violations of slave trade laws. Vessels charged with engaging in the slave trade included the brig *Elvira,* 1858; the *C. Perkins,* 1858; the brig *Ardennes,* 1858; the *Tavernier,* 1859; and the *Atlantic* and the *St. Jago de Cuba,* 1859.

206.6. Closed cases (miscellaneous), 1812–1915, arranged alphabetically, include papers (3 in.) relating to the slavers *Julia Deane,* 1858–60, and the *William G. Lewis,* 1858–59.

Record Group 207

General Records of the Department of Housing and Urban Development

207.1. The Department of Housing and Urban Development (HUD) succeeded the Housing and Home Finance Agency (HHFA), which had been established in 1947 to coordinate Federal housing activities and then was made responsible for implementing the Housing Act of 1949. The HHFA had, in turn, replaced the National Housing Agency (NHA), established in 1942 to coordinate wartime housing activities. In the same year some of the housing functions of the Office of Emergency Management had been transferred to the NHA. Included within the HHFA were the Federal Housing Administration (see RG 31); the Public Housing Administration (see RG 196); the Federal National Mortgage Association (see RG 294); the Urban Renewal Administration and the Community Facilities Administration, which were established as constituent units by the HHFA Administrator in 1954; and the Home Loan Bank Board, which became independent in

1955 as the Federal Home Loan Bank Board (see RG 195). Under provisions of the Housing Act of 1954, the National Voluntary Mortgage Credit Extension Committee was created with the HHFA Administrator as Chairman. The 1965 act creating HUD transferred the functions, powers, and duties of the HHFA to the Department. Many of the records relate to housing problems encountered by blacks.

Predecessor Agencies

Office for Emergency Management

207.2. Among the **general records** ("subject file"), **1940–42** (6 ft.), arranged alphabetically by subject or type of record, of the Division of Defense Housing Coordination (Office for Emergency Management) is one folder entitled "Housing–Negroes" (¼ in.), which contains information about the availability of housing for black workers in various locations and about Government housing policies and priorities. There is a memorandum entitled "Negro Participation in Defense Housing" dated August 27, 1940, and a "Statement Concerning the Effect of Priorities on USHA-Aided Projects for Negro Occupancy," n.d.

National Housing Agency

207.3. Included among the **general records of NHA, 1942–47** (29 ft.), arranged by subject categories, is the folder "Racial Relations" (2 in.). It contains a report entitled "Negro Share of Priority Housing—Private and Public as of December 31, 1944," a number of memorandums with the subject heading "Programming Negro Housing," and correspondence and reports pertaining to restrictions on defense production due to problems of race relations. **NHA's subject file of the war housing program, 1943–46** (5 ft.), arranged by a subject-numeric classification scheme, includes one folder, "Negro" (#2–2–1–1, 1 in.). It contains information on black occupancy in public war housing; a report of black participation in wartime employment, migration, and housing; and charts and correspondence relating to race relations.

207.4. The Research and Statistics Division of the Federal Housing Administration gathered current economic and housing market data for cities with a population of 5,000 or more in order to forecast housing demands and market values. The resulting records are called the **city data file, 1938–45** (30 ft.), arranged alphabetically by State and thereunder by city. The study of each city is divided into four large sections: general characteristics, demand factors, supply factors, and demand versus supply. The second and third sections have detailed information that is sometimes broken down into race, place of birth, age, occupation, and salary. The city data file should be used in conjunction with the Home Owners Loan Corporation city survey file (see RG 195).

Housing and Home Finance Agency and the Department of Housing and Urban Development

207.5. A variety of records pertaining to black history are scattered among the **subject correspondence files of HHFA Administrators, HUD Secretaries, and their deputies, 1942–69** (290 ft.), arranged by subject. They concern public housing; racial relations services; urban problems; minority housing; a youth opportunity campaign in Watts, Calif.; equal employment opportunity; the model cities program; low-income housing; and housing for the elderly.

207.6. Robert C. Weaver, who was HHFA Administrator from 1961 to 1965 and the Secretary of HUD from 1966 to 1968, was the first black man to become a member of a Presidential Cabinet. His **subject correspondence files, 1961–68** (128 ft.), are arranged annually and thereunder alphabetically by subject headings. The subject headings vary in style and order from year to year. Weaver's records include topics such as equal opportunity in the Armed Forces, in housing, and in employment; equal opportunity in HUD operations and programs; rehabilitation of urban slums; and the model cities program. Included are race and educational statistics and information about the President's Advisory Commission on Civil Disorders, the Commission on Civil Rights, the National Committee Against Discrimination in Housing, and the President's Committee on Equal Employment Opportunity. There is correspondence with the Urban League, the NAACP, Tuskegee Institute, Massachusetts Senator Edward Brooke, and the Houston Negro Chamber of Commerce.

207.7. There are some audiovisual records relating to Robert C. Weaver. Motion pictures, 1963–69 (43 reels), document the creation of the Department of Housing and Urban Development and the appointment by President Lyndon B. Johnson of Weaver as the Department's first Secretary; they show several ceremonies relating to the establishment and early activities of the Department. Sound recordings, 1966–68 (#207-6, 7, 10, 11, 15–20), consist of radio spot announcements and speeches by Secretary Weaver.

207.8. The **race relations program correspondence files** consolidated from the records of various HUD predecessors, **1946–58** (3 ft.), are arranged alphabetically under subject headings. Some of the subject headings are "Advisory Conference on Housing for Minority Families," "National Urban League," "Urban Renewal," "President's Committee on Government Contracts," "Public Housing Administration Racial Relations Officers," "Publications," "Housing Programs," "Speeches," "Building Trades Training," "Minority Group Opportunities," and "Housing Problems in Large Urban Areas," such as San Francisco and Detroit.

207.9. The **records of the voluntary home mortgage credit program, 1954–65** (15 ft.), consist of the files of the national committee that administered the program with the aid of regional subcommittees. This program helped people in areas with a shortage of lending resources (primarily rural areas) and minority group members (primarily in local areas where loans were not as readily available to them as to others) obtain private mortgage credit through Federal Housing Administration-insured and Veterans Administration-guaranteed loans. The records include various series of correspondence, organization and operation materials, National Committee meeting records, and reports relating to the regional subcommittees (various arrangements).

Record Group 208

Records of the Office of War Information

208.1. The Office of War Information (OWI) was established in the Office for Emergency Management (OEM) by Executive Order 9182 of June 1942 to coordinate the Government's war information program. It assumed the coordinating functions and related records of the OEM Division of Information and the functions and records of the Office of Government Reports (and predecessor agencies dating from 1933), the Office of Facts and Figures, and the Office of the Coordinator of Information units concerned with foreign propaganda activities. The OWI formulated and carried out programs to disseminate information in the United States and abroad about the progress of the war and Government policies, activities, and objectives. Duties of the OWI included coordinating informational activities of other Government agencies, issuing necessary directives for accurate and consistent Government information, reviewing and approving proposed motion picture and radio programs sponsored by Federal agencies, and maintaining liaisons between the Government and the radio and motion picture industries and United Nations information offices. The OWI was terminated December 31, 1945, by Executive order. Many of these records relate to the participation of blacks in the war effort.

Records of the Office of the Director and Predecessor Agencies

208.2. The Director of OWI had general charge of all phases of the programs of the organization. The **records of the Director, 1942–45** (4 ft.), arranged alphabetically by subject, include the folder "Racial Relations" (½ in.), which contains information about the various responses of the black community to the war effort, especially the responses of the black press. There is some correspondence with black organizations, such

Willa Beatrice Brown, the first black woman to be commissioned a lieutenant in the U.S. Civil Air Patrol, was the head of the Coffey School of Aeronautics in the United States during World War II. At the school, pilots were trained for the U.S. Army Air Force. Date and photographer unknown. RG 208, Records of the Office of War Information. (208-FS-793-1).

as the NAACP, and with Government agencies, such as the Committee on Fair Employment Practice (FEPC). One letter in the "Racial Relations" folder mentions the resignation of Theodore M. Berry. He was a black lawyer from Ohio who served briefly as OWI liaison officer with the black community. There are several folders pertaining to the organization of OWI. Some of the charts and narrative reports give information about the Negro News Section, which was part of the OWI News Bureau and was headed by Theodore Poston, a black newspaperman.

208.3. The **miscellaneous records of the Advertising and Intelligence Division of the Office of Facts and Figures, 1941–42** (5 ft.), arranged chronologically, include a folder entitled "Negroes" (2 in.), which contains a number of reports. "Negroes in a Democracy at War" (29 pp.) includes sections on militancy, black organizations, black newspapers, grievances, discrimination, blacks in the Armed Forces, blacks and civilian defense, black appraisals of the war, and the attitudes of blacks toward the Japanese and the Germans. Other reports in the folder are "The Negro Looks at the War" (65 pp.), "Report on Negro Morale" (25 pp.), "Blueprint of Program for Strengthening Negro Morale in War Effort" (25 pp.), and a two-part report (14 pp.) entitled "Negro Organizations and the War Effort,'' with one part about the Detroit ''Sojourner Truth Housing Crisis.''

208.4. The **records of the Director of the Office of Facts and Figures, 1941–42** (10 ft.), are arranged according to a decimal filing scheme. The classification ''Negroes'' (#002.11; 3 in.) includes correspondence from black individuals and organizations, such as Walter H. White and Roy Wilkins of the NAACP; Carl Murphy, Claude A. Barnett, and John H. Sengstake—members of the black press; and Mary McLeod Bethune, T. Arnold Hill, William H. Hastie, Alfred Edgar Smith, and Robert C. Weaver—blacks who served in the Federal Government. Materials in these files pertain to the employment of blacks in defense industries, the low morale of black citizens, discrimination, racial violence and lynching, entertainment for black troops, the FEPC, and agitation of black leaders for equal rights and representation on Federal Government policymaking boards.

208.5. The **records of the Historian, 1941–45** (16 ft.), are arranged by subject or by organizational unit. Included among these records are correspondence of the Historian with officials of the OWI regarding OWI history as well as some historical studies written by the Historian and other employees of the OWI. Many of them pertain to OWI activities overseas. Among the Historian's records for OWI's Motion Picture Bureau (4 in.) are a few reports, some correspondence, and several clippings relating to films designed to lift the morale of the black population that were produced or reviewed by OWI. They include ''The Negro Soldier'' (#111–M–6022), ''Henry Brown, Farmer'' (#16–665), ''Negro Colleges in Wartime'' (#208–7), and newsreels and other films directed to blacks. Some reports list newsreel items about the baby daughter of Sgt. and Mrs. Joe Louis, Liberian officials at the Casablanca Conference, black trainees learning radio codes, and black history week; other reports list three films that were in the process of being researched by Metro-Goldwyn-Mayer Studios pertaining to the training and combat experiences of black pilots, the life of Crispus Attucks, and the career of Marian Anderson.

208.6. The **subject file of the Office of Facts and Figures, the Committee on War Information, and the Censorship Policy Board, 1941–42** (8 ft.), arranged according to a decimal filing scheme, includes several folders entitled ''Negro'' (totaling 3 in.). The primary area of concern in these records is the low morale of black civilians and soldiers. To address this problem, OWI organized a March 20, 1942, conference with a number of black leaders from all over the United States who could provide ''counsel and advice'' for ''securing unity of thought and action in this war for democracy.'' The folders include copies of letters to black leaders announcing that Theodore M. Berry had recently become a staff officer in OWI's Liaison Bureau and inviting black leaders to the conference. The correspondence in these folders also includes a December 21, 1941, letter from Richard Wright, a black author, to OWI offering his services to the Office of Facts and Figures. Other correspondence relates to the black press, the appointment of a black war correspondent, the 1941 March on Washington, Theodore Poston, William Alexander (a black newspaperman who worked in OWI's Press Division), the "Negro Problem and Radio," and various other matters. There is a copy of the *New Negro World,* a periodical dated December 1941, and some correspondence about hiring a black staff member for OWI in the folder "Racial Relations" (¼ in.).

Records of the Domestic Operations Branch

208.7. The records of the Office of the Director of the Domestic Operations Branch include the **correspondence of Director Palmer Hoyt, 1943** (1 ft.), arranged by subject or alphabetically by name of correspondent. A folder entitled "Negro Committee" includes a few letters between Hoyt and John H. Sengstake, who was president of the Robert S. Abbot Publishing Co. (which published the *Chicago Defender*) and president of the Negro Newspaper Publishers Association. A letter from Hoyt to Sengstake dated July 21, 1943, states that OWI was prepared to appoint "an Advisory Committee of Negro Newspaper Publishers."

208.8. The **letters sent by the Executive Director of the Branch, 1942–45** (1 ft.), arranged alphabetically by name or subject, include folders entitled "American Council on Race Relations" and "Committee on Fair Employment Practice," both of which contain only a few letters relating to race relations, rumor control, and blacks in the Armed Services.

208.9. The **speeches of Government officials, 1942–45** (28 ft.), arranged alphabetically by name of speaker, include one brief speech by Theodore M. Berry, one by Theodore Poston, and several by Francis J. Haas, who served as Chairman of the FEPC.

Records of Deputy Directors

208.10. The deputy directors of the Domestic Operations Branch were assigned fields of war information and served as the principal representatives of OWI to various Federal war agencies with respect to their particular fields. They were responsible for the adequacy of the information available to the press in their respective fields and for policy decisions on information matters in those fields.

208.11. The **records of the Deputy Director for Military Information, Nicholas Roosevelt, 1943** (3 ft.), arranged alphabetically by subject, include a folder labeled "Negro Activities" (1 in.), which contains copies of comments by black labor leader A. Philip Randolph and black attorney William H. Hastie on the Army's race policy, information about the news coverage of black troops overseas, and copies of a few press releases. The file includes information about antiblack feelings among U.S. white troops, interracial violence, the treatment of Dorie Miller (the black naval hero), and the concerns of Theodore Poston of the Negro Press Section. The file also contains a copy of *Negroes and the War* by Chandler Owen, which was published by OWI. A June 18, 1943, letter from Nicholas Roosevelt to Gen. A. D. Surles states: "The Negro newspapers are protesting to us vociferously against an Army bottleneck which they allege is holding up release of stories concerning the activities of the all-Negro 99th Pursuit Squadron."

208.12. The records of the Deputy Director for Labor and Civilian Welfare include the **files of Natalie Davidson, Program Manager for Homefront Campaigns, 1943–45** (4 ft.), arranged alphabetically by name of campaign. A folder entitled "Negro" (1 in.) includes a collection of press releases relating to blacks that were generated by various Government agencies. They relate to a number of subjects, such as the participation of blacks in the war bond drives, the FEPC, blacks in the Navy and the Marine Corps, black women war workers, Frances Williams' appointment as special assistant to Price Administrator Chester Bowles, and the Interracial Section of the War Finance Division in the Treasury Department.

208.13. The **records of Deputy Director for Pacific Operations Capt. Waldo Drake and other OWI officials, 1944–45** (10 in.), are arranged by subject. These records concern many diverse aspects of acquiring and dispatching war news. A folder entitled "Negro Press" (¼ in.) includes several photographs of black enlisted men and a few press releases.

208.14. The records of the Senior Deputy Director for Production and Manpower include the **files of the Program Manager for the Recruitment of Women, 1944–45** (1 ft.), arranged alphabetically by subject. Media campaigns to reach black women through the black press are mentioned in various reports and correspondence.

Records of the News Bureau

208.15. This Bureau was responsible for preparing and distributing war-related information to all segments of the U.S. press, including the black press. The Negro Press Section (also called the Negro News Section) was established July 28, 1942, to serve the black press with all available information on the participation of blacks in the war effort and to obtain wider recognition for the black press.

208.16. The **general records of the News Bureau, 1941–43** (6 ft.), arranged according to a numerical filing scheme, include correspondence of Theodore Poston, Chief of the Negro Press Section, interspersed throughout the correspondence of the Bureau (#095). For example, in the file folder entitled "National" (½ in.) is correspondence between Poston and the National Negro Business League, the National Association of Negroes in American Industry, the National Negro Congress, the National Negro Insurance Association, the National Newspaper Publishers Association, and the Urban League. Most of this correspondence

Basic and advanced flying school for Negro Air Corps cadets, Tuskegee, Ala. January 1942. Wilfred Morgan, photographer. RG 208, Records of the Office of War Information. (208-FS-872-1).

was written in 1943. There is also a folder for Charles Alston, a black artist who drew cartoons for OWI. There are a number of vouchers for payments to Alston and a copy of the contract between Alston and OWI. The audiovisual records for OWI (described in paragraph 208.26) include some of Alston's original drawings. The folder labeled ''Charles Alston'' also contains some photographs of black workers in war industries and a photo story of Clara Carroll, a young black woman who came to Washington, D.C., to work during World War II and lived in Lucy Diggs Slowe Hall, a dormitory for black women war workers that later became a part of Howard University.

208.17. Interoffice memorandums of the News Bureau, 1945 (4 in.), are arranged chronologically by month and thereunder by section. These memorandums give information about the operations of various sections of the News Bureau, including the Negro Press Section. There is a January 19, 1945, memorandum from Poston inquiring about admission of blacks to the Presidential inauguration and a March 22, 1945, memo from Poston giving a brief history of the Negro News Section. Other Poston memos list news releases sent to the black press and give a brief summary of their contents. In a few cases, press releases—most of which pertain to blacks and the Seventh War Loan Drive—are attached to the memos.

208.18. The **general subject file of the Chief of the News Bureau, 1944–45** (2 ft.), is arranged alphabetically by subject. The folder "Negro" (⅛ in.) includes a few pieces of Poston correspondence relating to blacks and the war effort, black employment in shipyards, and maritime stories for the black press.

208.19. The News Editing Division of the News Bureau kept a **record set of press releases, 1942–45** (42 ft.), arranged by agency and thereunder chronologically by release number. The **alphabetical subject index to news releases, 1941–45** (13 ft.), includes numerous cards under the heading "Negroes." Most of the releases directed to the black press were prefaced with an "N" and then given a number. The index indicates that there was a total of over 1,600 releases on various subjects. Some of the earliest releases are listed in the **alphabetical index to miscellaneous press releases, 1942–43** (1 ft.), under "Negroes."

208.20. The records of the Negro Press Section include the **general correspondence of Theodore Poston, Chief of the Section, 1943** (1 in.), arranged by subject. Included is correspondence with the black press and with other black organizations and individuals. Some of the materials deal with features, photographs, and cartoons for the black press; the launching of naval ships named after blacks; and black newspapers releasing news stories in advance of the release dates.

208.21. A number of photographs were collected by the Section. There is one group of pictures of blacks in industry and Government, 1941–45, that depicts blacks in shipbuilding and other war industries, black employees of Government agencies, and the activities of blacks in connection with bond rallies.

208.22. There is also a series of photographs of the activities of black personnel in the Navy, 1944–45, showing both enlisted and civilian personnel. These are official photographs taken at Naval installations in the United States and overseas. Included are photographs of black personnel of the Navy, the Marine Corps, the Navy Department, the Treasury Department, the Office of Price Administration, and other Government agencies. There are also photographs of black military personnel in the Army, n.d.

Records of the Motion Picture Bureau

208.23. The **reference file of the Chief of the Motion Picture Bureau, 1943–44** (1 ft.), includes a folder entitled "The Negro Soldier" (⅛ in.). There is a March 8, 1944, cable from OWI to Paramount Picture Studios saying that "The Negro Soldier" (#111–OF–51) was approved for release. The file also includes a November 30, 1943, memorandum stating that the participation of blacks in the war was shown in the following OWI films: "Suggestion Box," "Divide and Conquer" (#208–304), "Ring of Steel" (#208–106), "Henry Brown, Farmer" (#16–665), and "Negro Colleges in Wartime'' (#208–7). The memo also mentions that black participation was depicted in "December 7," (#226–1), a film produced by the Navy.

208.24. Summaries of film production activities, 1942–43 (3 in.), arranged by type of film, include a summary for "Negro Colleges in Wartime," with information about research, shooting, release, and cost; the names of the writer and director; and a copy of the script. The shooting locations for the film were Tuskegee Institute and Howard University.

208.25. The **general file of the chief of research, 1941–42** (1 ft.), arranged alphabetically by subject or name of correspondent, includes the folder "N–Negro" (¼ in.), which contains information about blacks in newsreels and gives the date of the newsreel, a brief summary of the content, and the name of the production studio. The folder includes a release about black fliers; information about the reception of films by black audiences; some correspondence of Theodore M. Berry and Leo C. Rosten; a "Memorandum on Negro Morale" prepared by Horace Cayton, a black sociologist; and a report entitled "Motion Picture," which lists theaters serving black audiences and films addressed to them.

Other Audiovisual Records

208.26. OWI photograph series are entitled "Life in the United States" and "Feature Stories" and contain both photographs and textual material about blacks that document education, war production, religion, theater, youth activities, the work of stevedores, and the lives of athletes. In addition, there are photographs of blacks in the "Allies and the Axis" and "Military Operations" series; a large number of artworks, cartoons, and posters done by black artists, such as Alston; and an extensive file of personalities for the World War II period in the "Unmounted Prints" series. (See also paragraph 208.16.)

208.27. One film, "Negro Colleges in Wartime," 1943 (#208.7), distributed by the War Activities Committee of the Motion Picture Industry, shows black students being trained for military and civilian occupations during World War II at Howard University, Tuskegee and Hampton Institutes, and Prairie View College. Many of the other films reviewed or distributed by OWI are also among the holdings of the National Archives.

208.28. Among the OWI audio documents is a 1943 radio address by Mary McLeod Bethune (#208–477A) speaking on the contributions of American blacks to freedom and democracy in a program broadcast to the British West Indies. There are also two dramatizations. One, based on Carl Sandburg's biography of Abraham Lincoln, *The Prairie Years* and *The War Years,* portrays Lincoln's attitudes toward slavery (#208–656). The other, the radio series "Freedom's People" (#208–690 and 208–691), sponsored by the Office of Education in cooperation with NBC and the Julius Rosenwald Fund, provides a musical dramatization of the freedom struggles of American blacks.

208.29. See also RG 44, Records of the Office of Government Reports.

Record Group 211

Records of the War Manpower Commission

211.1. The War Manpower Commission (WMC), 1942–45, was established within the Office for Emergency Management by an Executive order that transferred to the WMC the Civil Service Commission's National Roster of Scientific and Specialized Personnel, the Office of Procurement and Assignment of the Office of Defense Health and Welfare Services, and the labor supply functions of the Labor Division of the War Production Board. The Committee on Fair Employment Practice (FEPC), the U.S. Employment Service (USES), the Apprentice Training Service, the Training Within Industry Service, and the National Youth Administration were all transferred to the WMC shortly after its establishment. The WMC recruited labor for war and essential civilian industries, trained labor for jobs essential to the war effort, analyzed manpower utilization practices to increase labor efficiency, and accumulated national labor market information. The WMC worked through a headquarters office, regional and State offices (which planned and supervised work), and area and local USES offices (which handled operations).

Records of the Chairman and Vice Chairman (Labor Relations)

211.2. Among the **general correspondence of the Chairman, 1943–45** (12 ft.), arranged by year and thereunder alphabetically by name of correspondent, are a few pieces of correspondence with Francis J. Haas, Chairman of FEPC, concerning 1943 discrimination hearings, discrimination reports, and a military service deferment for Robert C. Weaver. The **Chairman's correspondence with Government officials, 1942–45** (3 ft.), is arranged in two parts—1942–44 and 1945—and thereunder alphabetically by name of official. Scattered references to black workers and soldiers appear among the reports and correspondence in the folders for the Women's Advisory Committee; the Committee for Congested Production Areas and its Director, Corrington Gill; and Charles M. Hay, who served as both Deputy Chairman and Executive Director of the WMC. The **speeches, radio addresses, interviews, and statements of Chairman Paul V. McNutt and other WMC officials, 1943–45** (2 ft.), arranged by name of official, include a radio statement by McNutt entitled "Negro Newspaper Week" (3 pp.). It was aired by the NBC network on February 26, 1944, at 3 p.m. from Des Moines, Iowa.

211.3. The **Vice Chairman's reference file, 1943–45** (2 ft.), arranged by subject or agency, contains a folder on discrimination (1 in.). It includes reports such as "The Negroes' Role in the War—A Study of White and Colored Opinions," a chapter on "Negroes in Selective Service" in Lewis B. Hershey's *Selective Service in Wartime,* and Marshall Field's "The Negro Press and the Issues of Democracy," a speech delivered before the First Annual Dinner of the Capital Press Club of Washington, D.C., June 21, 1944.

Records of the Management-Labor Policy Committee

211.4. The **index to summary minutes of national MLPC meetings, 1942–45** (¼ in.), arranged alphabetically by subject, refers to at least eight meetings during which the subject of discrimination was discussed. The **index to summary minutes of State and area management-labor policy committees, 1942–45** (4 in.), is arranged alphabetically by State or area and thereunder alphabetically by subject. Although the card index is incomplete, cards for southern California; San Diego; Portland, Oreg.; and Detroit include subjects such as discriminatory practices, FEPC, minority groups, organized labor discrimination, and discriminatory practices in transportation. The **general records of the Executive Secretary of the Management-Labor Policy Committee, 1942–46** (8 ft.), are arranged for the most part alphabetically by subject, type of material, agency, or name of person. At the beginning of the series is a list of folder headings, which includes "Discrimination" and "Developments in the Employment of Negroes in War Industries, October 16, 1943."

Records of the Women's Advisory Committee

211.5. The **summary minutes of meetings of the Women's Advisory Committee (WAC), 1942–45** (8 in.), arranged chronologically, include information about the need to tap the labor supply provided by black women, hiring irrespective of sex or race, opportunities for black veterans, full employment, and problems of minority unemployment in peacetime. Some of the dates of these discussions are June 15 and October 11, 1944, and January 16, 1945. The **correspondence of the Chairman and the Executive Secretary, 1942–45** (1 ft.), arranged alphabetically by name of correspondent or by subject, consists chiefly of correspondence with WAC members, other Government agencies, women's organizations, and the general public. In the file folder containing biographies of committee members is a resume for Maudelle Bousfield, principal of the Wendell Phillips High School in Chicago, Ill., and "a foremost Negro leader." These records indicate that she was the first black woman to receive a Bachelor of Arts degree from the University of Illinois. There is a file folder entitled "Bousfield" (⅓ in.), mostly pertaining to WAC meeting attendance. In the folder of correspondence with women's organizations (1 in.) is a February 9, 1944, letter to Mary McLeod Bethune of the National Council of Negro Women pertaining to attendance at a conference.

Records of the Review Committee on Deferment of Government Employees

211.6. The **deferment case files, 1943–47** (46 ft.), arranged alphabetically by agency and thereunder by name of employee, concern Goverment employees who did not hold key positions but whose deferment was requested by their agencies because they were considered essential to the war effort. Some black employees can be identified by the fact that they attended predominantly black colleges or universities, the names of which are listed on the applications.

Records of the Offices of the Deputy Chairman and the Executive Director

211.7. Agenda for the Executive Director's staff meetings, 1942 (¼ in.), arranged chronologically, include an August 8, 1942, discussion of the general relationship of FEPC with other units of the WMC and an undated statement of duties of "Negro Manpower and Minority Group Services and Their Representatives in Regional Offices" (3 pp.). Among the records of the Executive Director, 1945, are **agenda for regional directors' conferences, 1944–45** (¼ in.), arranged chronologically. Subjects discussed concerning black workers include proposed policies on discrimination, problems of minority groups between VE Day and VJ Day, and recruitment and placement services for minority groups.

Records of the Office of the Deputy Executive Director

211.8. The **guides to field instructions, 1943–45** (1 in.), arranged by subject, include an alphabetical subject index to instructions, covering numbers 1–782 only. Under the heading "Minority Groups" are the following subheadings: "Estimates of In-Migrants," "Reports of Discriminatory Training Practices," "Black Applicants for the Training Programs," and "Utilization of Minority Groups." Under the heading "Discrimination" is the subheading "Orders Containing Discriminatory Requirements."

Records of the Office of the Assistant Executive Director for Field Service

211.9. Among the **records of May Thompson Evans,** special assistant in this office, **1942–45** (7 ft.), arranged by subject, is a folder on the Massachusetts antidiscrimination bill, March 8, 1945, which includes some correspondence and copies of the proposed legislation. Scattered references to black employment are made in the **regional directors' reports, 1942–45** (2 ft.), arranged by region number and thereunder chronologically. These reports were addressed primarily to the Deputy Chairman and Executive Director but were received and reviewed by the Field Service staff. The reports concern labor market conditions and recruitment and placement of workers. A North Carolina report, for example, includes the "Region IV Progress Report—with Reference to Negro Participation in Defense Training and Employment," March 3, 1942, by Lawrence A. Oxley, placement specialist for black workers.

Records of the Reports and Analysis Service

211.10. The records of the Analysis Division, Industry Section, include **industry labor market reports, 1942–44** (3 in.), which are arranged alphabetically by industry. Reports on specific industries, prepared by the Analysis Division and its predecessors, present information on production and employment trends, labor shortages, housing and transportation facilities, utilization of black labor, hours of work, labor turnover, and absenteeism. They also contain recommendations for the alleviation of labor market problems.

211.11. The **subject-classified general records of the Historical Analysis Section, 1940–46** (45 ft.), are arranged according to a numeric-subject classification scheme and contain material pertaining to FEPC (1 ft.). Much of the material about black workers pertains to fair employment practices for minority groups, manpower allocation, Government policies in hiring, contracting and advertising, and activities of the Minority Groups Unit. There is correspondence with military leaders, employers, and unions pertaining to full participation of all workers regardless of race in the war effort and to the elimination of discriminatory specifications in advertising; there are reports on compliance. There are also reports and publications pertaining to black workers, such as *Minorities in Defense* (jointly published by the FEPC and the Negro Employment and Training and the Minority Groups Branches of the Office of Production Management), October 15, 1941, and "Employment and Training of Negroes for Defense Industries," April 26, 1941. There is also a transcript of a February 19, 1943, protest hearing concerning black leaders' concern over the management of FEPC. Government representatives included Paul V. McNutt, Chairman of the WMC, and Attorney General Francis Biddle. Some of the representatives of minority group organizations were Lester Granger of the Urban League; P. B. Young, editor of the *Norfolk Journal and Guide;* A. Phillip Randolph of the March on Washington Committee; and Walter H. White of the NAACP.

Cadet Nurse Corps of the U.S. Public Health Administration at graduation exercises. Date and photographer unknown. RG 208, Records of the Office of War Information. (208-NP-4FF-1).

Records of the Legal Service

211.12. The **general records of the Legal Service, 1942–45** (21 ft.), are arranged by subject, type of record, agency, or private organization. Materials relating to discriminatory employment practices are scattered throughout the records. The **general records of Bernard C. Gavit and Charles M. Hay, 1942–44** (6 ft.), arranged by subject, also include scattered information about discriminatory employment practices.

Records of the Bureau of Placement

211.13. The Bureau of Placement was established in December 1942 within the WMC to develop programs and policies with respect to the recruitment, placement, clearance, and transfer of workers for industry and agriculture; to develop local USES office procedures and standards required for the effective application of these programs and policies; and to coordinate civilian recruitment activities of all Government agencies with the policies and standards of the WMC.

211.14. The creation of the Bureau brought into one department several WMC divisions and services—the Industrial and Agricultural Employment Division, the Minority Groups Service, the National Roster of Scientific and Specialized Personnel, and the Procurement and Assignment

Service. The Minority Groups Service assisted WMC operating divisions and field offices with problems arising from the employment of minority groups and maintained liaison with FEPC. There are no separate records for the Minority Groups Service, but some of the records in the Bureau include information about blacks.

211.15. The **Bureau's publications and issuances, 1942–45** (2 ft.), arranged by subject, include a handbook entitled *The United States Employment Service and the Negro Work Applicant,* WMC, 1944.

211.16. Among the records of the Industry Section is a series relating to **forges and foundries, 1943–45** (3 ft.), arranged by subject. There is a four-page report about the percentage of non-whites employed in forges and foundries, listed by region, name and location of forge or foundry, percent of non-whites employed, and percent of their terminations. The percentages of non-whites employed were reported to range between 9.9 percent and 80.1 percent. **Records relating to the cotton textile industry, 1943–45** (5 in.), arranged chronologically, consist mainly of materials relating to production and manpower problems in the cotton textile industry, labor relations, and utilization of women and minority groups in the mills.

Records of the Bureau of Manpower Utilization

211.17. The Bureau of Manpower Utilization was established by the WMC in January 1943 on the recommendation of the Management-Labor Policy Committee. It was responsible for implementing the program of manpower utilization by encouraging the most productive use of the minimum amount of labor necessary for production under working conditions that would maintain worker effectiveness and morale. The **general records of the Office of the Director, 1943–45** (7 ft.), arranged by subject, agency, or region, include a folder (¼ in.) for the FEPC.

Records of the Bureau of Training

211.18. The Bureau of Training was established in WMC to coordinate the Government's training efforts. The **general records, 1940–45** (16 ft.), are arranged by subject and name of person or agency according to a subject filing scheme. One folder, "Minority Groups" (1 in.), includes an article by Robert C. Weaver entitled "The Negro Comes of Age in Industry," which is reprinted from *Atlantic Monthly,* September 1943; a bibliography on the "Negro Worker and the War"; correspondence and reports of Weaver; reports on black employment in certain plants, including Firestone, United Aircraft, and Ford Motor Co.; the policy statement of the Office of Production Management on the employment of blacks in defense industries, especially directed to employers with defense contracts; and reports on training opportunities for black workers. There is also a folder of reports by Sidney Hillman (2 in.), which includes information about training for black workers.

211.19. The **records relating to field operations, 1940–45** (42 ft.), are arranged by district number and thereunder in several categories, one of which is titled "Minority Groups" (about ¼ in. for most districts). There is also a folder for each district relating to discrimination against blacks, usually with only a few documents.

Record Group 212

Records of the Committee for Congested Production Areas

212.1. The Committee for Congested Production Areas, 1943–45, was established in the Executive Office of the President to coordinate Federal, State, and local governmental activities in congested production areas, especially with regard to plant and site availability, local labor supply, and transportation, housing, social service, recreational, and commercial facilities. It designated critical areas and prescribed binding policies and programs for the Federal agencies involved.

212.2. Records relating to black people in congested areas concern the lack of facilities for this group of urban in-migrants. The lack of housing and recreational areas sometimes led to racial violence. In the Detroit area, for instance, inadequate housing for blacks led to interracial tension that contributed to the race riot of June 20 and 21, 1943, and was a direct cause for action on the part of the Committee in designating Detroit as a congested production area.

212.3. Correspondence with other Government agencies, 1943–44 (2 ft.), arranged alphabetically by name of Federal agency and thereunder chronologically, includes scattered information (about 2 in.) about the problems of the black population. There are reports about black employment and housing situations, a report on the Detroit riot, surveys of other racial problems, and lists of black public housing projects, recreational services, and school facilities. Of special interest is a report on housing for blacks in Detroit prepared by Nelson Foot of the Office of Facts and Figures in the Bureau of Intelligence.

212.4. The **records relating to the operation of area offices, 1943–44** (36 ft.), are arranged alphabetically by the name of the area office and thereunder alphabetically by subject, name of person, or type of material. Included are files of the various area offices (consolidated later with related headquarters materials) documenting all phases of field operations. Scattered records (about 10 in.) relate to various problems affecting the black community, such as juvenile delinquency, racial tensions, recreation, schools, and housing. Included are reports of interviews with local officials, surveys of congested areas, and reports from area representatives on such urgent problems as medical care, child care, and restaurant and shopping facilities for the black population.

212.5. Among the **records relating to undesignated congested production areas, 1943–44** (2 ft.), are materials about war production areas with congestion problems that were not severe enough to warrant official designation as congested areas. The records are in two parts: one arranged alphabetically by name of State and thereunder by name of city, area, or private organization; the other arranged alphabetically by name of Federal agency. These records contain information concerning black communities (about 1 in.) similar to that found in the series on congested areas. Sanitation, education, hospital facilities, segregation, and employment policies are the main subjects of reports and correspondence relating to various local areas.

212.6. There is a National Archives finding aid for this record group entitled *Calendar of Negro-Related Documents in the Records of the Committee for Congested Areas in the National Archives* (1949), which was compiled by Elaine C. Bennett for the American Council of Learned Societies.

Record Group 214

Records of the Office for Emergency Management

214.1. The Office for Emergency Management (OEM) was established in the Executive Office of the President in 1940 to assist the President in clearing information on defense measures and to maintain liaison with national defense agencies. In 1941 OEM became responsible for keeping the President informed about emergency activities of Government agencies, assembling and analyzing information concerning additional measures, and assisting in the preparation of recommendations for legislation. The Office was discontinued in 1944.

214.2. The **general records of the Liaison Officer for Emergency Management, 1941–43** (9 ft.), are arranged in two parts: one alphabetically by subject and the other alphabetically by initial name of correspondent. These records include a folder entitled "Negro" (1 in.), which contains information about blacks and defense activities and the establishment of the Committee on Fair Employment Practice. The folder includes correspondence with Walter H. White of the NAACP, Mary McLeod Bethune of the National Council of Negro Women, and others. Other materials pertain to local community problems such as housing and discrimination, health problems in the black community, defense contractors and black employees, the role of Robert C. Weaver in OEM, and an illustrated article in the New York daily paper *PM* for May 7, 1941, entitled "Governor, Mayor and Fifty-Eight Prominent Citizens Protest Discrimination Against Negroes in Defense Program" (pp. 11–19).

214.3. The **correspondence with Government agencies, 1941–44** (1 ft.), arranged alphabetically by the name of agency, includes a folder for the Committee on Fair Employment Practice (¼ in.). Most of the correspondence is with Francis J. Haas, the third Chairman of the Committee, and pertains to various aspects of discrimination against black workers. (See also RG 228.)

Record Group 215

Records of the Office of Community War Services

215.1. The Office of Community War Services (OCWS), 1943–47, was established in the Federal Security Agency to aid in the coordination of all health, welfare, nutrition, recreation, and related fields of activity affecting national defense. In the field, regional directors of the Social Security Board served as regional directors for OCWS and its predecessors (the Office of Defense Health and Welfare Services (ODHWS) in the Office for Emergency Management and the Coordinator of Health, Welfare, and Related Defense Activities of the Council of National Defense) and as chairmen of regional advisory councils. Because many war services were segregated, there are some separate files relating to black health, welfare, and recreation.

215.2. The **subject-classified central files, 1940–47** (209 ft.), are arranged in two groups (1940–44 and 1944–47), thereunder by four main headings ("General," "Regional," "State," and "Foreign"), and thereunder according to a subject-numeric scheme. The records pertain to the organization, functions, and administration of the ODHWS and the OCWS; their relationships with other Federal agencies and their contracts with associations and organizations other than cooperating agencies; their operation of various programs and services; and community problems in war areas. Records about black participation in the war effort are scattered throughout this series, particularly among the regional records. OCWS was concerned about the availability of recreational facilities for black workers and ser-

Hattie McDaniel (center), chair of the Negro Division of the Hollywood Victory Committee, leads a caravan of entertainers and hostesses to Minter Field in Bakersfield, Calif., for a show. Date and photographer unknown. RG 208, Records of the Office of War Information. (208-S-4264-5).

vicemen. In the series is a folder for the Urban League (#801, ½ in.). The Urban League worked with OCWS in the areas of industrial and labor problems, housing, health, recreation, and welfare among blacks and helped identify possible racial conflict areas in the Nation. There are four folders with materials for black history in the file "Recreation–Negroes" (#845.33), one file for each of the years 1941, 1942, 1943, and 1944 (totaling 3 in.). The records document the lack of recreational facilities outside of military camps as causes of racial tensions in some areas for black soldiers, for Bahamian and Jamaican migratory laborers on the east coast, and for defense workers. In order to know where recreational facilities for blacks were most needed, the Office kept track of the location of black servicemen and women and defense workers. An OCWS staff member, James W. Greater, himself a black man, supervised two black representatives on the recreation staff. In addition to information about the location of the black population, he kept press releases relating to blacks, lists of blacks working in the Federal Government, names of members of black community churches and organizations who were willing to provide recreational services to black men, locations of United Service Organizations (USO) providing for the needs of black servicemen, and reports on problems of black youth, transportation, and health. The subject of recreation for blacks is under the same heading (#845.33) in the regional records of this series.

215.3. The **general records of the Office of the Director, 1941–45** (7 ft.), arranged alphabetically by subject, include a folder on race relations and areas of racial tension (3 in.). There is a *Monthly Summary of Events and Trends in Race Relations* compiled by Fisk University in Nashville, Tenn., for the months of August and September of 1943 and for February, March, May, and June of 1944. There are also reports from various local areas about the size of the black population, racial conflicts, recreational facilities, housing, and employment. Some of the local areas are Cincinnati, Ohio; Kansas City, Mo.; Portland, Oreg.; Vancouver, Wash.; Richmond, Calif.; Gary, Ind.; St. Louis, Mo.; New Orleans, La.; Los Angeles, Calif. (particularly concerning the Los Angeles Railway Co.); San Francisco, Calif.; Chicago, Ill.; and Evansville, Ind. The records in this folder also relate to work with the American Council on Race Relations and include some of their newsletters, publications, correspondence, and reports. There is also some information about recreation for black children. Other articles, clippings, and publications pertain to race relations.

215.4. The **general records of the Office of the Director of the Recreation Division, 1941–46** (5 ft.), arranged by subject, relate mainly to administrative and personnel matters; the construction of recreation centers as war public-service projects and their disposition by the Federal Works Agency; and recreation problems affecting industrial workers, children, servicemen, and black Americans. One folder entitled "Negroes" (1 in.) includes correspondence from James W. Greater to black groups that sponsored recreational activities for black soldiers or workers. There is a clipping from the November 1, 1944, *Atlanta Daily World,* a black-owned newspaper, with the headline "Ninety-Five Recreation Buildings Built by FSA for Race." The buildings were located in 29 States. There are other clippings and articles about blacks and the war effort, information about USO facilities for black servicemen and women, Negro Recreation Conference programs for Mississippi and Florida, and material about health, employment, and housing for the black population in North Carolina; Benton Harbor, Mich.; and Memphis, Tenn. Another folder, "Centers of Negro Population" (1 in.), consists of information about recreational facilities for blacks in various locations and related urban conditions, such as housing, employment, the number of defense workers, type of labor available to blacks, educational opportunities, employment and unemployment, number of black-owned papers in the area, and labor union participation by blacks. Some reports include maps. There are general reports for North Carolina, West Virginia, Virginia, and New York. There is a more extensive report that includes information on Jacksonville, Daytona Beach, Tallahassee, and Pensacola, Fla., and Dothon, Ala. Separate reports exist for Camden, Newark, and Elizabeth, N.J., and Harrisburg, Pa.

The most extensive report is for Philadelphia.

215.5. The **general records of the Social Protection Division, 1941–46** (4 ft.), are arranged alphabetically by subject. This Division was responsible for organizing and conducting a national program to check the spread of venereal disease (VD) and to suppress prostitution in defense areas. Some records pertaining to blacks are in folders entitled "Negro and White VD Rates" and "Negro Groups" (totaling ½ in.). The former includes reports such as "The Negro Community's Share in Prevention," 1944, by Edward V. Taylor, a staff member of the Division, and "A Brief Resume of Correlative Factors in the Incidence and Prevalence of Venereal Disease," by Ira DeA. Reid, which discusses low income, housing inadequacy, poor education, and lack of health insurance as factors for the presence of venereal disease among blacks. Another folder contains information about a National Committee on Venereal Disease among blacks and a 1943 report from the Office of the Army Surgeon General with information about VD among black troops, participation by various black community groups in educating blacks about VD, means of suppressing prostitution, and National Negro Health Week in 1941. One report emphasized that "about half of the venereal disease in this nation is found in the Negro tenth of its population."

215.6. The series of **statistics and studies, 1941–45** (3 ft.), conducted by the Division, are arranged by type of material and include scattered statistics about blacks, including information about venereal disease rates, the incidence of VD in the Armed Forces, prostitution within defense communities, and the number, age, and race of women held for prosecution on charges of prostitution.

215.7. The **Division's publications file, 1941–45** (2 ft.), arranged alphabetically by title or subject, includes an article and an address pertaining to blacks (about ½ in.). Both of them are by Nelson C. Jackson, social protection representative for Region VII of the Federal Security Agency. One, entitled "Social Protection Among Negroes," was printed in the *Journal of Social Hygiene,* May 1945, and the other, "Community Organization Activities Among Negroes for VD Control," was an address delivered by Jackson before the eighth annual meeting of the Southern Sociological Society in Atlanta, March 1944. These files also contain the minutes of the National Venereal Disease Committee for 1944 and 1945 (¼ in.). Black members of the Committee included Mordecai Johnson of Howard University; Mabel K. Staupers of the National Association of Graduate Nurses; R. R. Wright, Jr., of the Fraternal Council of Negro Churches; and John H. Sengstake of the Negro Newspaper Publishers Association. The minutes include some information about the availability of VD treatment centers to blacks and about the employment of black staff and black workers by the Public Health Service.

215.8. The **public relations file, 1942–46** (3 ft.), arranged alphabetically by name of correspondent or by subject, includes one folder entitled "Negro VD Reports" (¼ in.). The records consist of correspondence and reports chiefly pertaining to local programs established to combat VD among blacks.

215.9. The records of the Field Operations Division contain **community reports, 1941–45** (7 ft.), arranged by region and thereunder by type of report. These are mainly reports prepared by the regional offices of the ODHWS and the OCWS relating to the impact of defense mobilization and war on certain communities, the ways in which the communities geared themselves to meet the resulting problems, and the unmet needs of these localities with respect to certain community facilities. Many files include information about the problems of local black communities in the areas of employment, housing, recreation, health, child care, nutrition, and transportation.

Record Group 216

Records of the Office of Censorship*

216.1. Immediately after the President's declaration of a state of national emergency on September 2, 1939, the military services began planning wartime censorship of international communications. Censorship operations were carried on by the War and Navy Departments from the time the United States entered the war until the Army and Navy personnel engaged in these operations were formally transferred to the Office of Censorship in 1942.

216.2. The Office of Censorship was established by an Executive order of December 19, 1941, to censor all communications between the United States and any foreign country or between foreign countries by means of transportation that touched U.S. territory. The Executive order also created the Censorship Policy Board to advise on policy and coordination and the Censorship Operating Board to arrange for other Government agencies to use information acquired through censorship. Voluntary censorship of information concerning the war effort by the domestic press and radio was initiated by the Director of the Office of Censorship. Some black-owned newspapers and other periodicals were censored. After Germany's surrender, the activities of the Office were greatly curtailed; they were terminated by an Executive order on September 28, 1945.

216.3. The **administrative subject file, 1941–45** (320 ft.), is arranged according to a subject-numeric classification scheme. The records include correspondence, memorandums, reports, and related material documenting the planning, organization, administration, and operations of the Office of Censorship and its component units. The records, originating in all the operating units of the Office and in the advisory boards, relate to the development of policies and programs for the examination of international communications and supervision of a voluntary censorship of the domestic press and radio; the allocation and distribution to interested Government agencies of useful information intercepted in the process of censorship; the handling of special types of communications, such as privileged mail, financial mail, philatelic mail, and prisoner-of-war mail; the consideration and disposal of complaints relating to delay or mishandling of international communications; the considerations of requests for special privileges in the transmitting of international communications; the preparation, revision, and interpretation of voluntary codes of wartime practices for press and radio and counseling with editors, publishers, and broadcasters as to the application of these codes; the monitoring of selected foreign-language broadcasts and the censoring of press dispatches and shortwave programs; the management and operations of field censorship stations; the demobilization of the Office of Censorship and plans for future censorship; legislation affecting censorship activities; activities of the Censorship Operating and Censorship Policy Boards; and the training of personnel, procurement of supplies, and other administrative services.

216.4. The administrative subject files include several subject headings for black history. "Restricted Information/Racial Problems" (#012–A/15, ⅛ in.) consists of correspondence concerning "inflammatory racial references" in black newspapers, which possibly affected racial relations in overseas theaters of operations. The folder "General Radio/Racial Discrimination" (#021–C/6, ⅛ in.) contains information about a Paul Robeson broadcast on NBC radio for June 27, 1943, and information about race riots, discrimination against black soldiers, and racial segregation of troops. "Troops and Troop Movement/Negro Troops" (#012–D/6, ⅛ in.) consists mostly of correspondence cautioning black newspapers about revealing the movements of black troops. Another folder about black troops, "Race Riots" (#012–D/6), includes three letters about black and white relations at Vallejo, Calif.

216.5. "General Press/Racial Discrimination (Special)" (#012–D/8, ¼ in.) consists of various reports about published accounts of race riots or about the racial situation in the United States. "General Press/Negro Press" (#012–D/8, ¼ in.) consists of correspondence with black newspaper publishers and the Negro Newspaper Publishers Association concerning the relationship between the black press, the Office of Censorship, and the National Negro Newspaper Week. "General Press/Racial Discrimination" (#012–D/8, 1 in.) includes reports about the black press for January and March of 1943 with information about the *Pittsburgh Courier,* Ira F. Lewis, editor; the *Washington Afro-American,* Carl Murphy, editor; the *Chicago Defender,* Louis C. Harper, executive editor; and *The People's Voice,* Adam Clayton Powell, Jr., editor. There are also two folders entitled "Afro-American Censorship Review" (#012–D, ⅛ in.), January 1944. These folders include correspondence and information about articles that were reviewed by the Office of Censorship. There are some cross-references.

216.6. "Personnel/Race Discrimination" (#017, ¼ in.) includes reports and correspondence about the race of Office of Censorship employees, a few pieces of correspondence with the NAACP, and correspondence with the Committee on Fair Employment Practice.

* *Restrictions may apply to this Record Group. Consult NARS staff.*

Record Group 217

Records of the U.S. General Accounting Office

217.1. The U.S. General Accounting Office (GAO) is headed by the Comptroller General of the United States, who is appointed for a 15-year term by the President. Although the agency was established in 1921, records dating from 1789 were transferred to it from predecessor agencies in the Treasury Department. The GAO is in the legislative branch of the Federal Government; it receives its direction from and reports its results to Congress rather than to the President. The chief duties of the GAO are to perform independent Government-wide audits and periodic investigations of receipts, expenditures, and use of public funds; settle fiscal accounts and certain claims by or against the United States; prescribe principles, standards, and related requirements for accounting by executive agencies; cooperate with the Bureau of the Budget and the Treasury Department in the joint program to improve Federal accounting; render legal decisions on fiscal matters; and report the results of its activities to Congress. Among the records of the GAO, 1776–1960, those of the following offices are relevant to research for black history.

Records of the Office of the First Comptroller

217.2. The Office of the First Comptroller was created in 1789. Its main functions were to superintend the adjustment of all accounts and claims, examine the accounts and claims settled by the Auditor, certify the balances to the Register, countersign warrants drawn by the Secretary of the Treasury, and establish regulations for the accountability for public moneys and the forms in which accounts were to be presented. The First

Comptroller was also responsible for directing the filing of suits against delinquent officers.

Records of the Division of Public Lands

217.3. These records include **registers of surety bonds for Land Office officials, 1805–1913** (6 vols., 9 in.). They are arranged by title of official and thereunder alphabetically by name of State in which the land office was located. There are registers of surety bonds of surveyors-general, special disbursing agents, registers, and receivers. Some of these officials were black men. For instance, there are bonds for Mifflin W. Gibbs of Little Rock, Ark., as special disbursing agent and receiver in 1881 and 1890; for Herschel V. Cashin of Huntsville, Ala., in 1897; and for John Leftwich of Montgomery, Ala., in 1897. Information from the registers can be used to find accounts for black officials among the **accounts of receivers of public moneys, 1811–94** (901 ft.), arranged by account number and thereunder chronologically.

Records of the Division of Miscellaneous Accounts

217.4. Among the records relating to accounts and claims is an **abstract of bounty claims for capture of slave ships, 1859–71** (1 vol., 2 in.), arranged alphabetically by initial letter of claimant's surname and thereunder by account number. These abstracts show account number, claimant's name and rank, names of the capturing and captured vessels, amount due, and to whom payable. Many other claims accounts are among the First Auditor's miscellaneous Treasury accounts. Two pages at the front of the volume were used to record captured ships libeled between March 8, 1856, and June 20, 1861; the pages show name of captured ship, dates libeled and condemned, port brought to after seizure, amount paid into the Treasury, and date and number of certificate of deposit or date of distribution of proceeds to officers and men on the capturing vessel.

Records of the Division of Bonds, Contracts, and Powers of Attorney

217.5. Among the civil contracts are **architectural blueprints of Freedmen's Hospital, Howard University, and the U.S. Pension Office, 1909–10** (81 items), arranged by building and thereunder chronologically by date of drawing. Floor plans, elevations, and utility system drawings for the Freedmen's Hospital and other buildings on the Howard University campus (63 items) are accompanied by the contract, specifications, and correspondence relating to the work for which the drawings were made.

Records of the Second Comptroller

217.6. The Office of the Second Comptroller was established in 1817 to improve accountability for public moneys. This act gave the Second

Comptroller the duties formerly exercised by the First Comptroller with respect to the review and approval of accounts and claims relating to military activities; countersigning warrants issued by the Secretaries of the War and Navy Departments; and regulating the preparation of accounts of a military nature.

Records of the Quartermaster Division

217.7. Among these records are **registers of reports about accounts and claims for subsistence, pensions, and accounts for the Bureau of Refugees, Freedmen, and Abandoned Lands** ("Third Auditor's reports, new series"), **1865–78** (18 vols., 6 ft.), arranged numerically by settlement number and thereunder chronologically by date of the Second Comptroller's approval. Each volume has an index arranged alphabetically by initial letter of officer's or claimant's surname. Register entries show settlement number, name of accountable officer or claimant, debit and credit entries, dates reported and approved, titles of appropriations to be charged and credited, and balance. The account numbers begin with No. 1 in both July 1868 and September 1875.

217.8. The general registers of and indexes to contracts include **Freedmen's Bureau contracts, 1867–70** (4 in.), arranged chronologically. The contracts show date, names of parties, terms, and cost. The contracts typically are for construction of schools in Florida, Kentucky, and South Carolina; construction of dormitories in the Washington, D.C., area; and supplies for Freedmen's Hospital.

Records of the Miscellaneous Claims Division

217.9. Included among these records are **abstracts of the settlement of accounts of disbursing agents for the Freedmen's Bureau** ("Freedmen's Bureau differences"), **1866–82** (1 vol., 3 in.), arranged in random order by name of officer and thereunder chronologically. They are also indexed by name of officer. The abstracts show the officer's name, adjusted balance of his accounts for disbursements of the Freedmen's Bureau, balance reported by officer, and explanation of differences.

217.10. The records also include **abstracts of payments to Colored Troops** ("disbursements of Freedmen's Bureau of Treasury certificates"), **1867–74** (5 vols., 1 ft.), arranged by military unit. Abstracts show name of military unit, soldier's name, number and amount of Treasury certificate issued, fees paid, amount paid to soldier, and total paid. The dates indicated above are the approximate payment dates of the Treasury certificates issued as reflected by the numerical range of the volumes.

Records of the Office of the Commissioner of Customs

217.11. The Commissioner of Customs, 1849–94, served as a "Third Comptroller" performing the duties formerly assigned to the First Comptroller with respect to accounts for customs receipts and disbursements and other disbursements of customs officials.

Records of the Miscellaneous Division

217.12. The origin of this Division is not known, but it is mentioned in an 1881 history of the Treasury Department as being the division in the Office of the Commissioner of Customs responsible for administrative matters, such as maintaining the general files of the Office, maintaining records of customs appointments, and keeping a file of oaths of office. The Division also settled claims about customs charges.

217.13. Among the records of this Division are **abstracts of decisions** ("index to decisions"), **ca. 1790–1851** (1 vol., 1 in.), arranged alphabetically by key word of subject. Among the subjects included are prohibitions on the use of slaves in the Navy.

217.14. Official and miscellaneous letters received from merchants, customs officials, and Cabinet-level Government officials, 1789–1892 (230 vols., 69 ft.), are arranged by source (primarily customs district) and thereunder chronologically. They relate to matters such as interpretation of regulations, administrative problems, refund of duties on merchandise, claims for damaged merchandise, and the filing of oaths, bonds, and contracts. There are some letters received from black customs officials, such as Christopher C. Wimbish, a surveyor of port in Atlanta; John H. Deveaux, collector of customs in Brunswick, Ga.; Robert Smalls, collector in Beaufort, S.C.; and Joseph E. Lee, a collector in Jacksonville, Fla. (See also RG 56.) Replies by the Commissioner of Customs are described in **official and miscellaneous letters sent, 1849–94** (74 vols., 14 ft.), and **letters sent to customs officials, 1849–94** (184 vols., 35 ft.).

Records of the Office of the First Auditor

217.15. The Office of the Auditor was authorized by an act of 1789. The Auditor was responsible for the receipt and settlement of all public accounts. An act of 1817 created the offices of four additional auditors and gave the original auditor the title of First Auditor with responsibility for all accounts accruing in the Treasury Department. The First Auditor also had jurisdiction over the accounts of the Department of Agriculture from 1868 to 1894 and of the Justice Department from 1849 to 1894. The Office was abolished in 1921.

Records Relating to Accounts and Claims

217.16. The **miscellaneous Treasury accounts, 1790–1894** (about 1,300 vols. and unbound records, totaling 8,300 ft.), are arranged numerically. One account in this series is for the Board of Commissioners for the Emancipation of Slaves in the District of Columbia, 1862–65 (#158 299, 3 bound volumes and unbound records, totaling 6½ ft.). These records have been reproduced as M520 (6 rolls). The records were transmitted to the First Auditor of the Treasury Department in 1866. An act of April 16, 1862, abolished slavery in the District of Columbia. Under section 3 of the act, the President was authorized to appoint a board of three commissioners who were residents of the District to examine petitions for compensation from former owners of freed slaves in the District. The records include minutes of the Board, a record of bound and unbound petitions, a docket book, a summary list of amounts awarded to claimants, and a final report by the Board dated January 14, 1863.

Records of the Office of the Second Auditor

217.17. The Office of the Second Auditor, 1792–1921, had its origins in an act of May 8, 1792 (1 Stat. 279), which authorized the appointment of an accountant for the War Department. The duties of the accountant were settlement of accounts for pay of the Army, subsistence of officers, bounties, expenses of recruiting, and incidental and contingent expenses of the War Department; settlement of claims for personal services; and settlement of military claims formerly filed with the Paymaster General and the Commissioner of Army Accounts. The Second Auditor was responsible for settlement of accounts for pay and clothing of the Army, subsistence of officers, bounties and premiums due soldiers, military and hospital stores, and contingent expenses of the War Department. His Office also filed the accounts and claims after approval by the Second Comptroller, kept a record of receipts and disbursements of public moneys as they related to the functions of his Office, and recorded warrants drawn by the Secretary of War. An act of 1894 changed the name of the Office to the Auditor for the War Department and assigned to his jurisdiction the settlement of all accounts and claims relating to the Department.

General Records

217.18. Among the general records of the Office relating to personnel is a **register of employees, 1817–1900** (1 vol., 1 in.), arranged alphabetically by initial letter of employee's surname and thereunder by year of appointment. The register shows name of employee, State where born and from which appointed, length of military service (if any), dates of appointment and later personnel actions, and date and cause of termination of service. Some of the employees have "colored" written after their names.

Records of the Paymaster, Ordnance, and Medical Division

217.19. Among the records relating to pay for military service is a **register of payments of Colored Troops** ("payments to discharged soldiers: U.S. Colored Troops"), **1863–68** (6 vols., 2 ft.), arranged alphabetically by initial letter of the soldier's surname and thereunder chronologically. The register of payments shows soldier's name, rank and military unit, period for which he was paid, amount paid, name of paymaster, account number, and date paid. Variations in pay—generally for travel pay, bounty, or stoppages of pay—are explained. Some entries are for claims for arrears of pay and were settled as late as 1889.

Records of the Pay and Bounty Division

217.20. The records relating to pay and bounty claims include a **register of payments to Colored Soldiers, 1867–85** (7 vols., 1 ft.), arranged by military unit and thereunder chronologically. This is a register of payments to members of the U.S. Colored Troops under provisions of Joint Resolution No. 23, dated March 29, 1867 (15 Stat. 26), which established procedures for settlement of approved pay and bounty claims for members of the U.S. Colored Troops. Entries show soldier's name and military unit; date of claim; certificate of settlement number; amounts due for pay and regular bounty; special bounty total due; amount paid claimant; and amount paid as attorney fees.

217.21. Another **register of claims of Colored Soldiers** is dated **1879–99** (1 vol., 2 in.) and is arranged alphabetically by initial letter of surname of soldier. The register entries show name of soldier and unit of U.S. Colored Troops with which he had served. Some entries are followed by the notation "returned to claimant" or "Mr. Smith, Room 74," followed by a date.

217.22. There are many case files for the **disallowed claims of U.S. Colored Troops, ca. 1864–93** (269 ft.), arranged by military unit and thereunder alphabetically by soldier's name. These case files of disallowed claims for additional bounty or other moneys consist usually of the original petition of the soldier or his heirs, affidavits, correspondence between the Auditor and War Department officials relating to possible basis for the claim, and a statement of the basis on which the claim had been rejected. The cover sheet for the claim shows the soldier's name and military unit.

Records Relating to Other Accounts and Claims

217.23. The **abstract of settled accounts of disbursing officers for the Freedmen's Bureau, 1874–82** (1 vol., 2 in.), is arranged by month of settlement and indexed by name of disbursing officer. It shows name and rank of disbursing officer, year and number of settlement, date of settlement, debit and credit entries (including names of persons to whom moneys were advanced or from whom moneys were received, titles of appropriations concerned, and amounts), and dates accounts were reported and confirmed. Most appropriations concerned were for pay and bounty for volunteers and for "colored soldiers."

Records of the Archives Division

217.24. The records relating to pay of volunteer units include **registers of payments to volunteer and special units during the Civil War, 1861–66** (4 ft.), arranged by State or type of unit. Register entries show identity of military unit and its commanding officer, period for which paid, name of paymaster, settlement number, account number, and voucher number. There are two volumes for payments to U.S. Colored Troops.

217.25. Records relating to pay of volunteer soldiers include a **selected list of personnel of volunteer military organizations, ca. 1863–65** (4 vols., 5 in.), arranged by military unit and thereunder alphabetically by initial letter of surname of officer or soldier. The list shows the identity of the organization and the names of persons. There are volumes for the U.S. Colored Troops.

Office of the Third Auditor

217.26. The Office of the Third Auditor was established to settle all accounts relating to the War of 1812 that remained unsettled in 1816. Other duties were added in later years, including claims for horses and other property lost in the military service of the United States (1849), for the loss of steamboats and other vessels in military service (1864), and for reimbursement to States for military expenses incurred in the Indian Wars and the Civil War (1890). An 1890 act also made the Third Auditor responsible for the Signal Corps accounts.

Land, Files, and Miscellaneous Division

217.27. The records of settled accounts and claims include **case files for claims approved by the Southern Claims Commission, ca. 1871–90** (211 ft.). They are arranged alphabetically by State and thereunder alphabetically by name of claimant. These are case files for approved claims of citizens of Alabama, Arkansas, Georgia, Louisiana, Mississippi, North Carolina, South Carolina, Tennessee, Texas, and Virginia who had suffered property damage or loss by Federal troops during the Civil War. Many of the claimants were black, especially those from the South Carolina Sea Island region. They were required to prove to the Commission that they had remained loyal to the Union during the war. The claims were paid from appropriations for "Claims of loyal citizens for supplies furnished during the Rebellion." A typical file includes the claimant's petition, inventories of supplies and property for which compensation was desired, testimony of the claimant and others (both favorable and adverse) relating to the claim, a copy of the Commission's report, and the Third Auditor's certificate of settlement. These files were formerly a part of the main series of settled accounts and claims. An index to claims acted on by the Commission was published under the title *Consolidated Index of Claims Reported by the Commissioners of Claims to the House of Representatives, From 1871 to 1880* (Washington: Government Printing Office, 1892).

217.28. Case files for disallowed claims are among the records of the U.S. House of Representatives (RG 233). Some claims originally disallowed by the Commission were later heard by the U.S. Court of Claims, and case files for these claims are among the records of that court (RG 123). Other records of the Southern Claims Commission are among the general records of the Department of the Treasury (RG 56). The Treasury records have been published on microfilm: *Records of the Commissioners of Claims (Southern Claims Commission), 1871–1880,* M87 (14 rolls).

217.29. Among the State claims is an **abstract of additional pay credited to soldiers of the Rhode Island militia for service in the Revolutionary War, April 1780** (5 sheets). It is arranged alphabetically by name of soldier. This abstract shows the name and rank of the soldier, his military unit, and amount due. An act of the Continental Congress passed April 10, 1780, provided that additional pay could be credited to soldiers because of depreciation of the currency. Some of these soldiers were black.

Office of the Fourth Auditor

217.30. The Office of the Fourth Auditor had its origins in a 1798 act that authorized the appointment of an "accountant for the Navy" within the Navy Department. The duty of the accountant was to settle accounts for moneys advanced and supplies and provisions issued or distributed and to report such settlements periodically to the accounting officers of the Treasury Department for review. In 1817 these duties were assigned to the Fourth Auditor, who was responsible for settling all accounts of or relating to the Navy Department, including those for payment of naval pensions; keeping accounts of receipts and disbursements of public moneys by the Navy Department; keeping accounts of debts due because of advances of public moneys; and filing settled accounts after final approval by the Second Comptroller. In 1822 the Office began registering warrants for disbursements for the Navy Department. After 1894 it ceased to settle accounts for paying naval pensions.

General Claims Division

217.31. Among these records are **abstracts of accounts of officers of the Freedmen's Bureau, 1874–82** (1 vol., 2 in.), arranged by name of officer and indexed by name of officer. The abstracts show name and rank of officer representing the Freedmen's Bureau, titles of appropriations from which he had disbursed funds in behalf of naval personnel, debit and credit entries, explanation, and number of settled account. Most of the moneys had been disbursed from appropriations to pay Navy salaries, bounties for service, prize money, and bounties for destruction of enemy ships. The accounts were to repay the Freedmen's Bureau for Bureau funds spent in behalf of naval personnel. Loosely inserted in the front of the volume is a list of payments to Gen. O. O. Howard by Navy paymasters C. C. Jackson and Edwin Stewart, May 4, 1867, to March 6, 1872, showing date paid, claimant's name, and amount paid. General Howard receipted for the moneys paid.

Records of the Record and Prize Division

217.32. The functions of the Division were the registering, indexing, and recording of general correspondence; settlement of claims for prize money; preparation of reports on naval personnel and reports requested by Congress, the courts, or the Secretary of the Treasury; administering personnel matters within the Fourth Auditor's Office; and maintaining the files of the Office. John R. Lynch, a black former congressman from Mississippi, served a term as Fourth Auditor from 1889 to 1893. Much of the correspondence of the Division for this period was addressed to him or sent out under his signature.

Office of the Fifth Auditor

217.33. The Office of the Fifth Auditor was established in 1817 to settle all accounts of the Department of State, of the Post Office Department (1817–36), and arising out of Indian affairs (1817–19). The duties of the Fifth Auditor relating to general superintendence of the lighthouse system began in January 1820 and were formalized in 1845. The Fifth Auditor became responsible for settlement of internal revenue accounts in 1864. In 1894 the Fifth Auditor was renamed Auditor for the State and other Departments and was made responsible for the settlement of accounts of the State and Justice Departments and other accounts not specifically assigned to another auditor.

Records of the Diplomatic and Consular Division

217.34. The Diplomatic and Consular Division was first specifically mentioned as a division in the Fifth Auditor's Office in a report on activities of the Office for the fiscal year beginning July 1, 1882. It may have been a division in the Office as early as 1868. Among the major types of accounts settled by the Diplomatic and Consular Division were those for salaries, fees, and contingent expenses of diplomatic and consular officers; expenses for care and transportation of destitute U.S. seamen; expenses relating to deceased seamen; and contingent and other expenses of the State Department.

217.35. It is believed that Ebenezer D. Bassett, who became Minister Resident and Consul General in Haiti in 1869, was the first black diplomat. Haiti and Liberia were recognized by the U.S. Government during the Civil War. From this time formal diplomatic representatives were usually black Americans. James Milton Turner served as the first black Minister Resident and Consul General to Liberia beginning in 1871. (See RG 59 and RG 84.) Among the records relating to accounts and claims are **alphabetical registers of diplomatic and consular accounts, 1854–96** (6 vols., 11 in.). The volumes are arranged chronologically. Within each volume, entries are arranged by initial letter of accountable officer's surname and thereunder chronologically. Black diplomats Bassett and Turner, as well as others, are listed in these volumes. Entries show officer's name, title, duty station, type and period of account, and date received. Among the types of accounts included are those for salaries and contingent expenses of U.S. diplomatic and consular officials and for relief of seamen. There are also other series relating to diplomatic and consular accounts.

Records of the Internal Revenue Division

217.36. Among the records relating to accounts are those pertaining to the direct tax of 1862. In the South Carolina Sea Island region, blacks constituted virtually the entire population. Consequently, the records for the South Carolina Direct Tax Commission for this period largely concern the Commissioners' interactions with the former slaves. **Accounts of the Direct Tax Commission for South Carolina, 1865–1885** (50 vols. and unbound records, totaling 5 ft.), are arranged chronologically. These files consist of some direct tax accounts, including audit reports, abstracts of disbursements of the Commissioners in behalf of the school system in South Carolina, and receipts for rents paid to the Commissioners. Report 12 was accompanied by receipt books and assessment books. They show location, description, and valuation of land, names of owners and taxpayers, and amounts of taxes paid. Other records of the South Carolina Commission are among RG 58.

217.37. The **journal of the Direct Tax Commission for South Carolina, 1871–76** (1 vol., 1 in.), is arranged chronologically. Entries for funds received relate typically to sale or rental of lands or buildings and show name of purchaser or renter, location and description of property, and amount paid. Entries for disbursements are chiefly for administrative expenses and show names of persons paid and explanation of services furnished to the Commissioners. Other entries relate to transfer of funds collected, applications for redemption of land, and the delivery of leases.

217.38. Records of the Beaufort, S.C., tax district, 1862–72 (6 vols., 11 in.), are arranged chronologically. These records consist of a statement of the assessed value of lands as determined by the Commission during the period November 3–25, 1862, occasionally showing actual payment of taxes; applications for redemption of plantations sold for taxes; land maps annotated to show the township, range, section, topographical features (such as swamps), and landmarks (such as houses and graveyards) of surveyed lands, along with surveyors' field notes; and copies of leases, which include name and address of person leasing the land, location and description of the property, and terms and special conditions of the lease.

217.39. The **list of South Carolina tax sale certificates, 1875–76** (1 vol., ½ in.), is arranged chronologically. Entries show the number and date of the certificate, name of purchaser, purchase price, and description of the property.

Record Group 220

Records of Temporary Committees, Commissions, and Boards*

220.1. Temporary committees, commissions, boards, and other bodies have been appointed from time to time by the President to serve in factfinding or advisory capacities or to perform policymaking or coordinating functions with regard to the work of other executive agencies. Committees can also be created by acts of Congress. This collective record group includes the records of a number of such bodies that have not been established as separate record groups. Excluded from this record group are records of Presidential committees, commissions, and boards that gained permanent status or whose functions and records were transferred to other agencies, those whose records have been interfiled with or otherwise have become part of the records of an agency that had them in its custody or of the President's files (now in Presidential libraries), and those established to serve the heads of other agencies rather than the President. Many of these records relate to black history, particularly to discrimination and segregation.

Records of the President's Committee on the Equality of Treatment and Opportunity in the Armed Services, 1948–50

220.2. This Committee, popularly known as the Fahy Committee, was established by Executive Order 9981 of July 26, 1948, to determine in what ways operations of the armed services might be altered or improved to ensure equality of treatment and opportunity for all members without regard to color, religion, or national origin. The Committee's final report was submitted to the President on May 22, 1950. The **records of the Committee, 1949–50** (5 ft. in the Harry S Truman Library in Independence, Mo.), arranged by subject, include transcripts of Committee meetings, correspondence, drafts of reports, newspaper clippings, and materials relating to rules and procedures followed by the Army, Navy, Air Force, and Coast Guard in utilizing personnel from minority groups.

Records of the President's Committee on Migratory Labor

220.3. The President's Committee on Migratory Labor was formally established in 1960 by Executive Order 10894. The Committee had existed previously as the Interdepartmental Committee on Migratory Labor, appointed by letter of the President on August 26, 1954. In 1955 the name was changed to the President's Committee on Migratory Labor. The Committee was terminated January 4, 1964, by the Secretary of Labor with the approval of the President. The purpose of the Committee was to assess the needs of migratory workers and to stimulate programs toward improving their living and working conditions. The **records of the Committee, 1960–64,** with some dated as early as 1938 and as late as 1966 (41 ft., in the Dwight D. Eisenhower Library, Abilene, Kans.), arranged by subject, include administrative correspondence, correspondence with State and local public and nonpublic organizations, speeches, reports, and publications. There are some references to black migrant workers. A folder for the NAACP includes an NAACP publication entitled *No Harvest for the Reaper: The Story of the Migratory Agricultural Workers in the United States,* by Herbert Hill with an introduction by Roy Wilkins (50 pp.). The publication pertains to migrant workers of all racial groups, but almost all of the photographs in this publication depict black migrant workers.

*Records of the President's Committee on Equal Opportunity in the Armed Forces**

220.4. The establishment of this Committee was set forth in a letter from President Kennedy to the Chairman, Gerhard A. Gessell, dated June 22, 1962. The Commission considered means of improving equality of opportunity, especially for black Americans, in the Armed Forces. The **records of the Committee, 1962–65** (10 ft., in the Lyndon B. Johnson Library, Austin, Tex.), arranged by subject, consist of drafts of the Committee's report, correspondence, research studies, and questionnaires with replies. Subjects include antidiscrimination policies, racial designations, equality of treatment and of opportunity for black military personnel stationed in the United States, minority groups in the Air Force, black cadets, integration and the black officer, use of race on personnel and reporting forms, complaints of discrimination, and civil rights report on family housing.

Records of the President's Committee on Equal Opportunity in Housing

220.5. This Committee was established November 20, 1962, by Executive Order 11063 to recommend general policies and procedures relating to the prevention of discrimination in housing in which the Government had a primary interest, to check on the progress made by the departments and agencies subject to this order, and to promote coordination programs for eliminating the causes of housing discrimination. It was terminated June 30, 1968. The **records of the Committee, 1962–68** (40 ft., in the Lyndon B. Johnson Library, Austin, Tex.), arranged by subject, consist of reports prepared for the President and the heads of various Government agencies; correspondence of the Chairman, the General Counsel, and other committee members; transcripts of meetings and conferences; copies of speeches; and material relating to housing discrimination against blacks in the United States.

Records of the President's Committee on Equal Employment Opportunity

220.6. This Committee was established by Executive Order 10925 of March 6, 1961, as amended by Executive Order 11114 of June 22, 1963. It studied employment practices of the Federal Government and large employers and recommended steps to completely eliminate discrimination in employment within the executive branch and by Government contractors. The Committee's functions were transferred to the Department of Labor by Executive Order 11126 of September 24, 1965. The **office files of Hobart Taylor, Jr.,** Executive Vice Chairman of the Committee, **1961–65** (2 ft.), arranged by subject, include memorandums about Committee deliberations; correspondence, chiefly of the White House Press Secretary with civil rights leaders; and case files concerning discrimination in large firms.

Records of the President's Committee on Public Higher Education in the District of Columbia

220.7. President John F. Kennedy announced on September 23, 1963, the creation of a Committee on Public Higher Education in the District of Columbia and requested that it consider what types of publicly supported institutions of higher learning should be established for the District. The Committee issued its report to the President in June 1964 and recommend the establishment of several publicly supported institutions of higher learning and a system of noncompetitive scholarships and special curricula. The **records of the Committee, 1963–64** (2 ft.), arranged by subject, include interspersed information about the black population in Washington, D.C., and about blacks in the school system and in the predominantly black institutions of higher learning—Howard University and the District of Columbia Teacher's College.

Records of the National Advisory Commission on Rural Poverty

220.8. The National Advisory Commission on Rural Poverty was appointed by President Johnson under Executive Order 11306 on September 27, 1966. The Commission was instructed to make a comprehensive study of rural life and rural poverty, evaluate programs, and submit recommendations to the President. The Commission's report is entitled *The People Left Behind: A Report by the President's National Advisory Commission on Rural Poverty* (1967). Experts on rural poverty in the United States prepared, under contract, 45 technical papers on all aspects of the prob-

Young women in a dance class at Atlanta University. 1936 or 1937. Kenneth F. Space, photographer. RG 208, Records of the Office of War Information. (208-LU-51C-3).

lem. A volume of these background papers was published separately under the title *Rural Poverty in the United States* (1968). One paper, written by Dr. Daniel O. Price, is entitled "The Negro Population of the South." The **records of the Commission, 1966–67** (7 ft., in the Lyndon B. Johnson Library, Austin, Tex.), arranged by subject, include the Commission staff's correspondence files relating to meetings, hearings, and preparation of the report; tapes of oral testimony from public hearings; transcripts of hearings, and meetings; manuscripts of contracted papers and drafts of the Commission report; and administrative data. Black history materials are interspersed.

Records of the President's Committee on Urban Housing

220.9. This Committee was appointed by the President on June 3, 1967, to prepare a report on ways to stimulate the rebuilding of depressed areas of U.S. cities. The study focused on the role of the private sector of the economy in rehabilitating deteriorated urban housing and on methods for enlarging the size and skills of the labor force available to rebuild depressed housing areas. The Committee was terminated when its report was submitted to the President on August 31, 1968. The **records of the Committee, 1967–68** (29 ft., in the Lyndon B. Johnson Library, Austin, Tex.), arranged by subject, include some black history materials pertaining to race riots, civil disorders, job discrimination, and other topics.

The files for the Committee include minutes, reports, correspondence, records relating to legislative research, housing goals, research and technology, manpower, and land.

Records of the National Advisory Commission on Civil Disorders*

220.10. The National Advisory Commission on Civil Disorders, commonly called the Kerner Commission from the name of its Chairman, Gov. Otto Kerner of Illinois, was appointed by President Johnson under Executive Order 11365 on July 29, 1967. The Commission was instructed to investigate and make recommendations concerning the origins of civil disorders; to recommend the appropriate role of local, State, and Federal authorities in dealing with civil disorders; and to consider any other matters the President might place before it. The Commission's report to the President was published March 1, 1968, as the *Report of the National Advisory Commission on Civil Disorders* along with supplementary studies.

220.11. All of the records of the Commission, 1967–68, some of an earlier date (350 ft., in the Lyndon B. Johnson Library, Austin, Tex.), are important for black history because the disorders investigated were confrontations between black and white citizens in various cities. The records include **transcripts and proceedings of the Commission, 1967** (3 ft.), which are arranged chronologically and include statements of witnesses, lists of participants, and agenda. **Exhibits used at Commission meetings, 1967** (4 ft.), are arranged chronologically and thereunder by exhibit number. They consist of statements by witnesses, newspaper clippings, analyses of the affected cities, and various types of background information. **Commission reports and drafts, 1968** (4 ft.), are arranged by volume number and consist of drafts of chapters for the final report. **Commission research studies, 1967** (2 ft.), are arranged alphabetically by title. The studies include investigations of discrimination in housing and education, of consumer protection for the poor, and of the participation of black youths in civil disorders.

220.12. The records also include **chronologies of disturbances in the affected cities, 1966–67** (5 in.), arranged alphabetically by city. These consist of a description of each city, data on disorders, events leading up to the disorders, and a draft of the analysis of the disturbances. There is also a file of **selected letters received by the Commission, 1967** (2 ft.), arranged alphabetically by subject. The letters include statements and suggestions on the problems of civil disorders from State officials, business leaders, churchmen, and others. The **general subject file of the Office of Information, 1967–68** (5 ft.), is arranged alphabetically by subject and consists of correspondence of the Commission staff with congressmen, business leaders, university professors, and others. Events leading up to the disorders, the riots, and their aftermath are the subjects of **newspaper clippings, 1967** (6 ft.), which are arranged alphabetically by name of city. The **still picture collection, 1875–1967** (5 in.), includes pictures of the cities in which the 1967 riots occurred, scenes of racial incidents in U.S. history, and prints of the Commissioners with President Lyndon B. Johnson.

Records of the National Commission on the Causes and Prevention of Violence

220.13. The Commission was established in 1968 after the assassinations of Rev. Dr. Martin Luther King, Jr., and Presidential candidate Robert F. Kennedy and the numerous riots and civil disturbances that followed their deaths. Executive Order 11412 of June 10, 1968, directed that the Commission investigate and make recommendations concerning the causes and prevention of lawless acts of violence in the United States, including assassinations, murder, and assault; of disrespect for law and order and for public officials; of violent disruptions of public order by individuals and groups; and of any other matters the President might place before it. Milton Eisenhower was appointed chairman and a black woman, Patricia R. Harris, a former ambassador, was a member of the Commission. The Commission was terminated after its report, *To Establish Justice, To Insure Domestic Tranquility,* was submitted to the President on December 10, 1969.

220.14. Many of the **records of the Commission, 1968–69** (157 ft., 10 rolls of microfilm, 1,663 audiovisual items, and 2 reels of machine readable records in the Lyndon B. Johnson Library, Austin, Tex.), relate to race relations, racial violence, and anti- and pro-black activist groups. One task force report is entitled *Shoot-Out in Cleveland: Black Militants and the Police.*

220.15. Audiovisual material includes photographs of disorders at the Chicago and Miami Presidential nomination conventions in 1968, disturbances in Cleveland, and disorders in Washington during the 1969 Presidential inauguration; of persons outside the Post Office Building in Richmond, Va., during the trial of black activist H. "Rap" Brown in 1968; and of miscellaneous subjects, some of which relate to black history. There are sound recordings (18 items) of a talk by Tom Anderson, publisher of agricultural periodicals, entitled "Bi-Partisan Treason"; of songs for the racial segregationist Presidential candidate George Wallace entitled "Wallace for President" and "Ride with Wallace"; and of speeches, songs, interviews, and radio programs concerning antiblack statements of the Ku Klux Klan. Included are tapes relating to disturbances at San Francisco State College.

Records of the 1970 White House Conference on Children and Youth

220.16. On October 26, 1969, President Nixon issued the call for the Conference to convene in Washington on December 13, 1970, and on December 5, 1969, he appointed Stephen Hess as National Chairman of the Conference. It was decided in January 1970 to hold two separate and distinct conferences: the Conference on Children (under 14 years of age), which was held in Washington, December 13–18, 1970, and the Conference on Youth (ages 14–24), which was convened in Estes Park, Colo., April 18–22, 1971. The Youth Conference had 10 task forces on such subjects as the draft, national service, and alternatives; drugs; the economy and employment; education; the environment; foreign relations; legal rights and justice; poverty; race and minority relations; and values, ethics, and culture. The combined Conference staff terminated its activities on June 30, 1971, and the final reports were submitted in May and December 1971. The **records of the Conference, 1960–72** (99 ft.), arranged by subject, include the National Chairman's subject files, correspondence, records relating to followup activities, and copies of official publications. These files include information about race relations and statistics about black children and youth. (This conference was one of a series of White House conferences on children. The first one was in 1909.)

Records of the National Commission on Marihuana and Drug Abuse

220.17. The Commission was established by title II of the Comprehensive Drug Abuse Prevention and Control Act of 1970 to conduct a comprehensive study of drug abuse and the use of marihuana in the United States. President Nixon appointed nine persons to the Commission. The first report of the National Commission, *Marihuana: A Signal of Misunderstanding,* was presented to the President and Congress in 1972, and its second and final report, *Drug Use in America: Problem in Perspective,* was presented a year later. The Commission was terminated May 21, 1973. The **records of the Commission, 1970–73** (31 ft. and 4 machine readable tapes), arranged by type of material, include transcripts of hearings, correspondence, subject files, studies and reports, questionnaires, and punched cards. There are also magnetic tapes that contain a comprehensive study of drug abuse in the United States. Some of the statistical information about drug users indicates race.

Records of the Commission on Population Growth and the American Future

220.18. The Commission was established by an act of March 16, 1970, pursuant to President Nixon's recommendation to Congress that a commission be established to study aspects of the projected growth of the population of the United States up to the year 2000. The Commission reported to the President and Congress in March 1972 and ended its activities in May 1972. The **records of the Commission, 1970–72** (15 ft.), arranged by subject, include the agenda and statements prepared for Commission meetings, transcripts of hearings, correspondence, studies, publications, newsclippings, press releases, copies and drafts of the interim and final reports, and a name and subject index to material in the reports. Some of the material includes racial statistics. One magnetic tape contains responses to a nationwide public opinion survey conducted for the Commission in 1971 by Opinion Research Corp., Princeton, N.J. It concerns individuals' demographic knowledge, their attitudes toward population policies, and the relation of these factors to sex, race, income, religion, education, and ethnic origin.

Records of the President's Commission on Campus Unrest, 1970

220.19. This Commission was established by Executive Order 11536 of June 13, 1970. Its duties included identifying the principal causes of campus violence; suggesting specific methods and procedures through which grievances could be resolved by means other than force; suggesting ways to protect academic freedom, to safeguard the right to obtain an education free from interference, and to ensure the right of peaceful dissent and protest; and proposing practical steps that could be taken to minimize dangers attendant upon expressions of dissent. The Commission's creation came in the wake of the tragedies of May 1970 at Kent State University in Ohio and at Jackson State College in Mississippi, which together had resulted in the deaths of six students and the wounding of several others. Jackson State College is a predominantly black school. **Records of the Jackson State College investigative team, 1970** (10 in.), are arranged by subject and include reference material gathered by the team, such as statements, speeches, official documents, maps, newspaper clippings, and items concerning the grand jury investigation of the incident. **Additional records of the Jackson State College investigative team, 1970** (7 ft.), are arranged by subject and thereunder alphabetically by name. The records include Federal Bureau of Investigation and team interviews and background reports on individuals in the protest and shooting, indexes, synopses, and tables of contents for the preliminary, supplementary, and final reports of the team; a printed report on the incident prepared by a committee created by the mayor of Jackson; material on physical evidence; and various other documents used by the team during its investigation at Jackson, Miss.

Records of the National Commission on the Financing of Postsecondary Education

220.20. This Commission was established by Public Law 92-318, approved June 23, 1972. Consisting of members appointed by Congress and the President, it was required to undertake studies of current sources of support for postsecondary education, the appropriate role of the States in its support, and student assistance programs. The Commission was terminated June 30, 1974. The **records of the Commission, 1972–74** (3 ft. and 5 machine readable tapes), arranged by subject, include the Commission's meetings and budgetary files, study plan files, copies of material distributed to its members and staff, press releases, and magnetic tapes containing data on enrollment, financial support, institutional characteristics, and student and faculty information. There is information about black colleges and universities and about black students.

Records of the President's Commission on Coal

220.21. President Jimmy Carter established the President's Commission on Coal by Executive Order 12062 of May 1978. The President had announced his intention to create such a committee in March of 1978 on the same day that he announced the settlement of an 111-day coal strike by the United Mine Workers of America. The Commission undertook to investigate several major areas of interest relating to the U.S. coal industry, mine safety, labor-management relations in the industry, and living conditions of the miners and their families.

220.22. The President appointed five voting Commission members, balancing them to represent the interests of labor, management, and the public sector. West Virginia Gov. John D. (Jay) Rockefeller IV was the Chairman. Data acquired through the hearings and field investigations were compiled, and a final report was sent to the President on March 3, 1980. In addition to the recommendations and summary findings that constituted the final report, the Commission also published several other compilations and special reports, including a coal data book, a summary of staff findings, and an illustrated volume entitled *The American Coal Miner: A Report on Community and Living Conditions in the Coalfields.*

220.23. The reports, transcripts, sound recordings, and correspondence of the Commission yield little statistical information about black coal miners, but the still picture collection and the photographs in the published report, *The American Coal Miner,* indicate that black miners were interviewed and their living conditions were investigated by the Commission. Interspersed among 108 black-and-white mounted slides and 22,337 contact prints (taken throughout U.S. coalfields by Commission photographers between May and November of 1979) are pictures that depict black

miners at work and their lifestyles in mining communities. There are some portraits of individual black miners as well as pictures that document occupational safety conditions, medical services and health facilities, roads, transportation, educational facilities, leisure-time activities, and living conditions of other minority miners, such as women, Indians, and Hispanics.
* *Restrictions may apply to this Record Group. Consult NARS staff.*

Record Group 224

Records of the Office of Labor (*War Food Administration*)

224.1. The Office of Labor was created March 1, 1943, and was responsible for farm labor supply, recruitment, and wage stabilization. It supervised importation of farmworkers from abroad and the transportation and care of both foreign and domestic interstate farmworkers. Its chief activity was the operation of camps for migratory and foreign farm laborers. When the War Food Administration was abolished in 1945, the Office of Labor was terminated. Some of its functions were continued by the Labor Branch of the Production and Marketing Administration of the Department of Agriculture until 1948.

224.2. The **general correspondence, 1943** (13 ft.), arranged according to a subject-numeric classification scheme, includes the file "Farm Labor–Negroes" (#1–19, ¼ in.). Correspondence in the file shows that two black men, Frederick D. Patterson and Claude A. Barnett, worked as special assistants to the director of the War Food Administration. The correspondence relates to the education of black farmers and various public relations matters. The folder includes a copy of the spring 1943 issue of *The Brown American,* a periodical published by the Philadelphia-based National Association of Negroes in American Industry. This issue includes articles on food conservation. The folder "Negro Press" (#1–1, ⅛ in.) contains several "Digests of Clippings on Agriculture from the Negro Press." These digests include information about farm laborers brought in from outside of the United States to help harvest crops. Many of these laborers were black people from the Bahamas and Jamaica. Their treatment as workers and in labor camps reflects the racial attitudes prevalent in the United States during the World War II period.

224.3. The **general correspondence** for the period **1943–44** (11 ft.), arranged by an alpha-numeric file classification scheme, also includes information about the treatment of Bahamian and Jamaican farm laborers. Material on this topic is interspersed throughout these records, but there is a concentration in file category 30–C61. The records pertain

Farmers chewing sugarcane. Meridian, Miss. September 1941. Forsythe, photographer. RG 83, Records of the Bureau of Agricultural Economics. (16-N-2558).

to racial discrimination, labor camps, riots and other racial disturbances, wage disputes, legal problems, and numerous other difficulties.

224.4. General correspondence for the period **1945–46** (19 ft.), arranged according to a subject-numeric classification scheme, also includes information under various categories about black farm laborers from the Bahamas and Jamaica.

Record Group 228

Records of the Committee on Fair Employment Practice

228.1. The first Committee on Fair Employment Practice (FEPC) was established in the Office of Production Management (OPM) by Executive Order 8802 of June 25, 1941. Executive Order 9346 of May 27, 1943, abolished that Committee and created a new Committee with the same name in the Office for Emergency Management. The National War Agencies Appropriation Act of 1946 provided funds for the second Committee until June 30, 1946. The Committee terminated its business on June 28 when it sent its final report to the President. The Committee formulated and interpreted policies to combat racial discrimination in employment; received, investigated, and adjusted complaints of such discrimination; and assisted Government agencies, employers, and labor unions with problems of discrimination. The jurisdiction of the Committee included complaints against all departments, agencies, and independent establishments of the Federal Government; complaints against all employers and the unions of their employees having contractual relations with the Federal Government; complaints against all employers engaged in the production of war materials; and complaints about defense training programs financed with Federal funds. If a case was within jurisdiction of the Committee, it could make recommendations, after adjudication, for remedial action to the appropriate Government agency or to the President. The vast majority—about 80 percent—of the FEPC records pertain to the history of the black work force.

Headquarters Records

228.2. The records of the Office of the Chairman include materials for Mark Ethridge, who served from July 1941 to March 1942; Malcolm S. MacLean, May 1942 to March 1943; Francis J. Haas, May 1943 to October 1943; and Malcolm Ross, October 1943 to June 1946. The Chairmen's records include the **summary minutes of Committee meetings, 1942–45** (½ in.), arranged chronologically, **Committee action summaries, 1942–43** (1 in.), arranged chronologically; **FEPC meeting agenda, 1941–45** (¼ in.), arranged chronologically; a **documents file, 1944–45** (3 in.), arranged chronologically, consisting of materials that were distributed to Committee members for consideration at FEPC meetings; **outgoing correspondence, 1941–45** (25 ft.), arranged in two sets—chronologically and alphabetically by addressee; **the reading file, 1943–45** (8 in.), arranged alphabetically by name of addressee, which consists of copies of letters and teletypes sent by the Chairmen and their staffs.; **interoffice memorandums, 1942–45** (3 in.), arranged alphabetically by name or subject; the **office files of Malcolm Ross, 1940–46** (3 ft.), arranged alphabetically by name and subject; and the **office files of Max Berking, assistant to the Chairman, 1944–45** (10 in.), arranged by subject in random order. Some of these series have indexes.

228.3. These series pertain to FEPC administration and operations; the employment, education, and training of black workers by the Federal Government; job discrimination; public opinion toward FEPC; black workers' relations with labor unions; discriminatory employment advertising; wage inequities; and urban migration of the black population. The records include some publications, such as the New York-based American Management Association's *The Negro Worker, An Analysis of Management Experience and Opinions on the Employment and Integration of the Negro* *in Industry* (1942); FEPC reports, such as "Racial Tensions in Industry" and "National War Labor Board Cases Involving Racial Discrimination"; a brief history of FEPC; an annotated bibliography of published studies pertaining to blacks in the labor force; and analyses of employment and racial situations in various urban areas, such as St. Louis, Detroit, and Kansas City.

228.4. Of special interest are Chairman Malcolm Ross' office files. They include background material and rough drafts for the FEPC *Final Report* of June 28, 1946. Among the numerous subjects included in the report are the national policy against discrimination in industry, domestic war morale, international aspects of discrimination in industry, the effectiveness of FEPC, an analysis of many of the most difficult cases, and information about the problems of reconversion to a peacetime economy.

228.5. The records of the Office of the Deputy Chairman include only those of George M. Johnson, a black lawyer who came to the Committee in 1941 from a position in Howard University Law School. He was the Director of the Legal Division throughout his service with FEPC and served as Deputy Chairman from October 1943 to February 1946. His records are in two series: **outgoing letters, 1942–45** (7 in.), arranged in two parts—one alphabetically by name of addressee and the other chronologically, and his **office files, 1941–45** (2 ft.), arranged alphabetically. The letters relate principally to complaints about discrimination in Government agencies, private employment, and defense training. The office files contain newspaper clippings (many of which are from black-owned newspapers), magazine articles, and bibliographies of materials related to black workers. The files also include information about FEPC caseloads, equal employment opportunity legislation, discrimination by labor unions, race relations, and compliance with FEPC directives.

228.6. The records of the Legal Division include **records relating to hearings, 1941–46** (24 ft.), arranged by type of case. The case files consist of the transcripts of hearings, exhibits, briefs, summaries of hearings with findings and directives, complaints, petitions, newspaper clippings, and questionnaires relating to discriminatory practices in Government agencies, private industry, and unions. There is an **alphabetical index to cases, 1941–45** (2 in.); a **chronological index to opinions, 1941–43** (½ in.); an **index to agreements with Government agencies arranged by name of agency, 1942–44** (¼ in.); and a **chronological index to FEPC policy, 1943–44** (½ in.). The **office files** for members of the Legal Division include those **of George M. Johnson, Director, 1941–45** (3 ft.); **Emanuel H. Block, hearing examiner, 1944–45** (1 ft.); **Maceo W. Hubbard, hearing examiner, 1943–45, and Acting Director, 1945–46** (5 in.); **Frank D. Reeves, trial attorney, 1942–45** (2 ft.); and **Evelyn N. Cooper, trial attorney, 1944–45** (5

Signs on Highway 84 at the outskirts of Eloy, Pinal County, Ariz. November 1940. Dorothea Lange, photographer. RG 83, Records of the Bureau of Agricultural Economics. (83-G-44323 BAE).

in.). These records are arranged alphabetically by subject with the exception of Cooper's files, which are arranged by subject in random order. Their files generally relate to enforcement and enforceability of remedial action for complaints of discrimination, the application of Executive orders forbidding discrimination, the jurisdiction of FEPC, and rules and regulations governing the conduct of hearings. The files also include press releases, information about caseloads, speeches, newspaper clippings, and materials about occupational opportunities for black workers with some emphasis on the postwar period. Among the cases with which they were concerned are those involving railroads, shipyards, the steel industry, the telephone industry, public transportation, the building trades, and organized labor.

228.7. The records of the Division of Budget and Administrative Management include the **central files of the FEPC, 1941–46** (77 ft.), arranged according to a subject-numeric classification scheme. The Division was responsible for the budget, personnel matters, and mail and file management. The files include correspondence, reports, transcripts of the proceedings of Committee meetings, summaries of conferences with representatives of Government agencies and private organizations, legal opinions, undocketed case files, accounting reports, newspaper clippings, and miscellaneous FEPC issuances.

228.8. The records of the Division of Review and Analysis include information about the black community during World War II. The Division was responsible for operational analysis, program planning, and research. The records consist of the **office files of John A. Davis, Director, 1941–46** (4 ft.); **Marjorie M. Lawson, Assistant Director, 1942–45** (4 ft.); **Wilfred C. Leland, Jr., consultant, 1943–45** (8 ft.); **Cornelius Golightly, compliance analyst, 1943–45** (2 ft.); **Carol Coan, compliance analyst, 1943–45** (2 ft.); **Joy P. Davis, compliance analyst, 1943–45** (10 in.); and **Walter L. Simmons, clerk-stenographer, 1943–45** (5 in.). These series are arranged alphabetically by subject with the exception of those of Davis and Simmons, which are arranged by subject in random order. The records include issuances of the FEPC and other agencies relating to the employment of black workers in the Federal Government, information about discriminatory help-wanted advertising and labor strikes resulting from the employment of black workers, regional studies of racial tension, and materials concerning Committee hearings in the boilermaking, shipbuilding, and railroad industries.

228.9. The records of the Division of Review and Analysis also include a **reference file, 1941–46** (10 ft.), which is divided into five parts—the publications file; books, periodicals, pamphlets, and newspapers; synopses of books and articles; studies and reports; and speeches and statements. The publication file, arranged alphabetically by subject, includes circulars, bulletins, press releases, reports, newspaper clippings, and other materials concerning discrimination. Books, periodicals, pamphlets, and newspapers, arranged by subject in random order, include reference materials covering such subjects as minorities in defense work, voting restrictions in Southern States, mortality among southern blacks, racial aspects of reconversion to a peacetime economy, and copies of FEPC pamphlets: *First Report, Fair Employment Practice Committee, July 1943–December 1944; FEPC: How It Operates;* and *Minorities in Defense.*

228.10. The reference file also includes synopses of books and articles, arranged alphabetically by name of author, and reviews or analyses of studies of minority group problems. Studies and reports, arranged by subject in random order, include materials issued by FEPC as well as those of other Federal agencies, local governments, and private organizations on discrimination in the shipbuilding industry, in housing, and in defense training; the discriminatory practices of the boilermakers union; and the Chicago mayor's committee on race relations. Speeches and statements, arranged by name of speaker in random order, are copies of addresses made by members of the Committee and the staff on topics that relate to black workers and the FEPC.

228.11. Other records for the Division of Review and Analysis are **materials relating to the *First Report* of FEPC, 1944–45** (10 in.), arranged by subject in random order, which include drafts, work papers, and tabulations. **Operational statistics for cases docketed and closed, 1944–45** (10 in.), arranged chronologically, consist of summary tables of statistical data concerning cases and show their regional distribution by type of discrimination, by party charged, and by reason for discrimination. **Final disposition reports, 1943–45** (2 ft.), arranged by type of disposition, are regional reports to the Director of Field Operations, submitted at the conclusion of a case. The **tension file, 1943–45** (6 ft.), arranged alphabetically by city, provides information on employment, housing, recreational facilities, industries, strikes, and postwar planning for areas in which racial disturbances were anticipated. **Issuances accumulated by Wilfred C. Leland, Jr., at meetings of the Production Readjustment Committee, 1943–45** (3 ft.), are arranged by type of material. This Committee was set up in the War Production Board to supervise cutbacks in military production incidental to reconversion to peacetime economy.

228.12. The Information Office was responsible for keeping the staff informed about current events relating to the Committee's work and for maintaining liaison with the press, radio, and other sources of public information and with Government agencies. The records include **files of Information Officer St. Claire T. Bourne, 1943–45** (2 ft.), arranged alphabetically by subject; **press releases, 1941–45** (3 ft.), arranged chronologically; **weekly news digests, 1943–45** (2 vols., 1 ft.), arranged chronologically and composed of FEPC releases concerning significant developments inside and outside the Government; **newspaper clippings, 1943–46** (10 ft.), arranged in two sets—alphabetically and chronologically; and **sound recordings, n.d.** (1 in.), consisting of four sound discs containing the radio script of a program entitled "Weapons for Victory." In order to dramatize the Committee's work, the script describes how black and white workers cooperated in the production of electric cable for the U.S. Armed Forces during World War II.

228.13. The Division of Field Operations administered FEPC's regional offices, which, at peak strength, totaled 13 regional and 5 subregional offices. It prepared techniques for investigation and disposition of complaints, and it negotiated and formalized operating relationships with other Government agencies whose work impinged on that of the Committee. The regional directors had authority to adjust all complaints, and only when all their efforts failed to achieve a settlement was a complaint referred to the Division of Field Operations in Washington, D.C. The headquarters records of the Division include the **office files of Will Maslow, Director, 1943–45** (5 in.), arranged by subject in random order; **Clarence M. Mitchell, Associate Director, 1943–46** (2 ft.), arranged alphabetically by subject; **Eugene Davidson, Assistant Director, 1941–46** (3 ft.), arranged by subject in random order; **Ernest G. Trimble, senior field representative, 1941–45** (10 in.), arranged alphabetically by subject; and **John Beecher, senior field representative, 1941–45** (2 ft.), arranged by subject or name of correspondent in random order. Their office files concern weekly and monthly workload reports, field letters and correspondence with staff members and regional offices relating to the status of the most important FEPC cases, agreements with unions to abolish racial discrimination, a liaison between FEPC and War Manpower Commission regional offices, materials relating to discriminatory hiring practices reported to the FEPC by the U.S. Employment Service, newspaper clippings, and correspondence with private organizations relating to national defense training for black workers.

228.14. There are also **correspondence with regional offices, 1943–46** (10 in.), arranged by region and thereunder chronologically; **memorandums sent to regional directors, 1943–45** (5 in.), arranged numerically; **field instructions, 1943–45** (10 in.), arranged numerically; and **field letters, 1943–46** (10 in.), arranged numerically. Each of the last three series has a subject index. The records concern cases handled by the regional offices and the transmission of FEPC policy information to the regions.

228.15. Other records of the Division of Field Operations are **active cases, 1943–46** (5 ft.), arranged by region and thereunder chronologically; **correspondence relating to cases, 1943–45** (3 ft.), arranged alphabetically; and **weekly reports, 1943–44** (10 in.), arranged by region and thereunder chronologically. There are also a number of indexes to cases, complainants, and companies.

Field Records

228.16. The field records include **active cases, 1941–45** (17 ft.), and **closed cases, 1941–46** (76 ft.), both arranged alphabetically by name of party charged. The series of **nondocketable cases, 1941–46** (8 ft.), arranged alphabetically by name of party aggrieved, includes information on cases involving complaints that were dismissed because the FEPC had no jurisdiction to handle them, anonymous complaints, and complaints that did not give essential facts or that alleged discrimination in matters other than employment. **Predocketed cases, 1941–45** (4 ft.), arranged alphabetically by name of party charged, consist of complaints of discrimination against employers in Region II (N.Y.). The complaints were under investigation before they were docketed, and some of them were dismissed because the FEPC did not have jurisdiction to handle them. Most of these series have alphabetical indexes to the names of complainants.

228.17. For **Region II** there are **general records, 1942–45** (1 ft.), arranged by subject in random order, and **correspondence relating to complaints, 1942–43** (3 ft.), arranged alphabetically by name of correspondent. The general records include radio scripts, newspaper clippings, pamphlets, information on participation of interracial civic groups in a drive to secure permanent FEPC legislation, and materials about cooperation with other Federal agencies in combating discriminatory hiring practices.

228.18. There are **fiscal records for Region III** (Pa., N.J., and Del.), **1942–46** (10 in.), arranged by type of material. For **Region IV** (D.C., Md., W.Va., N.C., and Va.) there are **general records, 1943–45** (10 in.), arranged alphabetically by subject. The folders contain materials such as interoffice memorandums relating to case activities, nondocketable complaints, reports on cutbacks in industrial production in the region during the final stages of World War II, and analyses of congressional bills designed to establish a permanent FEPC.

228.19. For **Region V** (Ohio, Ky., and Mich.) there are **general records, 1942–46** (7 ft.), arranged alphabetically by subject, and the **general file of the Cincinnati office, 1945–46** (5 in.), also arranged alphabetically by subject. The records consist of correspondence, reports, and press releases relating to satisfactory adjustments of complaints of discrimination against local employers, requests for Committee action in deadlocked cases, and advice on developments in race relations. For **Region VI** (Ill., Ind., Wis., N. Dak., S. Dak., Nebr., Minn., and Iowa) there are **general records, 1941–46** (2 ft.), arranged alphabetically by subject, and **general correspondence, 1943–46** (3 ft.), arranged alphabetically by name of correspondent.

228.20. There are **general records for Region VII** (Ga., S.C., Tenn., Ala., Fla., and Miss.), **1943–45** (3 ft.); **general records for Region IX** (Kans., Mo., Okla., Ark., Colo., Idaho, Wyo., Mont., and Utah), **1941–46** (2 ft.); and **general records for Region XII** (Calif., Wash., Oreg., and Nev.), **1941–45** (4 ft.). The records are arranged alphabetically by subject or type of material and are concerned with public relations, administrative matters, caseload activities, support of FEPC by minority group organizations, and contacts with central office and other FEPC regional offices.

Record Group 233
Records of the U.S. House of Representatives*

233.1. The U.S. House of Representatives shares legislative power with the Senate. The House originates all bills for raising revenue and, by custom, general appropriation bills. The House has sole power to impeach U.S. civil officers, and it judges elections, returns, and qualifications of its members. Many of the congressional records have been published by the U.S. Government. In some cases no unpublished records pertaining to particular actions have survived. The records described below are primarily the unpublished records of the U.S. House of Representatives. The printed records are part of RG 287, Publications of the U.S. Government. A brief synopsis of the published records of Congress appears at the end of the description of the Records of the U.S. Senate, RG 46. Included among the printed records are *Journals,* the official record of business transacted on the floor; as such, they give abstracts of proceedings and indicate the committees to which matters were referred. Since the records of Congress are arranged by committee, the *Journals* can be an indispensable tool for researchers.

Committee Reports and Papers

233.2. Many of the records relating to black history are among the **committee reports and papers, 1789–1974** (16,276 ft.), arranged by the number of Congress and thereunder alphabetically by the name of the committee. The committee records described below illustrate the broad range of issues that relate to black history and the wide variety of committees that handled these matters.

233.3. Before the Civil War, black history materials generally pertain to slavery, abolition, the slave trade, the colonization of blacks in Africa, the status of free blacks, and fugitive slaves. For example, during the 6th Congress (1799–1801) there was a Select Committee on Fugitive Slave Laws. Questions pertaining to these laws or their repeal were also considered by the Committee on the Judiciary during the 28th, 32d, and 33d Congresses (1843–45, 1851–53, and 1853–55). The Committee of the Whole House also considered the repeal of the Fugitive Slave Law and the exclusion of the slave trade in the Territories, 33d Congress (1853–55).

233.4. The Committee on the District of Columbia discussed slavery, the slave trade, and abolition in the District from the 20th (1827–29) through the 34th (1855–57) Congresses. Other committees that debated the question of slavery in the District include two Committees of the Whole

The Sam McCall family of Wilcox County, Ala. 1910. M.A. Crosby, photographer. RG 83, Records of the Bureau of Agricultural Economics. (83-FB-5005-BAE).

House, one in the 20th Congress (1827–29) and another in the 33d (1853–55), and the Select Committee on the Abolition of Slavery in the District of Columbia in the 23d and 24th Congresses (1833–37). The Committee of the Whole House considered abolition in the entire United States during the 29th Congress (1845–47). This Committee also debated about the slave trade during the 15th Congress (1817–19).

233.5. Many other aspects of the slavery question were addressed by House committees. From the 27th to the 36th Congresses (1841–61) the Committee on the Judiciary considered abolition, the sale of slaves for debts due the United States, slavery in the Territories, and the freeing of slaves by purchase. The Committee on the Territories considered slavery in the Territories during the 30th Congress (1847–49). The Committee on Foreign Affairs discussed payment for the freedom of the Africans who had captured the slave ship *Amistad,* 33d Congress (1853–55; see also RG 60 for more information about the *Amistad* mutiny). There were several committees that dealt with the slave trade and its suppression, including select committees on the subject during the 14th, 17th, and 19th Congresses (1815–17, 1821–23, and 1825–27). The Committee on Commerce considered the matter of the slave trade in the 26th Congress (1839–41), and both the Committee on the Judiciary and the Committee on Foreign Affairs discussed the suppression of the slave trade during the 36th Congress (1859–61).

233.6. The colonization of free blacks in Africa or elsewhere was a frequent topic of discussion. Colonization was addressed by the Select Committee on the Protection and Colonization of Free People of Color during the 15th, 19th, and 20th Congresses (1817–19, 1825–27, and 1827–29). The Committee on Commerce discussed the protection of Liberia during the 28th Congress (1843–45), and the Committee on Ways and Means considered the colonization of blacks during the 32d Congress (1851–53). Another matter involving free blacks, addressed by the Committee on the District of Columbia, was the imprisonment of these blacks and the sale of such persons as unclaimed slaves for jail fees and other charges, 19th Congress (1825–27).

233.7. Slavery and emancipation continued as important questions for the House committees well into the Civil War. In the 37th Congress (1861–63) the Committee on Ways and Means discussed the suppression of the African slave trade; the Committee on the Judiciary considered the abolition of slavery in the District of Columbia and the United States; and the Committee on Military Affairs dealt with the question of slavery. During the 38th Congress (1863–65) the Committee on the Judiciary proposed an amendment to the Constitution to abolish slavery, and a Select Committee on Emancipation was formed.

233.8. During the Civil War and its aftermath the House committees addressed issues such as slavery and emancipation, black troops in the war effort, the plight of the freedmen, civil rights for blacks, and contested elections that involved black Congressmen-elect. The question of black participation in the war effort, for instance, was considered by the Committee on Military Affairs in the 37th and 38th Congresses (1861–65). During the 39th Congress (1865–67) select committees were formed to investigate the New Orleans and Memphis riots of 1866. A number of blacks were killed and wounded during these disorders.

233.9. Committee records include information about various aspects of the lives of emancipated blacks. Numerous problems of the Freedmen's Bureau were addressed by the Committee on Military Affairs during the 40th and 42d Congresses (1867–69 and 1871–73) and by the Committee on Education and Labor during the 41st Congress (1869–71). The Freedman's Savings and Trust Co. was investigated by a select committee during the 43d Congress (1873–75), and the Committee on Ways and Means proposed legislation to secure the savings of the depositors in that bank during the 46th Congress (1879–81). A Committee on Freedmen's Affairs was established during the 39th Congress and continued in the 40th and 42d Congresses (1865–67, 1867–69, and 1871–73). This committee considered such matters as local conditions of blacks, freedmen's affairs in various States, the functions and operations of the Freedmen's Bureau and the Freedman's Savings and Trust Co., and the emigration of blacks to

Liberia. The subject of emigration to Liberia was also addressed by the Committee on Education and Labor, 45th Congress (1877–79), as well as by the Committee on Appropriations, 49th Congress (1885–87).

233.10. Several House committees were concerned with the poverty and lack of education among the freedmen. The Select Committee on Reconstruction was made aware of the problem of starvation of freedmen in South Carolina during the 40th Congress (1867–69). The Committee on Appropriations was interested in the education of black youths in the District of Columbia, 41st Congress (1869–71), as was the Committee on the District of Columbia, 42d Congress (1871–73). The Committee on Appropriations also discussed the relief of destitute black women and children, 46th Congress (1879–81).

233.11. During the Reconstruction period several committees dealt with issues relating to civil and political rights for black Americans. The Committee on the Judiciary handled matters pertaining to civil rights legislation during the 43d and 45th Congresses (1873–75 and 1877–79). During the postwar period many blacks were voting and running for public office. The Committee on Elections dealt with many contested elections, some of which involved blacks. In the following list of contested elections, black contestants are indicated by an asterisk.

Congress	Years	Contestants and State
42d	1871–73	Silas L. Niblack v. Josiah T. Walls*, Florida
43d	1873–75	George A. Sheridan v. P. B. S. Pinchback*, Louisiana
44th	1875–77	Jesse J. Finley v. Josiah T. Walls*, Florida
		G. H. White* v. John A. Hyman, North Carolina
		Frederick G. Bromberg v. Jeremiah Haralson*, Alabama
		Samuel Lee v. Joseph H. Rainey*, South Carolina
		James T. Rapier* v. Jeremiah N. Williams, Alabama
		Roderick Seal v. John R. Lynch*, Mississippi
45th	1877–79	Jeremiah Haralson* v. Charles M. Shelley, Alabama
		John S. Richardson v. Joseph H. Rainey*, South Carolina
		John R. Lynch* v. James R. Chalmers, Mississippi
46th	1879–81	James E. O'Hara* v. William H. Kitchin, North Carolina
47th	1881–83	Robert Smalls* v. George P. Tillman, South Carolina
		John R. Lynch* v. James R. Chalmers, Mississippi
50th	1887–89	Robert Smalls* v. William Elliott, South Carolina

51st	1889–91	John M. Langston* v. E. C. Venable, Virginia Thomas E. Miller* v. William Elliott, South Carolina
52d	1891–93	Thomas E. Miller* v. William Elliott, South Carolina
54th	1895–97	Henry P. Cheatham* v. Frederick A. Woodward, North Carolina George W. Murray* v. William Elliott, South Carolina
55th	1897–99	George W. Murray* v. William Elliott, South Carolina

233.12. Congressional committees addressed themselves to numerous issues concerning black Americans during the 20th century. At the turn of the century, during the 56th Congress (1899–1901), the Committee of Military Affairs examined the case of 2d Lt. Henry O. Flipper, the first black graduate of West Point. During the same Congress, the Committee on the Judiciary discussed legislation against lynching, a subject that repeatedly occupied the Committee's time until the 80th Congress (1947–48).

233.13. Several committees examined problems of violence and discrimination against black people. In the 66th Congress (1919–21) the members of the Committee on the Judiciary discussed equal rights and discrimination. During the 67th Congress (1921–23) they discussed the crimes of the Ku Klux Klan. Racial violence was addressed during the 65th Congress (1917–19) by the Select Committee to Investigate Conditions in Illinois and Missouri Interfering with Interstate Commerce between these States: Race Rioting in East St. Louis, Illinois, 1917. The committee issued a report with exhibits and photographs, which has been reproduced as M1167. The Committee on Military Affairs investigated the Houston riot during the 67th Congress (1921–23). During 1917 a battalion of the 24th Infantry, U.S. Colored Troops, had fought with white residents of Houston, and 17 whites and 2 blacks had died.

233.14. Complex legal matters affecting blacks were considered by various House committees. The Committee on the District of Columbia held a hearing on Negroes in the District of Columbia, intermarriage of whites and Negroes, and Jim Crow bills during the 64th Congress (1915–17); a similar hearing was held during the 66th Congress (1919–21). The Committee on Immigration and Naturalization considered definitions of race during the 75th Congress (1937–38), when it discussed color and racial tests in the immigration and naturalization laws of the United States. Anti-poll-tax legislation was considered by the Judiciary Committee during the 77th, 79th, and 80th Congresses (1941–42, 1945–46, and

1947–48) and by the House Administration Committee during the 80th Congress (1947–48). During the 84th and 85th Congresses (1955–58), and even more recent Congresses, questions about rights for black Americans have often come under the umbrella terms "civil rights" and "equal rights." These rights have been discussed by the Committee on Rules and the Judiciary Committee.

233.15. Some 20th-century material concerns fairs, memorials, and celebrations for blacks. The Committee on Industrial Arts and Expositions discussed plans for the National Negro Fair in Mobile, Ala., in 1909, 60th Congress (1907–9). This committee also considered the Celebration of the Semicentennial Anniversary of the Emancipation Act, 63d Congress (1913–15). The Committee on the Interior and Insular Affairs reviewed the proposal for the establishment of a Booker T. Washington National Monument in Virginia during the 84th Congress (1955–56). During the 66th Congress (1919–21) the Library Committee held a hearing about a Negro soldiers and sailors memorial. The Foreign Affairs Committee considered the erection of a monument in France to commemorate the valiant services of the all-black 93d Division of the American Expeditionary Forces, 69th Congress (1925–27).

233.16. Some of the issues reviewed by House committees during the 20th century concern various aspects of the economic life and education of black Americans. The Committee on Banking and Currency discussed claims against the Freedman's Savings and Trust Co. during the 61st Congress (1909–11). The Committee on the Judiciary considered the creation of a "Negro Industrial Commission" during the 67th, 68th, and 74th Congresses (1921–23, 1923–25, and 1935–36). Various matters pertaining to the Committee on Fair Employment Practice (which was not a House committee but an agency of the executive branch; see RG 228) were deliberated by the Committee on Labor, the Committee on Education and Labor, the Committee on the Civil Service, and the Select Committee to Investigate Acts of Executive Agencies Beyond the Scope of Their Authority, 78th through the 81st Congresses (1943–50).

233.17. Education and facilities for black students at Howard University were reviewed by the Committee on Education from the 68th through the 70th Congresses (1923–29) and by the Committee on Public Works, 80th Congress (1947–48).

233.18. The House Select Committee on Assassinations, 94th and 95th Congresses (1975–76 and 1977–78), for the greater part under the chairmanship of black Representative Louis Stokes, investigated the circumstances surrounding the assassinations and deaths of President John F. Kennedy and civil rights activist Dr. Martin Luther King, Jr. The select committee submitted to the House on March 29, 1979, the report containing its findings on both investigations (printed as H. Rept. 95–1828, 95th Congress, 2d session, 686 pp.). The select committee, in addition, printed evidence and testimony that it received in the course of its investigation. The select committee devoted the latter part of its report to presenting its findings on the assassination of Dr. King and attached published copies of the *Hearings* and other evidence that it received on King's murder as appendixes. There are a number of films and sound recordings that were collected as a part of the evidence of the select committee, including King's speech about the garbage strike in Memphis, Tenn., before his assassination, interviews with his convicted assassin James Earl Ray, and numerous other interviews pertaining to the assassination.

Petitions and Memorials

233.19. Petitions and memorials, 1789–1972 (2,093 ft.), are arranged by number of Congress and thereunder alphabetically by name of the committee to which they were submitted. Some petitions—such as those that were tabled, "handed in," or otherwise not referred to a committee—are arranged by Congress and thereunder alphabetically by subject. The petitions and memorials are accompanied by supporting documents from individuals and organizations and deal with private and public matters. Black history topics among the petitions generally parallel those of the committees (described in paragraphs 233.2–233.18) (especially those topics such as slavery, abolition, colonization, and lynching) that were considered over a period of years.

233.20. Some petitions that are of special interest are the petition from Paul Cuffee that is among the records of the Committee on Commerce and Manufactures, 13th Congress (1813–15), and the voluminous collection of antislavery petitions. In 1836 the House adopted a "gag rule," which prevented discussion of antislavery measures, to hold back the flood of antislavery petitions that came in as a result of the rise of antislavery sentiment in the Nation. The rule was not rescinded until 1844. During this period, from the 24th through the 28th Congress (1836–45), antislavery petitions were simply "handed in" and are filed with the tabled petitions. During the 28th Congress (1843–45) a petition to amend the Constitution by eliminating slaves from the ratio of representation was tabled. The Committee on the Judiciary received advice during the 37th Congress (1861–63) from some Massachusetts citizens "to drop the Negro question and return to the business of the country." The 38th Congress (1863–65) tabled a petition to place "colored soldiers on the same footing as white soldiers as regards pay and allowances." A commission to "inquire into the condition of colored people in the United States" was the subject of a petition submitted to the Committee on Labor during the 57th Congress (1901–3)

* *Restrictions may apply to this Record Group. Consult NARS staff.*

Record Group 234

Records of the Reconstruction Finance Corporation*

234.1. The Reconstruction Finance Corporation (RFC), 1932–57, was created to extend aid during the Depression to agriculture, commerce, and industry by direct loans to banks, other credit agencies, and, with approval of the Interstate Commerce Commission, to railroads or receivers of railroads. Subsequent legislation authorized the RFC to purchase capital stock of banks and insurance companies; make loans to businesses and other classes of borrowers; and, with the advent of World War II, acquire strategic and critical materials, provide financing for plant conversion and construction, and undertake many other activities related to the war effort. Some black business owners applied for RFC loans.

234.2. Most of the records for the RFC are arranged by type of business or industry. It is necessary to know the name of a black-owned business in order to ascertain whether there is any information about it in these records. Below are several examples. In the RFC **card index to business loans, 1934–57** (210 ft.), arranged alphabetically by the name of borrowing company, is an entry for "Colored Funeral Home, Minden, Louisiana, 6/4/47." Among the **card index to loans made to public works and public agencies, 1932–55** (5 ft.), arranged alphabetically by name of State, thereunder alphabetically by name of city or town, and thereunder alphabetically by name of public agency, are two cards for the Florida Agricultural and Mechanical College for Negroes, Tallahassee, Fla., 1939–42.

234.3. Among the **project files, 1941–47** (31 ft.), of the Defense Homes Corporation, a subsidiary of RFC, arranged alphabetically by name of project, is a file for the Mayfair Corporation in Washington, D.C. (1 in.). A cover letter in the file reads, "Early in 1941, a group of colored people headed up by Elder L. S. Michaux and Albert I. Cassell, an architect, started planning a large scale housing project in recognition of the need in Washington, D.C. for habitable housing for colored families."

* *Restrictions may apply to this Record Group. Consult NARS staff.*

Record Group 235

General Records of the Department of Health, Education, and Welfare

235.1. The Department of Health, Education, and Welfare (HEW) was established in 1953. The Federal Security Agency (FSA), created in 1939, was abolished, and its functions and components were transferred to HEW. HEW administered Federal and Federal-State programs in public health, education, and social and economic security. It also carried out Federal responsibilities in relation to the American Printing House for the Blind, Gallaudet College, and Howard University.

235.2. The records of the Office of the Administrator of FSA include the **general classified file, 1939–44** (45 ft.), arranged in four parts: an alphabetical decimal file, a general decimal file, a regional decimal file, and a State decimal file. The general classified file, maintained for the Federal Security Administrator and the various units of his Office, consists mainly of correspondence pertaining to the organization, functions, and administration of the units and of the Agency as a whole. The records are basically organized in accordance with a decimal classification scheme. Several categories refer to blacks: "Racial Problems" (#000.8), "Population–Sex, Age, Color" (#051.2), "Excluded Groups–Domestic Labor" (#054.13), "Personnel–Race" (#222.2), "Administration–Freedmen's Hospital" (#322.2), "Administration–Howard University" (#321.1), "Howard University Scholarships" (#480.1), "Negro–Recruitment and Placement" (#533.15), "Race Discrimination" (#533.225), "Negro–Training" (#533.404), "Public Assistance to Negroes" (#600.0413), and "Subcommittee on Negro Health" (#814). Other subjects mentioned in the records are recreational facilities for black soldiers during World War II, black employment in the Federal Government generally (not only HEW), and blacks in health professions and training facilities for them.

235.3. The **general classified files, 1944–50** (141 ft.), are arranged in four parts corresponding to the four parts in the general classification files for 1939–44, except that the decimal classification scheme was modified. Many of the same black-related subjects are covered. Among the alphabetical segment (095) of the 1944–50 files is a folder for the NAACP and one for the Urban League (totaling about ½ in.). These folders pertain to conferences, participation of minority groups in planning and training programs for defense, recreation for black soldiers, segregation, discrimination in Federal Government employment, conferences for the training of black doctors, discrimination against blacks in all phases of the medical profession, and job recommendations.

235.4. General classified files, 1951–55 (164 ft.), were accumulated partly under the Office of the Administrator of FSA and partly under the Office of the Secretary of HEW. They are arranged in four parts also, but with a further modification of the classification scheme. Several headings for black history are "Civil Rights" (#000.9), "Fair Employment Practice Program" (#255.2), and "Freedmen's Hospital" (#325.1). Among the alphabetical files is a folder for the National Council of Negro Women and one for the Urban League (totaling about ½ in.). These folders pertain to conferences, meetings, child welfare, employment in HEW, and service to blacks by the Public Health Service.

235.5. Among the **survey reports, 1946–50** (1 ft.), which are arranged alphabetically, is a report by Drs. Robin Beurki and Basil MacLean entitled, "A Study of Freedmen's Hospital, Washington, D.C.," 1947 (1 in.).

Record Group 241

Records of the Patent Office

241.1. The granting of patents for inventions was made a function of the Federal Government by the Constitution. In 1790 the first patent act created a board consisting of the Secretaries of State and War and the Attorney General to issue patents. It placed related administrative responsibility in the Department of State. The board was abolished in 1793 and its functions were given to the Department of State. The Patent Office was set up in 1836 in the Department of State and was transferred to the Department of the Interior in 1849 and to the Department of Commerce in 1925. The Patent Office administers patent laws and Federal trademark laws. A number of patents have been issued to black inventors.

241.2. Records relating to numbered patents consist mainly of **patent application files, 1837–1900** (7,781 ft.), which are arranged chronologically and include inventors' specifications; **interference case files, 1836–1905** (927 ft.), arranged after 1849 by case number; and the **digest of assignment of property rights in patents, 1837–1900** (416 vols., 83 ft.). The digest entries are arranged alphabetically by first letter of surname of assignor or assignee and thereunder chronologically. These records rarely have any racial identifications. However, Henry E. Baker, assistant examiner, U.S. Patent Office, conducted a survey to locate black inventors and subsequently wrote an article entitled "The Negro in the Field of Invention," which was published in the *Journal of Negro History* in

1917. He stated that "more than a thousand authentic cases were fully identified by the name of the inventor, date and number of patent and title of invention, as being patents granted for inventions of Negroes." There are also some more recent publications relating to black patentees, such as *Black Inventors of America,* by McKinley Burt, Jr. (Portland, Oregon: National Book Co., 1969).

Record Group 245

Records of the Solid Fuels Administration for War

245.1. In 1941 the President named the Secretary of the Interior the Solid Fuels Coordinator for National Defense. The Office of the Coordinator was basically an information-gathering and advisory body. It was replaced in 1943 by the more powerful Solid Fuels Administration for War. The Administration was the chief Government instrument for wartime control of solid fuels industries. It issued and enforced policy and operating

Miner eating ice cream. This man worked at the Westland Mine in Washington County, Pa., which was owned by the Pittsburgh Coal Co. June 12, 1946. Photographer unknown. RG 245, Records of the Solid Fuels Administration for War. (245-MS-257).

directives to those industries, recommended to the Office of Price Administration maximum prices for solid fuels, advised other agencies on such matters as transportation of solid fuels and manpower needs of solid fuels industries, and formulated general policies and specific programs for development, conservation, distribution, and use of coal and coke. The Administration also participated in the operation of Government-seized coal mines. The audiovisual records include a large collection of still pictures (4,100 items) depicting mines, mining communities, and working conditions for miners. Some of these photographs show black miners, their families, and their living conditions.

Record Group 252

Records of the Office of the Housing Expediter

252.1. The Office of the Housing Expediter (OHE) originated in 1945, when the President appointed a Housing Expediter in the Office of War Mobilization and Reconversion to plan, coordinate, and expedite postwar housing programs. An Executive order in January 1946 authorized the Expediter to plan a veterans housing program and coordinate activities of executive agencies in implementing that plan. Congressional authorization for the OHE was given in the Veterans Emergency Housing Act of 1946. In 1947, functions relating to the veterans emergency housing program and the rent control functions of the Office of Price Administration (OPA) were transferred to OHE. The veterans emergency housing program stimulated production of building materials, directed those materials into housing construction, and provided veterans with priorities for houses so built. The OHE was terminated by an Executive order in 1951, and its functions were transferred to the Office of Rent Stabilization (ORS) of the Economic Stabilization Agency and to the Housing and Home Finance Agency. Because of the prevalence of segregated housing, OHE generated some files relating to the availability of housing for blacks.

252.2. The **central files of OHE, 1946–51** (117 ft.), arranged annually and thereunder by a duplex-numeric classification scheme, include several files relating to racial relations. File classifications for folders (totaling about 3 in.) pertinent to black history are "Personnel–Racial Relations" (#2–1–2–5), 1946; "Program–Negro" (#2–2–1–1), 1946; "Racial Relations" (#650), 1947; and "Racial Relations" (#640), 1948. There is information about housing programs for black veterans, black workers and students in the building trades, housing conditions, protests by black organizations about housing, the OHE Racial Relations Service, and public housing for minorities.

252.3. The ORS Deputy Director for Information **administrative files, 1947–52** (19 ft.), arranged alphabetically by subject, include two folders about housing: "Negro Organizations" and the "National Urban League" (totaling about 1 in.). The folders contain names and addresses of local representatives of the NAACP, the Urban League, and the National Association of Consumers as well as Urban League press releases, correspondence, and reports.

252.4. The **subject files of Ivan D. Carson, 1942–47** (7 ft.), arranged alphabetically by subject, contain a folder entitled "Negro Correspondence" (1 in.). Carson was ORS Deputy Administrator for Rent. Some of these records belonged to his OPA predecessor, Paul A. Porter. The correspondence contains material on black participation in the work of war price and rationing boards, black employment in OPA field offices, OPA relations with minority groups, rent control for blacks, and field reports from T. Arnold Hill, special assistant to the OPA Senior Deputy Administrator for Rent, on rent prices, tenant conditions, and rationing in cities such as New York, Dayton, Philadelphia, Baltimore, Pittsburgh, Louisville, Indianapolis, and Terre Haute.

Record Group 256

Records of the American Commission To Negotiate Peace

256.1. The American Commission To Negotiate Peace, organized in November 1918, consisted of five commissioners plenipotentiary of the United States headed by the President, a secretariat, administrative officers, and technical advisers. In December 1918 its Division of Territorial Economic and Political Intelligence absorbed most of the specialists of The Inquiry, a group assembled in the fall of 1917 by Col. Edward M. House at the request of President Wilson to prepare for the peace conference after World War I. The Commission ceased to exist in December 1919, and the Department of State arranged and bound its records.

256.2. The **general records of the American Commission To Negotiate Peace, 1918–31** (537 vols., 158 ft.), are arranged according to a decimal classification scheme and are accompanied by an **alphabetical card index, 1918–31** (102 ft.). In the index there are two cards referring to W. E. B. DuBois, director of the NAACP. One card concerns his 1919 request for "six representative American Negroes" to receive passports to enable them to "attend at Paris a conference to present claims of Negroes of the world" with the members of the Peace Conference; the other card concerns his statement about the desirability of holding a Pan African Conference in Paris to discuss problems and interests of the black race. There are five cards referring to the Pan African Congress (or Conference) in 1919. The information refers to the attitude of the French and U.S. Governments toward the meeting scheduled to take place in Paris for 3 days in February.

Record Group 257

Records of the Bureau of Labor Statistics

257.1. The Bureau of Labor Statistics (BLS) originated as the Bureau of Labor, established in the Department of the Interior in 1884. In 1888 the Bureau became an independent Department of Labor without Cabinet status. It was incorporated into the Department of Commerce and Labor in 1903 as a bureau, and when the present Department of Labor was organized in 1913 the Bureau was transferred to it as the Bureau of Labor Statistics. As the Federal Government's principal factfinding agency in the field of labor economics, the Bureau gathers and analyzes data and publishes reports concerning the labor force, employment, and unemployment; long-range occupational employment prospects, wage rates, earnings, hours of work, and labor productivity; industrial hazards, accidents, and work injuries; rent; labor unions; collective bargaining; work stoppages; and foreign labor conditions. The Bureau is also the principal Government agency concerned with price statistics outside the field of agriculture. It publishes periodic indexes of consumer and wholesale prices and conducts studies of consumer expenditures and incomes. The various consumer surveys that were made by BLS yield information about black families, such as the number of children, occupation of husband and wife, educational level, work history, frequency of work, wages, ages, and addresses. Daily expenditures as well as rent, mortgages, and utility and other costs are reported in minute detail in many of these surveys.

257.2. Early records that relate to blacks include a few pieces of correspondence from the Commissioner of Labor to W. E. B. DuBois at Atlanta University pertaining to studies that DuBois compiled for the Bureau. The letters are interspersed among the **letters sent, 1889–96** (4 ft.), arranged chronologically. Among the **papers of Ethelbert Stewart, Commissioner of Labor, 1904–31** (7½ ft.), arranged by subject, is a folder entitled "Race Question" (½ in.). It consists principally of copies of Ray Stannard Baker's magazine articles called "Following the Color Line," mostly for the years

1906 and 1907. There are also clippings and articles from other periodicals.

257.3. Most of the BLS surveys that are among the holdings of the National Archives include information about the race of the respondents. The **"Family Disbursements of Salaried Workers" survey, 1935–36** (290 ft.), is arranged by city. For selected cities, such as Birmingham, Cincinnati, Indianapolis, Philadelphia, Pittsburgh, New York City, and Portsmouth, N.H., there are surveys that were made in a random selection of black families (18 ft.).

257.4. There are three separate **consumer purchases studies:** one for **1934–36** (132 ft.), arranged alphabetically by city, and two for the years **1935–36**—one arranged randomly by city (220 ft.) and the other arranged alphabetically by city (167 ft.). Several more limited surveys were taken: **cost of living schedules for urban families, 1918–19** (2 ft.), arranged by schedule number, and **cost of living of Federal employees in Washington, D.C., 1932–33** (3 ft.), arranged by schedule number. Each of these surveys provides a wide variety of information about black families. Most have a box where the BLS agent checked "white" or "Negro." All types of expenditures are detailed. Some of the surveys include the amounts of money that were spent for recreation, tobacco, occupational costs, and education as well as food, shelter, utilities, and other basic necessities.

Record Group 262

Records of the Foreign Broadcast Intelligence Service

262.1. The Foreign Broadcast Intelligence Service (FBIS), originally called the Foreign Broadcast Monitoring Service, was established in the Federal Communications Commission in February 1941 to record, translate, and analyze foreign broadcast programs and to report on them to interested Government agencies. Monitoring stations intercepted broadcasts of foreign news, intelligence, or propaganda emanating from belligerent, occupied, and neutral countries. This record group comprises records created by FBIS until 1947 and the records of the Service's predecessors.

262.2 The FBIS central files include **radio reports on the Far East, 1942–45** (3 ft.), which are arranged numerically. A November 10, 1944, report entitled "Japan's Race Propaganda" (#58, about 125 pp.) gives information about Japan's allegations of U.S. and British racial prejudice toward the darker races, especially the yellow race. To illustrate their view, Japanese broadcasts often pointed to the exploitation of blacks in the United

States by whites, the discrimination against blacks in the Armed Forces and labor, attempts to keep blacks "in their place," race riots, and U.S. efforts to colonize blacks in Africa. The report states that in much of the Japanese propaganda "the cause of the Negro in the United States is vigorously championed and with increasing intensity in English language broadcasts."

Record Group 267

Records of the Supreme Court of the United States*

267.1. The Supreme Court of the United States was established in 1789. The Court's jurisdiction extends to all cases in law or equity arising under the Constitution, the laws of the United States, and treaties made under their authority; all cases affecting ambassadors, other public ministers, and consuls; all cases of admiralty and maritime law; and controversies in which the United States is a party between two or more States, between a State and citizens of another State, between citizens of different States, between citizens of the same State claiming lands under grants of different States, and between a State or its citizens and foreign states, citizens, or subjects. In all cases involving ambassadors, ministers, and consuls, and those in which a State is a party, the Supreme Court has original jurisdiction. Its appellate jurisdiction is defined in various statutes. The Supreme Court consists of the Chief Justice of the United States and the number of Associate Justices determined by Congress. This number has ranged from five to nine, but since 1869 has been fixed by law at eight.

267.2. Appellate jurisdiction case files, 1792–1975 (13,428 ft.), are arranged numerically by case number through the October term 1933; by term and numerically by term through the October term 1970; and by term and case file number beginning in the October term 1971. The records consist of petitions for writs of error or certiorari of lower courts, writs of error or certiorari, transcripts of records from lower courts, and amendments or supplements to the transcripts. Also included are exhibits, citations to appellees to appear in the Supreme Court, appeal bonds, assignments of error, agreements of counsel, briefs, depositions ordered to be taken by the Supreme Court as additional evidence, motions, orders, decrees, judgments, mandates, correspondence, and other papers. Among the many famous cases for black history are *Dred Scott* v. *Sandford* (19 Howard 393) and *Plessy* v. *Ferguson* (163 U.S. 537). Files on more recent cases include those for *Brown* v. *Board of Education of Topeka* (347 U.S.

483). There is a **card index to the case files, 1792–1909** (100 ft.), arranged alphabetically by names of parties to cases. This index provides case title, file number for case, date case was filed, and date it was decided.

267.3. Opinions, 1808–1913 (139 ft.), are arranged numerically by case file number. There are numerous gaps in the sequence of numbers. The records consist of manuscript and revised printed opinions, including both majority and dissenting opinions. Most of the opinions before 1850 are in the handwriting of members of the Court, with some clerks' copies; after 1850, printed opinions became more common, and only printed opinions are found after 1870. Both manuscript and printed opinions contain revisions.

267.4. For the period from 1955 through the 1969 terms, audio tape recordings of oral arguments before the Supreme Court are in the custody of the National Archives. These recordings serve as audio documentation of every case argued relating to the legal status of black Americans in the areas of education, due process, jury service, forced confession, housing, public accommodations, transportation, recreation, and voting rights.

* *Restrictions may apply to this Record Group. Consult NARS staff.*

Record Group 269

General Records of the General Services Administration

269.1. The General Services Administration (GSA) was established as an independent agency by the Federal Property and Administrative Services Act of 1949. The act consolidated and transferred to the GSA certain real and personal property and related functions formerly assigned to various agencies. Its purpose is to provide an economical and efficient system for managing Government property and records, including such services as constructing and operating buildings, procuring and distributing supplies, disposing of surplus property, managing traffic and communications, stockpiling strategic and critical materials, and managing, preserving, and disposing of records. "Partners in Progress" (#269.1), a 1971 motion picture, relates to GSA's efforts to utilize minority businesses for Federal purchases and to GSA's experimental use of natural gas powered automobiles.

Record Group 272
Records of the President's Commission on the Assassination of President Kennedy*

272.1. The President's Commission on the Assassination of President Kennedy, commonly called the Warren Commission from the name of its Chairman, Earl Warren, was appointed by President Lyndon B. Johnson by Executive Order 11130 on November 29, 1963. Its purpose was to investigate the assassination of President John Fitzgerald Kennedy on November 22, 1963, in Dallas, Tex. President Johnson directed the Commission to evaluate matters relating to the assassination and the subsequent killing of the alleged assassin and to report its findings and conclusions to him. On December 13, 1963, Congress passed Senate Joint Resolution 137 (Public Law 88-202) authoriziing the Commission to subpoena witnesses and obtain evidence concerning any matter relating to the investigation. The resolution also gave the Commission the power to compel the testimony of witnesses by granting immunity from prosecution to witnesses testifying under compulsion. The Commission, however, did not grant immunity to any witnesses during the investigation. The *Report of the President's Commission on the Assassination of President Kennedy* was presented to the President on September 24, 1964. The publication of the *Report* at that time was soon followed by the publication of the 26 volumes of the Commission's *Hearings.* They consist of 15 volumes of testimony and 11 volumes of exhibits.

Subject-Numeric Files and Related Records

272.2. The **numbered Commission document file, 1963–64** (30 ft.), is arranged numerically by Commission document number, 1–1555. Among the investigative reports is a May 25, 1964, interview (#997, 3 pp.) with Abraham Bolden, "the first Negro to serve on the White House Secret Service Detail" (*New York Times,* May 22, 1964).

272.3. Records relating to "key persons," 1963–64 (30 ft.), are arranged alphabetically by surname. Some black men were looking at the Presidential procession from the window immediately below the one in which Lee Harvey Oswald stood. There are files for Bonnie Ray Williams, James Earl Jarman, and Harold Dean Norman, the three black witnesses (totaling ½ in.), which include affidavits and some correspondence.

272.4. Records relating to other individuals and organizations involved or interviewed, 1963–64 (17 ft.), are arranged alphabetically by name of person, organization, or establishment. There is a file for the Ku Klux Klan (¼ in.) containing statements alleging that the assassination was a "right wing conspiracy." The aim of the Klan stated in the correspondence was "to promote white supremacy and to combat integration of the races."

Records Relating to Testimony

272.5. The series of **exhibits and other evidence, 1964** (70 ft.), is arranged, in part, numerically by FBI item number and by Commission exhibit number and alphabetically by name of person giving the deposition. Pictures in the published *Hearings* depict the three black witnesses mentioned above seconds after the assassination at the window below Oswald and a reenactment of the incident (vol. 17, pp. 199–209). The *Hearings* also include some references to Abraham Bolden (vol. 5, 454–455, 457).

* *Restrictions may apply to this Record Group. Consult NARS staff.*

Record Group 274
National Archives Collection of Records of Inaugural Committees

274.1. Inaugural committees, chairmen of which have been appointed by the President-elect since 1948, are organized into several staff offices and special committees to stage traditional public ceremonies in Washington, D.C., to honor the newly elected President and Vice President. The committees also provide accommodations for guests; compile guest lists; arrange for newspaper, radio, and television coverage of inaugural activities; and sell souvenirs. The Federal and the District of Columbia governments provide aid and facilities to the committees. Preinaugural committees, first appointed in 1956, and inaugural planning committees, first appointed in 1960, procure office space and make other preliminary arrangements for the inaugural committees. The location of many early inaugural committee records is largely unknown, but some records relating to inaugurations are in the Library of Congress, the District of Columbia Public Library, Georgetown University, the Smithsonian Institution, and the Art and Reference Library of the Office of the Architect of the Capitol.

274.2. There are some records relating to black participation as members of inaugural committees, balls, and parades. The records of the 1957 Inaugural Committee include among the files of the office of the general chairman **reports from officers and committees, 1956–57** (10 in.), arranged by subject. One file is entitled "Negro Participation" (⅛ in.). The file contains a few letters, "A Report of Negro Participation in the Inaugural Committee, 1957" (4 pp.), and photographs and a clipping from the *Pittsburgh Courier* for February 2, 1957, about black guests at the Inaugural Ball.

274.3. The Publicity Committee of the 1961 Inaugural Committee produced a series of **press releases, 1960–61** (5 in.), arranged by number of press release. Release number I 158 is about Negro participation in the inaugural activities.

274.4. The **general files, 1964–65** (7 in.), of the office of the executive director of the 1965 Inaugural Committee are arranged by subject. A folder entitled "Complaints" includes several letters about racial discrimination sent by the District of Columbia Improvement Association.

274.5. For the 1973 inauguration a Special Groups Committee was established. The **records for the committee, 1972–73** (1 ft., 3 in.), include plans for the participation of minorities and ethnic groups. One representative on the committee was black. The committee's primary responsibility was planning a "Heritage Day."

Record Group 276
Records of the U.S. Courts of Appeals

276.1. The courts of appeals are intermediate courts created by an act of March 3, 1891, to relieve the Supreme Court of considering appeals in cases originally decided by Federal trial courts. They are empowered to review final and certain interlocutory decisions of district courts except where the law provides for direct review by the Supreme Court. The courts of appeals also review and enforce orders of Federal administrative bodies, such as the Securities and Exchange Commission and the National Labor Relations Board. Decisions of the courts are final except when subject to discretionary review or appeal to the Supreme Court. The United States is divided into 11 judicial circuits, with the District of Columbia constituting a separate circuit; there is a court of appeals in each circuit.

276.2. The **records of U.S. courts of appeals, 1891–1951** (9,292 ft., in the archives branches of the Federal records centers), are arranged geographically by name of circuit court and thereunder by type of record. The records are appellate court case files, including mandates, stipulations, orders and decrees of the court, records of petitions for review, briefs for petitioners and respondents, transcripts of records of cases heard in lower courts before appeal, and judgments of the courts. Court cases involving black Americans are interspersed throughout these records; most of them must be located by name, by the nature of the case, or by racial designations within the records.

276.3. Records of the court of Judge William H. Hastie, who was appointed to the Third Circuit Court of Appeals in Philadelphia in 1949, are among the files in the Archives Branch, Philadelphia Federal Archives and Records Center.

Record Group 279

Records of the Indian Claims Commission

279.1. The Indian Claims Commission was created by an act of August 13, 1946, to hear and determine claims against the United States on behalf of any tribe, band, or other identifiable group of American Indians residing in the United States. The Commission consisted of a chief commissioner and four associate commissioners appointed by the President. Hearings were conducted by one or more commissioners and could be held anywhere in the United States. The act establishing the Commission provided that it should receive claims for a period of only 5 years after the date of approval of the act and that all such claims be heard and decided within a further 5-year period. This period was extended several times. The Commission was terminated and pending cases were transferred to the U.S. Court of Claims on September 30, 1978.

Closed Docketed Case Files

279.2. The **case files, 1949–67** (197 ft.), are arranged by docket number. Some of these cases were filed by Indian freedmen from the Five Civilized Tribes—the Choctaw, Chickasaw, Creek, Cherokee, and Seminole. Treaties after the Civil War stipulated that these tribes would allot land or money or both to the former slaves who lived among them. Some of the freedmen did receive land or money as provided by the treaties. Other freedmen's claims were rejected. Some of those whose claims were rejected and those who felt that they had not received their fair share of lands or money from the tribes brought suit. Litigation continued well into the 20th century as freedmen attempted to prove their claims.

279.3. Much of the information about freedmen's claims is interspersed among the case files for the Five Civilized Tribes. However, there are two specific cases dealing with freedmen: ***Creek Freedmen Association*** v. ***the United States*** (#25, ½ in.), and ***Cherokee Freedmen and Cherokee Freedmen's Association*** v. ***the United States*** (#123, 4 in.). Both of these cases give information about the history of the interaction between the Indians and the freedmen. Each case file includes some or all of the following documents: original, amended, and supplementary petitions; motions; briefs; transcripts of hearings; powers of attorney; findings; opinions of the Commission; and appeals.

279.4. See also RG 48, Records of the Office of the Secretary of the Interior, and RG 75, Records of the Bureau of Indian Affairs.

Record Group 280

Records of the Federal Mediation and Conciliation Service

280.1. The Federal Mediation and Conciliation Service (FMCS), created in 1947, assumed the functions that had been performed by the U.S. Conciliation Service since 1913. The Conciliation Service had been established in the Department of Labor under provisions of an act of 1913 that authorized the Secretary of Labor to act as a mediator or to appoint commissioners of conciliation in labor disputes. The FMCS has no enforcement authority. Its mediators assist representatives of labor and management in settling disputes. The National Labor-Management Panel, which equally represents management and labor, advises the Director of the Service. Some of the case files relate to labor disputes involving black laborers.

280.2. The FMCS records include **dispute case files, 1913–48** (1,049 ft.), and **arbitration case files, 1937–48** (108 ft.). Both are arranged numerically by file number. The dispute and arbitration case files are indexed together in the following indexes: a geographic card index arranged alphabetically by name of State and thereunder by name of town or city; a name index arranged alphabetically by name of person, organization, or firm; a subject index arranged alphabetically by subject; a conciliator index arranged alphabetically by name of conciliator; two arbitrator indexes arranged alphabetically by name of arbitrator; and an arbitration index, arranged alphabetically by name of individual or firm. In the subject index there are cards labeled "Colored Employees," "Negro(es)," "Racial Discrimination," "Pullman Porters," and "Red Caps Union #20342." The cases listed in each of these categories concern black workers. Other case files probably have additional information. A memorandum (3 pp.) in one case file (#170–6626, ¼ in.) concerning crabmeat pickers, dated September 18, 1931, to the Director of Conciliation from Karl F. Phillips, a commissioner of conciliation, pertains to a strike in Crisfield, Md. He reported that 700 black and 100 white employees were involved in the strike. There are several cases concerning labor problems within the meatpacking industry. One case pertaining to Chicago packinghouses in 1920 (#170–1365, 8 in.) includes a 1921 memorandum to Hugh Kerwin from George E. Haynes, Director of Negro Economics in the Labor Department, about the proportion of blacks employed in meatpacking plants in Chicago, January 1916 to February 1919. During this period black employees composed more than one-third of the work force in some of the plants.

Record Group 287
Publications of the U.S. Government

287.1. This record group is composed of the record set of U.S. Government publications transferred from the Government Printing Office (GPO) Library and of publications directly accessioned from departments and agencies. Generally, publications printed for purely administrative and internal use by an agency are not included. Although the collection is not complete, especially for the period before the GPO established the Office of Superintendent of Documents in 1895, this collection appears to be the most complete collection of U.S. Government publications in existence.

287.2. The **publications of the Federal Government, 1789–1976** (22,000 ft.), include about two million items. Thousands of these relate to various aspects of black history. The publications are arranged according to the Superintendent of Documents classification scheme, a system that reflects the organizational structure of the agency or office responsible for the original publication. An explanation of the system and a general description of Government documents will be found in Laurence F. Schmeckebier and Roy B. Eastin, *Government Publications and Their Use,* 2d ed., rev. (Washington, D.C.: Brookings Institution, 1969), and in U.S. Superintendent of Documents, *Checklist of United States Public Documents,* Vol. 1 (Washington, D.C.: Government Printing Office, 1911).

287.3. Publications relating to black history cover various topics. Pre-Civil War publications basically concern various aspects of slavery, such as the slave trade, emancipation, slave States, slaveholders, fugitive slaves, laws pertaining to slaves, and freed slaves. Others concern the civil rights of freed blacks, efforts to colonize them, and attempts to prevent their kidnapping and reenslavement.

287.4. Post-Civil War topics for black history among U.S. Government publications concern the economic, political, and legal status of black Americans; education of black Americans; blacks in the military; and numerous other matters. The collection includes publications of the Civil Rights Commission, the Colored Troops Bureau (War Department), the Equal Employment Opportunity Commission, the National Advisory Commission on Civil Disorders, and the Bureau of Refugees, Freedmen, and Abandoned Lands. All of these have concentrated information for black history. Other black history materials are interspersed among the publications of various agencies and departments.

287.5. Many publications relating to black history are among the series of congressional publications. Some early documents relating to slavery and colonization are among the *American State Papers,* 38 vols. (Washington, D.C.: Gales and Seaton, 1832–61). The *American State Papers* is an official reprint edition of the documents of the first 14 Congresses. Later records are included in the *Serial Set,* which begins with the 15th Congress in 1817 and continues to the present. The *Serial Set* is an ongoing collection of Federal Government publications compiled under the authority of the U.S. Congress. The *Serial Set* includes the *Journals* of the House and the Senate, congressional reports on public and private legislation, reports from special committees, reports submitted annually from various departments and agencies, and selected reports on nongovernmental agencies.

287.6. A few of the wide variety of black history topics included in the *Serial Set* are colonization, petitions of free blacks, abolition of slavery in the District of Columbia, sale of blacks by the Seminole Indians, Quaker petitions for abolition, claims for slaves captured by Great Britain during the War of 1812, illicit introduction or importation of slaves, prohibition of slavery in various territories, women's petitions against slavery, blacks in the military, treatment of black sailors at southern ports, adoption of blacks into the Chickasaw Nation, protection of emancipated slaves and freedmen, Indian freedmen, Freedmen's Hospital, Freedmen's Village, Freedmen's University, Freedman's Savings and Trust Co., and the Freedmen's Bureau. Several other topics of interest are claims from black soldiers and sailors for pensions or bounties, intermarriage between blacks and whites, migration of blacks from the South to the North, education of the black population, the Brownsville Affray, discrimination in employment, integration of the Coast Guard, Black Muslims, equal employment opportunity, and civil rights.

287.7. Both the *American State Papers* and the *Serial Set* have been indexed in the *CIS U.S. Serial Set Index, 1789–1969,* 36 vols. (Washington, D.C.: Congressional Information Service, 1979). Lists of black history materials appear under "Negro," "Colored," "Africa," "Freedmen," "Slavery," "Race," "Discrimination," "Civil Rights," "Integration," "Fugitives," "Indentured Servants," "Missouri Compromise," "Wilmot Proviso," "Servitude," and other headings.

287.8. The *Serial Set* does not include congressional committee hearings and prints. However, the hearings and prints are a part of this record group. They date from about the 48th Congress in 1884 and include information about many standing committees and some select and special committees no longer in existence. Much of this material is important for the study of black history.

287.9. Printed black history materials often supplement the unpublished records among the holdings of the National Archives. Sometimes the printed material gives information about black history topics for which there are no unpublished records. The following is a random sample of articles published from 1901 to 1903 that supplement the black history material among the records of RG 12, Records of the Office of Education: P. G. Barringer, "Negro Education in the South"; A. D. Mayo, "Work of Certain Northern Churches in Education of Freedmen, 1861–1900"; and Kelly Miller, "Education of the Negro." All of these articles appear in the *Education Bureau Report* for 1901–2. Titles for the years 1901–3 that supplement black history materials in RG 174, General Records of the Department of Labor, include J. B. Laws, "Negroes of Sinclare Central Factory and Calumet Plantations, Louisiana"; R. R. Wright, Jr., "Negroes of Xenia, Ohio—Social Study"; and W. T. Thom, "True Reformers." Laws' and Thom's articles appear in the *Labor Department Bulletin* for 1902, and Wright's in 1903.

287.10. A sampling of articles published in 1931–33 include a group written by a black Office of Education official, Ambrose Caliver, and published as Education Office Bulletins: *Background Study of Negro College Students,* Bulletin 8, 1933; "Education of Negroes," a segment of Bulletin 20, 1931; *Rural Elementary Education Among Negroes under Jeanes Supervising Teachers,* Bulletin 5, 1933; and *Secondary Education for Negroes,* Bulletin 17, 1932. A Census Bureau publication for 1933 was *Fifteenth Census of the United States, 1930, Census of Agriculture, Negro Farmers in the United States,* compiled by Charles E. Hall. The U.S. Public Health Service published the periodic newsletter *National Negro Health News.* In 1933 E. M. Shinn of the Federal Extension Service published a *Survey of Methods Pursued by Supervisors of Negro Agricultural and Home Economics Extension Work in Developing Programs and Plans of Work,* Miscellaneous Extension Publication 12.

287.11. Late 19th- and 20th-century black history publications can be located by using the *Documents Catalog,* 25 vols (Washington, D.C.: Government Printing Office, 1893–1940); the *Monthly Catalog of United States Government Publications* (Washington, D.C.: Government Printing Office, Jan. 1895–); and the *Cumulative Subject Index to the Monthly Catalog of United States Government Publications, 1900–1971* (and subsequent updates), compiled by William W. Buchanan and Edna M. Kanely, 15 vols. (Washington, D.C.: Carrollton Press, 1973).

Record Group 288
Records of the National Foundation on the Arts and the Humanities

288.1. The general purpose of the National Foundation on the Arts and the Humanities is to encourage and support national progress in the humanities and the arts. The Foundation was created as an independent agency in 1965 and consists of a National Endowment for the Arts, a National Endowment for the Humanities, and a Federal Council on the Arts and the Humanities. Each endowment has its own council, composed of the endowment chairman and 26 other members appointed by the President, which advises the chairman about policies and procedures, reviews applications for financial support, and makes recommendations thereon. The National Endowment for the Arts awards grants to individuals, State and regional arts agencies, and nonprofit organizations representing the highest quality in the fields of design arts, dance, expansion arts, fold arts, literature, media arts, museums, music, theater, and the visual arts. The National Endowment for the Humanities provides grants for the study of language, linguistics, literature, history, jurisprudence, philosophy, archaeology, and the history, criticism, theory, and practice of the arts and some aspects of the social sciences. The Federal Council on the Arts and Humanities coordinates the activities of the two endowments.

288.2. Black history materials are interspersed throughout the **Foundation's records, 1966–77** (about 65 ft.). Most of the correspondence files include some letters from members of the faculties and staffs of various predominantly black colleges and universities or from blacks in the arts.

Record Group 302
Records of the National Capital Housing Authority

302.1. The National Capital Housing Authority (NCHA), the public housing agency for the District of Columbia, was established as the Alley Dwelling Authority by Executive Order 6868 of October 9, 1934, in accordance with the District of Columbia Alley Dwelling Act of June 12, 1934. It was given its present name in 1943; the Office of the Commissioner of the District of Columbia was designated the National Capital Housing Authority in 1968; and the functions of the Authority were delegated to the Commissioner's assistant at that time. An act of December 24, 1973 (87 Stat. 779; D.C. Code 5-103a), provided that the Authority become an agency of the District of Columbia government, effective July 1, 1974. Originally the Authority reclaimed District of Columbia slums in squares containing inhabited alleys, but in 1938 amendments to the Alley Dwelling Act enabled the Authority to provide low-rent housing for low-income families under the auspices of the U.S. Housing Authority and in accordance with the U.S. Housing Act of 1937, as amended. The wartime objective of the Authority was to provide housing for war workers under the Lanham Act and other legislation. When slum reclamation in the District was resumed after the war, it was made the responsibility of the District of Columbia Redevelopment Land Agency. At present the chief function of the Authority is to assure an adequate supply of proper dwellings for low-income families at rents commensurate with their income.

302.2. Most of the records relating to alley dwelling and slum clearance relate to the housing conditions of blacks in the District of Columbia. The speeches, statements, and related records of **John Ihlder, Executive Director of the Authority, 1934–52** (4 ft.), are arranged alphabetically by title or type of record. In an undated speech entitled "Development of the Inhabited Alleys of Washington," Ihlder wrote "at the close of the Civil War, between 30,000 and 40,000 emancipated slaves came to Washington," adding that these were in addition to the number of other blacks who had attached themselves to military establishments in and near the city. No provision was made for the housing of these freed men and women. Some squatted on public ground and others constructed makeshift dwellings and lived in alleys. Some landlords also built inexpensive housing in the alleys and rented it cheaply to blacks. Some of these old houses were still inhabited in 1934, although they were in a dilapidated condition. The purpose of the Alley Dwelling Authority was to tear down the slum areas and build low-income housing for the former occupants.

302.3. There is a folder among Ihlder's records for "Hopkins Place, a Low Rental Housing Development" (½ in.), which was the Authority's first low-rent housing project. A speech was delivered at the dedication ceremony in October 1936 by Emmett J. Scott, the secretary of Howard University. He was introduced at the ceremony in this way: "Because the housing of low income families in Washington is so largely a problem of the Negroes, we wish to hear from one who can speak for them."

302.4. The **general records maintained by the central files unit, 1935–49** (5 ft.), are arranged alphabetically by subject or type of record. Information about housing for the black community of Washington, D.C., is interspersed throughout the records. For example, the folders for the Washington Housing Association (5 in.) include a December 1939 speech by John Ihlder in which he describes the seven construction projects with 2,000 housing units that were funded at that time. Of the seven sites, five were scheduled for black occupants and two for whites. There were also three proposed sites for black occupancy. Other correspondence and reports in these folders include information about redlining (the practice by some bankers and realtors of drawing on a map a red line around housing districts closed to blacks), housing for blacks provided by the U.S. Housing Authority, and opposition by whites and tenant organizations to the various housing projects.

302.5. The **administrative records, 1935–51** (8 ft.), are arranged alphabetically by subject or type of record. The folder "Negro Housing Conference" is for the conference held April 18, 1936, sponsored by a nongovernment organization called the Washington Committee on Housing. Maj. Campbell C. Johnson, a black man who was later appointed Executive Assistant to the Director of the Selective Service System, was the chairman of the subcommittee that organized the conference. Johnson was also the compiler of the *Report of the Conference on Better Housing among Negroes,* which was published by the Washington Committee on Housing and which is among these records. The report includes the excerpted remarks of the addresses made to the conference by Eleanor Roosevelt; Robert C. Weaver, the Advisor on Negro Affairs in the Department of the Interior; Roscoe C. Brown, Director of National Negro Health Week at the U.S. Public Health Service; Hilyard R. Robinson, chief architect of the Langston low-rent housing project, which was sponsored by the Housing Division of the Public Works Administration; and numerous others, many from Howard University.

302.6. Other administrative records include specifications for various housing projects, correspondence with municipal housing and welfare organizations, housing surveys, requests for publications, legislation, and reports about the constitutionality of public housing laws.

Record Group 306

Records of the U.S. Information Agency

306.1. The U.S. Information Agency (USIA) was established in 1953 to help achieve U.S. foreign policy objectives by influencing public attitudes in other nations and by advising the President, his representatives abroad, and various departments and agencies on the implications of foreign opinion for present and contemplated U.S. policies, programs, and official statements. There are approximately 700,000 photographs in this record group.

306.2. There are more than 600 **Press Service (PS) photographs, ca. 1948–60,** that deal directly with black Americans. Typical subjects are blacks distinguishing themselves in various fields, blacks and whites working together in a variety of jobs in military and civilian life, black people in settings intended to display their economic prosperity, and the functioning of programs designed to improve economic and social conditions for black Americans.

306.3. Pictorial documentation for the study of black history is also contained in the photograph series from the ***New York Times* (NT) Paris Bureau files, 1900–50.** These photographic files were purchased by the Economic Cooperation Administration in 1950, when the *Times* Paris Bureau was discontinued, and were later turned over to the U.S. Information Agency. There are photographs documenting various forms of black protest, progress toward racial equality, daily life in Harlem, cultural life, participation in Olympic games, black members of the Communist Party of America, blacks and the police and the judicial system, and blacks in the labor movement and in the military during World War II, the postwar period, and the occupation of Europe.

Record Group 318

Records of the Bureau of Engraving and Printing

318.1. Acts of February and July 1862 authorized the engraving of signatures on Treasury notes and the imprinting of the Treasury Department seal on notes made for the Department by private firms; it also empowered the Secretary of the Treasury to have the notes engraved at the

Department, to purchase equipment, and to employ necessary personnel. As early as 1866 the First Division in the Office of the Comptroller of the Currency, created by an act in 1863, was informally referred to as the Bureau of Engraving and Printing. The Bureau designation was officially adopted in 1869, when the unit was administratively separated from the Office. The first legislative recognition of the Bureau as an organizational unit of the Department of the Treasury was made in an appropriation act of 1874. The Bureau designs, engraves, and prints for the Federal Government and U.S. insular possessions all paper currency, bonds, notes, bills, and certificates; Federal Reserve notes; obligations of Government-owned corporations; revenue, customs, postage, and savings stamps; Government checks; and other engraved documents. Bureau operations are financed by reimbursements to a working capital fund authorized by law. The Bureau has retained most of its records. General correspondence between the Secretary of the Treasury and the Director of the Bureau, correspondence about Bureau appointments, and personnel registers are among the general records of the Department of the Treasury (see RG 56).

318.2. Among the records pertaining to personnel is an **index to applications, 1869–1912** (3 vols., 6 in.), arranged alphabetically by name. The applications themselves are described in paragraph 56.16. However, the index may be used to locate other information about employees, a few of which are designated in the index as "colored."

318.3. The **central subject file, 1913–39** (120 ft.), is arranged by year and thereunder alphabetically by subject. For 1913 there is a folder entitled "Segregation" (¼ in.), which includes correspondence about white and black employees of the Bureau working side by side. There are several other folders (totaling about 2 in.) pertaining to black history in this series: "Segregation," 1914; "Employees–Colored," 1920; "Civil Service," 1920; and "Employees–Colored," 1921, 1930, 1935, 1936, 1937, 1938, 1939. These folders contain information about the percentage of black employees in the Bureau, their grades or job titles, and other related information.

Record Group 325

Records of the Committee on Government Contract Compliance

325.1. The Committee on Government Contract Compliance, established by a 1951 Executive order, was composed of representatives of industry, labor, the general public, and several Government agencies, including the Departments of Defense and Labor, the Atomic Energy Commission, the General Services Administration, and the Defense Materials Procurement Agency. The purpose of the Committee was to improve ways of obtaining compliance with the provisions in Federal contracts that prohibited discrimination on account of race, color, or religion. The Committee became inactive after publication of its final report, *Equal Economic Opportunity,* in January 1953, and it was officially abolished by an Executive order of August 13, 1953, which established the Government Contract Committee and transferred to it all property and records of the Compliance Committee.

325.2. Virtually all of the records in this group relate to black history. The Committee worked to prevent or solve problems of racial discrimination in hiring, wages, and promotional opportunity. The antidiscrimination clause in Federal contracts had been a feature sine 1941. The Committee could confer with and make recommendations to the contracting agencies concerning procedures to further the prevention of discrimination. The Committee collected a file of over 300 allegations of violations of the antidiscrimination clause.

325.3. Records relating to Committee meetings, 1952–53 (4 in.), are in two parts: (1) mainly communications and telephone memorandums of the Executive Director with Committee members, but including some letters and telegrams of the Chairman to members of the staff about meetings, arranged alphabetically by name of Committee member; (2) summaries of Committee meetings, arranged chronologically. **Issuances of the Committee, 1951–53** (10 in.), consist mainly of records pertaining to Committee activities, such as plans and procedures to carry out its mission, a questionnaire on compliance sent to Government agencies, summaries of reports on various aspects of the nondiscrimination clause, photographs, press releases, and printed copies of the Committee's final report. These records are arranged by subject. **Weekly progress reports, 1952–53** (1 in.), arranged chronologically, were prepared for the Chairman by the Executive Director; the reports summarize the activities of the staff and the Committee.

325.4. Staff working papers, 1952 (7 in.), are divided into two parts: (1) copies of questionnaires, correspondence, memorandums, drafts, and summary reports prepared chiefly by the staff in connection with the establishment of Government contract compliance procedures to be used by Federal agencies in processing complaints of discrimination and in enforcing the nondiscrimination clause and (2) copies of background material such as civil rights surveys. The first part is arranged by code number from 1–32 to 1–36; the second part is arranged by subject.

325.5. There are three administrative series. **Administrative records, 1952–53** (3 in.), arranged by subject, include such fiscal material as salary and housekeeping accounts; **personnel papers, 1952–53** (7 in.), arranged alphabetically by name of applicant or staff member, consist of applications for employment and personnel files of staff members; and **miscellaneous records, 1951–53** (3 in.), arranged by subject, contain correspondence requesting information on various phases of the Committee's work, mailing lists, and personnel matters.

325.6. Materials relating to the Committee's final report, 1952–53 (8 in.), arranged by subject, include the draft of an unpublished interim report, drafts for the final report, and the responses from newspapers, magazines, and the general public about the report. **Reference materials, 1952–53** (2 ft.), of an educational nature were collected by the staff to provide background information on discrimination and the means of combatting it. The materials include descriptions of films; various articles and reports; information about discrimination in the Armed Forces; discriminatory practices in housing, employment, and labor unions; and discriminatory measures in Federal and State legislation.

325.7. The Committee and its staff conducted **correspondence with Federal contracting agencies, 1952** (6 in.), to survey their compliance methods. These records are arranged alphabetically by name of Federal agency. The **Committee's chronological file, 1952–53** (5 in.), includes copies of letters sent by the Executive Director to Committee members and officials of Federal agencies, weekly reports, announcements of meetings and hearings, and daily memorandums. There is also a series of **correspondence with municipal commissions, 1952–53** (1 in.), arranged alphabetically by name of city and code number from 2–D–3 to 2–D–9. The correspondence contains summaries of field interviews, municipal issuances, and related material pertaining to employment discrimination in several cities.

325.8. There are **records relating to Committee hearings with Federal agencies, 1952–53** (6 in.); **with State commissions, 1952–53** (3 in.); and **with private organizations, 1952–53** (5 in.). The records are arranged alphabetically by name of agency, State, or organization. The records include preparatory correspondence, lists of participants, transcripts or summaries of the proceedings, and summaries of interviews. The hearings relate to training and apprenticeship programs, State antidiscrimination legislation, and the effectiveness of various nondiscrimination programs. There is also a **complaints case file, 1952–53** (5 ft.), arranged alphabetically by name of company and by code number. The files contain mainly abstracts of allegations of discrimination against 326 companies whose names were obtained in Committee hearings with private organizations. Many of the allegations were submitted by the Urban League.

Record Group 328
Records of the National Capital Planning Commission

328.1. The National Capital Planning Commission was created by an act of July 1952 to succeed the National Capital Park and Planning Commission, established in 1926, and its predecessor, the National Capital Park Commission, established in 1924. The National Capital Planning Commission was created as the central agency for the Federal and District of Columbia governments for planning the development and redevelopment of the National Capital and the conservation of its natural and historical features. The 12-member Commission is composed of officials of the Federal and District governments and private citizens. Washington, D.C., historically had a large black population. In 1860, 19.1 percent of the population was black, 28.5 percent was black by 1910, and 53.9 percent by 1960. Consequently, many of the records relating to housing, slum clearance, and urban renewal in the District of Columbia pertain to black neighborhoods. The **transcripts of proceedings and minutes of the meetings of the National Capital Planning Commission and its predecessors, 1926–72** (35 ft.), arranged chronologically, include some information about blacks in the District of Columbia. Specific information can be found by using these records in conjunction with the planning files.

328.2. The **planning files, 1924–67** (78 ft.), are arranged in a numeric-subject classification scheme. The file "Housing" (#545–45) includes information about alley dwelling, public housing, and the work of the National Capital Housing Authority. One category under "Housing" is urban redevelopment, which includes records pertaining to Barry Farms, a community that was initially formed by freed slaves; to other black housing areas; and to slum prevention. The records pertaining to sites for expansion and buildings (#545–55) include information about Howard University and Freedmen's Hospital.

328.3. The planning files also include a category on playgrounds and recreation (#545–85). There is information about some segregated facilities, such as the Langston Recreation Center, and about efforts to integrate recreational areas. Under the category for the public works program (#545–88) is a file on race discrimination and segregation (2 in.); the file includes information about discrimination in many areas of life besides public works. It includes correspondence from political and civic groups as well as from individuals and contains a number of statements of racial policy in the District. There is information about recreational facilities and about alleged efforts of the National Capital Planning Commission to maintain racial segregation patterns in the District. There are a number of records throughout the planning files surveying the population, income levels, and public school and housing situations in the city.

328.4. The **office files of the National Capital Park and Planning Commission Chairman Frederic A. Delano, 1926–42** (5 ft.), arranged alphabetically by subject, include some information relating to blacks in the files on housing, population, family income, and other subjects.

328.5. The **office files of Director John F. Nolen, Jr., 1926–58** (29 ft.), arranged alphabetically by subject, include information about income, housing, alley dwelling, slum clearance, recreation centers, and redevelopment.

328.6. The **records relating to urban renewal, ca. 1952–67** (45 ft.), contain information about housing patterns of the black population, community reactions to renewal plans, responses by black activist groups to renewal plans, and plans for Howard University and Federal City College. Among the records are feasibility studies, cost estimates, and agreements and contracts drawn up by the Commission.

328.7. The records of the **Washington Civil Disorder Survey, 1968–69** (15 ft.), arranged by subject, include material relating to an "inquiry into the economic and social characteristics of privately and publicly owned real properties which sustained damage or loss" during the April 4–15 civil disturbances in the District set off by the assassination of civil rights activist Dr. Martin Luther King, Jr. The records are primarily lists of damaged properties and completed questionnaires giving names of owners and addresses of damaged properties, extent and type of damage, data on employees within damaged businesses, future plans of owners, and other information.

Record Group 350

Records of the Bureau of Insular Affairs

350.1. The Bureau of Insular Affairs had its origin in 1898 as the Division of Customs and Insular Affairs in the Office of the Secretary of War, created to assist in administering customs and other civil affairs in Puerto Rico, Cuba, and the Philippine Islands. It was named the Bureau of Insular Affairs in 1902 and was transferred to the Department of the Interior in 1939. The functions of the Bureau and its predecessors included supervising civil affairs of the Governments of the Philippine Islands, Puerto Rico, and Cuba. The Bureau also supervised the Dominican and Haitian Customs Receiverships and performed duties relating to the Panama Canal.

350.2. The **general classified files, 1898–1945** (527 ft.), arranged numerically, include some materials for black history. "Negroes" (#1846, 1¼ in.) contains information about prejudice toward black Americans in the Philippines, inquiries about the employment of black Americans there, questions about possibilities for black farmers and colonists in the Islands, and some information on the number of black Americans actually working in the Islands. There is a file relating to the black educator Carter G. Woodson (#8898, 1 in.), who worked as General Superintendent of Education for the Philippines from 1903 to 1907. In this file there is also some correspondence after 1907 with Woodson that includes applications for reemployment with the Bureau, resumes, and biographical information. There is a file about "Negroes" (#26691, ⅛ in.) that includes only a few pieces of correspondence, which relate to the employment of black Americans in Puerto Rico, to invitations to black Puerto Ricans to attend meetings and conferences held by blacks in the United States, and to racial relations in Puerto Rico.

Record Group 351

Records of the Government of the District of Columbia

351.1. The District of Columbia, created by acts of 1790 and 1791 from lands ceded by Virginia and Maryland, was permanently established as the seat of the Federal Government in 1800. In 1846 Congress returned to Virginia its part, including both the city and county of Alexandria. The Constitution of the United States gave Congress power to legislate for the capital of the United States, and the first District of Columbia government was established under an act of 1802, which provided for a mayor appointed by the President and a city council elected by District residents. The charter was modified by later acts and in 1871 was revoked. Congress then established a territorial form of government for the District headed by a governor. In 1874 three commissioners were appointed by the President to govern the District. In 1967 a reorganization plan provided for a commissioner (informally called mayor) of the District of Columbia and a District city council composed of a chairman, vice chairman, and seven other members, all appointed by the President with the advice and consent of the Senate. The Home Rule Act of 1973 provided for an elected mayor and city council. These records include information about the black community in Washington, D.C.

351.2. The **annual reports of the commissioners, 1874–1941** (66 vols., 30 ft.), arranged chronologically, are printed reports usually containing detailed accounts of the operation of all departments and offices of the District government. Although the contents of the reports vary from year to year, they generally include a comprehensive account of the finances of the local government and its departments, health and crime statistics, and reports concerning charitable institutions, public improvements, and public education. Much of this information includes racial statistics.

351.3. The **general files, ca. 1924–68** (189 ft.), arranged according to a decimal classification system, include numerous subjects for black history. The District of Columbia's growing black population exceeded the size of the white population by the middle of the 20th century. Consequently, many of the records pertaining to education, housing, urban renewal, and slum clearance relate to black neighborhoods. Other records relate to the population of the District of Columbia, home rule, protest marches and demonstrations, an Emancipation Proclamation memorial, a Frederick Douglass memorial, and black churches in the District of Columbia. Public relations records include correspondence with black organizations, such as the Prince Hall Grand Lodge, the National Council of Negro Women, and the National Association of Colored Women's Clubs. There are records relating to race relations, discrimination in the District of Columbia government, racial restrictions in community covenants, racial advancement, the NAACP, the Washington Urban League, anti-black organizations, antidiscrimination laws, and the integration of the fire department and District schools.

351.4. The general files also have information about the National Negro Opera Company, the Washington *Afro-American* newspaper, Freedmen's and Howard University Hospitals, Howard University, Federal City College, and the Jack and Jill Clubs. There is also information about interracial recreational activities, the District's policies on racial segregation on playgrounds, the integration of penal institutions, police discrimination, and the Fair Employment Practice Act.

351.5. Transcripts of public hearings, 1947–74 (14 ft.), arranged alphabetically by subject, include hearings about racial discrimination, housing, crime, urban renewal, and home rule.

351.6. The **hearing files of the District city council, 1967–74** (20 ft.), arranged alphabetically by subject, contain information on civil disorders, including the mayor's report on the use of tear gas and the enforcement of curfew in June 1968, when riots erupted after the assassination of Dr. Martin Luther King, Jr. There are materials pertaining to Nichols Avenue being renamed Martin Luther King, Jr., Avenue, and other records relating to housing and urban renewal.

351.7. The records relating to fiscal affairs include **general assessment books, 1814–79** (37 vols., 11 ft.), arranged mainly by square and lot numbers. Entries vary from volume to volume. One of the 1829 volumes and the 1839 book give assessments for ownership of personal property, slaves, and carriages. The **taxbooks, 1824–79** (159 vols., 36 ft.), arranged by ward or by initial letter of surname, give an annual record of the payment of taxes on real and personal property. Frequently in the earlier volumes there are also entries relating to the payment of such special taxes as the tax on slaves and carriages or special assessments levied for sinking wells, erecting pumps, and setting curbstone or pavements.

351.8. The fiscal records also include **registers of licenses, 1818–76** (24 vols., 2½ ft.). The arrangement within each volume varies. The act of 1802 that incorporated the city of Washington also empowered the corporation to license and regulate certain activities, including auctions, the retailing of liquor, hackney carriages, wagons, carts, drays, pawnbrokers, theatrical productions, and other amusements. The list of occupations or other activities requiring a license from the city grew over the years to include slaveowners, lotteries, insurance agencies, groceries, and many others.

351.9. The records relating to land include **deedbooks of the Office of the Recorder of Deeds, 1792–1869** (551 vols., 112 ft.), arranged chronologically by the date the document was recorded. The deeds record transfer of real property as well as other legal documents, such as letters of attorney, leases, bills of sale, mortgages, deeds of manumission of slaves, and certificates of freedom establishing the free status of blacks.

351.10. The records of the metropolitan police include volumes with **daily returns of precincts, 1861–78 and 1887** (38 vols., 9 ft.), arranged chronologically and thereunder by precinct. The individual entries of sergeants' daily reports of arrests include name of person arrested; time of arrest; arrestee's age, race, nationality, occupation, martial status, and literacy; nature and disposition of the complaint; and name of complainant.

351.11. The **arrest books, 1869–1906** (6 vols., 10 in.), arranged chronologically, list arrests for some precincts. The entries usually give date and time of arrest; name, age, race, nationality, occupation, martial status, and literacy of person arrested; complaint; name of complainant; name of arresting officer; and disposition of the case.

351.12. The **record of juvenile arrests in the third precinct, 1908–18** (1 vol., 1 in.), arranged alphabetically by initial letter of surname of person arrested and thereunder chronologically, shows date; name of juvenile arrested and his address, age, and race; charge; name of complainant; arresting officer; and disposition of the case.

351.13. The miscellaneous records of the metropolitan police include a **register of lodgers, 1891–95 and 1898** (1 vol., ½ in.), arranged chronologically. Entries show date, name, age, race, occupation, and home city of lodger. This volume was maintained by the third precinct.

351.14. The records relating to charitable and reformatory institutions include the **history of committed feebleminded children, 1884–1907** (2 vols., 3 in.), arranged chronologically. Congress by an act of 1880 authorized the Secretary of the Interior to take care of indigent, feebleminded children in the District of Columbia and, after having them examined, to place them in institutions in Pennsylvania or elsewhere for the education of feebleminded children. These volumes give the personal and family background—including race—of those children committed to the Pennsylvania Training School for Feebleminded Children in Elwyn, Pa., 1884–1907, and to the Virginia Home and Training School for Feebleminded Children in Falls Church, Va., 1894–1907.

351.15. The **record of children received by the Board of Children's Guardians, 1893–1912** (1 vol., 1½ in.), arranged chronologically, includes a list of children placed in the custody of the Board, giving date taken in charge; name of child; race; from whom received; basis for the commitment; religion of the parents; and information about the parents' birthplaces and character and whether living or dead.

351.16. The **children's history, 1893, 1897–1906, and 1909–13** (7 vols., 1½ ft.), arranged chronologically by date of commitment, includes background and progress reports on children placed in the custody of the Board. The entry for each child gives the date taken in charge; name, age, and race; the name and last known address of the parents; date and place of birth; remarks on physical, mental, and moral condition; and a general history of the ward and his family, including an account of the circumstances that led to the ward's commitment. There is also a record of visits to the child during the period in custody (with remarks concerning the child's progress) and records of the various homes and institutions in which the child was placed.

351.17. The **directory of placed-out children, 1893–1908** (1 vol., 1½ in.), arranged chronologically, is a list of children placed in foster homes by the Board of Children's Guardians and the terms of their placement. The information given in the list varies through the years, but there is generally information about the child's family and race.

351.18. The **record of children in temporary custody, 1897–1909** (3 vols., 6 in.), arranged chronologically, includes information for each child placed in temporary custody of the Board of Children's

Guardians. Each entry gives the date the child was placed in the custody of the Board; age, name, and race; name and last known address of the parents; place and date of birth; physical, mental, and moral condition; from whom received; cause of the placement; where temporarily placed, length of stay, and financial charges; final disposition of the case; and remarks, usually elaborating on the background of the child and the reasons for his commitment.

351.19. Congress, by an act approved April 27, 1904, appropriated funds for locating a site and planning the building for an Industrial Home School for Colored Children. The school, which was originally placed under the control of the Board of Charities, was opened at Blue Plains in August 1907. It came under the control of the Board of Public Works when that organization was created in 1926. The **minutes of six staff meetings, 1927–28** (1 vol., 1 in.), presided over by the superintendent of the school, are arranged chronologically. The minutes consist largely of routine announcements to the staff, discussions of rules and regulations, and instructions to the matrons. Also included are conduct reports on individual children for 1923, with a record of misconduct reported to "the Office." The reports are arranged alphabetically by name of child. In the back of the volume is an index to names of children; in the front of the volume is a list of pupils by grade for some unidentified year.

351.20. The records of the Health and Welfare Council Committee on Junior Village include the minutes of the **meetings of the executive committee of the Council, 1958–59** (1 vol., 1 in.), arranged by type of meeting and thereunder chronologically. In addition to the minutes there are summaries of discussions of problems and proposals for action resulting from meetings between the Committee and other persons involved with the problems of dependency, including a meeting with the executive secretary of the Urban League.

351.21. The records of the City of Georgetown include **general assessment books, 1800–19 and 1835–79** (21 vols., 5 ft.). The arrangement varies from volume to volume. The volumes for 1800 to 1819 include assessments levied on such personal property as furniture, slaves, merchandise, horses, cows, and carts.

351.22. The records of the County of Washington also include general assessment books, 1855–64 and 1868–79 (12 vols., 2½ ft.). The arrangement varies from volume to volume. The assessors' lists of taxable property for 1855 include entries for assessments of personal property such as furniture, cows, wagons, carts, carriages, and slaves.

Record Group 360

Records of the Continental and Confederation Congresses and the Constitutional Convention

360.1. The First Continental Congress, which met in Philadelphia on September 5, 1774, included representatives from all of the Thirteen Colonies except Georgia. Convened to discuss and address grievances to the British Crown and Parliament, the Congress elected Peyton Randolph as President and, as Secretary, Charles Thomson, who served in that capacity until the Federal Government was established in 1789. In contrast to the First Continental Congress, which adjourned on October 26, 1774, after having been assembled less than 2 months, the Second Continental Congress met over a period of almost 6 years. Meeting for the first time on May 10, 1775, at Philadelphia, it convened successively at Baltimore, Philadelphia, Lancaster (one day only), York, and Philadelphia. With the final ratification of the Articles of Confederation on March 2, 1781, a new central government was created by a series of Confederation Congresses. The final business of the last Congress under the Articles was transacted October 11, 1788, and on March 4, 1789, the First Congress of the United States met in New York City.

360.2. It should be noted that the records allocated to this record group are not, for the most part, organized in a manner that reflects the identity, structure, or function of each of the Continental and Confederation Congresses. They were arranged and bound by previous custodians, chiefly by type of record—such as journals, committee reports, correspondence, memorials, and petitions—and thereunder chronologically or alphabetically. In many instances the date span of individual series encompasses all Continental and Confederation Congresses. In addition, groups of closely related records and even parts of essentially the same body of documents are widely separated in the numbered series, while collections of unrelated records constitute a single volume of a series. It should not be assumed that all records of a given type are to be found in a particular series, nor that the title of a series always accurately reveals either its principal or its total contents.

360.3. Most of the records of the Continental and Confederation Congresses, 1774–89, are arranged in a numerical sequence of 196 series referred to as "item numbers." There are also miscellaneous records that are not among the numbered series. The records consist of the *Journals* of Congress, reports of its committees, memorials and petitions, papers submitted by State governments, and correspondence of its Presidents and other officers with diplomatic representatives of the U.S. abroad, officers in the Continental Army, State and local officials, and private persons. There are copies of the Declaration of Independence, the Articles of Confederation, the Northwest Ordinance, the Constitution, and other documents instrumental in molding the new government; drafts of treaties and commercial agreements; papers relating to expenditures and to domestic and foreign loans; reports of military progress during the Revolution; and papers relating to Indian treaties and tribes. The documents are accessible for research through five microfilm publications and the printed edition of the manuscript journals (Items 1–8) of the Congress. For the printed journals, there is the *Index: Journals of the Continental Congress, 1774–89,* compiled by Kenneth Harris and Steven D. Tilley (Washington, D.C.: National Archives and Records Service, 1976). The manuscript journals and the remainder of the records (Items 9–196 and the miscellaneous papers) are reproduced on the five microfilm publications, as mentioned above, and are indexed in *Index: The Papers of the Continental Congress, 1774–1789,* 5 vols. (Washington, D.C.: National Archives and Records Service, 1978).

360.4. In the *Index* to the Journals, records for black history are found under the headings "Negroes," "Mulattoes," "Slaves," "Slavery," and "Slave Trade." The records pertain to the enlistment of free blacks for service in the Revolutionary War, petitions and addresses for the abolition of slavery and the slave trade, ways to enumerate blacks and mulattoes in the population, slave revolts, British-instigated slave insurrections, the disposition of captured fugitive slaves and blacks taken by U.S. vessels, attempts to get South Carolina and Georgia to raise 1,000 able-bodied black troops, the return of slaves captured by the British, taxes on slaves, slavery in the Northwest Territory, calls for Indians to return all fugitive and other slaves, and applications to the Governor of East Florida to return fugitive slaves.

360.5. The *Index* to the Papers includes the following headings for black history: "Africa," "Mulattoes," "Negroes," "Slaves," "Slavery," and the "Slave Trade." In addition, the names of various individuals are identified as "(Negro)" in the *Index.* Much of the material for black history concerns the evacuation of blacks by the British in 1783. Lists of those who left with the British are called "Inspection Rolls" and are dated June 13 and 25; July 8, 10–16, and 29–31; August 13–22; September 5–13 and 22; and November 19, 1783. These inspection rolls were created so that reparations could be made to the owners of the slaves at a later date. Consequently, careful information about each evacuee was kept, such as age, description, former owner's name and address, and the name of the person in whose custody they were traveling (if any). Other subjects among the records are similar to those in the Journals.

Record Group 362
Records of Agencies for Voluntary Action Programs

362.1. ACTION was established as an independent agency in the executive branch by Reorganization Plan No. 1 of 1971. The purpose of the agency is to strengthen the impact and appeal of citizen participation in programs providing personalized services to people in need, both at home and abroad. ACTION provides centralized coordination and administration of domestic and international volunteer activities sponsored by the Federal Government. Included in the activities of the agency are: the Peace Corps, Volunteers in Service to America (VISTA), Foster Grandparent Program, Retired Senior Volunteer Program (RSVP), Service Corps of Retired Executives (SCORE), Action Corps of Executives (ACE), University Year for Action (UYA), and the National Student Volunteer Program (NAVP).

362.2. There are a number of motion picture films (144 items) created, commissioned, or acquired by the Peace Corps and other predecessor agencies of ACTION that document volunteer programs, international conditions, or subjects of international interest. The films include some black history topics. "Toby Town, U.S.A.: A Way of Life" (#362–123) is a black and white television documentary that explores a black town in the affluent Washington, D.C., suburb of Montgomery County, Md. The residents of the town expressed the need for better housing, more educational opportunities, and some job training programs. A VISTA volunteer inspires and helps them to improve their community. Included are a film entitled "The Negro and the American Promise" (#362–72), an appeal for the Peace Corps by Harry Belafonte on the Dinah Shore Show (#362–24), a 13-minute speech by President John F. Kennedy on equal rights (#362–148), and scenes in other films that relate to black history.

362.3. There is a **subject file of photographs of VISTA volunteers and programs, 1964–69** (15,452 items). Many of the pictures depict the living conditions of low-income people in urban and rural areas, a number of whom are black. Some pictures show blacks working on a tobacco farm, others document the aftermath of the Detroit race riots, and many relate to a wide variety of VISTA activities among the black population.

Record Group 365

Treasury Department Collection of Confederate Records

365.1. Although most Confederate Treasury records that came into the possession of the U.S. Government passed into and remained in the custody of the War Department, some were acquired by the Treasury Department through special agents appointed to regulate commerce in areas recaptured by Federal forces and to superintend captured and abandoned Confederate property. These records were supplemented by purchases in 1872 and 1873 and the transfer of a small quantity of records from the War Department. This collection comprises records of the central office of the Confederate Treasury Department, records of local officials of the Confederate Treasury and Justice Departments and of Confederate State governments, records of the Confederate War Department's Trans-Mississippi Department cotton bureaus, and records of the U.S. Treasury Department relating mainly to attempts after the war to secure Confederate property abroad. Indexes prepared after the records were acquired by the U.S. Treasury Department are included. The Confederate Treasury Department was established February 21, 1861, by an act of the Confederate Congress. Its internal structure, patterned after that of the Federal Treasury, included Offices of the Secretary of the Treasury; Assistant Secretary; Treasurer, Comptroller, First, Second, and Third Auditors; Register; Commissioner of Taxes and Deposit; and the Produce Loan, Treasury Note, and Lighthouse Bureaus.

365.2. The **register of military claims in the records of the Second Auditor, January 3–November 14, 1862** (1 vol., 1 in.), includes entries arranged chronologically and numbered from 1 to 1900. These are claims for the pay of deceased noncommissioned officers and soldiers, for the hire of slaves, for medical services, and for food and lodging of soldiers. Shown are the name of the civilian or soldier who filed a claim; rank, company, and regiment of the soldier; date the claim was filed in the Office of the Second Auditor; name of next of kin or attorney; nature of claim; and amount of claim minus any allowances. For additional information about the use of blacks as laborers on military works for the Confederate Army in the field and in hospitals and as a source of military manpower by impressment and recruitment, consult the War Department Collection of Confederate Records (RG 109, not described in this guide).

Record Group 366

Records of Civil War Special Agencies of the Treasury Department

366.1. The Civil War special agencies of the Treasury Department were established under an act of July 1861 to regulate trade in the insurgent areas of the South controlled by the U.S. military and in adjacent areas of loyal States. Special agents were first appointed by the Secretary of the Treasury at places where there were no customs officers, but between 1863 and 1864 a system of special agencies having geographical jurisdictions was established. Special agents issued "authorities" for merchandise transported to or from restricted areas; collected and received captured, abandoned, and confiscable property within their agencies and from military and naval personnel; and were responsible for the employment and welfare of freedmen until the creation of the Bureau of Refugees, Freedmen, and Abandoned Lands. Purchasing agents bought products of insurgent States for the United States. Special agencies ceased to function soon after June 1865, when the Secretary—acting on a Presidential order that ended restrictions on commerce in the South—rescinded Treasury regulations governing captured and abandoned property. Duties of the purchasing agents were terminated at about the same time.

366.2. Correspondence and standard forms that include information about freedmen are interspersed throughout these records. There are no series that include information solely on blacks. The records of the Third Special Agency, for example, include the **alphabetical correspondence file of special agent Benjamin F. Flanders, 1863–66** (1 in.). Among the letters are a few with information about his dealings with military officials in regard to freedmen before the establishment of the Freedmen's Bureau. These records include many standard application forms filled in by persons desiring to establish plantations or businesses in the Confederate States. Most of the forms include a provision for the protection of the freedmen. The "Oath of Applicants for Family and Plantation Supplies" reads in part: "I solemnly swear, that all goods ordered by me through my Agent Mr. __________ of __________ are intended solely for ______ white and ______ negroes [sic], in the Parish of __________ State of __________." Other similar applications include oaths and affidavits for the employment of freedmen, the leasing of land to them, or agreements to respect all the acts of Congress referring to the former slaves. There were nine different special agencies, and records of this type are common for each of them.

Record Group 368

Records of Agencies Concerned With Recreation and Historic Preservation

368.1. One of the agencies concerned with recreation was the Outdoor Recreation Resources Review Commission (ORRRC). It was established in 1958 to conduct a nationwide inventory and evaluation of outdoor recreation resources and opportunities; to determine the amount, kind, quality, and location of outdoor recreation facilities that would be required by the U.S. public by 1976 and by 2000; and to recommend policies and programs to satisfy such future requirements. The Commission made a series of studies to develop background information. ORRRC submitted its final report in January 1962 and terminated its activities later in the same year. On May 15, 1962, the ORRRC transferred its records to the newly created Bureau of Outdoor Recreation (BOR). BOR was succeeded by the Heritage Conservation and Recreation Service of the Department of the Interior in 1978. This record group includes records for these agencies as well as those for the Advisory Council on Historic Preservation, an independent advisory agency within the Department of the Interior.

368.2. The **reports and correspondence of ORRRC, 1958–62** (50 ft.), include some information about blacks in large metropolitan slum areas and the recreational needs of such areas. The folder for staff member Morton Grodzins (2 in.), for example, contains an article written by him entitled "The Metropolitan Area as a Racial Problem" (28 pp.).

Record Group 381

Records of Agencies for Economic Opportunity and Legal Services

381.1. One of the agencies primarily concerned with economic opportunity was the Office of Economic Opportunity (OEO), 1964–75, which was established to "mobilize the human and financial resources of the nation" and to strengthen, supplement, and coordinate efforts to "eliminate poverty in the midst of plenty by opening to everyone the opportunity for education and training, the opportunity to work, and the opportunity to live in decency and dignity." Many organizational changes took place in OEO between 1964 and 1972. Although funds were appropriated for the agency in fiscal years 1973 and 1974, a number of its programs were transferred to other agencies. By provisions of an appropriation act, OEO was supplanted on January 4, 1975, by the Community Services Administration. Although the records contain mostly narrative and statistical reports about the poor, there are some records of Job Corps and Community Action Programs (CAP) and some records pertaining to civil rights policies and public affairs. Much of the information pertains to minority groups, especially black Americans.

Records of the Office of the Director

381.2. Among these records are five series generated by Special Assistant for Civil Rights Samuel Yette. His office advised the OEO Director on matters pertaining to civil rights legislation and on the formulation and implementation of policy. He was also responsible for receiving and processing civil rights complaints and for administering a program of equal employment opportunity within OEO. The records include the **alphabetical correspondence file of Samuel Yette, 1964–66** (3 ft., 3 in.); **program files, 1964–67** (1 ft., 5 in.), arranged alphabetically by subject; **records relating to the administration of the civil rights programs in OEO regions, 1965–66** (4 ft., 11 in.), arranged numerically by OEO region; the **local problems area file, 1966** (½ in.), arranged chronologically, which includes mostly intra-agency memorandums and reports about local and regional racial problems in OEO programs; and **memorandums to regional coordinators, 1965–67** (3 in.), pertaining mostly to instructions on procedures for making weekly reports and processing civil rights complaints.

Records of the Office of Operations

381.3. There are several series of records that relate to programs for migrant workers. Many of these workers, particularly in the eastern part of the United States, are black. Materials include **records of the public relations of the Migrant Division, 1965–71** (11 in.), arranged by subject. The records contain data on the life of migrants, their participation in OEO programs, and migrant-related legislation. The **migrant workers' program State files, 1966–72** (5 ft., 7 in.), are arranged alphabetically by State and thereunder by program; the files concern education, prevocational training, rehabilitation, housing, and health and legal services. There are also **records relating to migrant workers' education programs,**

1967–69 (10 in.), arranged by program and thereunder alphabetically by geographic region. These programs were conducted in various States for the education of adults and children of migrant workers' families and were overseen by institutions of higher learning and other educational organizations.

381.4. The **press clipping file on the War on Poverty, 1968–69** (1 ft., 3 in.), arranged by title and subject, is a part of the records of the Planning Systems Division of the Office of Operations. This collection pertains to student activists, urban problems, racial disturbances, black community activities, and reform and revolutionary philosophies in the United States.

Records of the Job Corps

381.5. The Director of the Job Corps, Otis A. Singletary, accumulated a **decimal file, 1965** (4 ft., 10 in.). The materials pertain to a variety of Job Corps administrative matters, to OEO responsibilities under the Civil Rights Act of 1964, and to such concerns of enrollees as admission, training, payment, entertainment, food, transportation, and placement. The **subject file of David Squire, 1965–66** (4 ft.), a Deputy Director of the Job Corps, is arranged alphabetically by subject. There are records concerning Job Corps operations and administration and policies regarding civil rights.

Records of the Community Action Program

381.6. The CAP was based on the principle that poor persons were themselves to be involved in the development and operation of the separate programs that were intended to help them. Therefore, under CAP, Federal grants were to be made to public or private nonprofit organizations that were broadly representative of the community. These groups were authorized to coordinate antipoverty programs developed locally for housing, health, civil rights, employment, training, and education. No blueprints for the programs were provided by OEO; the community action agencies (as they were commonly called) could devise solutions to local problems derived from or causing poverty. There are **narrative progress reports, 1966–67** (11 ft.), for this program. They are arranged chronologically and demonstrate the many different types of programs funded by OEO. There are programs such as day-care centers, legal services, credit unions, dental and health clinics, job training and placement, small business development, Head Start, adult education, and neighborhood multiservice centers. Many of the programs were developed by and for black communities.

381.7. A **computer tape master file of CAP grantee organizations, 1964–71** (1 reel), gives the name and phone number of the executive director of the Community Action Program and the addresses and the phone numbers of CAP group representatives by racial or ethnic group. The information is arranged numerically by OEO region code and thereunder by grantee number. The *Community Action Agency Atlas,* 1971, arranged by OEO administrative region, is a published set of maps showing the area served by each community action agency.

Records Relating to OEO Surveys

381.8. In order to find out where the poor of the Nation were located and what their needs were, OEO did a number of surveys. Most of them were computer tabulations, and many were based on Federal census data. The Office of Planning, Research, and Evaluation prepared **computer tapes for comparison of nonwhite social, demographic, and economic characteristics with those of the total population, 1967** (2 reels). This survey is also known as the 1967 Survey of Economic Opportunity. Data on each household in the survey include the location, characteristics of the dwelling, and number of families, persons, and adults in the households; the financial status of the family; age, sex, race, years of education, and family relationship of each person; and employment pattern, occupation, health status, income, marriage, and childbearing histories of each adult female.

381.9. The **computer tapes for the experiment in performance contracting, 1970–72** (4 reels), was also an OEO Office of Planning, Research, and Evaluation study done in cooperation with 100 schools in 20 school districts to determine whether performance contracting in education (paying private contractors in proportion to their success in raising pupil academic achievement levels, in this case the reading and mathematical levels) was more cost effective than other programs designed to improve the skills of low-scoring students. The data are divided into four subseries. The file, which contains the test results, gives information on grades, race, sex, absenteeism, and responses from the Parent Questionnaire.

381.10. The **machine tabulation of poverty characteristics in Appalachia in 1960** (1 item), is arranged alphabetically by State and thereunder by county. This computer printout, prepared by OEO's Information Center, is entitled "Total and Poor Population for All Races and Non-Whites by State and County in Appalachia."

381.11. Community profiles, 1967 (66 ft.), which were compiled by the Information Center, are reports on 3,135 U.S. counties and are arranged alphabetically by State and thereunder alphabetically by county. They were designed to provide basic information to government officials seeking solutions to community problems. The reports contain mostly statistical information but also narrative and interpretive demographic, geographic, social, and economic information. There is some emphasis on characteristics of the poor population. Racial information is included. (NARS has deposited in each regional archives branch reference copies of the reports that relate primarily to the geographic region served by the branch.)

381.12. Among the records of the Office of Operations are **computer tapes containing racial and demographic tabulations of poverty statistics extracted from the 1960 census** ("Putnam file" and "Putnam aggregate file"), **1965** (2 reels). Each file is arranged in numeric sequence by OEO region code. Israel Putnam of the Office directed the project to identify the extent and patterns of poverty at the State and county/city levels. The "Putnam file" focuses on poverty from the individual and family standpoint and analyzes income data in terms of age, sex, race (white and nonwhite only), and family size. The "Putnam aggregate file" focuses on poverty from a geographic and residential standpoint.

381.13. A similar tabulation is the Putnam summary of **fourth-count (socio-economic) summary tapes for counties and States from the 1970 census of population, 1970** (12 ft.). These compilations, arranged alphabetically by State and thereunder alphabetically by county, include four pages of tables for every State and county, one each containing data for all residences—urban, rural nonfarm, and farm—including racial information. (NARS has deposited in each regional archives branch reference copies of the tables that relate primarily to the geographic region served by the branch.)

381.14. **"Dimensions of Poverty in 1964," part II, 1965** (20 ft.), is a tabulation prepared by the Bureau of the Census for the Office of Operations. It arrays the minor civil divisions and census tracts in each State on the basis of the number of families falling into the lowest three deciles of income for that State. The tabulations, arranged by State, show not only the tracts and civil divisions containing the largest number of poor persons but also other characteristics of those areas. There is information about nonwhites. There is a summary description of parts I and II at the beginning of the series. Another report by the Office of Operations is a **"Preliminary Profile of the 1965 Poor by OEO Region and Nationally," 1968** (4 in.), which is arranged by geographic region. These mainly statistical reports, based on an OEO survey in 1966 of 1965 incomes, were intended to assist headquarters personnel in their review of the regional program budget estimates and justifications for fiscal year 1970. The data for each of the regions refer to the total poor and their residences, mobility, and family type or size. The data are given in various breakdowns, one of which is race.

381.15. The Office of Operations enlisted the Bureau of the Census to do **current population survey tabulations, 1970–73** (1 ft., 3 in.).

These are special income-class tabulations, arranged chronologically by survey, which show the number of persons and families at the various income levels. The data are broken down by ethnic group. The Bureau also compiled **"Low Income Neighborhoods in Large Cities," 1973** (4 ft.). These tabulations, arranged alphabetically by city, contain information from more than 100 cities. The tables compare the statistical data for census tracts that have populations of at least 20,000, of whom at least 20 percent are poor. Racial information is included.

381.16. Among the records of the Job Corps' Policy Development and Review Division are **computer tapes containing county and State poverty statistics extracted from the 1970 census** ("ten tables") **by the Bureau of the Census, 1972–74** (38 reels). This series, arranged in numerical sequence by State code, includes summary data tables relating to the poverty status of persons and families by age, sex, education, work experience, home value, the presence of plumbing, the number of persons per room, and sources of income. It also contains data on ethnic groups of at least 25 persons in a given location.

Audiovisual Records

381.17. Some of the documentary and training motion pictures (654 items) produced or acquired by OEO relate to its programs for combating racism and poverty in the United States. The Job Corps, VISTA, and Head Start are the principal OEO programs depicted and discussed in the films. The bulk of the films were circulated to low-income and minority groups or to other persons interested in the problems of racism and poverty. The films illustrate conditions of poverty in rural areas and cities and among Indians, Chicanos, blacks, and whites. Some of the films that deal specifically with blacks are "What's a Man Worth" (#381–28), which concerns opportunities for blacks in employment and housing and explores the problems of discrimination, welfare, crime, and city life; "Marked for Failure" (#381–71), a film that pertains to the education of underprivileged children in New York City; and "Phyllis and Terry" (#381–44), which is about the lives of two black teenage girls in New York City. "The Way It Is" (#381–32) is a film about a poverty-stricken black community in Louisville, Ky., and "Keep It Cool" (#381–52) depicts juvenile gangs in Chicago, Ill. "Everything in Its Place" (#381–58) explores racial problems between a white bank supervisor and a black youth in the Job Training Program. "The Peace Corps that Never Left Home" (#381–65) documents the work of two VISTA volunteers in a Philadelphia black community. In the film "117th Street, New York, New York" (#381–74), correspondents interview residents in Harlem about recent riots against the police. A number of other films explore various problems for poor black communities in the inner cities and rural areas, such as recreational facilities, substandard

Ray Brown (left) and his wife Ella Fitzgerald, the well-known jazz singer, perform with alto saxaphonist Louis Jordan. Date and photographer unknown. RG 306, Records of the U.S. Information Agency. (306-PS-50-14874).

housing, drug addiction, education, dropouts, job discrimination, race relations, crime, and other subjects.

381.18. Some of the sound records (835 reels) also relate to black history. The Voice of VISTA radio series, 1965–71 (#381–VoV–1 to 247), arranged chronologically, was produced by M. A. Mangum Co. for OEO. Its hosts were Willis Conover and Gene Klavan. The programs, which had as their purpose recruitment for VISTA, featured interviews with and recordings of performances by musicians and other entertainers, many of whom were black. Some of them are Louis Armstrong, Duke Ellington, Odetta, Lionel Hampton, Quincy Jones, Carmen MacRae, Godfrey Cambridge, Nina Simone, Count Basie, Otis Redding, Julian "Cannonball" Adderly, Sarah Vaughan, Earl "Fatha" Hines, Leslie Uggams, The Fifth Dimension, Peaches and Herb, Flip Wilson, Lou Rawls, Ella Fitzgerald, Dionne Warwick, Ray Charles, O. C. Smith, Bill Cosby, Jerry Butler, Gladys Knight and the Pips, Johnny Mathis, and Curtis Mayfield.

381.19. Other OEO sound recordings relating to the war on poverty include the recording of an impromptu press conference held by black residents of Washington, D.C., to protest welfare cuts by President Nixon (#381–87), discussions by Olympic boxing champion George Foreman about his career plans and the benefits of his Job Corps training (#381–127, 274, 299), and an address by Supreme Court Justice Thurgood Marshall on the subject of legal services for the poor as related to the 14th amendment (#381–154). Some recordings include statements by Martin Luther King, Sr. (#381–113); Adam Clayton Powell, Jr. (#381–309, 310); Dr. Beneta Washington, head of the Women's Job Corps Centers (#381–161); interviews with blacks from Watts, Calif. (#381–213, 220), and Canton, Ohio (#381–217); and an interview with a Selma, Ala., organizer of a local farmer's cooperative (#381–216). There is a recording of a discussion of popular black recording artists (with musical interludes) on the advantages of OEO programs (#381–348), and recordings from delegations from the "Poor People's March on Washington" (#381–238, 239).

Record Group 398

General Records of the Department of Transportation

398.1. The Department of Transportation (DOT) was established by an act of October 15, 1966, effective in April 1967. The primary function of DOT is "to assure the coordinated, effective administration of the transportation programs of the Federal Government" and to develop "national transportation programs and programs conducive to the provision of fast, safe, efficient, and convenient transportation at the lowest cost consistent therewith." The Department of Transportation is administered by the Secretary of Transportation, who is the principal assistant to the President in all matters relating to Federal transportation programs. The Secretary from 1975 to 1977 was William T. Coleman, Jr., a black lawyer. The **general subject files, 1973–75** (7 ft., 90 rolls), which document the Department's policies, programs, and procedures, include a small amount of material from the Coleman administration. The records include correspondence between the Department's highest officials and the President and officials of the White House Staff, other Cabinet members, Members of Congress, foreign governments, and others. The records are arranged chronologically by date of final action in each transaction.

398.2. There are a number of sound recordings of Coleman's addresses and interviews, including statements at news conferences, policy statements, and testimonies at congressional hearings (e.g., #398.013, .022, and .024–.028). There are 1975 speeches to the NAACP convention (#398.043) and to the Urban League meeting at Atlanta (#398.056), and 1976 speeches at a workshop on civil rights (398.084), at a minority business conference (#398.134), and on the program "Black Perspective on the News" (#398.085). There is also a 5-minute film segment of Secretary Coleman's appearance on the television talk show "Good Morning America" (#398.002).

Record Group 403

Records of the Equal Employment Opportunity Commission

403.1. The Equal Employment Opportunity Commission (EEOC) was created by title VII of the Civil Rights Act of 1964 and became operational on July 2, 1965. The purposes of the Commission are to end discrimination based on race, color, religion, sex, or national origin in hiring, promoting, firing, paying, and all other conditions of employment and to promote voluntary action programs by employers, unions, and community organizations to put equal employment opportunity into operation. There are five Commissioners appointed by the President, with the advice and consent of the Senate, for 5-year terms. The President designates one member as chairman and one member as vice chairman.

403.2. The records consist of **materials accumulated in connection with EEOC litigation against the American Telephone and Telegraph Company and its subsidiaries before the Federal Communication Commission (FCC), 1971–73** (80 ft.), arranged by subject. They consist mostly of verbatim transcripts, of proceedings before the FCC during 1972, exhibits introduced by EEOC, and other legal documents and publications. The case, referred to by some EEOC officials as the most important proceeding in the Commission's history, resulted in an agreement in which the company agreed to pay over $20 million to those of its employees who had "presumably" been discriminated against in terms of promotions and career advancement opportunities. Most of these employees were minorities and women.

Record Group 418

Records of St. Elizabeths Hospital

418.1. In the Civil and Diplomatic Appropriation Act approved in August 1852, Congress appropriated funds to enable the Secretary of the

Interior, under the direction of the President, to purchase a site in the Washington, D.C., region "for the erection, furnishing and fitting up of an asylum for the insane." In March 1855 a subsequent act officially organized the institution, provided that it be called the Government Hospital for the Insane, and stated that the purpose of the hospital was to provide human care and treatment for the insane of the Army and Navy of the United States and indigent insane residents of the District of Columbia. Insane patients from the District also could be accepted on a paying basis if vacancies existed. Since the Civil War, the hospital has been called St. Elizabeths after the tract of land near which it is located. The hospital was under the supervision of the Department of the Interior until it was transferred to the Federal Security Agency (FSA) in 1940. When the FSA was abolished in 1953, St. Elizabeths Hospital was transferred to the Department of Health, Education, and Welfare (HEW).

418.2. The records of the Medical Records Branch, 1855–1955, include the **case files of patients, 1855–1950** (about 370 ft.), arranged numerically by case number. Many of the patients were black. The folders for the cases of some individuals have the abbreviation "Col." for "colored" beside the patient's name, or the race of the patient is indicated on the records in the folders. A typical file contains correspondence with patients' relatives, guardians, lawyers, and other interested parties as well as medical records, including commitment papers, summaries of the personal and medical history of the patient, notes concerning mental and physical examinations, laboratory reports, data sheets on therapy, ward notes, autopsy reports, case summaries, and other pertinent records. Frequently included are a photograph of the patient and newspaper clippings if the case was noteworthy.

418.3. There are registers that serve as indexes to the case files. The **register of cases, 1855–1941** (12 vols., 2 ft.), is arranged numerically by case number. Some of the volumes include an alphabetical index to names in the front of the book. Entries vary over the years but usually show case number; date of admission; name, age, sex, race, marital status, birthplace, religion, and occupation of patient; and basis for admission. Admissions through 1936 also give a tentative diagnosis for each case.

418.4. The **register of female patients, 1866–1933** (1 vol., 3 in.), is arranged in rough alphabetical order by surname of patient and thereunder chronologically by date of admission. Entries show case number, name of patient, date of admission, date of discharge, basis for admission, and comments concerning the patient (recovered, died, discharged, unimproved, etc.). "Col." for "colored" is listed beside the names of many of the women or in the remarks column.

418.5. Because a number of patients were black, racial statistics can be found in many of the other records in this group.

Record Group 452

Records of the American Revolution Bicentennial Administration

452.1. Congress enacted legislation creating the American Revolution Bicentennial Commission (ARBC) to plan and develop the celebration of the bicentennial of U.S. independence. It operated from 1966 through 1973, and its successor agency, the American Revolution Bicentennial Administration (ARBA), operated from 1974 through September 1977. The records of both ARBC and ARBA are in this record group. Public Law 89-491 (80 Stat. 259), signed by President Lyndon B. Johnson on July 4, 1966, established the ARBC. The Commission consisted of 34 members selected equally from public and private life. Public figures were chosen from Congress and the executive branch, while private members were chosen from the cultural and business sectors of society as well as from the news media. The first full ARBC meeting was held on February 22, 1967, but the first funding was not approved until July 9, 1968. As a result of various accusations made in 1972, independent investigations of the ARBC were conducted by the General Accounting Office, Congress, and the Department of the Interior. The investigations absolved the Commission of the charges against it but revealed weaknesses in its work and organization. On December 11, 1973, President Richard M. Nixon signed Public Law 93-179 (87 Stat. 697), which abolished the Commission and established the Administration.

452.2. The climax of the bicentennial was the 200th anniversary of the signing of the Declaration of Independence. The Administration made its final report to Congress on June 30, 1977, and went out of existence on September 30, 1977. The report, *A Final Report to the People: The Bicentennial of the United States of America* (Washington, D.C.; Government Printing Office, 1977), recounts the main themes and events of the celebration and lists State and local celebrations.

Programs, States, and Communities Division

452.3. The ethnic-racial program was designed to involve black Americans and other racial and ethnic groups in various bicentennial events. **General correspondence of the ethnic-racial program, 1975–76** (4 in.), is arranged chronologically. The **program records, 1975–76** (1 ft., 3 in.), arranged alphabetically by program, include correspondence and other materials relating to program plans along with printed materials used during the events.

452.4. The **miscellaneous subject files of the ethnic-racial program, 1975–76** (1 ft., 3 in.), arranged by subject, include folders pertaining to a report about ethnic-racial bicentennial activities, ethnic participation, the Afro-American Bicentennial Corporation, and black colleges and universities.

452.5. The **program records of the National Bicentennial Ethnic-Racial Coalition (BERC), 1974–76** (1 ft., 6 in.), are arranged by subject. This is a general subject file including minutes of the steering committee, correspondence with regions, summaries of activities, and miscellaneous correspondence. **Correspondence with the Coalition, 1975–76** (10 in.), arranged alphabetically by name, consists of letters, reports, and memorandums with BERC member organizations and with committee members (1 in.). The subject files of BERC, arranged by subject, include a folder on the organization of the committee, press releases, resolutions, briefings, agenda and transcripts of various meetings, resumés of committee meetings, and some correspondence.

Audiovisual Records

452.6. There are 2,802 photographs and slides of prominent individuals, bicentennial activities, historic buildings, and the "World of Franklin and Jefferson" exhibit; 131 audio recordings of speeches, meetings, and conferences; and 29 motion pictures and 7 videotapes produced or acquired by ARBA. Many of these audiovisual records depict phases of the black experience or black people. There are photographs of some prominent black personalities—such as Senator Edward Brooke of Massachusetts and Congressional Black Caucus members Ronald Dellums, Shirley Chisolm, Charles Diggs, and Walter Fauntroy—and notables such as Vernon Jordan, Charley Pride, Walter Washington, Hank Aaron, and Sugar Ray Leonard. The sound recordings include a press conference following a Multi-Ethnic Coalition meeting, June 28, 1974 (#452–4); a recognition program led by Senator Brooke (#452–7–5); and Afro-American bicentennial speakers of the Federal Agency Panel (#452–7–8).

452.7. The motion pictures include "Many Voices" (#452.10), which was made for ARBA under contract. It focuses on the ethnic and racial heritage of America and urges participation in the Bicentennial ethnic and racial councils. "Here to Stay" (#452.30A) shows how blacks and Puerto Ricans formed Connecticut's first neighborhood corporation in order to build new housing, run social services, and launch an experimental school. The film "Come on in and Help Us Do It" (#452.31) depicts public leaders and average citizens explaining the Hampton, Va., government's open door system while focusing on downtown development and school integration as examples of collaborative efforts between the people and their government. "Staying Together" (#452.33) is about the Cleveland Heights, Ohio, Community Congress working with the challenge of racial integration and economic-social stability coexisting in the suburbs. There are also some other films with information about the "grass-roots" community organizations and with information for black history, though not specifically about blacks.

Record Group 453

Records of the Commission on Civil Rights

453.1. The Commission on Civil Rights was created by the Civil Rights Act of 1957. The Commission holds public hearings and collects and studies information on discrimination or denials of equal protection of the laws because of race, color, religion, sex, age, handicap, national origin, or in the administration of justice. Voting rights, enforcements of Federal civil rights laws, and equality of opportunity in education, employment, and housing are among specific Commission factfinding efforts. The Commission makes findings of fact but has no enforcement authority. Findings and recommendations are submitted to both the President and the Congress.

453.2. The records of the Commission include a number of sound recordings, most of which are of public hearings on civil rights issues held by the Commission in various cities from 1966 to 1968 (#453–1 through 7). The sound recordings of the Public Affairs Unit of the Commission include a 1961 press conference on discrimination in housing (#453–8); a 1967 "Florida Forum" on busing, segregation, and housing (#453–9); a 1967 interview with W. L. Taylor on busing and public schools (#453–10); and a 1967 interview with Frankie Muse Freeman entitled "Eye on St. Louis" (#453–11), about the personnel of the Commission and about racial segregation.

Appendix

Audiovisual records found in record groups covered in the **Black History** guide.

p–photographs *s–sound recordings* *f–films*

RG 3, *p*	RG 65, *s*	RG 121, *p*	RG 233, *f, s*
RG 12, *s, p*	RG 66, *p*	RG 130, *s*	RG 245, *p*
RG 16, *f*	RG 69, *p, f, s*	RG 135, *p*	RG 267, *s*
RG 26, *p*	RG 83, *p*	RG 171, *s*	RG 269, *f*
RG 30, *p*	RG 86, *p*	RG 174, *s*	RG 306, *p*
RG 33, *p, f*	RG 88, *p*	RG 188, *p*	RG 362, *f, p*
RG 35, *p*	RG 90, *p, f*	RG 200, *p, f, s*	RG 381, *f, s*
RG 41, *p*	RG 106, *s*	RG 207, *f, s*	RG 398, *s, f*
RG 43, *f*	RG 115, *p*	RG 208, *p, f s*	RG 452, *p, f s*
RG 48, *f, s*	RG 119, *p, f*	RG 220, *s, p*	RG 453, *s*
RG 59, *f*		RG 228, *s*	

Index

This guide is arranged in Record Group (RG) number order and each paragraph in the RG is sequentially numbered.

Entries in this index refer to the relevant Record Group or Record Group and paragraph number.

ex: Marshals, U.S., RG 118

ex: Refugee slaves, 76.3
Record group — Paragraph number

When the index citation shows the formal Record Group title, it will appear in bold face and appear as in the following:

ex: **Children's Bureau,** RG 102

If there are other references to the agency in the guide, the RG citation may be accompanied by other references.

ex: **Secret Service, U.S.,** RG 87, 272.2